Stochastic Modeling and Optimization Methods for Critical Infrastructure Protection 1

Series Editor
Nikolaos Limnios

Stochastic Modeling and Optimization Methods for Critical Infrastructure Protection 1

Stochastic Modeling

Edited by

Alexei A. Gaivoronski
Pavel S. Knopov
Vladimir I. Norkin
Volodymyr A. Zaslavskyi

iSTE

WILEY

First published 2025 in Great Britain and the United States by ISTE Ltd and John Wiley & Sons, Inc.

ISTE Ltd
27-37 St George's Road
London SW19 4EU
UK

www.iste.co.uk

John Wiley & Sons, Inc.
111 River Street
Hoboken, NJ 07030
USA

www.wiley.com

Library of Congress Control Number: 2025931326

British Library Cataloguing-in-Publication Data
A CIP record for this book is available from the British Library
ISBN 978-1-83669-027-6

Contents

Preface

The book presents mathematical models and tools for enhancing critical infrastructure protection against natural threats and adversarial attacks. The book consists of two volumes; the first is devoted to stochastic modeling of various critical sectors of economics and their interconnections, and the second considers mathematical tools for enhancing critical infrastructure protection.

These two volumes offer new results on risk assessment methods, taking into account the large number of systemic connections between the structures of the modern technosphere and the graded nature of damage probability from natural and human-made disasters. The cumulative effect from various risk sources will be investigated, which becomes an important generator of uncertainty and instability due to the nonlinear increase in system vulnerability and a decrease in its adaptation capabilities, when small impacts cause unstable system behavior. The generalizations of the attack and defense antagonistic game, and the rational distribution of defense resources are considered, and methods for solving the corresponding optimization problems are proposed. New mathematical methods of machine learning, based on quasi-gradient methods of stochastic programming, are reviewed.

The research is based on the authors' results on the theoretical foundations of stochastic systems with aftereffect, stochastic optimal control theory, robust methods of non-smooth and stochastic optimization for solving special optimization problems with a large number of variables and constraints, methods of multi-criteria dynamic optimization, methods of solving two-level stochastic programming problems, stochastic minimax game problems, and graph theory optimization problems. Basic concepts, methods and directions of cryptographic protection of information are considered. The working principles of classical cryptography ciphers and the main results of Shannon's theory of secret systems are presented. The obtained theoretical results will be applied to solving important problems of risk assessment and monitoring the state of critical infrastructure objects.

The chapters are the result of a series of international projects involving leading scientists from various research institutes in Austria, Norway, Ukraine and other countries in the field of modern stochastic optimization and decision making. These projects were aimed at developing a curriculum for risk management at the master's and doctoral levels. The studies included in this book contain new research results and also take into account the requirements of research-based education on these topics.

Acknowledgments

Work on parts of the book was supported by the grant CPEA-LT-2016/10003 "Advanced collaborative program for research based education on risk management in industry and services under global economic, technological and environmental changes: enhanced edition" of Norwegian Directorate for Higher Education and Skills (HKDIR), managed by the Norwegian University of Science and Technology (NTNU), Trondheim, Norway. It was also supported by the project 2020.02/0121 "Analytical methods and machine learning in control theory and decision-making in conditions of conflict and uncertainty" funded by the National Research Foundation of Ukraine. The work was also supported by the joint project between the International Institute for Applied Systems Analysis (IIASA) and the National Academy of Sciences of Ukraine (NASU) on "Integrated robust modeling and management of food-energy-water-land use nexus for sustainable development" (22-501) and by the projects 0122U00052 and 2.3/25-P of the National Academy of Sciences of Ukraine.

Alexei A. GAIVORONSKI
Pavel S. KNOPOV
Vladimir I. NORKIN
Volodymyr A. ZASLAVSKYI
March 2025

PART 1

Model-Based Risk Management in Critical Economic Sectors

Introduction to Part 1

Integrated solutions and procedures for combining distributed models for security modeling and management in the food, energy, water and environment sectors are proposed. The links between two-stage stochastic optimization and machine learning problems are discussed, and a new model using quantile regression for assessing the impact of land use practices on the environment is proposed. Also, new mathematical models for studying the vulnerabilities of critical infrastructure are proposed.

A multi-stage, multi-horizon stochastic equilibrium model for analyzing energy markets is studied, with particular attention applied to infrastructure development and renewable energy policy in perfect and imperfect market structures.

This section also proposes new approaches to managing energy systems – important objects of critical infrastructure. The task of optimizing the structure of the energy production portfolio is solved in order to combine various energy production technologies to maximize the value of the portfolio, ensure its safety and prevent the occurrence of critical situations.

Introduction written by Alexei A. GAIVORONSKI and Pavel S. KNOPOV.

1

Integrated Solutions and Distributed Models' Linkage Procedures for Food–Energy–Water–Environmental Nexus Security Modeling and Management

This chapter discusses a new modeling approach enabling the linkage of distributed individual food, energy, water optimization models under joint (e.g. water and land) resource constraints, uncertainty and asymmetric information (ASI). The approach is based on an iterative stochastic quasigradient (SQG) solution procedure of, in general, non-smooth, non-differentiable optimization. The SQG procedure organizes an iterative computerized negotiation between individual food–energy–water (FEW) systems (models) representing intelligent agents. The convergence of the procedure to the socially optimal solution is based on the results of non-differentiable optimization providing a new type of machine learning algorithm. The linkage problem can be viewed as a general endogenous reinforced learning problem. The models act as "agents" that communicate with a "central hub" (a regulator) and take decisions in order to maximize the "cumulative reward". In this way, they continue to be the same individual models and different modeling teams do not need to exchange information about their models – instead, they only need to harmonize the inputs and outputs that are part of the joint resource constraints. In this way, the agents link their models into an integrated model (IM) under ASI.

The convergence of the solution of the linked models to the solution of the hard-IM is discussed. Application of the approach is illustrated with a case study linking distributed agricultural, water and energy sector models. This approach can be effectively used for decentralized, deregulated planning of interdependent agricultural, energy and water systems.

Chapter written by Tatiana Y. ERMOLIEVA, Anatoly G. ZAGORODNY, Viacheslav L. BOGDANOV, Petr HAVLIK, Elena ROVENSKAJA, Nadejda KOMENDANTOVA and Pavel S. KNOPOV.

1.1. Introduction

The increasing interdependencies among food–energy–water–environmental (FEWE) sectors require integrated coherent planning and coordinated policies for sustainable development and nexus security. The sectors become more interconnected because they utilize common, often rather limited, resources, both natural (e.g. land, water and air quality) and socioeconomic (e.g. investments and labor force). For example, land and water are needed not only for agricultural production but also for hydropower generation, coal mining and processing, power plants cooling, renewable energy and hydrogen production.

Detailed sectoral and regional models have traditionally been used to anticipate and plan desirable developments of respective sectors and regions. These models operate with a set of feasible decisions and aim to select a solution optimizing a sector- or region-specific objective function. When interdependencies between sectors and regions are increasing, such an independent analysis without accounting for interconnections can become misleading and even dangerous. Hence, it is necessary to link the sectoral (regional) models together to derive truly integrated solutions. Interdependent FEWE security goals contribute immensely to signifying the nexus security between sectors and regions (Zagorodny et al. 2020, 2024; Ermolieva et al. 2021a, 2021b).

In this chapter, we consider the problem of linking individual sectoral and/or regional linear programming (LP) models into a cross-sectoral IM in the presence of joint constraints, when "private" information about the models is not available or it cannot be shared by modeling teams (sectoral agencies), that is, under ASI. This approach provides a means of decentralized cross-sectoral coordination and enables us to investigate policies in interdependent systems in a "decentralized" fashion. This enables more stable and resilient systems' performance and resource allocation as compared to the independent policies designed by separate models without accounting for interdependencies.

Limited resources can be allocated between systems (sectors/regions) in many ways. For example, Böhringer and Rutherford (2009) consider integrating mathematical programming models of the energy system into a general equilibrium (GE) model of the overall economy. Unfortunately, the convergence of the iterative procedure integrating the models could not be proven. For resource and production allocation with the generalized Nash equilibrium (GNE) approach, the existence, uniqueness and stability of the GNE, and a realistic large-scale implementation of this concept cannot be guaranteed. Ermoliev and von Winterfeldt (2012) demonstrate the complexity of the game-theoretic approaches, for example, the Stackelberg leadership model, emerging due to quite unrealistic assumptions that each player (sector/region) possesses knowledge about other players.

Traditional integrated deterministic optimization modeling incorporates goals, constraints and data of all models into a single code (hard integration), which can be considered as a multi-criteria optimization problem (Ogryczak 2000). In the case of separate distributed models and ASI, the linkage requires (see sections 1.2.2–1.2.4) specific non-smooth optimization methods. Problems under ASI are addressed with the agency theory (Gaivoronski and Werner 2012), in particular, on how to motivate information exchange. In this chapter, we consider, in a sense, the opposite and minimize the necessity to exchange information.

Our approach for linking separate optimization models under ASI is based on the parallel solving of equivalent non-smooth optimization models by an iterative stochastic quasigradient (SQG) procedure (Ermoliev 1976, 2009), based on subgradients or generalized gradients (Ermoliev 1976; Rockafeller 1981; Ermoliev and Norkin 1997) converging to an optimal welfare maximizing linkage solution, that is, to the solution of a "hard-integrated" model (Ermoliev et al. 2022). This approach does not require us to share details about models' specification. We can assume that there is a network of distributed computers connecting individual computer models with the computer of a "social planner" (decision-makers or regulatory agencies), who attempts to achieve the best result for all sectors/regions (parties) involved. The linkage procedure can be interpreted as a kind of a "decentralized market system" (Ermoliev et al. 2015, and references therein). According to this procedure, the optimization of sectoral/regional goals under individual constraints is performed independently and in parallel, without considering joint constraints. Joint constraints can be imposed on total production, natural and financial resource use, emissions, pollution and joint FEWE security targets. The constraints can establish supply–demand relationships between the systems enabling us to estimate optimal production, resource use and emission quotas for each system. The balance between the total energy (including biofuels) production and demand defines energy security, agricultural production and consumption reflect food security, and total emissions and pollution constraints correspond to environmental security. The joint FEWE constraints satisfaction establishes the FEWE security nexus (Zagorodny and Ermoliev 2013; Ermolieva et al. 2016, 2021a; Zagorodny et al. 2020, 2024). After the independent optimization using initial approximations of various (e.g. production, resource use and emission) quotas, the sectors/regions provide a social planner with the information on their actual production, resource use and respective shadow prices. The planner checks if the joint constraints are fulfilled. If not, that is, there is "excess demand" or "excess supply" (i.e. total resource use, production and emissions by all systems are higher/lower than required), the planner revises the individual systems' quotas via shifting their current approximation in the direction defined by the corresponding dual variables. Thus, shadow prices signal systems to adjust their activities accordingly. Formally, the procedure is described in sections 1.2.3–1.2.5.

In this way, the linkage allows us to avoid "hard linking" of the models in a single code, which is not possible because the systems (agencies) may not want to share the information or because the individual models are too detailed and complex to be "hard-linked". The approach saves reprogramming efforts and enables parallel distributed (decentralized) computations of sectoral models instead of a large-scale integrated (centralized) model. This also preserves the original models in their initial state for other linkages. The use of detailed sectoral and regional models instead of their aggregated simplified versions enables us to also account for critically important local details. Similar computerized, decentralized "negotiation" processes between distributed models (agents) have been developed for the design of robust carbon trading markets (e.g. Ermoliev et al. 2015, and references therein). The linkage procedure can be considered as a new machine learning algorithm, namely, as a general endogenous reinforced learning problem of how software agents (models) take decisions in order to maximize the cumulative reward (total welfare) (Ermolieva et al. 2021b)

This chapter is organized as follows. Section 1.2 discusses the problem of models' linkage under joint constraints. Section 1.2.1 presents a short overview and main shortfalls of several existing approaches. Section 1.2.2 formulates the problem of distributed LP models' linkage in the presence of joint resource constraints and ASI. Sections 1.2.3–1.2.5 outline the details and the main properties of the linkage solution procedure based on the parallel solving of the equivalent non-smooth optimization model following a simple iterative subgradient algorithm. Section 1.3 illustrates the application of the methodology to link detailed energy and agricultural production planning models under joint constraints on water and land use. In addition, the joint constraints can impose restrictions on total energy production by energy sector (electricity, gas, diesel, etc.) and land use sector (biodiesel and methanol), total energy use by energy and agricultural sectors, and total agricultural production by distributed farmers/regions. Section 1.4 concludes and outlines potential further extensions of the approach, for example, to include more details of energy and natural resources dynamics in general.

1.2. Linking distributed optimization models under joint resource constraints

1.2.1. *Social equilibrium game*

In the absence of coordination between systems (sectors and regions), they can act selfishly and aim at maximizing their own objective function. They can attempt to secure as high resource quotas as possible. Such a situation can be modeled using the non-cooperative game-theoretic framework. For example, social equilibrium games (Harker 1991) have been formulated to include joint constraints. The GNE solution, if it exists, allocates production and resources among systems (sectors/regions) fulfilling the joint constraint. However, the decisions are made independently and collective efforts for managing common resources are ignored. Importantly, the existence, uniqueness and stability of the GNE, as well as a realistic large-scale implementation of this concept, cannot be guaranteed as emphasized by Harker (1991). Moreover, in Harker (1991), it is highlighted that the GNE solutions set is rarely connected. Hence, a complete analysis of equilibriums in this case is a complex task, requiring additional assumptions.

The analysis can become even more complex if the joint constraints are based on the equilibrium (optimality) conditions arising from the problem formulated in the form of a principal–agent game or a leader–follower Stackelberg game (Ermoliev and von Winterfeldt 2012). For example, in the case of non-smooth goal functions required for linking systems under ASI (distributed models' optimization), the use of optimality conditions would require implicit sets of generalized gradients. Due to the computational complexity, heuristic methods are often used; however, they are lacking a rigorous convergence proof.

Böhringer and Rutherford (2009) discuss linking bottom-up mathematical programming models of the energy system into a top-down GE model of the overall economy. The paper shows that the formulation of market equilibrium conditions by using complementarity equations permits integration of models, but the convergence of the iterative procedure integrating the models cannot be guaranteed. In specific cases, models of GE are reduced to optimization problems (Norkin 1999).

Ermoliev and von Winterfeldt (2012) demonstrate that the complexity of the game-theoretic approaches is due to quite unrealistic assumptions that each player (sector/region) is in the possession of knowledge with regard to exact and unique responses of other players. Therefore, even in the simplest linear cases, this assumption leads to extremely complex discontinuous problems. More realistic assumptions of uncertain response functions in combination with a concept of robust decisions results in stable large-scale solutions.

A vast literature exists regarding important problems and methods for distributed systems' optimization (Yang et al. 2019) under joint constraints, for example, optimal control and economic dispatch in smart grids (Prakash and Nygard 2017), agricultural production planning for the multi-farmer systems (Alemany et al. 2021), network optimization (Liang et al. 2019) and optimal transportation problems (Dean and Cortés 2015; Galichon 2016). However, these approaches consider optimization of a total objective function representing a sum of individual objective functions of the involved systems. Thus, the problems assume full information is available to a social planner about the systems. They are formulated similarly to the traditional integrated "centralized" optimization modeling combining goals, constraints and data of all models into a single code.

Our problem is more complex as it deals with the coordination of decentralized systems' models in the presence of joint constraints and ASI. In this case, the approach is based on a specific iterative non-smooth optimization procedure (see sections 1.2.3–1.2.5). As we noted, integrated solution of separate LP models under ASI cannot be accomplished by LP methods. In section 1.2.2, we formulate the problem of distributed systems optimization in the presence of joint resource constraint under ASI, and in sections 1.2.3–1.2.5, we discuss the models' linkage algorithm and its convergence characteristics.

1.2.2. *LP models under joint constraints*

The basic problem of distributed individual sectoral (or regional) LP models optimization under joint resource constraint can be formulated as follows.

Assume that there are K systems' models formulated in the following LP form:

$$\langle c^{(k)}, x^{(k)} \rangle \to max, \tag{1.1}$$

$$x^{(k)} \geq 0, \tag{1.2}$$

$$A^{(k)} x^{(k)} \leq b^{(k)}, \tag{1.3}$$

where components of vector $x^{(k)}$ are unknown variables, vector $b^{(k)}$ defines system-specific demand or resource constraints and vector $c^{(k)}$ corresponds to net unit profits, $k = 1,2,\dots,K$. The common resource constraint [1.4] connects the systems through a common unknown (linkage) variable $y^{(k)}$

$$B^{(k)} x^{(k)} \leq y^{(k)}, \tag{1.4}$$

where $y^{(k)}$ defines resource quota allocated to system k. In this formulation, equation [1.3] defines individual systems' constraints and formula [1.4] establishes systemic supply–demand relationships among systems by distributing resources $y^{(k)}$. If matrix $D^{(k)}$ defines the marginal resource use by system k and d is the total available resource, $d \geq 0$, then the quotas $y^{(k)}$ fulfill the joint resource constraint on the common resources use

$$\textstyle\sum_{k=1}^{K} D^{(k)} y^{(k)} \leq d. \tag{1.5}$$

Thus, the overall problem is to maximize the individual objective function [1.1] for each system k by choosing $x^{(k)}$ and $y^{(k)}$ from the feasible set defined by [1.2] and [1.3], so that [1.4] and [1.5] are also fulfilled.

In the presence of full information about systems, the problem of models' linkage can be formulated and solved by a central planner (regulator) as a total net profit maximization

$$\sum_{k=1}^{K}\langle c^{(k)}, x^{(k)}\rangle \rightarrow \max \qquad [1.6]$$

s.t. to constraints [1.2–1.5], $k = 1,2,\dots,K$. The net profits can be defined as total net profit of production costs, possible taxes and other expenses.

If the information about parameters $b^{(k)}$, $c^{(k)}$, $A^{(k)}$, $B^{(k)}$, $x^{(k)}$ of systems k is not available to the planner, the integrated LP model [1.2–1.6] under ASI cannot be solved by the LP method due to the lack of common information about submodels.

In this situation, the consistent approach for linking distributed optimization models is based on the parallel solving of an equivalent non-smooth optimization model following a simple iterative subgradient algorithm. The convergence and other properties of the algorithm are presented in section 1.2.4. The proposed linkage approach does not require us to know full information about models' specification, and it can be seen as an endogenous reinforced learning algorithm describing how distributed agents (models) can take decisions to maximize the "cumulative reward". Sections 1.2.3–1.2.5 outline various aspects of the algorithm.

1.2.3. *Non-smooth model and linking algorithm*

A core part of the algorithm is a central hub computer that recalculates the resource quotas y by shifting their current approximation in the direction defined by the corresponding vectors of dual variables (shadow prices of resources) from the primal optimization problems. These quotas are received by sectorial/regional computers enabling parallel computations of solutions and fast adjustments of vector y. Ermoliev (1980) initially introduced the idea of this algorithm and current computer capacities enable its implementation in large-scale models used to support decisions.

Consider the main implicit maximization problem. For a given vector $y = (y^{(1)},\dots,y^{(K)})$, let us denote the optimal value of function [1.6] under constraints

[1.2–1.4] by $F(y)$; in other words, in this function $x^{(k)}(y)$ are optimal solutions to [1.1] under [1.2–1.4], ignoring joint constraints [1.5]. Therefore,

$$F(y) = \sum_{k=1}^{K} f^{(k)}(y),$$

where $f^{(k)}(y) = c^{(k)}, x^{(k)}(y))$ are concave non-differentiable (continuously) or non-smooth functions.

The following algorithm defines a rule for adjusting y toward an optimal y^* that maximizes function $F(y)$ under the joint constraints [1.5] defining the feasible set Y.

Consider an arbitrary feasible solution $y^s = (y^{s(1)}, \ldots, y^{s(K)})$ for iteration $s = 1,2, \ldots$ of the algorithm. For given quotas $y^s = \left(y^{s(1)}, \ldots, y^{s(K)}\right)$, independently and in parallel, computers of sectors/regions solve primal models [1.1–1.4] and obtain primal solutions $x^{s(k)} = x^{s(k)}(y^s)$ together with the corresponding shadow prices of resources, that is, solutions $(u^{s(k)}, v^{s(k)})$ of the dual problems

$$\left\langle b^{(k)}, u^{(k)} \right\rangle + \left\langle y^{(k)}, v^{(k)} \right\rangle \to min, \qquad [1.7]$$

$$A^{(k)} u^{(k)} + B^{(k)} v^{(k)} \geq w_k c^{(k)}, \qquad [1.8]$$

$$u^{(k)} \geq 0, v^{(k)} \geq 0, \qquad [1.9]$$

$k = 1,2, \ldots$, where vectors $v^{s(k)}$ are the driving force of algorithm [1.10].

The next approximation of quotas $y^{s+1} = \left(y^{s+1(1)}, \ldots, y^{s+1(K)}\right)$ is derived by the computer of the central hub by shifting y^s in the direction of vector $v^s = (v^{s(1)}, \ldots, v^{s(K)})$, that is, optimal dual variables (shadow prices) corresponding to constraints [1.4]. Hence, we have an iterative procedure defining, in a sense, the artificial "intellect" of the designed solution system:

$$y^{s+1} = \pi_Y(y^s + \rho_s v^s), = 1,2, \ldots, \qquad [1.10]$$

where ρ_s is an iteration-dependent multiplier, which is a method's parameter, and $\pi_Y(\cdot)$ is the orthogonal projection operator onto set Y (see, for example, Ermoliev 1976, 1980, 2009).

The orthogonal projection y^{s+1} of vector $\bar{y}^s = y^s + \rho_s v^s$ onto Y is calculated by minimizing the quadratic function $\|y^s + \rho_s v^s - y\|^2$ subject to joint constraints [1.5]. This minimization is very fast due to $\rho_s v^s \to 0$, as vectors v^s are bounded optimal dual solutions and if y^s is used as an initial approximation for y^{s+1}.

Vector v^s defines sub-gradient of the continuously non-differentiable function $F(x)$. This, and the convergence of solutions y^s to an optimal solution of the linkage problem [1.2]–[1.6] as $s \to \infty$ is analyzed in section 1.2.4. The step-size ρ_s is chosen from rather general and natural requirements: $\rho_s \geq 0$, $\sum_{s=1}^{\infty} \rho_s = \infty$, because generalized gradients are not the increasing directions of functions.

Although the standard sub-gradient projection method converges without condition $\sum_{s=1}^{\infty} \rho_s^2 < \infty$, the proposed linkage algorithm for problems under ASI [1.10] requires this additional condition to enable the convergence of not only function $F(y^s)$, but also solutions y^s. This allows us to propose a simple stopping criterion enabling the independent optimization of interdependent sectors by [1.10].

1.2.4. *Convergence of the linking algorithm (stopping criterion)*

Assume there exist solutions $x^{(k)}(y)$ of all K sectoral/regional models for feasible y satisfying constraints [1.5].

Then:

a) Functions $f^{(k)}(y) = (c^{(k)}, x^{(k)}(y))$, $F(y) = \sum_{k=1}^{K} f^{(k)}(x^{(k)})$ are concave continuously non-differentiable functions for all k.

b) The dual problem [1.7]–[1.9] has a solution $(u^{(k)}(y), v^{(k)}(y))$ for all k, and these solutions satisfy the stopping criterion of the linkage algorithm:

$$f^{(k)}(y) = (c^{(k)}, x \quad (y)) = (b^{(k)}, u \quad (y)) + (y, v \quad (y)).$$

This proposition leads to the following important fact (Ermoliev 1976, 1980, 2009), which is fundamental for solving the linkage problem through maximizing non-differentiable function $F(y)$ by algorithm [1.10]:

c) For any feasible solution z and y, $f^{(k)}(y) - f^{(k)}(z) \geq (v^{(k)}(y), y - z)$, that is, $v^{(k)}(y)$ is a subgradient of the concave non-differentiable function $f^{(k)}(y)$. Vector $v(y) = (v^{(1)}(y), \ldots, v^{(K)}(y))$ is a subgradient of function $F(y) = \sum_{k=1}^{K} f^{(k)}(y)$, $F_y(y) = v(y)$, that is, $F(y) - F(z) \geq (v(y), y - z)$.

Therefore, the procedure [1.10] is a specific subgradient algorithm for maximizing the (continuously) non-differentiable concave function $F(y)$.

The following proposition shows that y^s converges (non-monotonic convergence) to an optimal linking vector y^*, maximizing $F(y)$ subject to joint constraints [1.5]. Let us denote this feasible set by Y. Assume that

1) The feasible set Y is bounded.

2) Step size ρ_s satisfies the conditions: $\rho_s \geq 0$, $\sum_{s=1}^{\infty} \rho_s = \infty$, $\sum_{s=1}^{\infty} \rho_s^2 < \infty$, say $p_s = 1/s$.

Then $lim\, y^s \in Y^*$ for $s \to \infty$.

The following sequence of ρ_s satisfies the conditions of the theorem: $\rho_s = \gamma_s/s$, $0 \leq \underline{\gamma} \leq \gamma_s \leq \overline{\gamma} < \infty$ for some positive constants $\underline{\gamma}$ and $\overline{\gamma}$.

Joint constraints [1.5] may have the following form:

$$\sum_{k=1}^{K} M^{(k)} x^{(k)} + \sum_{k=1}^{K} D^{(k)} y^{(k)} \leq \delta \qquad [1.11]$$

with some matrices $M^{(k)}$. However, problems [1.1]–[1.4] and [1.11] can be reformulated similar to problems [1.1–1.5]. Let us define vectors $y^{(K+k)}$ such that $M^{(k)} x^{(k)} = y^{(K+k)}$, $k = 1, \ldots, K$. Now it is possible to rewrite [1.11] as $\sum_{k=1}^{K} D^{(k)} y^{(k)} \leq \delta - \sum_{k=k+1}^{2K} y^{(k)}$ and after some renotation, derive the problem in the form [1.1–1.5].

1.2.5. *Distributed computation*

The linkage algorithm can be summarized as follows. Imagine there is a network of distributed computers connecting submodels, say sectors, with a computer of a social planner. At the initial step, sectors k, $k = 1, \ldots, K$, use arbitrary chosen vectors $y^{0(k)}$ of resource quotas. They submit the information on $y^{0(k)}$ to the central computer. The computer updates quotas $y^0 = (y^{0(1)}, \ldots, y^{0(K)})$ by projecting them onto the set Y defining a first feasible approximation $y^1 = (y^{1(1)}, \ldots, y^{1(K)})$. All sectors independently solve models [1.1–1.4] with resource quotas y^1, calculate shadow prices $v^{1(k)}$ of common resources (constraint [1.4]) and submit to the central computer. The central computer calculates $y^1 + \rho_1 v^1$ with a step-size ρ_1 such that the product $\rho_1 v^1$ corresponds to the scale of y^1. Vector $y^1 + \rho_1 v^1$ is projected onto Y to derive quotas y^2. At the iteration $s + 1$, the algorithm derives the next approximation of quotas $y^{s+1} = (y^{s+1(1)}, \ldots, y^{s+1(K)})$ by shifting y^s in the direction of vector $v^s = (v^{s(1)}, \ldots, v^{s(K)})$, according to procedure [1.10].

At each iteration, all sectors independently calculate stopping criteria $\varepsilon_k(s) = (b^{(k)}, u^{s(k)}(y^s)) + (y^{s(k)}, v^{s(k)}(y^s)) - w_k(c^{(k)}, x^{s(k)}(y^s))$ and submit values $\varepsilon_k(s)$ to the central computer. If $\sum_k \varepsilon_k(s) \leq \varepsilon \geq 0$, where ε is an admissible accuracy, then the algorithm stops. Otherwise, it continues further. The convergence of the parallel independent optimization (linkage) of sectoral/regional models according to this algorithm, without revealing sectoral/reginal information, is possible due to the additional requirement $\sum_s \rho_s^2 < \infty$. This allows us to prove the convergence of solutions (linkages) y^s rather than the convergence of objective function $F(y^s)$. The convergence of the proposed linkage algorithm under ASI is based on the theory of (continuously) non-differentiable optimization (for more details, please see Ermoliev (1980)).

1.3. Linking energy and agricultural models for FEW nexus

The proposed iterative algorithm has been applied for linking energy and agricultural sectoral models under joint constraints on water and land use. Both models can be used for optimal energy and agricultural production and allocation planning. In the following, we only briefly outline the models. Further details can be found in some previous studies (Havlik et al. 2011; Ermolieva et al. 2016, 2021a; Gao et al. 2018; Ermoliev et al. 2022; Zagorodny et al. 2024). The models are spatially explicit, which allows us to link the models across locations and thus control local drivers having significant implications on the overall results of models' integration.

The energy model (Ermoliev et al. 2023) incorporates the main stages of energy flows from resources to demands: energy extraction from energy resources, primary energy conversion into secondary energy forms, transport and distribution of energy to the point of end and conversion into products for end users to fulfill specific demands. The structure of the model is such that it can incorporate various energy resources such as coal, gas, crude oil and renewables. Primary energy sources include coal, crude oil, gas, solar and wind; secondary energy sources are fuel oil, methanol, hydrogen, electricity, ammonia, etc.; final energy products are coal, fuel oil, gas, hydrogen, ammonia, methanol, electricity, etc. Demands for useful energy products come from main sectors of the economy: industrial, residential, transport, agricultural, water and energy. Each technology is characterized by unit costs, efficiency, lifetime, emissions, etc. Additional sectoral (and cross-sectoral joint) constraints are imposed to capture the requirements and the limitations on the natural resource use and availability, and investments. The model can include the existing technologies, as well as the new zero-carbon green technologies, at the beginning of implementation or even in the research stage, for example, various renewable and carbon capturing technologies.

The agricultural model (Havlik et al. 2011; Ermolieva et al. 2016, 2021a) can include main crops and livestock production and management systems, characterized by systems-specific production costs, water and fertilizers requirements, emission factors and other parameters. The supply of crops and livestock products need to cover food, feed and biofuel demands and fulfill security constraints. The food security constraint requires that the energy and nutrients consumption from grain and livestock products is not less than the required kilocalories and nutrients needed to satisfy dietary requirements in cereals, vegetable and animal products (meat and dairy products). Livestock feeds fulfill the livestock dietary requirements in energy intake measured in megacalories. Biofuels production from crops (and agricultural residues) have to fulfill biofuel mandates. In the model, land uses comprise agricultural (crop and pasture) land, grass land and natural land. Land use changes can be regulated by setting regulatory constraints on land expansion and conversion. Security constraints introduce competition for limited natural resources (land and water) among different land uses.

Energy and agricultural sectors compete for common land and water resources. Assume that regional planners, decision makers and sectoral authorities pursue a goal to minimize costs and maximize profits from energy and agricultural production under various joint balance (supply–demand) and resource constraints to fulfill the energy and agricultural demands. Namely, the goal is to choose a portfolio of energy technologies to be installed and operated to produce, convert and transfer energy products among locations, and a portfolio of agricultural technologies and management systems to produce and transfer among locations, agricultural commodities fulfilling constraints on natural resources, environmental pollution and end-products demands. The models include relevant risk-related systems performance criteria. These performance measures enable better understanding of how systems (individually and jointly) can perform in an uncertain environment in the presence of climate change, weather variability, market uncertainties, etc. The understanding of interdependencies of energy–water–agricultural systems can motivate regional and sectoral planners, experts, and involved stakeholders to make cross-sectoral coherent and risk-adjusted robust decisions.

1.3.1. *Energy, water and agricultural security nexus: case study in China*

In the case study in Shanxi province, China (Gao et al. 2018), the energy model was customized to include only coal-based industries and processes, that is, mining, washing, chemical production and power generation. The coal-based technologies consume vast amount of water, for example, for coal mining and washing, coal power plants cooling and steam production.

In the context of coal-based energy production, the integrated energy–agricultural–water model is formulated as follows. The problem is to decide how much coal x_{ijlmt} of type $i, i = 1, \dots, I$, to extract in location $j, j = 1, \dots, J$, transport to location $m, m = 1, \dots, M$, and convert by technology $t, t = 1, \dots, T$, to cover coal-based products (electricity, heating, cooling, pharmaceutical industry, etc.) demands.

Agricultural model decisions z_{kjm} concern agricultural commodities production, $k = 1, \dots, K$, in location j and transported to location m. The overall goal is to minimize the total costs of energy and agricultural production, transportation and conversion.

Individual sectoral goal functions are formulated as follows:

$$\sum_{i,j,k,m,t}\left[c_{ij}^{CP} + c_{ijm}^{CT} + c_{ijt}^{CC}\right]x_{ijmt} \rightarrow min \quad [1.12]$$

and

$$\sum_{i,j,k,m,t}\left[c_{kj}^{AP} + c_{kj}^{AT}\right]z_{kjm} \rightarrow min \quad [1.13]$$

for energy [1.12] and agricultural [1.13] sectors. Production costs c_{ij}^{CP} define all components of coal production costs, including extraction and washing, of a unit (ton) coal of type i in location j, transportation costs c_{ijm}^{CT} represent all costs associated with transporting a unit coal i from location j to location m, c_{ijt}^{CC} define conversion costs of a unit coal i by technology t in location j, c_{kj}^{AP} denote agricultural production cost per unit (ton) agricultural commodity k in location j and c_{kjm}^{AT} stand for transportation costs of a unit agricultural commodity k from j to $m, i = 1, \dots, I, j = 1, \dots, J, m = 1, \dots, M, t = 1, \dots, T, k = 1, \dots, K$.

The energy security constraints ensure that the demands for coal-based end products (electricity, heat, coke, gas and oil) are fulfilled:

$$\sum_{ijt} \alpha_{imt}^{d} x_{ijmt} \geq D_m^d, \quad [1.14]$$

where α_{ijt}^{d} denotes the conversion coefficient of coal i in location j by technology t, and D_j^d stands for the end product d demand.

Agricultural production fulfills food security constraints, which can be calculated according to nutrients and kilocalories norms for population by age groups:

$$\sum_j z_{kjm} \geq D_{km}^A, \quad [1.15]$$

where D_{km}^A is the demand for agricultural commodity k in location m to meet food security requirements.

Sectoral land use constraints

$$\sum_{i,m,t} x_{ijmt}\left(1 - r_{ij}\right)\ \Delta l_j S_{ij} + g \sum_{i,m,t} x_{ijmt} \leq L_j^C \quad [1.16]$$

and

$$\sum_{k,m} l_{kj} z_{kjm} \leq L_j^A \quad [1.17]$$

incorporate land demand by coal [1.16] and crop [1.17] production activities, where L_j^C and L_j^A are land use constraints for coal and agricultural sectors in location j, respectively. Parameter S_{ij} in [1.16] defines the area that may become unusable as a result of coal mining, Δl_j is a portion of agricultural land overlapping with a coal field in location j, parameter r_{ij} for coal i in location j defines plausible land reclamation rate and g_{ij} is a parameter allowing us to calculate the land under coal reject material. In equation [1.17], parameter l_{kj} defines the area required for a unit crop k production in location j. Equation [1.18] introduces the restriction on the total land use in location j by energy and agricultural sectors

$$\sum_{k,m} l_{kj} y_{kjm} + \sum_{i,m,t} x_{ijmt} (1 - r_{ij}) \ \Delta l_j l_{ij} + g_{ij} \sum_{i,m,t} x_{ijmt} \leq L_j. \quad [1.18]$$

Total available water W_j for both sectors and sectoral water quotas (W_j^E and W_j^A) significantly affect the choice of coal and crop (energy) production technologies through water utilization constraints:

$$\sum_{i,m,t} [w_{ij}^P + w_{ij}^d] x_{ijmt} \leq W_j^E \quad [1.19]$$

and

$$\sum_{k,m} w_{kj}^c z_{kmj} \leq W_j^A \quad [1.20]$$

where W_j^E and W_j^A are quotas on water use by coal and agricultural activities in location j, w_{ij}^P defines water requirement for a unit coal i production in location j, w_{ij}^d is water required for a unit coal i conversion in location j and w_{km}^c is water required for a unit crop k production in location j. Water use W_j^E for coal and W_j^A for agricultural production are constrained by total water W_j available in j:

$$W_j^E + W_j^A \leq W_j. \quad [1.21]$$

In the condition of ASI, the planner does not have full information about separate LP energy ([1.12], [1.14], [1.16] and [1.19]) and agricultural ([1.13], [1.15], [1.17] and [1.20]) submodels. To link the models under joint constraints [1.18] and [1.21], we implement procedure [1.10]. At the initial step of the procedure s = 0, individual sectoral models are solved using initial sectoral land and water quotas $L_j^C(0)$, $L_j^A(0)$ and $W_j^C(0)$, $W_j^A(0)$. Resource quotas $y^s = (L_j^C(\mathrm{s}), L_j^A(\mathrm{s}), W_j^C(\mathrm{s}), W_j^A(\mathrm{s}))$ at step s are adjusted according to [1.10] using shadow prices (dual variables) of energy and agricultural sectors land and water resource constraints

$$\sum_{i,m,t} x_{ijmt} (1 - r_{ij}) \Delta l_j S_{ij} + g \sum_{i,m,t} x_{ijmt} \leq L_j^C (s - 1) \quad [1.22]$$

$$\sum_{k,m} l_{kj} y_{kjm} \leq L_j^A(s-1) \qquad [1.23]$$

$$\sum_{i,m,t} w_{ij}^P x_{imlt} + \sum_{i,m,t} w_{ij}^d x_{ijmt} \leq W_j^C(s-1) \qquad [1.24]$$

$$\sum_{k,m} w_{kj}^c y_{kmj} \leq W_j^A(s-1) \qquad [1.25]$$

and constraints [1.18] and [1.21].

1.3.2. *Selected results*

Results were calculated and compared for three scenarios: (1) separately optimized energy and agricultural models, (2) hard-linked IM (one-code model) and (3) separate models integrated via the linkage procedure [1.10]. In the first scenarios, the net profits can be higher than in other two scenarios because the sectors are not restricted by joint constraints. This result is misleading the resource allocation analysis. In scenario 3, the solution of the iterative linkage process converges rather quickly (only in 10 iteration steps) to the solutions of the hard-integrated model, scenario 2.

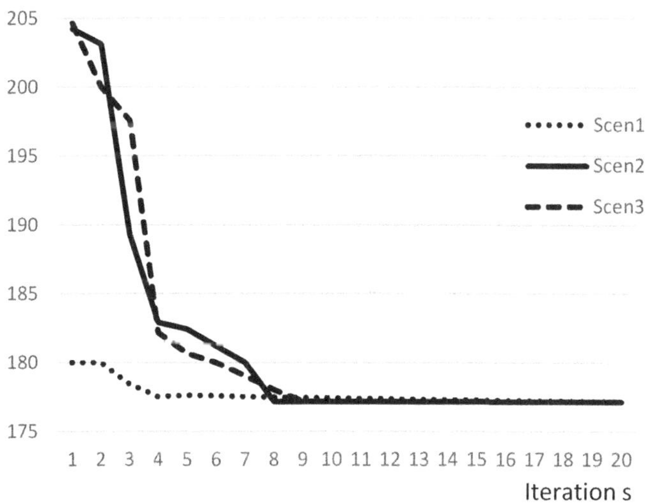

Figure 1.1. *Convergence of the iterative linking procedure in terms of the goal function values $F(y^s)$. Vertical axis displays net profits, and the iteration step is marked on the horizontal axis. The three curves (Scen1, Scen2 and Scen3) correspond to three different initial land and water quota scenarios at s = 0.*

Figure 1.1 illustrates the non-monotonic convergence of the linkage algorithm for three different scenarios of initial y^0 quotas allocated to energy and agricultural sectors. The choice of the step-size ρ_s in [1.10] affects the convergence rate, and the value of the product $\rho_s v^s$ must correspond to the value of solutions y^s.

1.4. Conclusion

In this chapter, we discuss the problem of linking distributed individual sectoral and/or regional optimization models into an inter-sectoral IM. The approach for linking models is based on an iterative SQG procedure of, in general, non-smooth non-differentiable optimization converging to a socially optimal solution maximizing an implicit nested non-differentiable social welfare function. The convergence of the algorithm relies on the duality theory and the non-differentiable optimization. The iterative solution procedure can be used for robust estimation and machine learning problems, in particular, it can be viewed as an endogenous reinforced learning problem.

The iterative SQG-based methods and their stochastic versions are intended for robust optimization of deterministic and stochastic systems with large number of decision variables and scenarios of uncertainties due to the ability of these methods to link scenario-simulation and optimization procedures. The proposed linkage method will be further developed for linking stochastic models enabling integrated management of global systemic risks.

The linkage of models is, in a sense, opposite to decomposition methods. While in the decomposition (e.g. Dantzig and Wolfe 1960; Kim and Nazareth 1991), we split an existing integrated optimization model into a number of smaller sub-models, in the linkage, we obtain an IM of the system by linking existing explicitly unknown sub-models. The proposed linkage procedure provides a flexibility enabling the simultaneous use of linkage and decomposition procedures; in other words, endogenously disaggregating models to make their further integration (linkage) more efficient.

1.5. Acknowledgments

The development of the methodologies and models is supported by EU PARATUS (CL3-2021-DRS-01-03, grant number 101073954) project on "Promoting disaster preparedness and resilience by co-developing stakeholder support tools for managing systemic risk of compounding disasters", by a joint project between the International Institute for Applied Systems Analysis (IIASA) and the National Academy of Sciences of Ukraine (NASU) on "Integrated robust modeling and management of food–energy–water–land use nexus for sustainable development" (22–501). Moreover, the work was supported by the project "Comprehensive analysis of robust preventive and adaptive measures of food, energy, water and social management in the context of systemic risks and consequences of COVID-19" (0122U000552) of National Academy of Sciences of Ukraine.

1.6. References

Alemany, M., Esteso, A., Ortiz, A., Pino, M.D. (2021). Centralized and distributed optimization models for the multi-farmer crop planning problem under uncertainty: Application to a fresh tomato Argentinean supply chain case study. *Computers and Industrial Engineering*, 153. doi: 10.1016/j.cie.2020.107048.

Böhringer, C. and Rutherford, T.F. (2009). Integrated assessment of energy policies: Decomposing top-down and bottom-up. *Journal of Economic Dynamics and Control*, 33(9), 1648–1661.

Cano, E.L., Moguerza, J.M., Ermolieva, T., Yermoliev, Y. (2016). A strategic decision support system framework for energy-efficient technology investments. *TOP*, 25(2), 249–270.

Dantzig, G.B. and Wolfe, P. (1960). The decomposition principle for linear programming. *Econometrica*, 29, 767–778.

Dean, R. and Cortés, J. (2015). Robust distributed linear programming. *IEEE Transactions on Automatic Control*, 60(10), 2567–2582.

Ermoliev, Y. (1976). *Methods of Stochastic Programming*. Nauka, Moscow.

Ermoliev, Y. (1980). Some problems of linkage systems. IIASA Working Paper WP-80-102. International Institute for Applied Systems Analysis (IIASA), Laxenburg.

Ermoliev, Y. (2009). Two-stage stochastic programming: Stochastic quasigradient methods. In *Encyclopedia of Optimization*, Floudas, C.A. and Pardalos, P.M. (eds). Springer-Verlag, New York.

Ermoliev, Y. and Knopov, P.S. (2006). Method of empirical means in stochastic programming problems. *Cybernetics and Systems Analysis*, 42(6), 773–785.

Ermoliev, Y. and Norkin, V. (1997). On nonsmooth and discontinuous problems of stochastic systems optimization. *Eur. J. Oper. Res.*, 101(2), 230–244.

Ermoliev, Y. and von Winterfeldt, D. (2012). Systemic risks and security management. In *Managing Safety of Heterogeneous Systems: Decisions under Uncertainty and Risks*, Ermoliev, Y., Makowski, M., Marti, K. (eds). Springer-Verlag, New York.

Ermoliev, Y., Ermolieva, T., Jonas, M., Obersteiner, M., Wagner, F., Winiwarter, W. (2015). Integrated model for robust emission trading under uncertainties: Cost-effectiveness and environmental safety. *Technological Forecasting and Social Change*, 98, 234–244.

Ermoliev, Y., Zagorodny, A.G., Bogdanov, V. L., Ermolieva, T., Havlik, P., Rovenskaya, E., Komendantova, N., Obersteiner, M. (2022). Robust food–energy–water–environmental security management: Stochastic quasigradient procedure for linkage of distributed optimization models under asymmetric information and uncertainty. *Cybernetics and Systems Analysis*, 58 (1), 45–57.

Ermoliev, Z., Komendantova, N., Ermolieva, T. (2023). Energy production and storage investments and operation planning involving variable renewable energy sources: A two-stage stochastic optimization model with rolling time horizon and random stopping time. In *Modern Optimization Methods for Decision Making Under Risk and Uncertainty*, Gaivoronski, A., Knopov, P., Zaslavskyi, V. (eds). Taylor & Francis, Oxfordshire. doi: 10.1201/9781003260196-2.

Ermolieva, T., Havlík, P., Ermoliev, Y., Mosnier, A., Obersteiner, M., Leclère, D., Khabarov, N., Valin, H., Reuter, W. (2016). Integrated management of land use systems under systemic risks and security targets: A stochastic Global Biosphere Management Model. *Journal of Agricultural Economics*, 67(3), 584–601.

Ermolieva, T., Havlik, P., Ermoliev, Y., Khabarov, N., Obersteiner, M. (2021a). Robust management of systemic risks and food-water-energy-environmental security: Two-stage strategic-adaptive GLOBIOM model. *Sustainability*, 13(2), 857. doi: 10.3390/su13020857.

Ermolieva, T., Ermoliev, Y., Obersteiner, M., Rovenskaya, E. (2021b). Two-stage nonsmooth stochastic optimization and iterative stochastic quasigradient procedure for robust estimation, machine learning and decision making. In *Resilience in the Digital Age*, Roberts, F.S. and Sheremet, I.A. (eds). Springer, Berlin. doi: 10.1007/978-3-030-70370-7_4.

Gaivoronski, A. and Werner, A. (2012). Stochastic programming perspective on the agency problems under uncertainty. In *Managing Safety of Heterogeneous Systems: Decisions Under Uncertainty and Risks,* Ermoliev, Y., Makowski, M., Marti, K. (eds). Springer, New York.

Galichon, A. (2016). *Optimal Transport Methods in Economics*. Princeton University Press, Princeton.

Gao, J., Xu, X., Cao, G., Ermoliev, Y.M., Ermolieva, T.Y., Rovenskaya, E.A. (2018). Optimizing regional food and energy production under limited water availability through integrated modeling. *Sustainability*, 10(6). doi: 10.3390/su10061689.

Harker, P.T. (1991). Generalized Nash games and quasi-variational inequalities. *European Journal of Operational Research*, 54, 81–94.

Havlík, P., Schneider, U.A., Schmid, E., Boettcher, H., Fritz, S., Skalský, R., Aoki, K., de Cara, S., Kindermann, G., Kraxner, F. et al. (2011). Global land-use implications of first and second generation biofuel targets. *Energy Policy*, 39, 5690–5702.

Kim, K. and Nazareth, J.L. (1991). The decomposition principle and algorithms for linear programming. *Linear Algebra and Its Applications*, 152, 119–133.

Knopov, P.S. and Kasitskaya, E.J. (1995). Properties of empirical estimates in stochastic optimization and identification problems. *Annals of Operations Research*, 56(1), 225–239.

Liang, S., Wang, L., Yin, G. (2019). Distributed smooth convex optimization with coupled constraints. *IEEE Transactions on Automatic Control*, 1. doi: 10.1109/TAC.2019.2912494.

Norkin, V. (1999). Reducing models of general economic equilibrium to optimization problems. *Cybern. Syst. Anal.*, 35(5), 743–753.

Ogryczak, W. (2000). Multiple criteria linear programming model for portfolio selection. *Annals of Operations Research*, 97, 143–162.

Prakash, R. and Nygard, K.E. (2017). *Distributed Linear Programming Models in a Smart Grid.* Springer, Cham.

Rockafeller, T. (1981). *The Theory of Subgradient and Its Application to Problems of Optimization: Convex and Nonconvex Functions*. Helderman Verlag, Berlin.

Yang, T., Yi, X., Wu, J., Yuan, Y., Wu, D., Meng, Z., Hong, Y., Wang, H., Lin, Z., Johansson, K. (2019). A survey of distributed optimization. *Annual Reviews in Control*, 47, 278–305.

Zagorodny, A.G. and Ermoliev, Y. (eds) (2013). *Integrated Modeling of Food, Energy and Water Security Management for Sustainable Social, Economic and Environmental Developments.* National Academy of Sciences of Ukraine, Kiev.

Zagorodny, A.G., Ermoliev, Y.M., Bogdanov, V.L., Ermolieva, T. (eds) (2020). *Integrated Modeling and Management of Food-Energy-Water Nexus for Sustainable Development.* Committee for Systems Analysis at Presidium of NASU-NMO of Ukraine at IIASA, Kiev.

Zagorodny, A., Bogdanov, V., Ermolieva, T., Komendantova, N. (2024). Modeling for managing food–energy–water–social–environmental–nexus security: Novel systems' analysis approaches. In *Nexus of Sustainability: Understanding of FEWSE Systems*, Zagorodny, A., Bogdanov, V., Zaporozhets, A. (eds). Springer, Berlin [Online]. Available at: https://link.springer.com/chapter/10.1007/978-3-031-66764-0_1.

2

Integrated Modeling for Managing Catastrophic Risks: Vulnerability Analysis and Systemic Risks Management

Catastrophic-dependent systemic losses have analytically intractable multidimensional probability distributions dependent on exogenous shocks, interactions among goals and constraints of the involved actors and systems, activities of economic sectors, structural and environmental standards, critical infrastructure in place, feasible mitigation and adaptation structural and financial measures, investment potentials, etc. In analyzing systemic risks, we argue for the design of proper decision support systems (DSSs) and integrated catastrophe analysis and management modeling approaches similar to integrated spatially explicit catastrophe risk management model (ISCRiMM) of IIASA. We discuss several important aspects and components of the ISCRiMM. This includes considerations of systemic risks, safety and security constraints, the necessity of robust ex ante loss reduction and ex post emergency response and building back better (BBB) actions, structural and financial measures, the need for stochastic catastrophe models (scenario generators) and proper stochastic optimization (STO) solution procedures to enable the decision-support regarding coherent systemic ex ante and ex post preventing and coping solutions for dealing with catastrophes. The diversion of capital from ex post measures to ex ante investments into structural loss reduction measures can essentially reduce the dependencies among losses and, hence, decrease overall vulnerability, stabilize insurance mechanisms, reduce the demand for ex post risk sharing and restoration efforts. One of the ISCRiMM submodels is the vulnerability assessment model. In this chapter, we discuss different methodologies and models for vulnerabilities analysis and modeling, and how they can be effectively integrated within ISCRiMM. In particular, vulnerability models can be based on AI, statistical and machine learning (ML) principles, which provide an effective means of incorporating them into ISCRiMM and designing optimal and robust interdependent ex ate and ex post measures decreasing vulnerabilities and increasing resilience and BBB capacities.

Chapter written by Nadejda KOMENDANTOVA, Tatiana Y. ERMOLIEVA, Taher ZOBEIDI, Iuliana ARMAS, Dragos TOMA-DANILA and Marcel HÜRLIMANN.

2.1. Introduction

The increasing vulnerability of the modern society is an alarming tendency. Losses from natural and human-made catastrophes are rapidly increasing. Catastrophes destroy communication systems, electricity supply and irrigation, and affect agricultural and energy production and provision systems.

One of the main reasons for the increasing losses due to natural and man-made catastrophes is the ignorance of risks and the lack of risk-based planning leading to the concentration of industries, infrastructure, wealth, people in risk-prone areas as well as the creation of new risk-prone areas. The trend becomes alarming especially because of the growing interdependencies among economic sectors and regions, the introduction of new policies and technologies, growing demands, and the increasing frequency and severity of floods, hurricanes, storms, droughts, landslides and prolonged heatwaves.

Continued urbanization and development in hazardous areas have been putting more people and wealth in harm's way. Urbanization and population concentration magnify impacts of hurricanes, windstorms, floods, heatwaves, epidemics and other natural catastrophes, exacerbated by the systemic risks within socioeconomic and environmental systems.

The alarming tendency of increasing losses due to the combination of natural and human-induced risks calls for risk-based approaches to economic developments and catastrophe management, for the design of robust interdependent ex-ante mitigation and ex-post adaptation options, to deal with the risks of all kinds. The measures aim to decrease societal vulnerabilities, increase resilience and BBB capacity.

For the analysis of the systemic risks, we argue for the design of DSSs and integrated catastrophe analysis and management modeling approaches similar to ISCRiMM of IIASA (Ermoliev et al. 1997, 2000, 2003, 2008, 2018; Ermolieva et al. 1997, 2016, 2023b; Amendola et al. 2013; see also the discussion in Atoyev et al. 2018). In section 2.2.1, we discuss several important aspects and components of the ISCRiMM. This includes considerations of systemic risks, safety and security constraints, robust interdependent ex-ante and ex-post (strategic and operational) mitigation and adaptation structural and financial measures, the need for stochastic catastrophe models (scenario generators) and proper STO solution procedures to enable the decision-support for dealing with catastrophes. Section 2.2.2 summarizes main features of systemic risks as a new type of risks that depend on the whole structure of systemic interactions (see, e.g. Ermoliev and von Winterfeldt 2012; Ermolieva et al. 2016a, 2016b, 2021a,b, 2023a,b). These risks are analytically intractable. They can be triggered by a combination of exogenous and endogenous shocks, that is, by natural hazards in combination with decisions of intelligent agents and, therefore, they cannot be described by a probability distribution. In section 2.2.3, we outline impact chains (ICs) approach as one of the existing ways to describing systemic interdependencies. However, the ICs methodology may not be sufficient to capture and manage the dynamics of systemic risks, possible delays, thresholds in the IC elements (risk factors, dependencies and elements at risk).

Management of systemic risks requires approaches incorporating individual and joint systemic safety and security constraints as it is discussed in section 2.2.4. The model can be revised and tuned to address specifics of case studies under investigation. For example, catastrophe funds (risk reserves) can be used for capital accumulation and further investments into structural retrofitting ex ante and reconstruction ex post, as well as for loss compensation after disaster events.

Systemic risks depend on socioeconomic and structural vulnerabilities, reliability and resilience of infrastructures, that is, the ability to prepare for and adapt to changing conditions and withstand and recover rapidly from disruptions. Section 2.3 makes an overview of different vulnerabilities as well as the existing approaches to vulnerabilities modeling. As an alternative or supplementing the traditional modeling methods, section 2.4 outlines statistical and ML approaches, the methodology and selected results. The section presents Risk&Vulnerability Scenario generator software being developed at International Institute for Applied Systems Analysis Cooperation and Transformative Governance group (CAT at IIASA), in particular, for PARATUS project (Promoting disaster preparedness and resilience by co-developing stakeholder support tools for managing the systemic risk of compounding disasters: https://www.paratus-project.eu/). The software aims to visualize socioeconomic and structural vulnerability scenarios simulated under alternative assumptions (projections) of vulnerability drivers, that is, population density, level of education, dependency ratios, population by age groups, buildings' codes/taxonomy and structural safety requirements. The software enables to test various mitigation preparedness and post-event reconstruction measures, which are briefly summarized in sections 2.5. Conclusions are presented in section 2.6.

2.2. Management of endogenous systemic risks: safety indicators and robust measures

2.2.1. *Structure of integrated catastrophe risk management model*

In this section, we briefly outline the structure of the ISCRiMM. The model consists, in principle, of three major interlinked submodels or modules (Ermolieva et al. 2023): a catastrophe module, an engineering vulnerability module and an economic multi-agent module.

A catastrophe module simulates (or takes into account the available) stochastic scenarios of natural hazards based on the knowledge of the event and scientific equations and variables describing it (Baranov et al. 2002; Amendola et al. 2012, 2015; Compton et al. 2013; Toma-Danila et al. 2015). The catastrophe models used in IIASA's case studies are based on Monte Carlo dynamic simulations of geographically explicit catastrophe patterns in selected regions.

The vulnerability module is used to estimate the degree of probability of elements at risk to suffer damages that may result from catastrophes. These can be direct and indirect damages depending on the goals of a case study. Shaking intensities, duration of standing water, water discharge speed or wind speeds and other characteristics of the natural hazard are the variables, which vulnerability modules can take from the catastrophe modules to calculate potential damages. The vulnerability module accounts for engineering principles. To calculate damages to buildings, for example, it can use structural vulnerability (or fragility) curves based on the buildings' taxonomy. It can also incorporate reduced forms of "damage" ("vulnerabilities") scenario generators using statistical and ML principles as is discussed in section 2.4. The vulnerabilities can be reduced through improvements of buildings codes and infrastructure safety regulations, construction of shelters, population relocation, loss compensation and reconstruction programs. The location and the level of the implemented measures depend on the goals and constraints of the risk management incorporated in ISCRiMM, for example, the safety constraints for systemic risks management (see discussion in section 2.2.4).

The economic multi-agent model is a stochastic dynamic welfare growth model. This model maps spatial economic losses/damages into gains and losses of the involved agents, that is, those who are affected by the disaster and those who are responsible for the implementation of preparedness, emergency response and recovery measures: central and local governments, infrastructure administration, water and energy systems authorities, private or/and public mandatory catastrophe insurance (catastrophe funds), investors, "individuals" (cells or regions), producers (farmers), etc., depending on implemented loss mitigating and sharing policy options.

GIS-based modeling of catastrophes and vulnerability coupled with multi-agent models, though still limited in use, is becoming increasingly important: to governments and legislative authorities for better comprehension, negotiation and management of risks; to insurance companies for making decisions on the allocation and values of contracts, premiums, reinsurance arrangements and the effects of mitigation measures; to households, industries, farmers for risk-based allocation of properties and values.

However, a scenario-by-scenario approach leads to different scenario-dependent strategies. The number of alternative decisions can be very large. The exploding dimensionality of the "if–then" analysis can be bypassed. The search for "robust" optimal combination of interdependent ex-ante preparedness and ex-post adaptative decisions can be done by incorporating the two-stage STO and the spatial adaptive Monte Carlo optimization procedure (based on stochastic quasigradient (SQG) procedure) (Ermoliev and Wets 1988; Ermoliev 2009a, 2009b, 2009c) into catastrophe modeling. The adaptive Monte Carlo search procedure enables the design of desirable robust solutions without evaluating all possible alternatives. The capacity of a region to deal with disaster losses ex post is built ex post.

Schematically, the model with an embedded optimization procedure is presented in Figure 2.1. Starting with some initial setting, policy variables are input into the "catastrophe model". The catastrophe model generates (or picks up) stochastic catastrophe scenarios and induced direct and indirect damages. The efficiency of the policies is evaluated with respect to safety and security performance indicators (block "indicators") of the agents, for example, insurers, the insured and governments. If these do not fulfill the requirements, that is, the goals and constraints (e.g. cause imbalances, failures or business interruption), they are further adjusted in the block "adaptive feedbacks". In this manner, it is possible to take into account complex interdependencies between damages in different locations, available decisions, resulting damage reductions, reconstruction demand, compensations, etc.

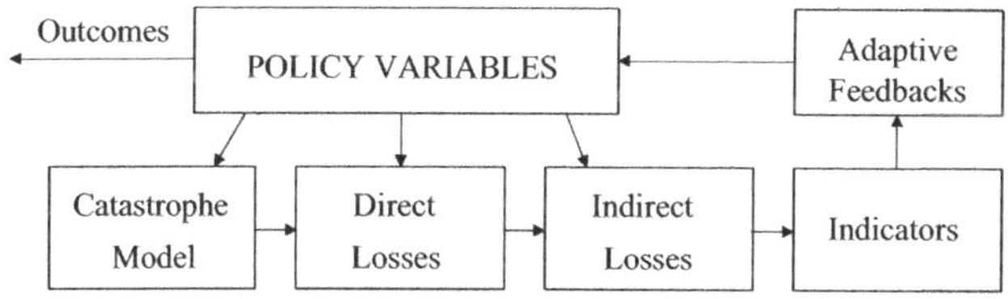

Figure 2.1. *Schematic representation of the models: adaptive Monte Carlo*

A crucial aspect is the use of appropriate risk indicators and safety constraints, for example, to avoid "bankruptcies" or "ruins" of agents.

2.2.2. *Systemic risks*

Systemic risks and security analysis include risks (threats), which are generated in interdependent food, energy, water, environmental, social (FEWES) and other systems due to failures in the systems, shortfalls of supply–demand relationships among the systems, exceedances of critical thresholds (e.g. lack of water for hydropower generation or for cooling a power station), etc. Examples of systemic risks are losses (damages) and costs incurred due to floods, which are often triggered by rain, hurricanes and earthquakes in combination with inappropriate land use planning, maintenance of flood protection systems and behavior of various agents. The construction of levees, dikes and dams may create an illusion of safety. However, in the absence of proper maintenance and further developments in the neighboring areas, these constructions can lead to catastrophic events of high consequences. Other examples include systemic risks in social, financial, economic, energy, food and water, and systems security management, for example, due to inadequate infrastructures (buildings codes), not satisfying the safety requirements.

Systemic risks in interdependent FEWES systems can be defined as the risks of a subsystem (a part of the system) threatening the sustainable performance of the whole system and the achievement of FEWES security goals. Thus, a shock in a peripheral subsystem induced (intentionally or unintentionally) by an endogenous or exogenous event can trigger systemic risks propagation with impacts, that is, instability or even a collapse, at various levels. The risks may have quite different policy-driven dependent spatial and temporal patterns. While standard risks analysis and assessment can rely on historical data, systemic cascading risks in FEWES systems are implicitly defined by the whole structure and the interactions among the systems, in particular costs, production and processing technologies, prices, trade flows, supply-demand balances, risk exposure, FEWES security requirements, risk measures and decisions of agents. The notion of systemic risks was introduced in relation to financial systems. The definition has been adopted for other natural and anthropogenic systems, for example, power grids and critical infrastructures, biodiversity, financial and insurance systems, and other natural and anthropogenic systems.

Prediction of systemic risks in integrated natural and anthropogenic policy-driven FEWES systems is a rather tedious task. The main issue in this case is robust management of the risks, which can be achieved by equipping the systems with precautionary (risk prevention and reduction) and operational (emergency and post disaster recovery) strategies enabling the systems sufficient flexibility and robustness to maintain sustainable performance and fulfill joint FEWES security goals independently of what systemic shock occurs (Ermoliev and Winterfeldt 2012; Ermolieva et al. 2016b, 2021).

In front of uncertainties, the strategies (decisions) can be of two main types: the ex-ante strategic precautionary anticipative actions (engineering design, building codes, shelters, resource allocation, technological investments, water and grain reserves) and the ex-post adaptive adjustments (inventory control, subsidies, prices, costs, reconstruction and BBB) that are made after the event occurrence.

A portfolio of robust interdependent ex-ante and ex-post strategies can be designed by using a two-stage STO approach incorporating both types of decisions (see, e.g. Ermoliev 2009a, 2009c; Ermoliev et al. 2000; Ermolieva et al. 2003, 2016, 2023 and references therein). The two-stage STO has been also applied in studies for dealing with systemic interdependent risks, for example, for agricultural risks management (Borodina et al. 2012, 2020), energy security management (Cano et al. 2014; Ermoliev et al. 2023), robust operation of multipurpose reservoirs (Ortiz-Partida et al. 2019) and climate change risk analysis (Ermolieva and Obersteiner 2005; O'Neil et al. 2006).

The management of systemic risks and security strongly depends on the individual and systemic safety and reliability regulations (standards, requirements) imposed on the systems' relationships and policies (measures) in place. Depending on the risks (earthquake, heavy precipitation, windstorm and heat wave), structural measures have to withstand the required earthquake shaking; shelters have to protect population; dams, dikes and levees have to confirm safety requirements; the measures have to be well operated, maintained and regularly monitored; water retention areas and channels have to be designed and maintained to protect against overtopping and/or flooding; policies need to be made for of a better land-use planning to preserve forests protecting areas against hurricanes, strong winds and precipitation runoff; discourage building in areas prone to catastrophes, etc.

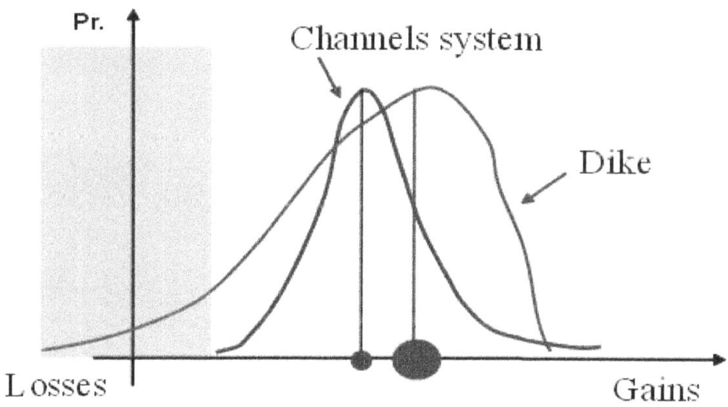

Figure 2.2. *Loss distribution depends on policies regarding dike or channel flood protection system: what risk is better? For a color version of this figure, see www.iste.co.uk/gaivoronski/stochastic1.zip*

Structural measures and their reliability can considerably reshape the risks. The measures can induce additional benefits. For example, construction of a dike motivates further regional developments. On the other hand, without proper maintenance, the measures can transform the risks to more severe and compound ones.

2.2.3. *Visualization of systemic risks with impact chains*

Natural disasters can cause direct and indirect structural damages. Houses can be knocked off their foundations and buildings can collapse, thereby causing roads blockage. Roads and bridges can be damaged or collapse either due to an earthquake or due to post-events like landslides or floods. Landslides can block roads and knock down energy utility poles or, more generally, energy infrastructure, taking out power in large areas. Power, gas and internet lines can rupture preventing sustainable businesses functioning. The interdependences, risks associated with each element and the systemic damage can be to a certain extent captured by ICs, for example, in Figure 2.3.

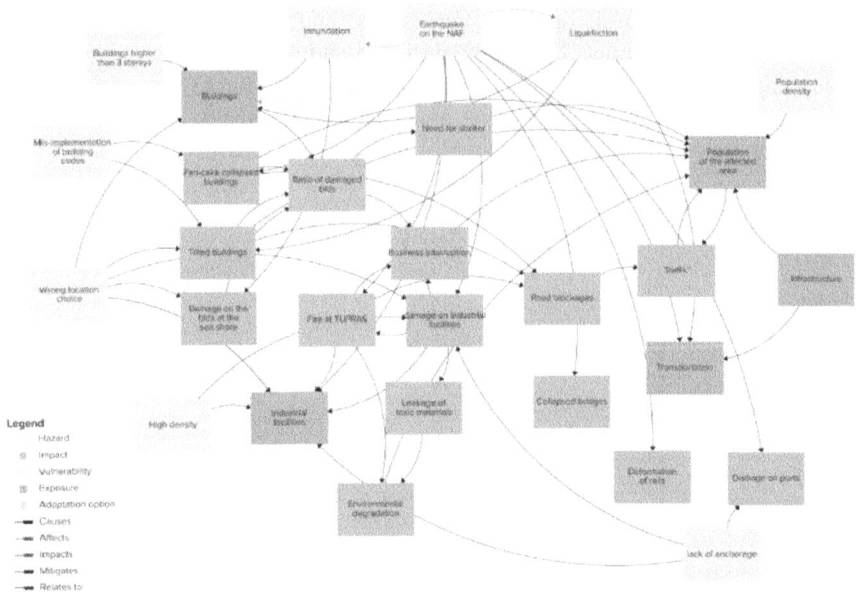

Figure 2.3. *Example of an IC for a region prone to earthquake risks. For a color version of this figure, see www.iste.co.uk/gaivoronski/stochastic1.zip*

ICs are being developed to explore cause and effect relationships to provide insights into the trigger events, systemic interdependencies and risks. They can show how one event leads to another. This is essential for understanding how the events are linked together. In many cases, uncertainties and ambiguity among the interdependent systems create difficulties for representing the dynamics of systemic risks, possible delays and thresholds. The inclusion of elements into ICs depends on stakeholders' knowledge and expertise. Thus, the development of ICs is not a straightforward task. A flood can be triggered by expansive deforestation in a region upstream beyond the IC diagram. Another example is a flooding upstream due to a bridge blockage preventing river flow downstream. Both situations can be overlooked in an IC.

Systemic risks can be addressed by safety regulations in combination with robust and interdependent precautionary and operational recovery measures through building-up the resilience with ex-ante measures minimizing occurrences of systemic failures and by expanding adaptive capacities to deal with the consequences ex post.

2.2.4. *Safety constraints for systemic risks management*

This section presents an example of how safety constraints for systemic risks management are integrated within the ISCRiMM. To account for multiple risk-exposed stakeholders and respective risk management options, the study region is subdivided into sub-regions or locations $j = \overline{1:m}$. Locations (or regions) can be characterized by a collection of households, a segment of a gas pipeline, flood-protection zone, municipality, etc. For example, in the flood-risk case study in the Netherlands (Ermolieva et al. 2016), the locations corresponded to dike-protected and non-protected areas. We assume that for each location j, an estimation W_j of the property value (corresponding to elements-at-risk (EAR)) or "wealth" of this location exists, which includes values of houses, lands, factories, etc.

Assume that the risks are mitigated and covered through a joint loss (re)construction and sharing program, and there are n agents, $i = \overline{1:n}$, (insurers, governments, re-insurers, funds, individuals, energy and water authorities), contributing to this program. They may have obligations (contracts in the case of insurers) with locations to cover losses/and finance retrofitting and post-event recovery projects. Each agent i has an initial fund, stock of money, or a risk reserve R_i^0 that depends on magnitudes of catastrophic events, loss-reduction measures in place, socioeconomic and structural vulnerabilities.

Assume that the planning horizon covers $t = 0,1...$ time intervals. The risk reserve (reconstruction fund) R_i^t at each t is calculated according to the following formula:

$$R_i^{t+1} = R_i^t + \sum_{j=1}^{m}(\pi_{ij}^t - c_{ij}^t(q_{ij}^t)) - \sum_{j=1}^{m} L_j^t(\omega_t)q_{ij}^t, \quad [2.1]$$

where q_{ij}^t is the loss coverage or reconstruction financing of a company (insurer, fund) i in location j at time t, $\sum_{i=1}^{n} q_{ij}^t \leq 1$, π_{ij}^t is the premium (tax) paid into a company i in location j at time t, $c_{ij}^t(q_{ij}^t)$ are transaction costs or administrative, running or other costs. $L_j^t(\omega_t)$ is the loss (damage) in location j caused by a catastrophe ω_t at time t.

Catastrophic events $\omega = (\omega_0, \omega_1, \ldots)$ may affect a random number of different locations. In general, a catastrophic event at time t is modeled by a random subset of affected locations j and its magnitude in each j. The losses $L_j^t(\omega_t)$ depend on the event ω_t, mitigation measures (e.g. dikes against flooding) and vulnerability of structural values in j (e.g. building codes, structural reliability requirements).

Decision variables q_{ij}^t and π_{ij}^t allow to characterize the differences in risks at different locations. It is assumed that all agents can cover different fractions of catastrophic losses from the same location. In the case of a catastrophe, a location j faces losses (damages) $L_j^t(\omega_t)$. Individuals at this location receive compensation $L_j^t(\omega_t)q_{ij}^t$ from a company i when such a loss occurs and pay insurance premiums (taxes) π_{ij}^t.

If W_j^0 is the initial wealth (property value) in location j, then the location's j wealth at time $t+1$ equals

$$W_j^{t+1} = W_j^t + \sum_{i=1}^{n}(L_j^t(\omega_t)q_{ij}^t - \pi_{ij}^t) - L_j^t(\omega_t)\, t = 0,1,\ldots \quad [2.2]$$

Let us note that random variables R_i^t and W_j^t implicitly depend on decision variables $x^k = (q^k, \pi^k)$, $q^k = \{q_{ij}^k, i = \overline{1{:}n}, j = \overline{1{:}m}\}$, $\pi^k = \{\pi_{ij}^k, i = \overline{1{:}n}, j = \overline{1{:}m}\}$, and random event ω_k, where $k = 0,1,\ldots,t-1$. For the sake of simplicity, we indicate in the following these path dependencies of R_i^t and W_j^t as $R_i^t(x,\omega)$ and $W_j^t(x,\omega)$.

The robustness of the loss sharing and reconstruction program depends on whether the accumulated risk reserve $R_i^t(x,\omega)$ at a random time $t = \tau(\omega)$ of a first catastrophic event avoids, in a probabilistic sense, the individual insolvency defined by events $E_{1i} = \left\{\omega : R_i^{\tau(\omega)}(x,\omega) < 0\right\}$, $i = \overline{1{:}n}$, and the joint insolvency defined by the combination of events

$$E_1 = E_{11} \cup E_{22} \cup \ldots \cup E_{1n}. \quad [2.3]$$

Individuals (locations and firms) are concerned with their wealth, which depends on whether the amount of taxes or premiums that they pay into the insurers or cat risk funds do not exceed the compensation of losses at time $\tau(\omega)$, that is, with the joint event E:

$$E_2 = E_{21} \cup E_{22} \cup \ldots \cup E_{2m} \quad [2.4]$$

where

$$E_{2j} = \left\{\omega: W_j^{\tau(\omega)}(x,\omega) < 0\right\} \text{ for } j = \overline{1:m},$$

are individual events.

Stability of the interdependent insurers, governments, households, firms, businesses, etc., depend on the joint fulfillment of constraints [2.3–2.4], that is, the events [2.3–2.4] determine the stability (resilience) of the regional program for protection against systemic risks, which can occur if one of the safety requirements is not fulfilled.

Therefore, a critical issue is to avoid these events with the highest possible probability. For example, by minimizing the expected uncovered losses $E\sum_j(1-q_j)L_j^{\tau(\omega)}$ under a probabilistic safety constraint of the type

$$Pr\,o\,b[E_1, E_2] \leq \overline{p}, \quad [2.5]$$

where $\overline{p}$ is a critical probability threshold of the program's systemic insolvency (failure, default) that may occur, say, only once in 100 years.

The notation $Pr\,o\,b[E_1, E_2]$ is used to denote a probability of insolvency as a general function of E_1, E_2. Another more relaxing example of constraints [2.5] may be constraints $Pr\,o\,b[E_1 \text{ or } E_2] \leq \overline{p}$.

Probabilistic constraints [2.5] in the ISCRiMM can be reformulated to define a convex STO problem with specific non-smooth risk (penalty) functions enabling to derive optimal and robust interdependent ex-ante and ex-post solutions. This problem is effectively solved by the linear programming methods. The safety and reliability constraints are central for large-scale integrated interdependent risk management problems.

2.3. Types of vulnerability and vulnerability analysis approaches

Direct and indirect damages and losses due to catastrophes depend on vulnerabilities of agents and structures. In what follows, we discuss different aspects of vulnerabilities and ways of their analysis and modeling as one of the components of the ISCRiMM.

The concept of vulnerability is addressed in many different disciplines. The definition depends on the area of research, such as disaster management, economics, finance, sociology, environmental sciences and engineering (Cutter 1996). Among the definitions is, for example, the following:

> The quality or state of being exposed to the possibility of being attacked or harmed, either physically or emotionally. The understanding of social and environmental vulnerability, as a methodological approach, involves the analysis of the risks and assets of disadvantaged groups, such as the elderly.

In relation to hazards and disasters,

> [...] the concept of vulnerability expresses the multi-dimensionality of disasters by focusing attention on the totality of relationships in a given social situation which constitute a condition that, in combination with environmental forces, produces a disaster (Oliver-Smith 2003).

It is also the extent to which changes could harm a system, or to which the community can be affected by the impact of a hazard or exposed to the possibility of being attacked or harmed, either physically or emotionally. According to UNISDR's (2009) terminology, vulnerability is "the conditions determined by physical, social, economic, and environmental factors or processes which increase the susceptibility of an individual, a community, assets, or systems to the impacts of hazards".

Liverman (1990) distinguishes between vulnerability as a biophysical condition and vulnerability as defined by political, social and economic conditions of society. Kasperson et al. (1990) defines vulnerability as the differential capacity of groups and individuals to deal with hazards based on their position within physical and social world. Cutter (1993) identifies vulnerability as the likelihood that an individual or group will be exposed to and adversely affected by a hazard. It is the interaction of the hazards of place (risk and mitigation) with social profile of communities. Blaikie et al. (1994) formulates the definition of vulnerability as the characteristics of a person or group in terms of their capacity to anticipate, cope with, resist and recover from the impact of a natural hazard. It involves a combination of factors that determine the degree to which someone's life and livelihood are put at risk by a discrete and identifiable event in nature or in society.

Measurement of vulnerability follows the advancements of the vulnerability concept (Cutter et al. 2003). One of the approaches is the "Vulnerability Hazards-of-Place Model" by Cutter (1996) and Cutter et al. (2000). This model focuses on describing the place-based interaction between biophysical vulnerability and social vulnerability. In this approach, it is explained how the vulnerability of a place is determined by factors such as socioeconomic status, urbanization status and demography. Another model, the earthquake disaster risk index (EDRI), defines vulnerability and hazard as a component in the context of risk.

The methodologies and models for analyzing and assessing vulnerability indicators are among the major research areas. These include the analysis and assessment of external exogenous factors such as sudden shocks and continued stresses, and internal endogenous factors such as dependencies, low incomes, unemployment, inability to cope with incapacities and inadequate infrastructures.

Different disciplines develop different vulnerability frameworks. In relation to natural disasters and the systemic risks, researchers are currently working to refine the definitions of vulnerability, measurement and assessment methods accordingly. In the presence of possible systemic-dependent chain risks, which are typical for densely populated areas with developed infrastructures (energy, water, transportation, etc.), the vulnerabilities account for multiple socioeconomic, demographic, environmental vulnerability components along with the vulnerabilities of critical physical infrastructure.

In urban areas,

> In addition to natural disasters, the entire possible loss and damage that may occur due to reasons such as general layout of a city, urban texture, usage areas, existing housing, transportation systems and infrastructure, planning and management weaknesses in a city (Erdogan and Terzi 2022; ISMEP 2014b, p. 12).

Urban vulnerability indicators can be divided into social, economic, environmental, physical and systemic vulnerability criteria. Cardona et al. (2012) grouped vulnerability under four different main criteria: environmental, social, economic and other criteria that interact and intersect. The methods for the improvement of vulnerability assessment in the European Union (MOVE) framework are discussed under six main criteria, such as physical, economic, social, cultural, environmental and institutional (European Commission 2015). Some of the main vulnerability types can be defined as follows:

– For structural (physical) vulnerability analysis, safety of buildings, roads and infrastructure systems are being evaluated to define weak infrastructure elements and areas (ISMEP 2014b; Karimzadeh et al. 2014). The safety and reliability of infrastructure during a disaster directly determines the injury or loss of life. FEMA (n.d.) definition of the social vulnerability "[…] is the susceptibility of social groups to the adverse impacts of natural hazards, including disproportionate death, injury, loss, or disruption of livelihood". As adopted by FEMA (n.d.) for the United States, the SVI (social vulnerability index) is a location-specific assessment of social vulnerability that utilizes 16 socioeconomic variables determining a community's ability to prepare for, respond to, and recover from hazards: below 150% poverty, unemployed, housing costs, no high school diploma, no health insurance, aged 65 and older, aged 17 and younger, civilian with a disability, racial and ethnic minority status, multi-unit structures, mobile homes, crowding, no vehicle, group quarters, single-parent households and English language proficiency (FEMA n.d.).

– Systemic vulnerability (also referred to as critical vulnerability) is the damage of subsystems in the urban system, rendering other systems inoperable (ISMEP 2014a, 2014b). The infrastructure elements that could be damaged and trigger further damages in the event of a disaster are the following: electric power supplies, gas and oil, telecommunications, banking and finance, transportation, water supply systems and emergency services.

2.3.1. *Social vulnerability in urban areas, Bucharest (Romania) and Istanbul (Turkey)*

A vulnerability analysis approach in urban areas of Bucharest, Romania, has been proposed in Armas et al. (2017). The socioeconomic vulnerability included "four social vulnerability dimensions – social, education, housing, and social dependence...".

> [These indicators] explained over 88% of the variance among relevant variables as estimated from the Principle Component Analysis and deriving a middling value for Kaiser–Meyer–Olkin (KMO) Measure of Sampling Adequacy. The four dimensions were further integrated into a criteria tree using the SMCE (Spatial Multi-Criteria Evaluation) module of the Ilwis software (ITC 2001) and weighted according to expert judgment and scenario testing.

This allowed us to distinguish areas (tracts) in Bucharest, Romania, by the level of their socioeconomic vulnerabilities. The four criteria were constructed based on the following subcriteria data: social such as dwelling population density, widows female population in total population, elderly (e.g. over 65 years), female population in total population, room occupancy per household; educational such as minimum level of education, unemployed population (inactive population), women with more than three children (in total women who gave birth); housing such as housing density, average room area per person on census tract, average household room area on census tract, average no. of private/owned houses, number of rooms, etc.

In the Istanbul urban area (Erdogan and Terzi 2022), the vulnerability assessment by neighborhoods of Istanbul, Turkey, identified four main criteria (critical urban services, infrastructure facilities, structural and socioeconomic) and then further subdivided into subcriteria. For example, the "socioeconomic" criterion comprised population density, daytime density, average household size, education status, average household income, population over 65, child population ratio and women population ratio. The "critical urban services" consisted of road blockage, distance to fuel stations, accessibility to fire stations (m), accessibility to police stations (m), accessibility to open spaces (m). The "infrastructure" criterion included damaged electricity line length (km), damage distribution of water pipelines (Rm (PGV): damage ration (points per km), damage distribution of natural gas pipelines (Rm (PGV):damage ration (points/km); and structural criteria included such subcriteria as building age, building construction type, building density (building/ha) and peak ground acceleration (PGA-gal). After the data on criteria-subcriteria were collected, the data were reclassified into 1–5 scale. After reclassification, each class was scored using 1–5 rating scale, the highest score is assigned to the class that models affects the seismic vulnerability. After the classes are scored, the analytical hierarchy process (AHP) method identified the weights of the criteria according to experts' opinion. In this process, experts determined the order of the importance among criteria in the pairwise comparison matrices score scale from one to nine and weights of the criteria and subcriteria are calculated for urban earthquake vulnerability analysis.

In real studies, the data at required resolutions (e.g. tracts, neighborhoods and households) can be difficult and costly to obtain. Therefore, the dynamic revision of vulnerability indices in the context of newly introduced risk mitigation measures can become difficult if at all possible. In some cases, missing historical data and indicator values can be substituted by expert estimates. For the development of future vulnerability scenarios when the necessary data can depend on multiple uncertain global and local drivers and trends, the analysis can rely on statistical and ML models (section 2.3.3).

2.3.2. *Structural (physical) vulnerability and building codes*

The overall vulnerability significantly depends on structural vulnerability, which is characterized by the compliance with infrastructure reliability norms, buildings codes, buildings density and magnitudes of the disasters, for example, of earthquakes. In the context of urban vulnerability assessment, the buildings vulnerability is especially important. In Armas et al. (2017 and references therein) as well as in other studies (Erdogan and Terzi 2022), residential buildings vulnerability was introduced as a separate criterion in the vulnerability analysis.

Building codes ensure buildings safety in cases of certain magnitudes disasters. They are introduced to limit the damages in exposed regions. The incompliance with building codes can trigger systemic losses in urban areas. There is an often-repeated phrase stating, "earthquakes don't kill people, buildings do" (FEMA n.d.). For example, in Istanbul, geoscientist Okan Tüysüz (2023) from Istanbul Technical University reminded us that:

> [...] approximately 1.2 million houses are located in the metropole. Some 70 percent of them are not earthquake resistant [...] nearly 90,000 buildings in the city should be either demolished and rebuilt, or strengthened. The first rule in earthquake is to reduce the risk. If even only one person resides in each of these buildings, 90,000 lives can be saved with this step.

The analysis of the structural vulnerability can start with the analysis of individual buildings. Especially in urban regions, it is very important to determine which areas of the city have the greatest residential building vulnerability. For example, in Bucharest:

> Only 855 buildings (located mostly in the city center) could be classified according to their vulnerability by the Bucharest General Municipality (2016), although the total number of residential buildings in Bucharest is 131,875. Approximately 40,000 of these structures are older than 1963; they date from a construction period when no seismic design regulations were available. In other words, reliable information about building vulnerability can only be found for 0.65% of the city's buildings" (Armas et al. 2017; Toma-Danila et al. 2015, 2017).

Because of data shortage, Toma-Danila et al. (2015, 2017) adopted a more generalized approach relying on analytical methods of improved displacement coefficient method (IDCM), as well as statistical data such as the number of buildings per construction period, building material and structure height. The buildings were classified into building typologies accounting for construction materials (such as adobe, reinforced or unreinforced masonry, wood and reinforced concrete), building height classes and construction periods representative for Romania. The typologies were customized and reclassified to reflect the specific of buildings in Bucharest. Vulnerability (also called fragility) functions were developed and adapted from the literature for each building typology to associate with each identified building typology. To address the question on which urban areas are more endangered, three seismic scenarios were used to calculate the respective damages to different buildings typologies. Two of these scenarios are based on real recorded values: for the 1990 and 1977, Vrancea earthquakes with moment-magnitudes of 6.9 and 7.4, respectively; for the maximum possible Vrancea earthquake, with a moment-magnitude of 7.8.

2.4. Statistical and ML approaches to analyze future vulnerabilities

Vulnerability analysis and assessment through regular collecting, updating and processing all of the relevant data and indicators can be both time and cost consuming. The necessary data can be missing at the required resolutions, for example, households level.

The development of future socioeconomic vulnerability scenarios can be restricted by data and projections availability, for example, projections of population by age and income groups or unemployment. For projecting structural (physical) damage and vulnerability, for example, the seismic fragility functions require large amounts of data, which are also not always available. Large uncertainties in the application of fragility curves stem from earthquake characteristics as well as variability in building attributes. Data scenarios, that is, the number of buildings by typology, population and incomes, can depend on multiple uncertain global and local drivers and trends.

Alternatively or supplementing the traditional methods described in previous section, the vulnerability analysis and prediction can rely on AI, statistical and ML methods. ML is an expansion of statistical learning theory (Vapnik 1995), which is regarded as one of the most developed branches of artificial intelligence. It provides the theoretical basis for many of today's AI ML algorithms.

Statistical and ML approaches are becoming popular for the vulnerability analysis. Mangalathu et al. (2019) uses ML to classify building damage for the 2014 South Napa earthquake. Nateghi et al. (2011) developed statistical methods for predicting indirect damages from natural hazards, particularly, hurricanes.

Approaches based on statistical and ML can be developed and applied to analyze future socioeconomic vulnerability based on vulnerability drivers. For example, Kalaycıoglu et al. (2023) develops a predictive model that allows to identify households with high social vulnerability. An ML social vulnerability model can rely on previously constructed social vulnerability indices and relevant variables (e.g. Toma-Danila et al. 2015, 2017; Armas et al. 2017).

Thus, the trained statistical model can serve as a scenario generator of plausible future structural and socioeconomic vulnerability scenarios accounting for changing new conditions and scenarios of relevant covariates for testing feasible mitigation precautionary and reconstruction BBB measures. The approach can reduce the time and costs for new data collection and revision of SVIs (Kalaycıoglu et al. 2023).

2.4.1. *The choice of covariates for statistical and ML model*

2.4.1.1. *Socioeconomic vulnerability predictors*

As presented in section 2.3.1, the predictors of socioeconomic vulnerabilities can be classified into four main indicator groups: social, educational, housing and social dependence. The drivers of these indicators are as follows: social such as dwelling population density, widows female population in total population, elderly (e.g. over 65 years), female population in total population, room occupancy per household; educational such as minimum level of education, unemployed population (inactive population), women with more than three children (in total women who gave birth); housing such as housing density, average room area per person on census tract, average household room area on census tract, average number of private/owned houses, number of rooms, etc. The ML model can be trained based on a pre-calculated SVI and relevant covariates. Then, it can be used to study future socioeconomic vulnerability assuming different scenarios of predictors.

2.4.1.2. *Structural vulnerability predictors*

Selection of predictors (also, independent variables, covariates, or drivers) is essential for explaining and predicting the target (dependent) variable. For modeling and predicting structural vulnerability, the number of building stories, building material, distance to epicenter and other variable characterizing structural and physical properties of buildings and earthquakes can be used in statistical methods to explain the damage volume. In some regions, foundation type, land type, roof type, ground floor type and superstructure type based on construction materials are considered as predictor variables.

The data for structural (physical) vulnerability (or damage) assessment can be compiled from the historical earthquake data or come from simulation models.

Detailed information about earthquake characteristics, building typology, position, foundation, floor and roof type, and site condition can be incorporated as input features in ML models to estimate the dependencies between, for example, damages and buildings typology. The methods can be used to predict the damages and the need for new types of buildings, buildings retrofitting and rehabilitation intervention.

2.4.2. *Methodology and selected results*

The truly integrative developments planning, foremost in urban areas, benefits from incorporating the statistical and ML methods into ISCRiMM (as discussed in section 2.2) for designing interdependent robust ex ante loss reduction and ex-post operational (emergency response and BBB) risk management options. Informed decisions based on the safety norms and a disaster-resistant systemic urban planning would decrease the damages and vulnerabilities of all types. The development of statistical and ML models for the analysis and prediction of future vulnerabilities can shed the light on the role of decisions, their contribution to the vulnerability decrease, increase of resilience and BBB capacity.

The development of the statistical and ML models aims to analyze the correlation between exploratory variables and the drivers. ML models are gaining popularity for the analysis of vulnerability to natural hazards, including random forest, neural networks, convolutional neural networks, recurrent neural networks, classification and regression tree, support vector machine, naïve Bayes and k-nearest neighbors. Because many of these models have a black-box nature, the tractability of the results is not straightforward. Also, the prediction accuracy is sensitive to model structure and parameter calibration, and it can be difficult to explain the accuracy or inaccuracy of the derived results.

In this study, we develop a linear regression model that enables easy tractability of individual independent variable's contributions to the total vulnerability indicator. Furthermore, the linear regression can be extended to the quantile (linear) regression to identify the quantiles of vulnerabilities based on various combinations of the drivers.

2.4.2.1. *Multivariate linear regression model*

Multivariate regression analysis has been extensively used in earthquake-related studies, including predictions, damage reduction strategies through various indicators, vulnerability detection and the development of more resilient structures and cities. Researchers such as Godschalk et al. (1998), Bostenaru and Armas (2015), Bostenaru et al. (2014), Rahman et al. (2023) and Mitsova et al. (2018) have emphasized the use of multivariate regression analysis to enhance the design and policy-making processes in urban planning related to natural disasters. They have demonstrated the relationships between disaster-resilient urban infrastructure, superstructure development and earthquake damage using this method. The multiple regression analysis has been utilized in Jia and Yan (2015), Bostenaru and Armas (2015), Bostenaru et al. (2014), Yariyan et al. (2020) and Saputra et al. (2017) to identify the factors influencing earthquake damage and to create earthquake vulnerability indices.

A (multiple) linear regression (MLR) can be considered as one of the statistical or ML algorithms, which is in fact one of the most popular models in ML. It is widely used because it is simple and tractable. The simplicity means it is easy to understand the responses of the dependent variables to each covariate, that is, the regression coefficient of an independent variable reflects the change in the dependent variable as a result of a unit change in the respective independent variables.

On the other hand, the MLR assumes that the residuals are normally distributed. The linear regression model for calculating the mean response takes the form

$$y_i = \beta_0 + \beta_1 x_{i1} + \beta_2 x_{i2} + \beta_3 x_{i3} + \cdots + \beta_m x_{im}, \qquad [2.6]$$

where $i = 1, \ldots n$ is a number of observations and m is a number of covariates. Coefficients of the MLR are found by minimizing the mean square error "Goodness-of-Fit" function

$$MSE = (y_i - (\beta_0 + \beta_1 x_{i1} + \beta_2 x_{i2} + \beta_3 x_{i3} + \cdots + \beta_m x_{im}))^2,$$

which gives the "best regression line".

To distinguish vulnerability by classes, that is, very high, high, moderate, low and very low, in response to various combinations of drivers, a quantile-based criteria instead of the mathematical expectation can be used (see, e.g. Golodnikov et al. 2010; Ermolieva et al. 2021, 2023; Pepelyaev et al. 2022). Quantile regression is an extension of linear regression that is used when the conditions of linear regression are not met (i.e. linearity, homoscedasticity, independence or normality).

For the quantile regression, it is assumed that the τth quantile is given as a linear function of the explanatory variables. Taking a similar structure to the linear regression model, the "best" quantile regression model equation for the τth quantile is

$$Q_\tau(y_i) = \beta_0(\tau) + \beta_1(\tau) x_{i1} + \beta_2(\tau) x_{i2} + \beta_3(\tau) x_{i3} + \cdots + \beta_m(\tau) x_{im},$$

where $i = 1, \dots n$ is a number of observations and m is a number of covariates (independent variables). Coefficients $\beta_m(\tau)$ are functions of the required quantile τ. They are defined as

$$\beta(\tau) = argmin_{\beta \in R^m}$$
$$\left\{\sum_{i|Y_i \geq \beta'(\tau)X_i} \tau|Y_i - \beta'(\tau)X_i| + (1-\tau)\sum_{i|Y_i < \beta'(\tau)X_i} |Y_i - \beta'(\tau)X_i|\right\},$$

where Y_i are observations of dependent variables, X_i is a vector of independent variables $X_i = (x_{i1}, \dots, x_{im})$, $\beta(\tau)$ is a vector of coefficients $\beta(\tau) = (\beta_1(\tau), \dots, \beta_m(\tau))$ and m is a number of observations.

2.4.2.2. *Socioeconomic vulnerability*

The dataset utilized for this study is based on studies in Armas et al. (2017) and Toma-Danila et al. (2015). For the socioeconomic vulnerabilities, we establish a relationship between, precomputed in Armas et al. (2017), human vulnerability indicators and the indicators reflecting social dependency, education and housing conditions. That is, the vulnerabilities computed for Bucharest (Romania) by Armas et al. (2017) are used to train the regression model.

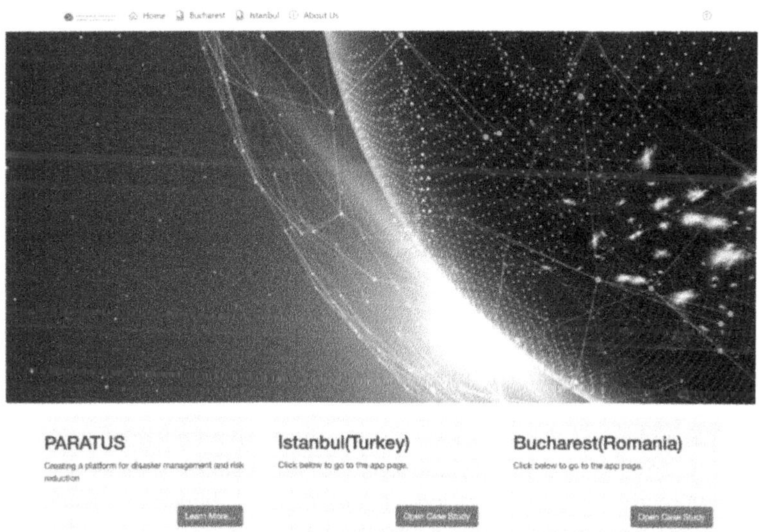

Figure 2.4. *Front page of the Risk & Vulnerability Scenario (RVS) generator, the software being developed by CAT group of ASA Program, IIASA. For a color version of this figure, see www.iste.co.uk/gaivoronski/stochastic1.zip*

The LR dependence between human vulnerability and the other four indices (social dependence, housing, education and social factor) is measured by $R^2 = 0.95$. From the four explanatory variables, most contribution to human vulnerability is due to social and social dependence factors composed of such variables as share of dependents, share of children in total population, population density, share of widows in total population, population over 65 years old, share of women in total population and room occupancy per household.

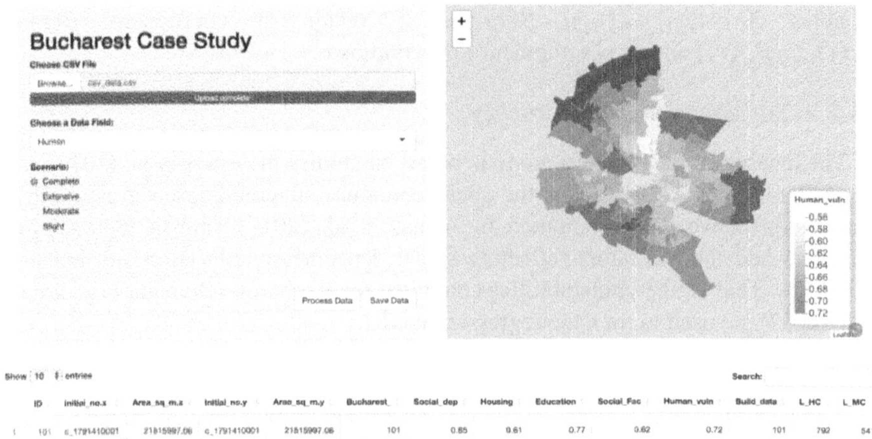

Figure 2.5. *Human vulnerability, LR estimate, data based on Armas et al. (2017). For a color version of this figure, see www.iste.co.uk/gaivoronski/stochastic1.zip*

In Figure 2.5, the human vulnerability indices are visualized with a Risk & Vulnerability Scenario (RVS) generator, the software being developed by Cooperation and Transformative Governance group of Advanced Systems Analysis Program (CAT-ASA, IIASA) for PARATUS project. Figure 2.4 displays the front page of the software providing an introduction into the PARATUS project.

The RVS within ISCRiMM allows for the interactive update of the covariates (vulnerability drivers) and recalculation of the vulnerability indices according to plausible alternative scenarios of population density, buildings typologies and buildings codes toward decreasing vulnerabilities. Thus, it allows for testing and designing robust vulnerability reduction decisions regarding ex-ante buildings and infrastructure retrofitting, population relocation, construction of shelters and other feasible structural and financial measures.

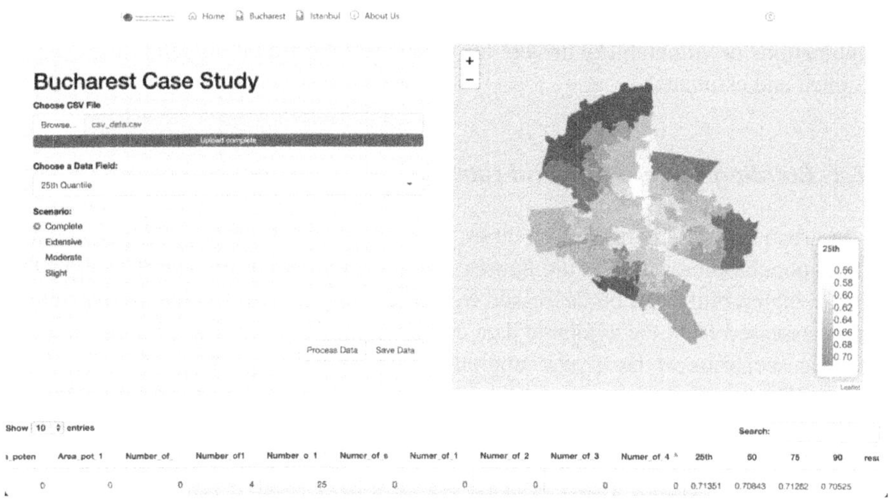

Figure 2.6. *Human vulnerability, 25th quantile. For a color version of this figure, see www.iste.co.uk/gaivoronski/stochastic1.zip*

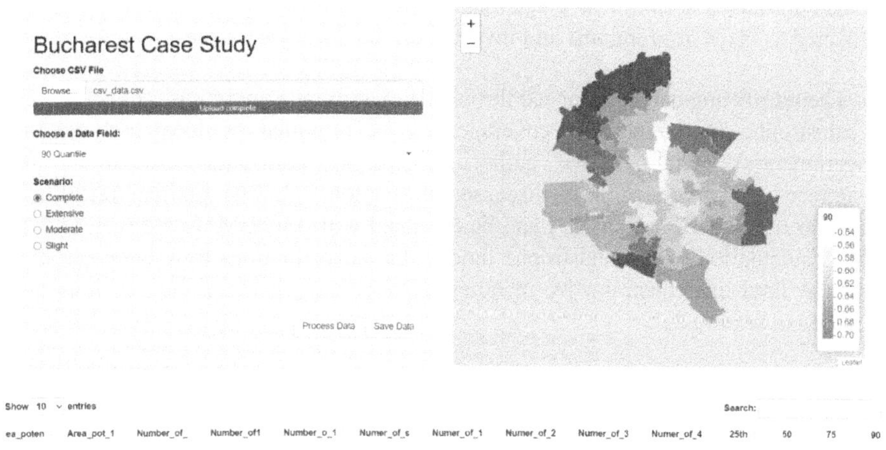

Figure 2.7. *Human vulnerability, 90th quantile. For a color version of this figure, see www.iste.co.uk/gaivoronski/stochastic1.zip*

2.5. Application of the ML regression model to future vulnerability scenarios testing

Using the developed ML regression models for the assessment of the vulnerabilities and damages based on historical data and model-based results reflecting socioeconomic, demographic, structural indicators, several scenario combinations of vulnerability drivers for the analysis of future vulnerabilities can be designed and estimated.

2.5.1. *Buildings upgrading and retrofitting*

In urban areas, centers of large cities, with a higher percentage of dependent and elderly population residing in old houses, the human vulnerability is rather high. The human vulnerability can be decreased by decreasing structural vulnerability, which can be assessed from the available data on structural damages. For example, several dynamic scenarios of buildings' upgrading and retrofitting can be considered in areas of Bucharest (Romania) and Istanbul (Turkey), which are most vulnerable to structural damages.

1) Do nothing scenario: no taxes/insurance premiums will be accumulated and, therefore, no retrofitting will be done.

2) Flat scenario: average annual losses from the previous events will be collected as taxes or premiums and invested equally in retrofitting.

3) Risk-based scenario: average annual losses from the previous events will be collected as taxes or premiums and invested on risk-based principle.

The retrofitting can be financed through tax (insurance premiums) collection into a catastrophe fund, and loss coverage can be provided by local and national government(s), administrative authorities, private and state companies, and insurance companies, as it is discussed in section 2.2. The optimal retrofitting scenario (risk-based scenario 3) can be designed with ISCRiMM (see section 2.2). The accumulation of the catastrophe fund and the contributions from the population into the fund are constraint by incomes, prices, running costs, etc., as it is also outlined in section 2.2.

2.5.2. *Construction of shelters*

A scenario of socioeconomic and human vulnerability decrease can assume construction of shelters for population protection and food storage in cases of disasters. For example, the building of earthquake evacuation shelters is an effective way to reduce earthquake disaster risk and protect lives. The shelters can be built in areas with highest population and infrastructure density and, for example, with high risk of structural damages. Urban earthquake evacuation shelters are safe places that provide evacuation protection and basic life support services after an earthquake. They can be classified into three categories: emergency shelter, fixed shelter and central shelter. Facility location models can address assessment of optimal places for locating earthquake evacuation shelters. The evacuation shelter location models are effective and suitable tools to assist in risk-based urban planning (Xu et al. 2016; Lomer et al. 2023; Qiu et al. 2024). Shelters can be built to protect also against other natural and systemic catastrophes.

2.5.3. *Population relocation*

Population relocation scenarios are relevant, particularly in volcanic eruption areas. Also, in cases of hurricanes, floods and earthquakes, millions of people have been forced to move away from their native places. One of such events is Hurricane Irma, which has brought devastation on the islands of the Caribbean as well as South Florida. In Indonesian, on Ruang island, the government's plans focused on permanently relocating almost 10,000 residents after a series of explosive eruptions of the Ruang volcano. On Caribbean islands, the island of Montserrat has been completed destroyed by a volcano and thus required population relocation. On the morning of April 9, 2021, the La Soufrière Volcano on the main island of St. Vincent and the Grenadines erupted, filling the sky with ash and transforming the lives, livelihoods and landscape of this small Southern Caribbean nation. More than 22,000 people were displaced from their homes, buildings including schools and businesses were damaged, livestock was destroyed and almost an entire population was cut off from clean drinking water and other basic necessities for 5 months. In total, the damage amounted to more than \$ 234 million; the impact of which was felt well beyond the main island to communities across the archipelago. Two years later, the ash from La Soufrière has settled, but the aftermath of the eruption continues to shape ordinary life and the development trajectory of this Small Island Developing State. Governments have a responsibility to protect their people, including from disasters and the effects of climate change.

Relocating people is a challenging task and it requires proper ex-ante planning and preparedness for occasions when it is absolutely necessary for people to be relocated.

2.6. Conclusion

This chapter discusses important aspects related to modeling and management of catastrophic risks, in particular, the risks, which can emerge in interdependent systems, that is, systemic risks. Systemic risks can be defined as a new type of risks that depend on the whole structure of systemic interdependencies, goals and constraints of the involved agents, safety and reliability standards, imbalances and thresholds. These risks are analytically intractable. They can be triggered by a combination of exogenous and endogenous shocks, that is, by natural hazards in combination with decisions of intelligent agents and, therefore, they cannot be described by a single probability distribution. They are hardly predictable, therefore require advanced risk-based approaches to the analysis and management. Systemic risks depend on socioeconomic and structural vulnerabilities in place. In particular, management of systemic risks requires approaches incorporating individual and joint systemic safety and security constraints increasing systemic resilience and BBB capacities, that is, the ability of complex systems to absorb disturbances, adapt to changing conditions and maintain essential functions.

In this chapter, we discuss the ISCRiMM, integrated catastrophe risk modeling and management model being developed at IIASA, which incorporates, among others, the vulnerability module to assist in designing optimal and robust ex-ante loss reduction and ex-post operational emergency response and BBB measures for dealing with risks. The vulnerability module can use vulnerability (fragility) curves. As an alternative, it can incorporate statistical and ML vulnerability models, enabling us to test and find optimal vulnerability reduction options. For case the study in Bucharest, Romania, we used the data on vulnerability drivers available from Armas et al. (2017) to develop a socioeconomic and structural vulnerability regression models.

The linear regression models allow for easy tractability of individual independent variable's (drivers and predictors) contributions to vulnerability indicators. The traditional linear regression model was estimated to predict socioeconomic vulnerability indices based on precomputed results. The quantile-based regression used same data to predict the lowest and highest possible vulnerabilities in the case study regions as functions of various factors (buildings safety, population density, dependence ratio, population by age groups, incomes, etc.), which, in turn, depend on feasible vulnerability reduction policies. For example, vulnerabilities can be reduced by buildings and infrastructures retrofitting, which can be financed through cat risk funds based on principles discussed in section 2.2. Building shelters is an important vulnerability reduction measure, especially in urban densely populated areas. This measure reduces population exposure and, therefore, human losses. Population relocation is also focused on decreasing the number of exposed people, however the measure is a complex undertaking and should be planned and implemented with special caution, perhaps, as a last resort, after other alternatives have been explored. Integrating the vulnerability models based on statistical and ML principles, the ISCRiMM serves an important tool for the analysis and management of catastrophic systemic risks. Alternative statistical and ML models will be further researched for the best tractability and representation of different types and aspects of vulnerabilities.

2.7. Acknowledgments

The development of the methodologies and models is supported by the EU PARATUS (CL3-2021-DRS-01-03, grant number 101073954) project on "Promoting disaster preparedness and resilience by co-developing stakeholder support tools for managing systemic risk of compounding disasters", a joint project between the International Institute for Applied Systems Analysis (IIASA) and the National Academy of Sciences of Ukraine (NASU) on "Integrated robust modeling and management of food-energy-water-land use nexus for sustainable development" (22-501). Moreover, the work was supported by the project "Comprehensive analysis o robust preventive and adaptive measures of food, energy, water and social management in the context of systemic risks and consequences of COVID-19" (0122U000552) of National Academy of Sciences of Ukraine.

2.8. References

Amendola, A., Ermoliev, Y., Ermolieva, T. (2000). Earthquake risk management: A case study for an Italian region. In *Proceedings of the 2nd European Conference on Global Change and Catastrophe Risk Management, Earthquake Risks in Europe*. IIASA, Laxenburg.

Amendola, A., Ermoliev, Y., Ermolieva, T. (2005). Catastrophe risk management: Vulnerability and equity. In *Integrated Risk and Vulnerability Management Assisted by Decision Support Systems*, Gheorghe, A.V. (ed.). Springer, Dordrecht.

Amendola, A., Ermolieva, T., Linnerooth-Bayer, J., Mechler, R. (eds) (2013). *Integrated Catastrophe Risk Modeling: Supporting Policy Processes*. Springer, Dordrecht.

Armas, I., Toma-Danila, D., Ionescu, R., Gavris, A. (2017). Vulnerability to earthquake hazards: Bucharest case study, Romania. *International Journal of Disaster Risk Science*, 8, 182–195. doi: 10.1007/s13753-017-0132-y.

Atoyev, A., Knopov, P., Pepeliaev, V., Kisala, P., Romaniuk, R., Kalimoldayev, M. (2017). The mathematical problems of complex systems investigation under uncertainties. In *Recent Advances in Information Technology*, Wojcik, W. and Sikora, J. (eds). CRC Press, Boca Raton. doi: 10.1201/9781351243179-6.

Bankoff, G., Frerks, G., Hillhorst, D.J.M. (2004). *Mapping Vulnerability: Disasters, Development and People*. Routledge, Oxford.

Baranov, S., Digas, B.V., Ermolieva, T.Y., Rozenberg, V.L. (2002). Earthquake risk management: A scenario generator. IIASA Interim Report, Laxenburg.

Birkmann, J. (ed.) (2006). *Measuring Vulnerability to Natural Hazards – Towards Disaster Resilient Societies*. UNU Press, Tokyo.

Blaikie, P., Cannon, T., Davis, I., Wisner, B. (1994). *At Risk: Natural Hazards, People's Vulnerability, and Disasters*. Routledge, Oxford.

Borodina, O., Borodina, E., Ermolieva, T., Ermoliev, Y., Fischer, G., Makowski, M., van Velthuizen, H. (2012). Sustainable agriculture, food security, and socio-economic risks in Ukraine. In *Managing Safety of Heterogeneous Systems*, Ermoliev, Y., Makowski, M., Marti, K. (eds). Springer, Berlin, Heidelberg.

Borodina, O., Kyryziuk, S., Fraier, O., Ermoliev, Y., Ermolieva, T., Knopov, P., Horbachuk, V. (2020). Mathematical modeling of agricultural crop diversification in Ukraine: Scientific approaches and empirical results. *Cybernetics and Systems Analysis*, 56(2), 213–222. doi: 10.1007/s10559-020-00237-6.

Bostenaru D.M. and Armas, I. (2015). Earthquake impact on settlements: The role of urban and structural morphology. *Natural Hazards and Earth System Science*, 15(10), 2283–2297. doi: 10.5194/nhess-15-2283-2015.

Bostenaru, D.M., Armas, I., Goretti, A. (2014). Earthquake hazard impact and urban planning – An introduction. In *Earthquake Hazard Impact and Urban Planning*, Bostenaru Dan, M., Armas, I., Goretti, A. (eds). Springer, Dordrecht. doi: 10.1007/978-94-007- 7981-5_1.

Cano, E.L., Moguerza, J.M., Ermolieva, T., Ermoliev, Y. (2014). Energy efficiency and risk management in public buildings: Strategic model for robust planning. *Computational Management Science*, 11(1–2), 25–44.

Cardona, O.D., Van Aalst, M.K., Birkmann, J., Fordham, M., McGregor, G., Rosa, P., Pulwarty, R.S., Schipper, E.L.F., Sinh, B.T., Décamps, H. et al. (2012). Determinants of risk: Exposure and vulnerability. In *Managing the Risks of Extreme Events and Disasters to Advance Climate Change Adaptation*, Field, C.B., Barros, V., Stocker, T.F., Dahe, Q. (eds). Cambridge University Press, Cambridge. doi: 10.1017/CBO9781139177245.005.

Compton, K., Ermolieva, T., Linnerooth-Bayer, J., Amendola, A., Faber, R., Nachtnebel, H. (2013). Modeling risk and uncertainty: Managing flash flood risk in Vienna. In *Integrated Catastrophe Risk Modeling: Advances in Natural and Technological Hazards Research*, Amendola, A., Ermolieva, T., Linnerooth-Bayer, J., Mechler, R. (eds). Springer, Dordrecht. doi: 10.1007/978-94-007-2226-2_2.

Cutter, S.L. (1996). Vulnerability to environmental hazards. *Progress in Human Geography*, 20(4), 529–539. doi: 10.1177/030913259602000407.

Cutter, S.L., Mitchell, J.T., Scott, M.S. (2000). Revealing the vulnerability of people and places: A case study of Georgetown county, South Carolina. *Annals of the Association of American Geographers*, 90(4). doi: 10.1111/0004-5608.00219.

Cutter, S.L., Boruff, B.J., Shirley, W.L. (2003). Social vulnerability to environmental hazards. *Social Science Quarterly*, 84(2), 242–261. doi: 10.1111/1540-6237.8402002.

Erdogan, S. and Terzi, F. (2022). GIS-based seismic vulnerability assessment for the Istanbul Historical Peninsula. *Journal of Design for Resilience in Architecture and Planning*, 3(1), 41–62. doi: 10.47818/DRArch.2022.v3i1043.

Ermoliev, Y. (2009a). Stochastic quasigradient methods in minimax problems. In *Encyclopedia of Optimization*, Floudas, C.A. and P.M. Pardalos (eds). Springer, New York.

Ermoliev, Y. (2009b). Two-stage stochastic programming: Quasigradient method. In *Encyclopedia of Optimization*, Pardalos, P.M. (ed.). Springer, New York.

Ermoliev, Y. (2009c). Stochastic quasigradient methods. In *Encyclopedia of Optimization*, Pardalos, P.M. (ed.). Springer, New York.

Ermoliev, Y. and Wets, R.J.-B. (eds) (1988). *Numerical Techniques for Stochastic Optimization*. Springer, Berlin, Heidelberg.

Ermoliev, Y. and von Winterfeldt, D. (2012). Systemic risk and security management. In *Managing Safety of Heterogeneous Systems*, Ermoliev, Y., Makowski, M., Marti, K. (eds). Springer, Berlin, Heidelberg.

Ermoliev, Y., Ermolieva, T.Y., Norkin, V. (1997). Spatial stochastic model for optimization capacity of insurance networks under dependent catastrophic risks: Numerical experiments. IIASA Interim Report, Laxenburg.

Ermoliev, Y., Ermolieva, T., MacDonald, G., Norkin, V. (2000). Stochastic optimization of insurance portfolios for managing exposure to catastrophic risks. *Annals of Operations Research*, 99, 207–225.

Ermoliev, Y., Ermolieva, T., Fischer, G., Makowski, M., Nilsson, S., Obersteiner, M. (2008). Discounting, catastrophic risks management and vulnerability modeling. *Mathematics and Computers in Simulation*, 79(4), 917–924.

Ermoliev, Y., Robinson, S., Rovenskaya, E., Ermolieva, T. (2018). Integrated catastrophic risk management: Robust balance between ex-ante and ex-post measures. *SIAM News*, 51(6), 4.

Ermoliev, Z., Komendantova, N., Ermolieva, T. (2023). Energy production and storage investments and operation planning involving variable renewable energy sources: A two-stage stochastic optimization model with rolling time horizon and random stopping time. In *Modern Optimization Methods for Decision Making Under Risk and Uncertainty*, Gaivoronski, A., Knopov, P., Zaslavskyi, V. (eds). Taylor & Francis, Abingdon. doi: 10.1201/9781003260196-2.

Ermolieva, T. and Obersteiner, M. (2005). Global change, catastrophic risks and sustained economic growth: Model-based analysis. IIASA Interim Report. Laxenburg.

Ermolieva, T., Ermoliev, Y., Norkin, V. (1997). On the role of advanced modeling in managing catastrophic risks. In *Proc. New Risk Frontiers: Conference for the 10th Anniversary of the Society for Risk Analysis – Europe*. The Center for Risk Research, Stockholm.

Ermolieva, T., Ermoliev, Y., Fischer, G, Galambos, I. (2003). The role of financial instruments in integrated catastrophic flood management. *Multinational Finance Journal*, 7(3–4), 207–230.

Ermolieva, T., Filatova, T., Ermoliev, Y., Obersteiner, M., de Bruijn, K.M., Jeuken, A. (2016a). Flood catastrophe model for designing optimal flood insurance program: Estimating location-specific premiums in the Netherlands. *Risk Analysis*, 37(1), 82–98.

Ermolieva, T., Havlík, P., Ermoliev, Y., Mosnier, A., Obersteiner, M., Leclère, D., Khabarov, N., Valin, H., Reuter, W. (2016b). Integrated management of land use systems under systemic risks and security targets: A stochastic global biosphere management model. *Journal of Agricultural Economics*, 67(3), 584–601.

Ermolieva, T., Ermoliev, Y., Obersteiner, M., Rovenskaya, E. (2021a). Two-stage nonsmooth stochastic optimization and iterative stochastic quasigradient procedure for robust estimation, machine learning and decision making. In *Resilience in the Digital Age*, Matos, F., Selig, P.M., Henriqson, E. (eds). Springer, Cham. doi: 10.1007/978-3-030-70370-7_4.

Ermolieva, T., Havlik, P., Ermoliev, Y., Khabarov, N., Obersteiner, M. (2021b). Robust management of systemic risks and food-water-energy-environmental security: Two-stage strategic-adaptive GLOBIOM model. *Sustainability*, 13(2), 857. doi: 10.3390/su13020857.

Ermolieva, T., Ermoliev, Y., Havlik, P., Lessa-Derci-Augustynczik, A., Komendantova, N., Kahil, T., Balkovič, J., Skalsky, R., Folberth, C., Knopov, P.S. et al. (2023a). Connections between robust statistical estimation, robust decision making with two-stage stochastic optimization, and robust machine learning problems. *Cybernetics and Systems Analysis*, 59(3), 33–47.

Ermolieva, T., Ermoliev, Y., Komendantova, N., Norkin, V., Knopov, P., Gorbachuk, V. (2023b). Linking catastrophe modeling and stochastic optimization techniques for integrated catastrophe risk analysis and management. In *Modern Optimization Methods for Decision Making Under Risk and Uncertainty*, Gaivoronski, A., Knopov, P., Zaslavskyi, V. (eds). Taylor & Francis, Abingdon. doi: 10.1201/9781003260196-2.

European Commission (2015). Final report summary – MOVE (Methods for the improvement of vulnerability assessment in Europe). Report, European Commission, Brussels [Online]. Available at: https://cordis.europa.eu/result/rcn/55194_en.html.

FEMA (n.d.). National risk index. Document, Federal Emergency Management Agency (FEMA), Washington, D.C. [Online]. Available at: https://hazards.fema.gov/nri/social-vulnerability [Accessed 10 September 2024].

Fischer, G., Ermolieva, T., Ermoliev, Y., Sun, L. (2009). Risk-adjusted approaches for planning sustainable agricultural development. *Stochastic Environmental Research and Risk Assessment*, 23(4), 441–450.

Flanagan, B.E., Gregory, E.W., Hallisey, E.J., Heitgerd, J.L., Lewis, B. (2011). A social vulnerability index for disaster management. *Journal of Homeland Security and Emergency Management*, 8(1), 1–22. doi: 10.2202/1547-7355.1792.

Godschalk, D.R., Beatley, T., Berke, P.R., Brower, D.J., Kaiser, E.J. (1998). *Natural Hazard Mitigation: Recasting Disaster Policy and Planning*. Island Press, Washington, D.C.

Golodnikov, A.N., Ermoliev, Yu, M., Knopov, P.S. (2010). Estimating reliability parameters under insufficient information. *Cybernetics and Systems Analysis*, 46(3), 443–459. doi: 10.1007/s10559-010-9219-9.

ISMEP (2014a). *Disaster-Resilient Urban Planning and Structuring*. Istanbul Seismic Risk Mitigation Project (ISMEP), Istanbul.

ISMEP (2014b). *Reduction of Urban Risks*. Istanbul Seismic Risk Mitigation Project (ISMEP), Istanbul.

Jia, J. and Yan, J. (2015). Analysis about factors affecting the degree of damage of buildings in earthquake. *Journal of Physics: Conference Series*, 628(1), 012062. doi: 10.1088/1742-6596/628/1/012062.

Johnson, L.A. and Mahin, S.A. (2016). The Mw 6.0 South Napa earthquake of August 24, 2014: A wakeup call for renewed investment in seismic resilience across California. Report, California Seismic Safety Commission, Sacramento [Online]. Available at: https://peer.berkeley.edu/sites/default/files/cssc1603-peer201604_final_7.20.16.pdf [Accessed 10 March 2024].

Jones, E., Doughorty, K., Brown, P. (2022). Building back better in the context of multi-hazards in the Caribbean. *Disasters*, 46(Suppl 1), 151–165.

Kalaycıoglu, O., Akhanlı, S.E., Mente, E.Y., Kalaycıoglu, M., Kalaycıoglu, S. (2023). Using machine learning algorithms to identify predictors of social vulnerability in the event of a hazard: Istanbul case study. *Nat. Hazards Earth Syst. Sci.*, 23, 2133–2156. doi: 10.5194/nhess-23-2133-2023.

Karimzadeh, S., Miyajima, M., Hassanzadeh, R., Amiraslanzadeh, R., Kamel, B. (2014). A GIS-based seismic hazard, building vulnerability and human loss assessment for the earthquake scenario in Tabriz. *Soil Dynamics and Earthquake Engineering*, 66, 263–280. doi: 10.1016/j.soildyn.2014.06.026.

Kasperson, R.E., Dow, K., Golding, D., Kasperson, J.X. (eds) (1990). *Understanding Global Environmental Change: The Contributions of Risk Analysis and Management*. The Earth Transformed Program, Clark University, Worcester, MA.

de Léon, V. and Carlos, J. (2006). Vulnerability: A conceptual and methodological review. Document, UNU-EHS, Bonn [Online]. Available at: https://collections.unu.edu/eserv/unu:1871/pdf3904.pdf.

Li, S.Q. (2023). Empirical vulnerability estimation models considering updating the structural earthquake damage database. *Soil Dynamics and Earthquake Engineering*, 169, 107864. doi: 10.1016/j.soildyn.2023.107864.

Liverman, D. (1990). Vulnerability to global environmental change. In *Understanding Global Environmental Change: The Contributions of Risk Analysis and Management*, Kasperson, R.E., Dow, K., Golding, D., Kasperson, J.X. (eds). The Earth Transformed Program, Clark University, Worcester, MA.

Lomer, A.R.B., Rezaeian, M., Rezaei, H., Lorestani, A., Mijani, N., Mahdad, M., Raeisi, A., Arsanjani, J.J. (2023). Optimizing emergency shelter selection in earthquakes using a risk-driven large group decision-making support system. *Sustainability*, 15(5), 4019. doi: 10.3390/su15054019.

Mangalathu, S., Sun, H, Nweke, C., Yi, Z., Burton, H. (2019). Classifying earthquake damage to buildings using machine learning. *Earthquake Spectra*, 36(1). doi: 10.1177/8755293019878137.

Mitsova, D., Esnard, A.M., Sapat, A., Lai, B.S. (2018). Socioeconomic vulnerability and electric power restoration timelines in Florida: The case of Hurricane Irma. *Natural Hazards*, 94, 689–709. doi: 10.1007/s11069-018-3413-x.

Nateghi, R., Guikema, S.D., Quiring, S.M. (2011). Comparison and validation of statistical methods for predicting power outage durations in the event of hurricanes. *Risk Analysis*, 31(12), 1897–1906.

O'Neill, B., Ermoliev, Y., Ermolieva, T. (2006). Endogenous risks and learning in climate change decision analysis. In *Coping with Uncertainty: Modeling and Policy Issues*, Marti, K., Ermoliev, Y., Makowski, M., Pflug, G. (eds). Springer, Berlin, Heidelberg.

Oliver-Smith, A. (2003). Theorizing vulnerability in a globalized world: A political ecological perspective. In *Mapping Vulnerability: Disasters, Development and People*, Bankoff, G., Frerks, G., Hillhorst, D.J.M. (eds). Earthscan, London.

Ortiz-Partida, J.P., Kahil, T., Ermolieva, T., Ermoliev, Y., Lane, B., Sandoval-Solis, S., Wada, Y. (2019). A two-stage stochastic optimization for robust operation of multipurpose reservoirs. *Water Resources Management*, 33(11), 3815–3830. doi: 10.1007/s11269-019-02337-1.

Pepelyaev, V.A., Golodnikov, A.N., Golodnikova, N.A. (2022). A new method of reliability optimization in the classical problem statement. *Cybernetics and Systems Analysis* 58(6), 917–922. doi: 10.1007/s10559-023-00525-x.

Qiu, J., Tan, H., Yuan, S., Lv, C., Wang, P., Cao, S., Zhang, Y. (2024). Selection of urban flood shelter locations based on risk assessment. *Water-Energy Nexus*, 7, 151–162. doi: 10.1016/j.wen.2024.04.003.

Rahman, M.M., Asikunnaby, N.J., Abdo, H.G., Almohamad, H., Al Dughairi, A.A., Al-Mutiry, M. (2023). Earthquake preparedness in an urban area: The case of Dhaka city, Bangladesh. *Geoscience Letters*, 10(1), 27. doi: 10.1186/s40562-023-00281-y.

Rotimi, J.O., Wilkinson, S., Zuo, K., Myburgh, D. (2009). Legislation for effective post-disaster reconstruction. *International Journal of Strategic Property Management*, 13(2), 143–152.

Rumpf, C.M., Hugh, L.G., Atkinson, P.M. (2017). Population vulnerability models for asteroid impact risk assessment. *Meteoritics & Planetary Science*, 52(6), 1082–1102.

Sanchez-Gonzalez, D. (2015). Physical-social environments and aging population from environmental gerontology and geography. Socio-spatial implications in Latin America. *Revista de Geografía Norte Grande*, 60(60), 97–114. doi: 10.4067/S0718-34022015000100006.

Sanchez-Gonzalez, D. and Egea-Jimenez, C. (2011). Social vulnerability approach to investigate the social and environmental disadvantages. Its application in the study of elderly people. *Pap. Poblac.*, 17(69), 151–185.

Saputra, A., Rahardianto, T., Revindo, M.D. (2017). Seismic vulnerability assessment of residential buildings using logistic regression and geographic information system (GIS) in Pleret Sub District (Yogyakarta, Indonesia). *Geoenvironmental Disasters*, 4(1), 1–33. doi: 10.1186/s40677-017-0075-z.

Smith, G.P. and Wenger, D. (2007). Sustainable disaster recovery: Operationalizing an existing agenda. In *Handbook of Disaster Research*, Rodríguez, H., Quarantelli, E.L., Dynes, R. (eds). Springer, New York.

Toma-Danila, D. and Armas, I. (2017). Insights on the possible seismic damage of residential buildings in Bucharest, Romania, at neighborhood resolution. *Bulletin of Earthquake Engineering*, 15(3), 1161–1184.

Toma-Danila, D., Zulfikar, C., Manea, E.F., Cioflan, C.O. (2015). Improved seismic risk estimation for Bucharest, based on multiple hazard scenarios and analytical methods. *Soil Dynamics and Earthquake Engineering*, 73, 1–16.

Tüysüz, O. (2023). Turkey: Building codes and the importance of regulations. WSRB [Online]. Available at: https://www1.wsrb.com/blog/turkey-building-codes-and-the-importance-of-regulation.

UNDRR (2015). Sendai framework for disaster risk reduction 2015–2030. United Nations Office for Disaster Risk Reduction (UNDRR) [Online]. Available at: https://www.undrr.org/publication/sendai-framework-disaster-risk-reduction-2015-2030.

Vapnik, V. (1995). *The Nature of Statistical Learning Theory*. Springer, New York.

Wolters, M.L. and Kuenzer, C. (2015). Vulnerability assessments of coastal river deltas – Categorization and review. *Journal of Coastal Conservation*, 19(3), 345–368.

Xu, J., Yin, X., Chen, D., An, J., Nie, G. (2016). Multi-criteria location model of earthquake evacuation shelters to aid in urban planning. *International Journal of Disaster Risk Reduction*, 20, 51–62.

Yariyan, P., Avand, M., Soltani, F., Ghorbanzadeh, O., Blaschke, T. (2020). Earthquake vulnerability mapping using different hybrid models. *Symmetry*, 12(3), 405. doi: 10.3390/sym12030405.

Zagorodny, A.G., Ermoliev, Y., Bogdanov, V.L., Kostyuchenko, Y.V., Ermolieva, T. (2020). Integrated robust management of food-energy-water-land use nexus for sustainable development. In *Integrated Modeling and Management of Food-Energy-Water NEXUS for Sustainable Development*, Zagorodny, A.G., Ermoliev, Y.M., Bogdanov, V.L., Ermolieva, T. (eds). Committee for Systems Analysis at Presidium of National Academy of Sciences of Ukraine, Kiev.

3

Robust Statistical Estimation and Two-Stage Stochastic Optimization: Quantile Regression EPIC Meta-Model of Soil Organic Carbon for Robust Decision Making with GLOBIOM

This chapter discusses the connections between two-stage stochastic optimization (STO) and robust statistical estimation. The main question related to statistical predictions is how to use the predictions to optimize the overall decisions and how current decisions can affect predictions. In general, problems of decision making, feasible solutions, concepts of optimality and robustness are characterized from the context of decision-making situations, that is, systems structure, goals, security constraints, safety norms, supply–demand relationships and thresholds. Robust statistical approaches can be effectively combined with disciplinary or interdisciplinary models, for example, land use model Global Biosphere Management Model (GLOBIOM), for effective decision making in the conditions of uncertainty, increasing interdependencies and systemic risks. We discuss a quantile-regression Environmental Policy Integrated Climate-based global gridded crop model (EPIC) meta-model for tracking dynamics and uncertainties of soil organic carbon (SOC), which is an important agri-environmental indicator. SOC levels (quantiles) can be controlled with GLOBIOM to analyze the costs of achieving robust land management practices to sequester SOC and fulfill food–energy–water–environmental (FEWE) nexus security goals. Quantiles identify critical SOC levels signaling how close a threshold or a targeted level is. The SOC–EPIC meta-model is developed using historical observations and results of the bio-physical model EPIC. It enables the analysis of SOC content and respective probabilities as a function of exogenous parameters such as monthly temperature and precipitation and endogenous, decision-dependent parameters, which can be altered by the land management decisions computed with GLOBIOM.

Chapter written by Tatiana Y. ERMOLIEVA, Petr HAVLIK, Andrey LESSA-DERCI-AUGUSTYNCZIK, Stefan FRANK, Andre DEPPERMANN, Andrè (Mahdi) NAKHAVALI, Juraj BALKOVIČ, Rastislav SKALSKY and Nadejda KOMENDANTOVA.

For a color version of all figures in this chapter, see www.iste.co.uk/gaivoronski/stochastic1.zip.

3.1. Introduction

Interdependencies among food, energy, water, environmental systems are increasing. Proper management (control) of such interdependent systems becomes a challenging multidisciplinary problem. Ensuring robust and sustainable performance of the systems in the face of uncertainty and risks is equivalent to equipping the systems with two types of coherent measures, that is, the measures that prepare the systems in advance and those that facilitate their proper adaptive (operational) responses to changing conditions, therefore minimizing chances of critical imbalances, thresholds' exceedance and thus systemic failures due to combinations of various possible uncertainty scenarios.

The robust interdependent ex ate and ex post decisions account for various risk-adjusted goals and constraints of the involved systems and agents (Ermoliev and Hordijk 2003; Ermoliev and von Winterfeldt 2012; Ermolieva et al. 2016, 2022). The risk-adjusted safety (or security) constraints are imposed as critical levels of vital socioeconomic, resource, environmental indicators analyzed by robust statistical and machine learning methods (Ermolieva et al. 2021). For example, quantiles identify different air and soil pollution levels and their respective probabilities signaling how close is the environmental pollution threshold. Quantile-based analysis of socioeconomic, environmental and demographic indicators allows us to distinguish population by their socioeconomic and environmental vulnerability levels, agricultural production by climatic factors and soil types. The quantile regression addresses the questions regarding what percentage of population leaves in highly polluted areas or in water-scarce regions, or the relation between the high air/water pollution and health indicators, or crop yield quantiles as functions of soil and climate characteristics (Ermolieva et al. 2023a). In interdependent natural and anthropogenic systems, it may be possible to control critical indicators by decisions. For example, agri-environmental indicators reflecting soil health characteristics depend on land use practices and, therefore, can be improved by robust and sustainable land use management.

Thus, in general, problems of robust decision making, feasible solutions, concepts of optimality and robustness are characterized from the context of decision-making situations, that is, systems structure, goals, constraints, safety norms, supply–demand relationships and thresholds. In statistics and machine learning, robustness property means that the solution/estimator is insensitive to outliers, that is, additional observations (data) cannot significantly affect the solution/estimator (Huber 1981; Vapnik 1995; Knopov 2002). Quantile regression estimators are more *robust* in the presence of outliers than the least square regression estimators. Quantiles divide the range of a probability distribution into intervals with equal probabilities.

Various problems of robust decision making under uncertainty, statistical estimation, big data analysis, artificial intelligence (AI) and machine learning can be formulated or reduced to the two-stage STO problems. For example, these are problems inherent to engineering, economics, finance, operations research, patter recognition, etc., which involve minimization or maximization of an objective or a goal function when randomness is present in a model's data and parameters, for example, observations, costs, prices, returns, crop yields, temperature, precipitation, soil characteristics, water availability, emissions and return periods of natural disasters. Uncertain parameters can be interpreted as environment-determining variables (Ermoliev 1976; Ermoliev and Wets 1988; Ermoliev and Hordijk 2003; Ermolieva et al. 2016, 2022; Gorbachuk et al. 2019; Borodina et al. 2020) that condition the performance of the system under investigation.

Stochastic variables can be characterized by means of probability distribution (parametric or non-parametric) functions or can be represented by probabilistic scenarios. Typically, in problems of managing environmental pollution, catastrophic risks, FEWE nexus security and probability distributions of stochastic parameters are non-normal, heavy tailed and even multimodal. For decision making, statistical estimation and machine learning problems in the presence of non-normal, heavy tailed and possibly multimodal probability distributions, it is appropriate to use quantile-based criteria instead of mathematical expectations. The problems can be formulated in the form of two-stage STOs with discontinuous chance (probabilistic or quantile-based) constraints defining vital threshold levels, for example, FEWE security indicators, used for robust decision making under uncertainty and risks and for FEWE nexus security management (Ermoliev and Hordijk 2003; Ermoliev and von Winterfeldt 2012; Ermolieva et al. 2016, 2021, 2022; Ren et al. 2018; Zagorodny et al. 2020, 2024; Gao et al. 2021).

3.1.1. *Two-stage decisions*

Often, decisions (actions) or parameter estimation has to be performed ex ante before the values (realizations) of the uncertain parameters become known or observed (Ermoliev 2009a; Ermolieva et al. 2022). Sometimes, the observations can be only partial or incomplete, that is, incomplete "learning". These situations happen, for example, in the process of agricultural production planning under weather variability and market risks (Ermolieva et al. 2021, 2022), water reservoir management (Ortiz-Partida et al. 2019), investments in irrigation and crop storage facilities (Ermolieva et al. 2022), energy technologies investments planning (Ermoliev et al. 2023) and in many other application problems.

The ex ante decisions may require revisions and corrections after receiving additional information (i.e. after "learning" or partial "learning" of uncertain parameters values). Therefore, the ex ante decisions/solutions can incur costs for their correction, revision or reversion. Thus, there are two types (two-stage) of decisions. The ex ante decisions x in the face of uncertainty may be a "here-and-now" decision, whereas ex post decisions y correspond to all future actions to be taken in different time periods in response to the environment created by the chosen x and the observed value of the uncertain parameter ω in that specific time period. The x and y solutions may represent sequences of interdependent ex ante and ex post control actions over a given time horizon. In the case of dynamical systems, there may also be an additional group of variables z characterizing states of the system in different time periods. These problems often emerge in operations research models, economics and system analysis in the theory of optimal control and its applications in engineering, inventory control, etc. Specific applications include deriving parameters of a statistical model (parametric or non-parametric) or training a machine learning model that maps an input to an output, based on examples of input–output pair through minimizing/maximizing a quantile-based "goodness-of-fit" criteria; deciding on optimal dynamic investments into new technologies (irrigation, energy, agricultural and water management) to minimize costs and/or maximize profits accounting for various norms and constraints; controlling water release from a multipurpose reservoir for hydroelectric power generation, agricultural and industrial production, household requirements, environmental constraints and determining food production to fulfill food security norms; defining insurance coverage and premiums to minimize risk of bankruptcy of insurers and risk of overpayments of individuals.

3.1.2. *Basic model of a two-stage decision making and parameter estimation*

Let us illustrate the concept of the two-stage decision making and robust statistical estimation problem with an example of a simplest two-stage STO model. The idea of this model is implemented in stochastic land use model GLOBIOM (Ermolieva et al. 2016, 2021). Assume that there are observations of an uncertain variable ω, which can be associated with a stochastic parameter, for example, demand for a certain product or resource (water level). The stochastic variable ω can define the uncertain level of pollution or catastrophe losses to be mitigated ex ante.

The choice of the decision $\bar{x} \geq x \geq 0$ to match the stochastic variable ω can be associated with a function $f(x, \omega)$ reflecting costs of overestimation and underestimation of ω. In the simplest case, $f(x, \omega)$ is a random piecewise linear function $f(x, \omega) = \max\{\alpha(x - \omega), \beta((\omega - x)\}$, where α defines the unit overestimation/surplus cost and β is the unit underestimation/shortage cost (associated with implementing measures ex post, which also can be interpreted as costs of imports, borrowing or costs of ex post emergency actions and recovery).

The problem is to find the level x that is "optimal", in a sense, for all foreseeable random scenarios/observations ω.

The expected cost criterion leads to the minimization of the following function:

$$F(x) = \max\{\alpha(x - \omega), \beta((\omega - x)\}$$

subject to $\bar{x} \geq x \geq 0$ for a given upper bound x. This stochastic minimax problem is also reformulated as a two-stage stochastic programming.

The optimal solution minimizing $F(x)$ and more general stochastic minimax problems defines quantile-type characteristics of solutions (Ermoliev 2009a, 2009b; Ermolieva et al. 2022), for example, CVaR risk measures. For example, if the distribution of ω has a density, $\alpha, \beta > 0$, then the optimal solution x minimizing $F(x)$ is the quantile defined as $Pr\{\omega \leq x\} = \beta/(\alpha + \beta)$.

The problem of minimizing $F(x)$ illustrates the essential difference between the so-called scenario analysis aiming at the straightforward calculation of $x(\omega)$ for various scenarios of ω and the STO optimization approach. The STO model produces one solution that is optimal ("robust") against all possible stochastic scenarios ω.

3.2. Concept of robustness in statistical and general decision-making problems

3.2.1. *Stochastic optimization and safety quantile-based constraints*

A rather general STO problem is formulated as the maximization (minimization) of the expectation function

$$F_0(x) = Ef_0(x, \omega) = \int f_0(x, \omega)P(d\theta), \qquad [3.1]$$

subject to constraints

$$F_i(x) = Ef_i(x, \omega) = \int f_i(x, \omega)P(d\theta) \geq 0, i = 1, \ldots, m. \qquad [3.2]$$

The choice of goal function $f_0(x, \omega)$ and indicators $f_i(x, \omega)$ is essential for the robustness of x. By choosing appropriate functions $f_0(x, \omega)$ and $f_i(x, \omega)$, STO models allow in a natural and flexible way to represent various risks, spatial, social and temporal heterogeneities, and the sequential resolution of uncertainty in time. Often, as shown in Example 3.1, constraints $f_i(x, \omega), i = 0, \ldots, m$ are analytically intractable, non-smooth and even discontinuous functions, and probability measure P is unknown, or only partially known, and may depend on decisions x.

Moreover, decisions x according to a two-stage STO can be composed of anticipative precautionary (mitigation) ex ante and adaptive (operational) coping ex post components, which allow us to model dynamic decision-making processes with flexible adaptive adjustments of anticipative decisions when new information is revealed.

The main challenge confronted by STO theory is that it may be practically impossible to evaluate exact values of $F_i(x)$, $i = 0,1,\ldots,m$ (see, for example, Example 3.1). As "deterministic" is a degenerated case of "stochastic", STO methods allow us to deal with problems that are not solved by standard deterministic methods.

EXAMPLE 3.1. (Pollution Control and Nutrients Balance Accounting).– A common feature of most models used in designing pollution-control policies and nutrients balance accounting (Balkovič et al. 2014; Atoyev et al. 2024; Ermolieva et al. 2024 and references therein) is the use of transfer coefficients a_{ij} that link the amount of pollution (nutrient) x_j released by source j to the pollution/nutrient concentrations $g_i(x,\omega)$ at the receptor location i as $g_i(x,\omega) = \sum_{j=1}^{n} a_{ij}x_j$, $i = 0,1,\ldots,m$. The coefficients often depend on meterorological conditions, soil properties, etc. In complex problems, the transfer coefficients a_{ij} are also stochastic values with intractable decision-dependent probability distribution.

The deterministic models ascertain cost-effective pollution or nutrients (for example, agricultural nitrogen and phosphorus) control strategies x_j, $j = 1,\ldots,n$ subject to achieving exogenously specified environmental targets, such as standard b_i at receptors (measurement points) $i = 1,\ldots,m$. These models can be improved by the inclusion of safety constraints that account for the random nature of coefficients a_{ij} and ambient standards b_i to reduce impacts of extreme events or exceedance of vital environmental thresholds:

$$F_i(x) = Prob\left[\sum_{j=1}^{n} a_{ij}x_j \le b_i\right] \ge p_i, i = 1,\ldots m. \qquad [3.3]$$

Namely, the probability that the accumulated nutrients level in each receptor (region, grid or country) i will not exceed uncertain critical load b_i with a given probability (acceptable safety level) p_i. The critical load b_i can be identified by experts or through the quantile-based robust statistical or machine learning approaches, as discussed in section 3.3.

Constraints [3.3] are known as chance constraints (Ermoliev and Wets 1988; Ermoliev and Hordijk 2003; Ermolieva et al. 2016, 2021, 2022, 2023). They can be written in the form of the standard STO model with discontinuous functions: $f_i(x,\omega) = 1 - p_i$ if $\sum_{j=1}^{n} a_{ij}x_j - b_i \le 0$ and $f_i(x,\omega) = -p_i$, otherwise. If $p_i = 1$, $i = 1,\ldots,m$, constraints [3.3] are reduced to constraints of deterministic robustness.

The main computational complexity confronted by STO methods is the lack of explicit analytical formulas for goal functions $F_i(x)$, $i = 0,1,\dots,m$. For example, consider constraints [3.3]. If there is a finite number of possible scenarios $\omega = (a_{ij}, b_i, i = \overline{1,m}, j = \overline{1,n})$ reflecting prevailing weather conditions, then $F_i(x)$ are piecewise constant functions, that is, gradients of $F_i(x)$ are 0 almost everywhere. Hence, the straightforward conventional optimization methods cannot be used.

Ignorance of risks defined by constraints [3.3] may cause irreversible catastrophic consequences. For example, although an average daily concentration of a toxicant in a lake is far below a vital threshold, real concentrations may exceed this threshold for only a few minutes and yet be enough to kill off fish. Safety constraints of the type [3.3] are also important for the regulation of stability in the insurance industry, known as the insolvency constraints. Safety concerns and constraints when operating a nuclear power plant require $p_i = 1 - 10^{-7}$, that is, a major failure occurs on average only once in 10^7 years.

3.2.2. *New problems of statistics and stochastic optimization*

Standard statistical problems are formulated as the minimization of the type [3.1] functionals in the case when the probability measure P is unknown but the sample ω^1, …, ω^N of observations drawn randomly according to P is available. It is assumed that P does not depend on X. In general problems of robust decision making, the exact evaluation of $F(x)$ can be practically impossible due to various reasons: probability measure $P(x, d\omega)$ is unknown or only partially known, random function $f(x,\omega)$ is analytically intractable, or the evaluation of $F(x)$ is analytically intractable, despite well-defined $f(x,\omega)$ and P.

Statistics (statistical decision theory) deals with situations in which the model of uncertainty and the optimal solution are defined by unknown sampling model P. The main issue is to recover P by using available samples. In other words, the desirable optimal solutions $x = x^*$ is associated with P (or its parameters), and the performance of x^* can be observed from available random data on its performance.

STO models were introduced for decision-making problems under uncertainty arising in operation research and systems analysis, which are typically described by a large number of decision variables and uncertainties. These models deal with fundamentally different situations. The uncertainty, feasible solutions and performance of the optimal solution are not given by the sampling model. All of these have to be characterized from the context of the decision-making situation. As a result, multiple performance indicators, constraints and dependencies among decisions and uncertainties play a key role. Thus, in STO, which in fact arose as an extension of linear and nonlinear programming with their sophisticated computation techniques, the accent is on solving problems [3.1] and [3.2] with large number of decisions variables, random parameters and constraints.

The classical statistics has been developed on the basis of asymptotic analysis requiring large samples of historical data. New, important problems in statistics and STO have to confront situations with small data samples, cases of missing observations or absence of direct observations. These new problems require explicit joint treatment of all relevant interdependent observable, partially observable and non-observable variables by using various prior information in the form of additional constraints describing these interdependencies. This leads to high dimensions. The key issue is the representation of interdependencies enabling us to organize pseudo-sampling based on proper characterization of probability measure P by using all available information.

Consequently, these new problems are formulated as general constrained STO problems where estimation of unknown probability measure P is directly associated with goals of overall decision-making problems. Since only specific data are essential for desirable decisions, the combined consideration of statistical estimation within overall decision-making problems can considerably reduce the quality and quantity of estimated information, for example, the accuracy of the true parameters of P including even requirements on the uniqueness of P.

Consider some important statistical estimation problems that can be formulated as STO model [3.1–3.2]. Instead of asymptotic analysis, this provides the natural criterion of efficiency that can be used to evaluate the convergence to optimal solutions with respect to the increasing number of real observations, resampling schemes and pseudo sampling procedures. This section also characterizes loss functions that are typical for statistics.

3.2.3. *Regression estimation*

Assume that a random function $u(v)$ for each element v from a set V corresponds a random element $u(v)$ of the set U. Assume that $V \subset R^l$, $U \subset R^1$. Let P be a joint probability measure defined on pairs $\theta = (u, v)$. The regression function is defined as the conditional mathematical expectation

$$r(v) = E(u|v) = \int uP(U|v). \qquad [3.4]$$

It is easy to see that $r(v)$ minimizes the functional (providing it is well defined)

$$F(x(v)) = E(u(v) - x(v))^2, \qquad [3.5]$$

where $Eu^2(v) < \infty$, $Ex^2(v) < \infty$.

It follows from the fact that

$$\min_{x(v)} F(x(v)) = E\min_{x} E[(u(v) - x)^2 | v],$$

$$\frac{d}{dx} = E[(u(v) - x)^2 | v] = -2(E(u|v) - x) = 0.$$

The estimation of $r(v)$ is usually considered in the set of functions given in a parametric form $\{r(x, v), x \in X\}$. In this case, the criterion [3.5] can be rewritten as

$$F(x) = E(u(v) - r(x, v))^2 = E(r(v) - r(x, v))^2 + E(u(v) - r(x, v))^2,$$

that is, the minimum of $F(x)$ is attained at the function $r(x, v)$, which is close to $r(v)$ in the metric $L_2(P)$ defined as $\sqrt{E(r(v) - r(x, v))^2}$.

3.2.4. *Quantile-based regression*

The conditional expectation $r(v)$ provides a satisfactory representation of stochastic dependencies $u(v)$ when they are well approximated by two first moments, for example, for normal distributions. For general (possibly, multimodal) distributions, it is more natural to use the median or other quantiles instead of the expectation.

Let us define the quantile regression function $r_\rho(v)$ as the maximal value y satisfying equation

$$P(u(v) \geq y | v) = \rho(v), \qquad [3.6]$$

where $0 < \rho(v) < 1$. It can be shown that function $r_\rho(v)$ minimizes the functional

$$F(x(v)) = E(\rho(v)x(v) + max\{0, u(v) - x(v)\}). \qquad [3.7]$$

This is due to the following. First of all, we have

$$\min_{x(v)} F(x(v)) = E\min_{x} E[\rho(v)x + max\{0, u(v) - x(v) | v\}].$$

Assume that probability $P(d\theta)$ has continuous density function $p(\theta)$, $P(d\theta) = p(\theta)d\theta$. Then, from the optimality condition for internal stochastic minimax problem follows that optimal solution x satisfies the following equation:

$$\rho(v) - \int_x^\infty P(d\theta | v) = 0, \qquad [3.8]$$

that is, indeed, it satisfies [3.6]. Let us note that the minimization of more general at the first glance functional

$$F(x(v)) = E(a(v)x(v) + max\{\alpha(v)(u(v) - x(u)), \beta(v)(x(v) - u(v))\})$$

is reduced to the minimization of [3.7] with $\rho(v) = (a + \beta)(\alpha + \beta)^{-1}$. The median corresponds to the case when $a \equiv 0$, $\alpha = \beta$. The existence of optimal solution requires $a < \alpha$.

3.3. Quantile-based machine learning regression model for tracking the dynamics and uncertainties of soil organic carbon in agricultural soils using multisource data

In this section, we introduce a quantile-based statistical (or machine learning) regression model for estimating and predicting annual SOC stocks and stock changes at plow depth under the variability and changing seasonal patterns of temperature and precipitation. SOC and soil organic matter (SOM) are important agri-environmental indicators characterizing soil health. The quantile-based linear regression (LR) is a two-stage STO model similar to that described in section 3.1.2. It enables estimation of quantiles, in particular, critical environmental loads and thresholds, as discussed in Example 3.1 of pollution/nutrients accumulation processes.

3.3.1. *Motivation*

The monitoring, modeling and mapping of agri-environmental indicators, in particular, SOC, are important for many reasons. SOC is an indicator for SOM content, which is a major determinant of soil quality and fertility for food production. Soils with higher SOC can better filter, degrade organic molecules and purify water. SOC accumulation can substantially contribute to climate change mitigation (see discussion and references in Ermolieva et al. 2024). SOC stock is a land degradation neutrality indicator used by the United Nations Convention to Combat Desertification (UNCCD).

Soils have recently become part of the global carbon agenda for climate-change mitigation and adaptation. The "4p1000 initiative" was launched at COP21 by UNFCC under the framework of the Lima-Paris Action Plan (LPAP) in Paris on December 1, 2015. The name of the initiative reflects that the proportional 4% increase in the global SOC stocks in top soils, excluding permafrost soils, would be similar in magnitude to the annual global net carbon dioxide (CO_2) growth.

The EU Mission Board for Soil Health and Food proposed a series of quantitative targets to make soils of Europe healthier. Among them, the aim is to reverse the current SOC concentration losses in croplands (0.5%/year on average at 20 cm depth) to an increase of 0.1–0.4%/year by 2030.

Thus, the quantiles (e.g. low and high) of SOC in agricultural soils can serve as targets in land use model GLOBIOM for estimating optimal and robust land use practices and respective costs of increasing SOC to required levels and achieving food–(bio)energy–water–environmental nexus security (Ermolieva et al. 2016, 2021).

3.3.2. *SOC quantile regression meta model*

The SOC meta-model operates at different spatial scales and provides an effective means for scaling biophysical and land use models' results to required resolutions. By introducing SOC constraints, for example, equal to the 50th or 75th quantile as estimated from the meta-model, the GLOBIOM model (Havlik et al. 2011; Ermolieva et al. 2016, 2021, 2022) can derive an optimal combination of land use practices increasing SOC to the desired level. SOC and other FEWE security constraints identify the overall costs of achieving the FEWE NEXUS security.

In our research, separate quantile-based SOC models are estimated for each EU NUTS2 regions using historical data and results of the bio-physical process-based model EPIC (Balkovič et al. 2014) available at the level of grid cells. The NUTS (Nomenclature of Territorial Units for Statistics) is the EU division of each EU country into three levels. NUTS2 is the level of country-specific basic regions.

NUTS2-specific SOC quantile models are approximated by fitting separate quantile-based regression models. In classical LR approaches, the regression coefficients (β coefficients) represent the mean increase in the response variable produced by one unit increase in the associated explanatory variables. The β-coefficients obtained from QR represent the change in a specific quantile of the response variable produced by a one unit increase in the associated driver. In this way, QR allows us to study how certain drivers affect median (most likely quantile $\tau = 0.5$) or extremely low (e.g. $\tau = 0.05$) or high (e.g. $\tau = 0.95$) SOC stock values. Therefore, it gives a more comprehensive description of the effect of SOC predictors on the whole SOC stock level and the probability distribution (i.e. not just the mean) and may be used to analyze differential SOC stock responses to land practices.

For a random sample $X_1, X_2, \ldots, X_n, \ldots$ with empirical distribution function $\hat{F}_X(x)$, the τth empirical quantile function can be defined as $\hat{Q}(p) = \hat{F}_X^{-1}(x) =$

$\inf\{x: \hat{F}_X(x) \geq \tau\}$. The τth empirical quantile is determined by solving the minimization problem

$$\hat{Q}(p) = argmin_x\{\sum_{i|X_i \geq x} \tau|X_i - x| + (1-\tau)\sum_{i|X_i<x}|X_i - x|\},$$

which is similar to the problem in section 3.1.2. For the linear quantile regression, we make an assumption that the τth quantile is given as a linear function of the explanatory variables. For quantile regression, it is possible to calculate any quantile (percentage) for particular values of the dependent variables. Solving the problem for all $\tau \in [0,1]$, it is possible to recover the entire conditional quantile function, that is, the conditional distribution function, of Y. Coefficients $\beta_m(\tau)$ are functions of the required quantile τ. They are defined as

$$\beta(\tau) = argmin_{\beta \in R^m}\{\sum_{i|Y_i \geq \beta'(\tau)X_i} \tau|Y_i - \beta'(\tau)X_i| + (1-\tau)\sum_{i|Y_i<\beta'(\tau)X_i}|Y_i - \beta'(\tau)X_i|\},$$

where Y_i are observations of dependent variables, X_i is a vector of independent variables $X_i = (x_{i1}, \dots, x_{im})$, $\beta(\tau)$ is a vector of coefficients $\beta(\tau) = (\beta_1(\tau), \dots, \beta_m(\tau))$ and m is a number of observations.

The QR models give much deeper insights into the complete conditional distribution of SOC stock values as a function of spatial and temporal predictors. By focusing on low (or high) quantiles, regression coefficients inform us about predictors that mainly influence the absence (or presence) of high/low SOC stock over space. By considering independent QR models for different values of τ, this allows for the possibility that the importance of certain predictors may change according to SOC level.

The estimates of the SOC quantile level $Q_\tau(y_i)$ in each SimUs within all NUTS2 regions and EU countries have a probability of

$$Prob\{Q_\tau(y_i) \leq \beta_0(\tau) + \beta_1(\tau)x_{i1} + \beta_2(\tau)x_{i2} + \beta_3(\tau)x_{i3} + \dots + \beta_m(\tau)x_{im}\} = \tau.$$

The equation means that $100\tau\%$ of the SOC observations/data are less than the value of the τ-quantile.

3.3.3. *Selected results*

The LR analysis of the relationship between the response variable (SOC) and the set of covariate variables (drivers) was carried out to establish the reference scenario for comparing the SOC quantiles with the mean value predictions.

Trained on EPIC model inputs and results, the estimated NUTS2-specific LR meta-models have an R^2 of about 0.9–0.98 for all NUTS2 regions. The estimated QR trends identify the ranges and the respective probabilities of possible SOC content in different years. Figures 3.1–3.4 display the SOC content change between the consequent years for NUTS2 regions in the period from 1980 to 2020 in mean change, the percentage difference between the 50th quantile and the mean value, the 75th quantile change and the 25th quantile change (t/ha).

In Figure 3.1, more brownish colors indicate the decrease in SOC between the years and the greenish colors point out to the NUTS2 regions with positive changes between the consequent years. In the upper-left panel of Figure 3.1, the mean changes in SOC are positive in Central Europe, that is, the SOC stocks increased. However, the decreasing accumulation of SOC stocks can be observed already in the period from 1985 to 1995; the upper-right panel has less green color when compared to the upper-left one. More of a rapid decumulation of SOC stocks is observed in the southern countries of Europe such as Spain and Portugal. The SOC loss slows down in the north, especially in Sweden, perhaps because of increasing ley farming and subsidies introduced in the early 1990s. This can reveal the strong impact of rather local socioeconomic policies on soil carbon storage, which can be captured by the QR meta-model at the resolution of the NUTS2 regions characterized by region- and country-specific characteristics. The policy-driven context needs to be considered in the models' design and applications. The slowing down of SOC decumulation in Sweden and Finland persists as time goes on, as it is shown in the panels of Figure 3.1. Figure 3.2 visualizes the percentage difference between the 50th quantile and the mean value of the SOC content change for NUTS2 regions from 1980 to 2020. Figure 3.2 shows that the mean value of the SOC content change, as estimated by the LR model, can differ from the most likely one, that is, the 50th quantile. The brownish colors in Figure 3.2 correspond to the locations (NUTS2 regions), where the mean value is lower than the 50th quantile and the greenish colors correspond to where it is higher. Thus, the brownish colors identify the NUTS2 with underestimated SOC changes, and the greenish with overestimated SOC changes by the traditional LR (using symmetrical or least square goodness-of-fit criteria) models as they cannot properly address the non-normality and the variability of the covariates.

The discrepancies between the 50th percentile and the mean value of the SOC content changes indicate that the interannual changes in the SOC content are non-normally distributed. The non-normality can be explained by the variability of the monthly precipitation and temperature patterns affecting components of SOC differently for different soil characteristics and land management practices. SOC meta-models have been estimated at the NUTS2 level, and, therefore, the discrepancies between the LR and the quantile estimates point to heterogeneities across SimUs within respective NUTS2 regions.

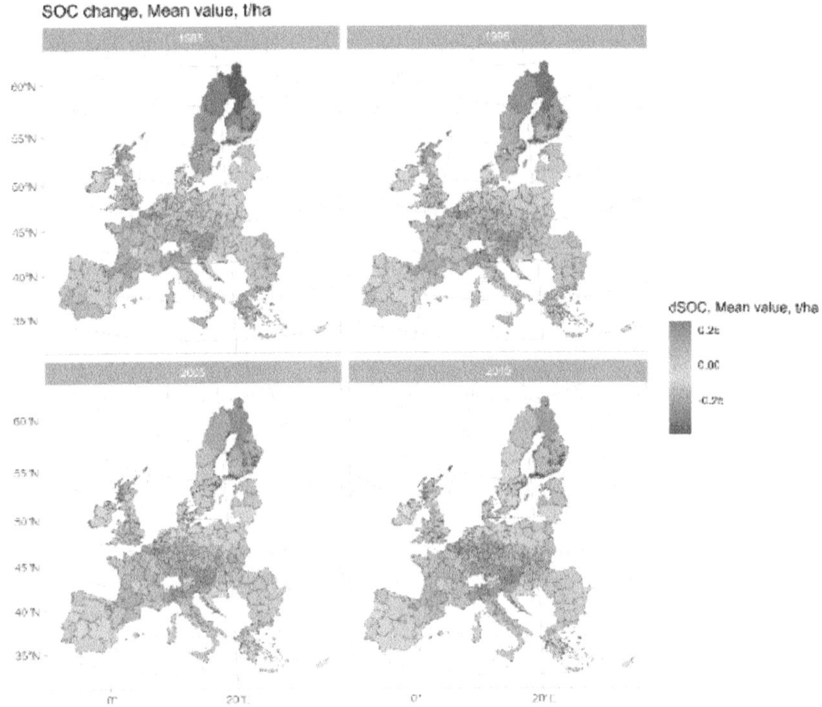

Figure 3.1. *Mean value of the SOC content change for 1980–2000*

The 50th quantile of the SOC content changes identifies the dominating response of the SOC labile fraction to the interannual variability of climatic indicators including the response to possible extreme weather conditions as well as the response to prevailing land practices. The effects of precipitation on different SOC fractions can be opposite at wet and dry sites. Both the soil DOC (dissolved organic carbon) and MBC (microbial organic carbon) concentrations can decrease at the wet sites but increase at the dry sites under increased precipitation conditions.

SOC accumulation is also influenced by interannual N response to changing climatic conditions in different soils under alternative land use practices. This determines the C:N ratio and, therefore, can significantly influence DOC degradability and leaching and, thus, affect SOC content. The combined effects of precipitation and temperature patterns and their variability on SOC content changes indicate the differing response mechanisms in different soils under alternative land use practices, which can be addressed by the quantile-based SOC meta-models.

Figures 3.3 and 3.4 show the 75th and the 25th quantiles of the SOC content changes, thus estimating the ranges and the respective probabilities of how slow and fast the SOC can change under varying exogenous drivers and local economic and policy conditions.

Figure 3.3, displaying the 75th quantile value, tells us that the SOC changes can be "better" than the 75th quantile value exhibited in the figure; however, only with a probability of 0.25. Correspondingly, the 25th quantile value in Figure 3.4 tells us that the SOC changes with the probability of 0.25 can drop below the 25th quantile value exhibited in Figure 3.4, that is, below 0.5 t/ha.

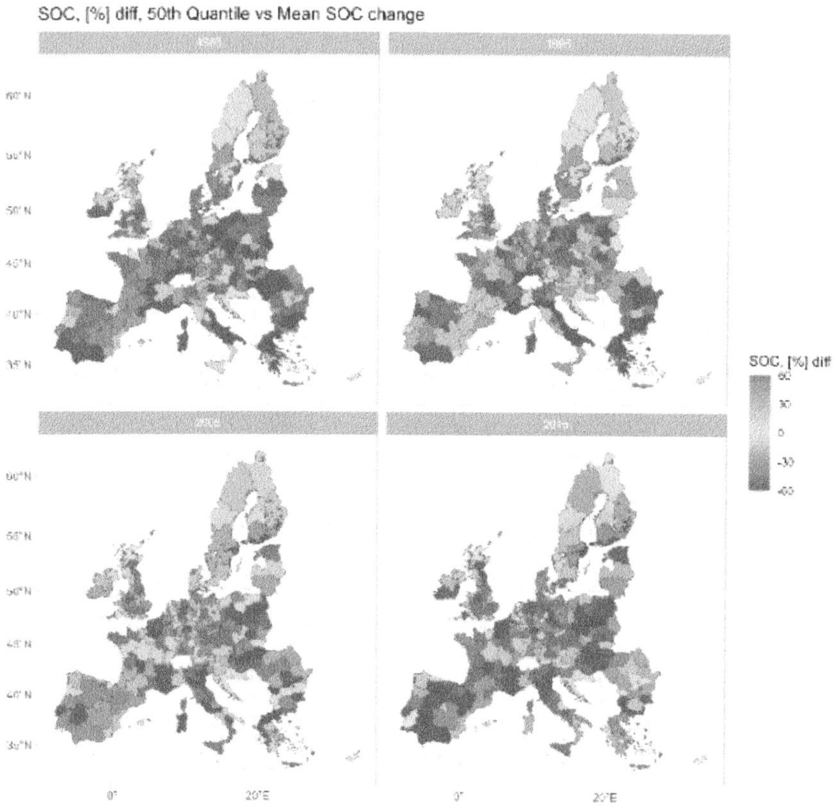

Figure 3.2. *Percentage difference between the 50th quantile and the mean value of the SOC content change for NUTS2 regions from 1980 to 2020*

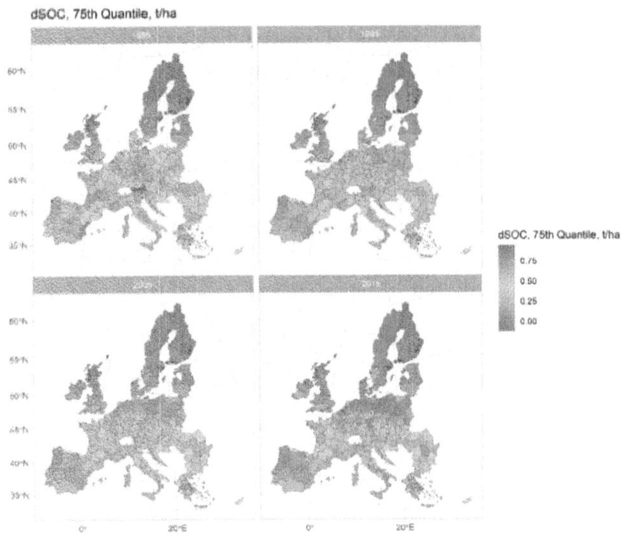

Figure 3.3. *The 75th quantile of the SOC content changes between the consequent years for NUTS2 regions from 1980 to 2020*

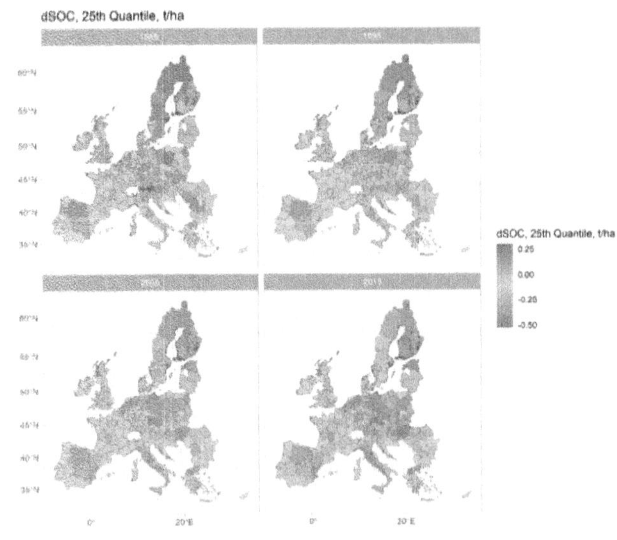

Figure 3.4. *The 25th quantile of the SOC content changes between the consequent years for NUTS2 regions from 1980 to 2020*

3.4. Conclusion

This chapter discusses the connections between the two-stage STO and robust quantile-based regression models. In general, problems of decision making, feasible solutions, concepts of optimality and robustness are characterized from the context of decision-making situations, that is, systems structure, goals, constraints, safety norms, supply–demand relationships and thresholds. The main question related to statistical estimation and predictions is how do we use these predictions to optimize the overall decisions and how can current decisions affect predictions?

In this chapter, we discussed quantile-based regression meta-model for tracking dynamics and uncertainties of SOC in agricultural soils as a function of exogenous parameters such as monthly temperature and precipitation and endogenous, decision-dependent parameters, which can be altered by land use decisions simulated with the GLOBIOM model. The SOC model is developed using historical observations and results of a bio-physical model EPIC, therefore meta-model. Thus, it emulates the EPIC model and can be explicitly linked with GLOBIOM, providing an effective means to analyze responses of environmental indicators to land management decisions computed by GLOBIOM. If incorporated as environmental targets into GLOBIOM, the quantiles of SOC enable the analysis of robust land management practices and the respective costs of increasing SOC content to targeted levels.

3.5. Acknowledgments

The development of the methodologies and models is supported by EU PARATUS (CL3-2021-DRS-01-03, grant number 101073954) project on "Promoting disaster preparedness and resilience by co-developing stakeholder support tools for managing systemic risk of compounding disasters", by a joint project between the International Institute for Applied Systems Analysis (IIASA) and the National Academy of Sciences of Ukraine (NASU) on "Integrated robust modeling and management of food-energy-water-land use nexus for sustainable development" (22-501). Moreover, the work was supported by the project "Comprehensive analysis o robust preventive and adaptive measures of food, energy, water and social management in the context of systemic risks and consequences of COVID-19" (0122U000552) of the National Academy of Sciences of Ukraine. This research has been funded by the European Union's H2020 Projects ENGAGE (Grant Agreement No. 821471) and COACCH (Proposal ID 776479), and European Union's Horizon Europe research and innovation action under grant agreement No. 101086179 (AI4SoilHealth). The results of the research have been used in project CPEALA-2012/10052 "Study program in optimal decisions under risk and uncertainty applied to information economics and response to terrorist threats".

3.6. References

Atoyev, K., Ermolieva, T., Knopov, P. (2024). Mathematical modeling of interconnections between ecological, food, and economic dimensions of security. In *Nexus of Sustainability: Understanding of FEWSE Systems*, Zagorodny, A., Bogdanov, V., Zaporozhets, A. (eds). Springer, Cham [Online]. Available at: https://www.springerprofessional.de/nexus-of-sustainability/27495702.

Balkovič, J., van der Velde, M., Skalský, R., Xiong, W., Folberth, C., Khabarov, N., Smirnov, A., Mueller, N.D., Obersteiner, M. (2014). Global wheat production potentials and management flexibility under the representative concentration pathways. *Global and Planetary Change*, 122, 107–121. doi: 10.1016/j.gloplacha.2014.08.010.

Borodina, O.M., Kyryziuk, S.V., Fraier, O.V., Ermoliev, Y.M., Ermolieva, T.Y., Knopov, P.S., Horbachuk, V.M. (2020). Mathematical modeling of agricultural crop diversification in Ukraine: Scientific approaches and empirical results. *Cybernetics and Systems Analysis*, 56(2), 213–222. doi: 10.1007/s10559-020-00237-6.

Ermoliev, Y. (1976). *Methods of Stochastic Programming*. Nauka, Moscow.

Ermoliev, Y. (2009a). Two-stage stochastic programming: Quasigradient method. In *Encyclopedia of Optimization*, Pardalos, P.M. (ed.). Springer-Verlag, New York.

Ermoliev, Y. (2009b). Stochastic quasigradient methods in minimax problems. In *Encyclopedia of Optimization*, Pardalos, P.M. (ed.). Springer-Verlag, New York.

Ermoliev, Y. and Hordijk, L. (2003). Global changes: Facets of robust decisions. In *Coping with Uncertainty: Modeling and Policy Issue*, Marti, K., Ermoliev, Y., Makowski, M., Pflug, G. (eds). Springer-Verlag, Berlin.

Ermoliev, Y. and Norkin, V. (1997). On nonsmooth and discontinuous problems of stochastic systems optimization. *Europ. J. Oper. Res.*, 101(2), 230–243.

Ermoliev, Y. and Wets, R.J.-B. (1988). *Numerical Techniques for Stochastic Optimization*. Springer-Verlag, Berlin.

Ermoliev, Y. and von Winterfeldt, D. (2012). Systemic risk and security management. In *Managing Safety of Heterogeneous Systems*, Ermoliev, Y., Makowski, M., Marti, K. (eds). Springer, Berlin, Heidelberg.

Ermoliev, Y., Zagorodny, A.G., Bogdanov, V. L., Ermolieva, T., Havlik, P., Rovenskaya, E., Komendantova, N., Obersteiner, M. (2022). Robust food–energy–water–environmental security management: Stochastic quasigradient procedure for linkage of distributed optimization models under asymmetric information and uncertainty. *Cybernetics and Systems Analysis*, 58(1), 45–57. doi: 10.1007/s10559-022-00434-5.

Ermoliev, Z., Komendantova, N., Ermolieva, T. (2023). Energy production and storage investments and operation planning involving variable renewable energy sources: A two-stage stochastic optimization model with rolling time horizon and random stopping time. In *Modern Optimization Methods for Decision Making Under Risk and Uncertainty*, Gaivoronski, A., Knopov, P., Zaslavskyi, V. (eds). Taylor & Francis, Oxfordshire. doi: 10.1201/9781003260196-2.

Ermolieva, T., Havlík, P., Ermoliev, Y., Mosnier, A., Obersteiner, M., Leclere, D., Khabarov, N., Valin, H., Reuter, W. (2016). Integrated management of land use systems under systemic risks and security targets: A stochastic global biosphere management model. *Journal of Agricultural Economics*, 67(3), 584–601.

Ermolieva, T., Ermoliev, Y., Obersteiner, M., Rovenskaya, E. (2021). Two-stage nonsmooth stochastic optimization and iterative stochastic quasigradient procedure for robust estimation, machine learning and decision making. In *Resilience in the Digital Age*, Roberts, F.S. and Sheremet, I.A. (eds). Springer, Berlin. doi: 10.1007/978-3-030-70370-7_4.

Ermolieva, T., Havlik, P., Frank, S., Kahil, T., Balkovič, J., Skalský, R., Ermoliev, Y., Knopov, P.S., Borodina, O.M., Gorbachuk, V.M. (2022). A risk-informed decision-making framework for climate change adaptation through robust land use and irrigation planning. *Sustainability*, 14(3), 1430. doi: 10.3390/su14031430.

Ermolieva, T., Havlik, P., Derci Augustynczik, A.L., Boere, E., Frank, S., Kahil, T., Wang, G., Balkovič, J., Skalský, R., Folberth, C. et al. (2023a). A novel robust meta-model framework for predicting crop yield probability distributions using multisource data. *Cybernetics and Systems Analysis*, 56, 844–858. doi: 10.1007/s10559-023-00620-z.

Ermolieva, T., Ermoliev, Y., Havlik, P., Derci Augustynczik, A.L., Komendantova, N., Kahil, T., Balkovič, J., Skalský, R., Folberth, C., Knopov, P.S. et al. (2023b). Connections between robust statistical estimation, robust decision making with two-stage stochastic optimization, and robust machine learning problems. *Cybernetics and Systems Analysis*, 59(3), 33–47.

Ermolieva, T., Havlik, P., Derci Augustynczik, A.L., Frank, S., Balkovič, J., Skalský, R., Deppermann, A., Nakhavali, A., Komendantova, N., Kahil, T. et al. (2024). Tracking the dynamics and uncertainties of soil organic carbon in agricultural soils based on a novel robust meta-model framework using multisource data. *Sustainability*, 16(16), e6849. doi: 10.3390/su16166849.

Gao, J., Xu, X., Cao, G.-Y., Ermoliev, Y., Ermolieva, T., Rovenskaya, E. (2021). Strategic decision-support modeling for robust management of the food–energy–water nexus under uncertainty. *Journal of Cleaner Production*, 292, e125995. doi: 10.1016/j.jclepro.2021.125995.

Gorbachuk, V.M., Ermoliev, Y., Ermolieva, T., Dunajevskij, M.S. (2019). Quantile-based regression for the assessment of economic and ecological risks. In *Proceedings of the 5th International Scientific Conference on Computational Intelligence*. Ministry of Education and Science of Ukraine, Uzgorod.

Huber, P. (1981). *Robust Statistics*. John Wiley & Sons, New York.

Knopov, P. (2002). *Empirical Estimates in Stochastic Optimization and Identification*. Springer-Verlag, Berlin.

Ortiz-Partida, J.P., Kahil, T., Ermolieva, T., Ermoliev, Y., Lane, B., Sandoval-Solis, S., Wada, Y. (2019). A two-stage stochastic optimization for robust operation of multipurpose reservoirs. *Water Resources Management*, 33(11), 3815–3830. doi: 10.1007/s11269-019-02337-1.

Ren, M., Xu, X., Ermolieva, T., Cao, G.-Y., Yermoliev, Y. (2018). The optimal technological development path to reduce pollution and restructure iron and steel industry for sustainable transition. *International Journal of Science and Engineering Investigations*, 7(73), 100–105.

Vapnik, V. (1995). *The Nature of Statistical Learning Theory*. Springer-Verlag, Berlin.

Zagorodny, A.G., Ermoliev, Y.M., Bogdanov, V.L., Ermolieva, T. (eds) (2020). In *Integrated Modeling and Management of Food-Energy-Water NEXUS for Sustainable Development*. Committee for Systems Analysis at Presidium of NASU–NMO of Ukraine at IIASA, Kiev.

Zagorodny, A., Bogdanov, V., Ermolieva, T., Komendantova, N. (2024). Modeling for managing food–energy–water–social–environmental–NEXUS security: Novel systems' analysis approaches. In *Nexus of Sustainability: Understanding of FEWSE Systems*, Zagorodny, A., Bogdanov, V., Zaporozhets, A. (eds). Springer, Berlin [Online]. Available at: https://link.springer.com/chapter/10.1007/978-3-031-66764-0_1.

4

A Multi-Stage Multi-Horizon Stochastic Equilibrium Model of Multi-Fuel Energy Markets

This chapter presents a multi-stage multi-horizon stochastic equilibrium model for analyzing energy markets, with particular attention paid to infrastructure development in perfect and imperfect market structures. By decoupling short-term operational decisions' feedback from long-term strategic investment decisions, the multi-horizon scenario tree approach allows us to consider long-term and short-term uncertainties while maintaining computational tractability. Numerical experiments demonstrate how considering long-term and short-term uncertainties affects infrastructure development. Independent of market structure, the investment in renewable production and transformation increases when considering the long-term uncertainty in gas production cost, but the investments are reduced when the uncertainty of renewable production is also considered. Moreover, we extend the concept of the value of the stochastic solution (VSS) to multi-horizon stochastic equilibrium problems. Numerical experiments show that the extended VSS can be negative, and such negative effects are more serious in a less competitive market structure. We think that strategic behaviors are the key reason.

4.1. Introduction

The transition from the global energy system toward a low-carbon economy is a major societal challenge of the 21st century. Deriving effective energy and climate policy measures to guide this transformation is difficult because of the many uncertain factors related to the energy system, such as technology cost, intermittent renewables and energy demand. The shale gas development in the United States over

Chapter written by Zhonghua SU, Alexei A. GAIVORONSKI and Asgeir TOMASGARD.

the last decade (Jacoby et al. 2011) has demonstrated the global impacts of local developments through the effect on international oil and gas prices and consumption. The fast development of renewable energy technologies together with rapid change in the use patterns of traditional fossil fuels make it more important than ever to understand the interplay between different energy carriers and sources in the energy system (Rhodes 2007).

This chapter presents a modeling approach for analyzing these dynamic and complex energy markets considering long-term and short-term uncertainties, with particular attention paid to infrastructure development for fossil and renewable energy supply in perfect and imperfect market structures. Such a model can analyze, for instance, the consequences of technology development, policy development and demand trends for which the long-term picture is uncertain, while considering the impact of an increased share of intermittent renewable energy that exposes the energy systems to high short-term variations in supply.

Often, energy system models use optimization or equilibrium modeling to analyze long-term investment and/or short-term operation in energy systems. For example, the TIMES model studies both investment and operation decisions under various economic and engineering constraints to reach the maximum economic surplus in the energy system (Loulou et al. 2005; Fodstad et al. 2022). Specifically, the core TIMES paradigm uses a single global linear programming, while the following model extensions use sequential linear programming, mixed integer programming (Ringkjøb et al. 2018), stochastic programming (Golombek et al. 2022), etc. Sometimes, when strategic behaviors of agents are considered in an energy system, equilibrium modeling is commonly applied. For instance, the LIBEMOD MP, a multi-market energy equilibrium model of Europe for eight energy goods, is applied in Aune et al. (2015) to analyze how in the European natural gas market, Russia exerts market power. However, in LIBEMOD MP, strategic behavior is assumed to only exist in international trade in electricity and natural gas, the production of electricity and the domestic distribution of energy. Investment is assumed to only occur in electricity production and transmission (Aune and Golombek 2021). Furthermore, a partial equilibrium model of the European energy system, PRIMES (E3MLab 2016), considers investments in all of the energy sectors and Nash–Cournot competition in the power/steam sector and gas sector.

Compared to energy system models, single- or double-fuel market models consider a high level of detail, for example, uncertainties, and infrastructure constraints. Yu et al. (2019) discuss the investment and operation planning of the electricity storage system under uncertainties in electricity production and load by developing a two-stage stochastic programming model. The numerical results illustrate that their stochastic model is at least 9.1% more economical than the deterministic model in contributing to the expected daily cost. Such advantage of a stochastic programming model (over the deterministic counterpart) has also been shown in, for example, Gupta and Grossmann (2014) (for the offshore oil field), Lima et al. (2018) (for the downstream oil supply chain) and Riepin et al. (2021) (for the European gas and electricity markets). When Hellemo et al. (2013) analyze investments in natural gas fields and infrastructure, they first propose a multi-horizon scenario tree approach to handle both long-term and short-term uncertainties of, for example, the gas composition and market demand. Later, Kaut et al. (2014) elaborate on the multi-horizon scenario tree structure and compare it with the traditional scenario tree approach. Furthermore, Maggioni et al. (2020) discuss bounds in multi-horizon stochastic programs. The multi-horizon scenario tree approach has also been applied in, for example, hydro-power planning (Abgottspon and Andersson 2016), and the European power system investments with renewable energy (Backe et al. 2022).

The above single- or double-fuel market models deal with optimization problems. When it comes to the strategic behaviors of market players, equilibrium problems much better reflect the interactions among all the energy market players. Specifically, each player has its own objective, possibly including shared constraints, while the players' problems are linked by market-clearing conditions (Gabriel et al. 2012). If this is a one-level game, the result is often a generalized nash equilibrium (GNE) (Facchinei and Kanzow 2007). There are many examples in the literature of a single- or double-fuel one-level equilibrium model, recast as a mixed complementarity problem (MCP). For instance, to investigate an electricity generation and transmission expansion planning problem in an integrated gas and electricity market, Rad et al. (2019) use a deterministic MCP approach and assume Cournot competition among electricity producers. Deterministic MCPs can also be found in, for example, Haftendorn and Holz (2010) for the coal market, Lynch et al. (2019) for the electricity market, and Berk and Çam (2020) for the global oil market. Devine and Bertsch (2018) examine the benefits of load shedding strategies in electricity markets by using a rolling horizon stochastic MCP, and they consider generators exercising market power and uncertainty in available online time of generators. Genc et al. (2007), Egging (2010, 2013) and Devine and Russo (2019) also use stochastic MCPs. Moreover, a conjectural variation (CV) approach (Giocoli 2005) to capture market power is applied widely, for example, Oliveira and Ruiz (2021) (for the electricity market), Berk and Çam (2020) (for the oil market) and Baltensperger et al. (2016) (for the natural gas markets).

In contrast to one-level games, multi-level games have not received much attention in the literature. For example, Kasina and Hobbs (2020) investigate the value of cooperation in interregional electricity transmission planning. Specifically, when there is only one regional planner (i.e. the leader) who makes transmission investments anticipating the response of the generators and consumers (i.e. the followers), this is a two-level Stackelberg game, modeled as a mathematical program with equilibrium constraints (MPEC). When there are multiple regional planners (acting as leaders), it results in an equilibrium problem with equilibrium constraints (EPEC). Multi-level games can also be found in, for example, Li et al. (2019) and Shafiekhani et al. (2019). Multi-level approaches quickly become intractable when increasing the problem size. Even modest sizes are difficult computationally and the interpretation of equilibria found is not straightforward. None of the approaches above is capable of reflecting the strategic behaviors of agents in multi-fuel energy markets and simultaneously address both long-term uncertainties in technology development, climate change, governmental policy on CO_2 emission and fuel mix, as well as short-term uncertainties, such as due to intermittent renewable generation, final demand or unexpected events (e.g. electricity blackouts).

In this chapter, we present a one-level multi-stage multi-horizon stochastic equilibrium model of multi-fuel energy markets, extending the deterministic model developed by Huppmann and Egging (2014). A main challenge for such a model is computational tractability. To address this, we customize the multi-horizon scenario trees introduced by Kaut et al. (2014) for equilibrium models. The multi-horizon scenario tree approach decouples investment decisions from the previously operational decisions, while it also decouples long-term uncertainty from the previously realized short-term uncertainty. To the best of our knowledge, this is the first stochastic, multi-horizon, multi-fuel, energy market equilibrium model.

This chapter is organized as follows. Section 4.2 discusses model-specific background and presents the mathematical model formulation. Section 4.3 introduces the market setup and three model variants. Section 4.4 analyzes the results. Section 4.5 concludes and considers future work.

4.2. Model formulation and model-specific background

This section presents the multi-stage multi-horizon stochastic equilibrium model of multi-fuel energy markets. We view the markets as a simultaneous game and characterize the equilibrium of this game as a GNE (Facchinei and Kanzow 2007). Every agent simultaneously makes a multi-stage investment strategy and/or operational strategy considering long- and short-term uncertainties (described in a multi-horizon scenario tree), forming rational expectations regarding the strategies of the other agents. The market equilibrium is illustrated in Figure 4.1 with key input information and decision variables of all types of agents (note that the market-clearing prices are endogenous in our model). From a mathematical perspective, the model is formulated as an MCP. In the following, we elaborate on the details of the model.

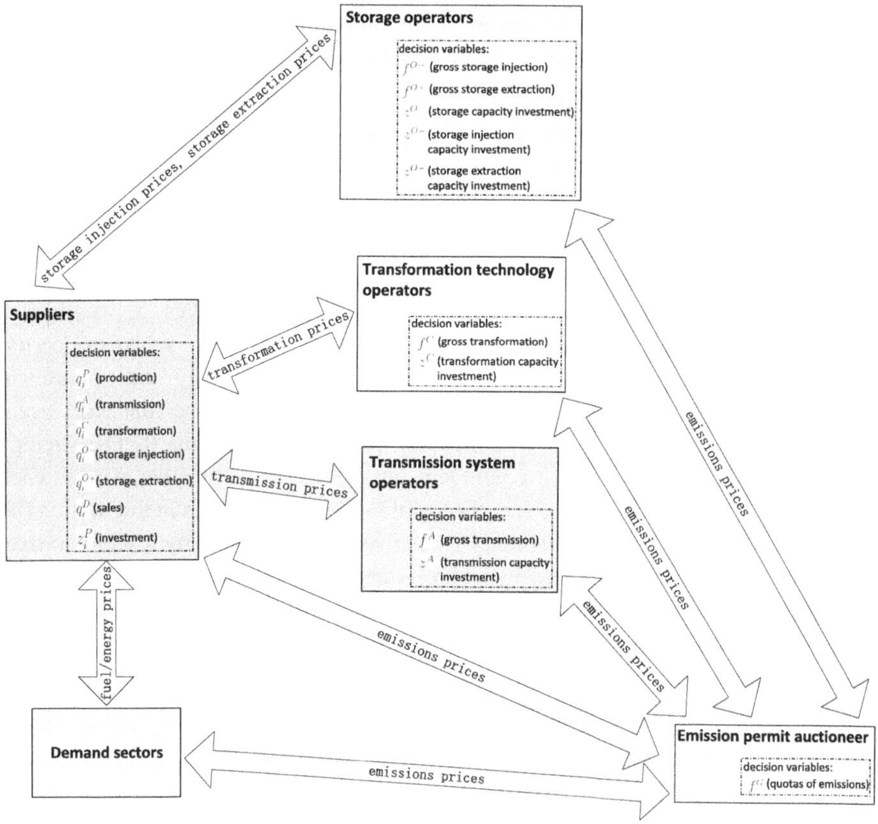

Figure 4.1. *The market equilibrium. For a color version of this figure, see www.iste.co.uk/gaivoronski/stochastic1.zip*

4.2.1. *The model in the context of game theory and stochastic programming*

From the perspective of game theory, our model depicts a simultaneous game. Every agent makes a multi-stage investment and/or operational strategy simultaneously based on symmetric common knowledge. A simultaneous game is sometimes called a static game, a one-level game or an open-loop game (no feedback of other agents' decisions). The simultaneous game equilibrium is illustrated in Figure 4.1 with key input information and decision variables of all the types of agents in the multi-fuel energy markets. Price signals are transferred among all of the agents making their decisions, which decisions in turn affect the prices. For instance, transmission prices link the problems of the transmission system operators (TSOs) (that provide transmission services) and the suppliers (that buy the transmission services), and the transmission prices, in turn, are affected by the gross transmission quantities. Overall, the equilibrium is established via the interplay of all of the agents. Moreover, there are "shared" constraints among suppliers in our model, and the resulting equilibrium is a GNE. To solve the problem, we include market-clearing constraints and derive the first-order optimality conditions for each agent's optimization problem. We can thus construct a MCP. To solve this MCP, we can find the GNE solution.

From the perspective of optimization, every agent solves a multi-stage multi-horizon stochastic program. For each agent (except the emission permit auctioneer and the final-demand sectors), the investment strategy and operational strategy are made simultaneously. Here, it is important to realize that each agent decides on its strategy for the whole planning time horizon at time 0. The strategy determines the actions/decisions contingent on the scenario. In other words, each agent's strategy is made at time 0 for all possible scenario outcomes in the future. The fact of that time passes and uncertainty is resolved is represented by a scenario tree. In Figure 4.2, this is exemplified by a three-stage traditional scenario tree. Though each agent's strategy is made at time 0, the implemented action/decision depends on which scenario is finally realized. Every time new information is available to the decision maker, and the predecided scenario-dependent action is implemented. In other words, decisions are contingent on the realization of uncertainty, and they do not change as a consequence of observing other agents' actions.

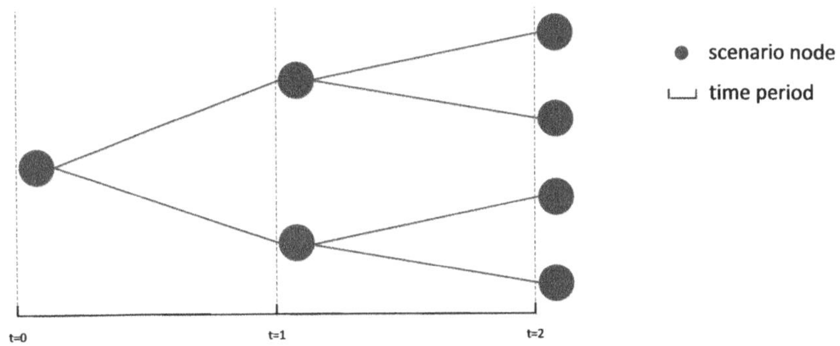

Figure 4.2. *The three-stage traditional scenario tree*

4.2.2. *The multi-horizon scenario tree approach*

The multi-horizon scenario tree is an alternative formulation for the traditional scenario tree (Hellemo et al. 2013). Note that the meaning of "multi-horizon" is different from that of “bi-scale”. The “horizon” denotes the furthest point in time your eyesight can reach if you are now standing in a scenario node (Kaut et al. 2014). Different short-term operational nodes may have different horizons, that is, “multi-horizon”. In a traditional scenario tree, the tree divides into branches, which correspond to different realizations of uncertainty, and all scenario nodes have the same horizon. If there are many uncertain events or possible realizations in every stage, the number of branches becomes very large, posing limits to the computationally tractability. In a multi-horizon scenario tree, we decouple the representation of short-term and long-term uncertainties. Hereby, we limit drastically the number of branches to end up with a much smaller, albeit approximate, scenario tree. Figure 4.3 shows an example of a multi-horizon scenario tree, with three long-term stages.

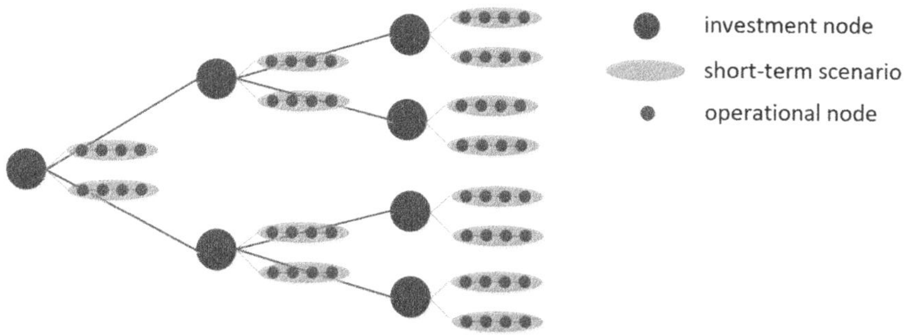

Figure 4.3. *The multi-horizon scenario tree. For a color version of this figure, see www.iste.co.uk/gaivoronski/stochastic1.zip*

The first big red dot on the left in Figure 4.3 represents the starting point of the main period, which is termed as (strategic) investment node or long-term scenario node. The big red dots together with the connecting red branches constitute the main tree, describing the long-term uncertainties. In this main tree, the time between uncertain events is typically one or several years. In the long-term scenario nodes, agents make investment decisions. Given the multi-year lead times for major infrastructure construction projects, capacity expansion decisions in one investment node will become available for use in its succeeding investment nodes. Connected to each investment node, there is a green sub-tree, representing the short-term uncertainties. The green ovals represent short-term scenarios. The blue dots in the ovals are representative short-term periods (for instance, hours, days or seasons). In these short-term nodes, agents make operational decisions such as production rates or storage injection rates.

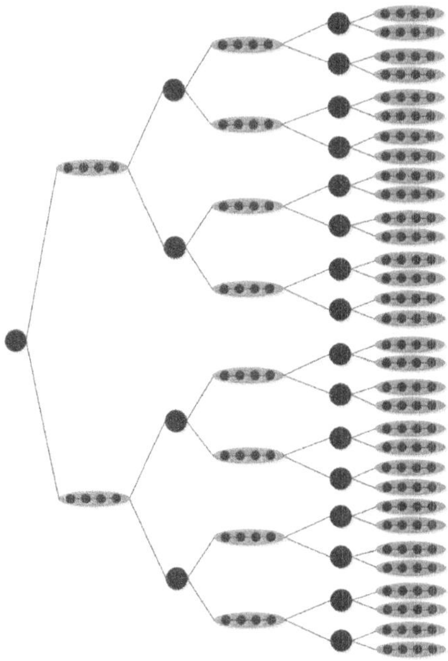

Figure 4.4. *The traditional scenario tree. For a color version of this figure, see www.iste.co.uk/gaivoronski/stochastic1.zip*

In the multi-horizon tree, the terminal leaves on an operational sub-tree are not linked to the succeeding investment and operational nodes. This decoupling of the short-term scenarios from the long-term main tree is the key difference from traditional scenario trees. For comparison, Figure 4.4 shows a traditional scenario tree where operational nodes are directly connected to the succeeding investment nodes. Consequently, the traditional approach creates a tree of much larger size to represent the same number of uncertain events.

Naturally, ignoring the connections of operational nodes with succeeding nodes has limitations. For example, natural gas in storage carried over from one time period to the next, hydro-power production levels affecting reservoir levels in future periods and the depletion of oil and gas reserves, cannot be captured accurately in this approach. This is the price for improving the computational tractability. We must consider how important this is in each specific application. However, many large-scale deterministic models also suffer from those same limitations, as well as stochastic models.

4.2.3. *Agents in the multi-fuel energy markets*

In the model, the following agents are represented: suppliers, TSOs, TTOs, storage operators, an emission permit auctioneer and final demand sectors. Specifically, suppliers produce fuels or energy carriers (e.g. biomass) and decide how much fuel to transmit abroad, transform, store and sell. Each TSO is responsible for transmitting a certain fuel or energy carrier from location A to B, for example, a gas pipeline. Each TTO converts one or more fuels (/energy carriers) into one or more other fuels (/energy carriers). For example, a biomass-based power generation plant transforms biomass into electric power. Each storage operator aids suppliers to store an amount of fuel for some time. An emission permit auctioneer allocates quotas for environmental emissions (e.g. CO_2) to the other agents. Each fuel (/energy carrier) can be used by final demand sectors with some efficiency to provide services.

Figure 4.5 exemplifies how we model a multi-fuel supply chain covering two countries, two suppliers, six fuels, etc. Country X and Country Y are modeled as two geographic nodes, which are connected by two directional transmission service facilities, that is, an oil pipeline and electricity cable. Supplier X located in Country X produces crude oil and natural gas. Crude oil can domestically be consumed by the industry sector and transformed into oil products in a refinery, while it can also be exported (via the oil pipeline) to Country Y, consumed, transformed (in a refinery) and stored (in oil storage) there. Crude oil after transmission, transformation and storage, is still owned by Supplier X, and in our model, such an assumption holds for the supplier of each primary energy. Note that a specific colored solid (/dashed) line represents the energy flow of a specific fuel/energy-carrier owned by Supplier X (/Supplier Y), for example, brown for crude oil. Natural gas can be domestically consumed by the industry sector and the other sectors and transformed into electricity. Both electricity and oil products can be consumed by all of the demand sectors in Country X, where electricity can also be stored. Country Y does not have its own crude oil production capacity but can produce biofuels and nuclear power. To model nuclear power, we make Supplier Y "produce" nuclear fuel, and a nuclear-power generation operator responsible for transforming nuclear fuel into electricity. Supplier Y can also produce biofuels, which can be directly used by all of the demand sectors and transformed into electricity. Electricity generated in Country Y can be exported to Country X via the electric cable, and then consumed and stored there.

Figure 4.5 is for illustration purposes. In fact, our modeling approach is flexible to depict one or several suppliers in a geographical node and a supplier located in one or several nodes.

1 Loading/unloading cycles are a flexible mechanism to connect sub-periods within short-term scenarios. For example, pumped storage is typically used to overcome short-term fluctuations, hence a loading cycle would connect sub-periods within a day. Underground natural gas storage

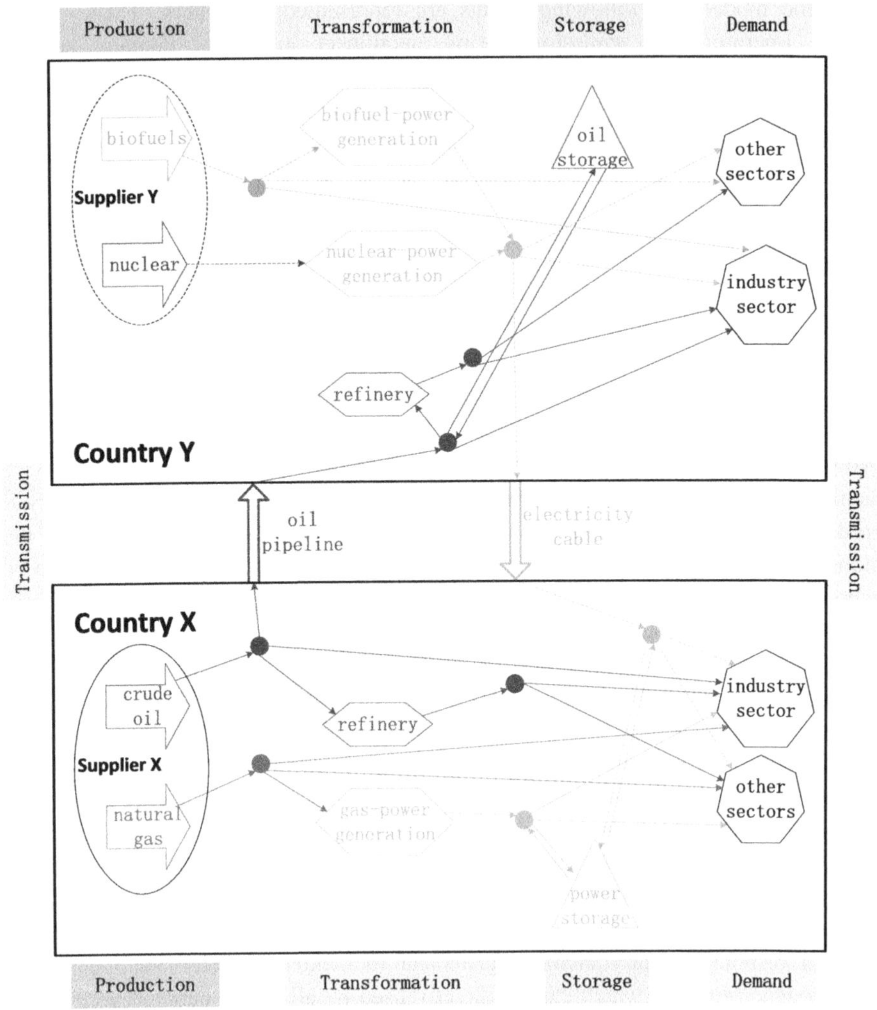

Figure 4.5. *Illustration of modeling a multi-fuel supply chain covering two countries, two suppliers and six fuels (a colored bullet, e.g. • representing the nodal mass balance regarding a certain fuel/energy from a supplier; colored lines: green for biofuels, yellow for electricity, purple for nuclear fuel, red for oil products, brown for crude oil, and blue for natural gas; line types: solid lines for fuel/energy owned by Supplier X, dashed lines for fuel/energy owned by Supplier Y). For a color version of this figure, see www.iste.co.uk/gaivoronski/stochastic1.zip*

Notation	Explanation
Sets:	
$a \in A$	Transmission arcs
$b \in B$	Short-term scenarios (see Figure 4.11)
$c \in C$	Energy transformation technologies (e.g. electric power plants)
$d \in D$	Final demand sectors
$e, f \in E$	Energy-carriers/fuels
$g \in G$	Environmental emissions
$n, k \in N$	Locations
$o \in O$	Storage technologies
$r \in R$	Regions
$s \in S$	Suppliers of fuels and energy
$u \in U$	Short-term scenario nodes representing operational periods (or *time slices*) (see Figure 4.11)
$v \in V$	Storage loading/unloading cycles[1]
$w \in W$	Long-term scenario nodes representing stages
Parameters:	
$b(u)$	Short-term scenario b that contains short-term operational node u
df_w	Discount factor
dur_u	Relative duration of a short-term period (hour/day/season) (with $\sum_{u \in U_b^B} dur_u = 1,\ \forall b \in B$) (if u represents all summer time in Norway, for example, from July to August during a year, then $dur_u = 60/365$)
pr_b^B	*Conditional* probability of the realization of short-term scenario b (given that the connected long-term scenario node is realized). This is used in the emission permit auctioneer problem only
pr_w^W	Probability of the realization of long-term scenario node w

Table 4.1. *Common notations*

4.2.4. *Optimization problem of each agent*

Each agent solves its own optimization problem, except that each final demand sector's problem is implicitly reflected by an inverse demand curve. We suppose that all of the agents have common knowledge of future uncertainties.

By solving this simultaneous game model, equilibria are reached, contingent on scenarios. Suppliers, TSOs, TTOs and storage operators make long-term investment decisions as well as short-term operational decisions. In contrast, the emission permit auctioneer and the final-demand sectors make operational decisions only. Suppliers can exert market power to affect the price of fuel/energy, modeled by a CV approach (Boots et al. 2004). Specifically, the CV approach aids us to capture a market structure from perfectly competitive markets to Cournot oligopoly markets (besides "intermediate" cases). Other than the suppliers, all of the agents in the model are price takers. In the following, we extend the deterministic formulation in Huppmann and Egging (2014) to allow for the representation of uncertainties and multi-horizon

is used to overcome seasonal fluctuations, hence a loading cycle would include all sub-periods wherein injection or extraction can take place.

scenario trees as discussed above. This involves a two-fold contribution to the modeling literature, as we point out in a later section. Generally, the changes concern variables to be scenario-node dependent instead of natural-time dependent. Moreover, in the objective functions, long-term scenario nodes w are weighed by the probability of the realization of long-term scenario node w, that is, pr_w^W, and short-term scenario nodes u by the conditional probability $pr_{b(u)}^B$. Table 4.1 shows the common notations used in the paper.

In the following, we present the optimization problems of all of the agents. We discuss the supplier's formulation extensively, and keep the discussion for the other agents succinct. For more details, the reader can refer to Huppmann and Egging (2014). The dual variables and the Karush–Kuhn–Tucker conditions for all of the agents' problems are presented in sections 4.6.2 and 4.6.4, respectively.

The supplier

Suppliers produce and sell fuels or energy carriers (e.g. biomass and electricity) using infrastructure services for transmission, transformation and storage. Each supplier maximizes its expected net profit over all investment and operational nodes. The optimization objective of supplier s is shown in equation [4.1]. See Table 4.2 for relevant notations.

The cost in each investment node is weighed by the absolute probability pr_w^W and discounted by df_w. Meanwhile, the revenue and cost in each operational node are weighed by the conditional probability $pr_{b(u)}^B$, the relative duration dur_u and also discounted. The supplier's profit comes from selling fuels to final demand sectors q^D, subtracting the costs of production $cost^P(\cdot)$, transmission q^A, transformation q^C, storage injection q^{O-} and extraction q^{O+}, investment in production capacity z^P and purchasing emission permits. In the summation term collecting the fuel transmission fees for fuel e, term $a \in A_{ne}^+$ represents the subset of arcs ending at location n.

Similarly, in the summation term for storage cost, $o \in O_e^E$ represent the subset of technologies for storing fuel e. As in the deterministic model, the supplier owns produced fuels or energy carriers throughout the whole value chain, after transmission, storage and transformation. In the supplier's objective, the value of $cour^S$ determines to what extent the supplier exerts market power. Values range from 0 to 1: a value of 1 represents a Nash–Cournot supplier and a value of 0 represents a perfectly competitive supplier.

$$\max_{\substack{q^P,q^A,q^C\\q^{O-},q^{O+}\\q^D,z^P}} \sum_{\substack{w\in W,u\in U\\n\in N,e\in E}} df_w dur_u pr_w^W pr_{b(u)}^B \Bigg\{ \sum_{d\in D} \bigg[cour_{wsnd}^S \Pi_{wunde}^D(\cdot)$$
$$+(1-cour_{wsnd}^S)p_{wunde}^D\bigg] q_{wusnde}^D - cost_{wusne}^P(\cdot)$$
$$-\sum_{a\in A_{ne}^+} p_{wua}^A q_{wusa}^A - \sum_{c\in C} p_{wunce}^C q_{wusnce}^C$$
$$-\sum_{o\in O_e^E} \left(p_{wuno}^{O-} q_{wusno}^{O-} + p_{wuno}^{O+} q_{wusno}^{O+} \right)$$
$$-\sum_{g\in G} p_{wb(u)ng}^G ems_{wsneg}^P q_{wusne}^P - inv_{wsne}^P z_{wsne}^P \Bigg\} \qquad [4.1]$$

$$\text{s.t.} \quad q_{wusne}^P \le avl_{wusne}^P \Big(cap_{wsne}^P + \sum_{w'\in W_w^{\leftarrow}} dep_{w'wsne}^P z_{w'sne}^P \Big) \qquad [4.2]$$

$$\sum_{u\in U_{vo}^V} dur_u q_{wusno}^{O+} = \sum_{u\in U_{vo}^V} dur_u (1-loss_o^{O-}) q_{wusno}^{O-} \qquad \text{if } v\in V_o^O \qquad [4.3]$$

$$(1-loss_{sne}^P) q_{wusne}^P + \sum_{c\in C, f\in E_c^{C-}} transf_{wncfe}^C q_{wusncf}^C$$
$$+\sum_{a\in A_{ne}^+} (1-loss_a^A) q_{wusa}^A + \sum_{o\in O_e^E} q_{wusno}^{O+} = \sum_{d\in D} q_{wusnde}^D$$
$$+\sum_{c\in C} q_{wusnce}^C + \sum_{a\in A_{ne}^-} q_{wusa}^A + \sum_{o\in O_e^E} q_{wusno}^{O-} \qquad [4.4]$$

$$z_{wsne}^P \le exp_{wsne}^P \qquad [4.5]$$

The supplier's problem includes several constraints (every time we display a constraint, and we omit the several ∀ statements for the constraint for readability). In the production capacity constraint (equation [4.2]), the production capacity cap^P including previous additions z^P (depreciation by dep^P) is weighted by the availability factor avl^P. [2] The storage injection/extraction constraint (equation [4.3]) specifies that within a loading/unloading cycle the fuel quantities injected q^{O-} (after injection loss $loss_o^{O-}$) and extracted q^{O+} must balance. Mass balance (equation [4.4]) contains, on the left-hand side, all supply sources and, on the right-hand side, all *sinks*. For each fuel e in location n, the total loss-corrected production, transformation output, import and extraction from storage q^{O+} must be covered by, hence be equal to, the total sales q^D, transformation inputs, export and storage

2 For conventional fuels, this will be a value close to and at most 1. For renewables, this value will be lower and depend on the type.

injection q^{O-}. Equation [4.5] stipulates that production capacity expansions z^p should not exceed limit exp^P. Compared to the deterministic model in Huppmann and Egging (2014), this chapter excludes fossil fuel reserve constraints. How to address such constraints in a multi-horizon scenario approach will be discussed in future work. Finally, for reference regarding the production cost functions (see Golombek et al. (1995)), see equation [4.6]. The derivatives are specified in section 4.6.1.

Notation	Explanation
Subsets and mappings:	
$a \in A^+_{ne}$	Subset of arcs transmitting fuel e ending at location n
$a \in A^-_{ne}$	Subset of arcs transmitting fuel e starting at location n
$e \in E^{C-}_c$	Subset of input fuel(s) e of energy transformation technology c
$(e, f) \in E^C_c$	Input-output fuel mapping of energy transformation technology c
$f \in E^{C+}_c$	Subset of output fuel(s) f of energy transformation technology c
$n^{A+}(a)$	End location of transmission arc a (singleton)
$n^{A-}(a)$	Start location of transmission arc a (singleton)
$o \in O^E_e$	Subset of storage technologies storing fuel e
$u \in U^B_b$	Subset of short-term scenario nodes along a short-term scenario b
$u \in U^V_{vo}$	Mapping among short-term scenario node, loading cycle and technology
$v \in V^O_o$	Subset of loading cycles with respect to storage technology o
$v^U(uo)$	Mapping among loading cycle, short-term scenario node and technology (singleton)
$W^{\rightarrow}_w$	Subset of successor nodes of long-term scenario node w
$W^{\leftarrow}_w$	Subset of predecessor nodes of long-term scenario node w
$x(w)$	Long-term scenario x that contains node w
Variables:	
q^P_{wusne}	Quantity produced
q^A_{wusa}	Quantity transmitted through arc a
q^C_{wusnce}	Quantity put into energy transformation technology c
q^{O-}_{wusno}	Quantity to be injected into storage o
q^{O+}_{wusno}	Quantity to be extracted from storage o
q^D_{wusnde}	Quantity sold to final demand sector d
z^P_{wsne}	Production capacity expansion
Parameters:	
avl^P_{wusne}	Availability factor of production capacity
cap^P_{wsne}	Existing capacity (before investment) of production
$cour^S_{wsnd}$	Cournot market power parameter of supplier s in sector d of location n
$dep^P_{ww'sne}$	Depreciation factor of production capacity expansion
ems^P_{wsneg}	Emission rate of type g during production process of fuel e in location n by supplier s
exp^P_{wsne}	Limit of production capacity expansion
gol^P_{wsne}	Logarithmic term in the production cost function ($gol^P \geq 0$)
inv^P_{wsne}	Unit cost of production capacity expansion
lin^P_{wsne}	Linear term in the production cost function ($lin^P \geq 0$)
$loss^P_{sne}$	Loss rate during production process of fuel e in location n
qud^P_{wsne}	Quadratic term in the production cost function ($qud^P \geq 0$)

Notation	Explanation
Functions:	
$cost^P_{wusne}(\cdot)$	Production cost function of supplier s for fuel e in location n (c.f. equation [4.6])
$\Pi^D_{wunde}(\cdot)$	Inverse demand curve (c.f. equation [4.25])

Table 4.2. *Notations relevant to the supplier*

$$\begin{aligned} cost^P_{wusne}(\cdot) &= (lin^P_{wsne} + gol^P_{wsne})q^P_{wusne} + qud^P_{wsne}(q^P_{wusne})^2 \\ &\quad + gol^P_{wsne}\left(\widehat{cap}^P_{wusne} - q^P_{wusne}\right)\ln\left(1 - \frac{q^P_{wusne}}{\widehat{cap}^P_{wusne}}\right) \\ \text{where } \widehat{cap}^P_{wusne} &= avl^P_{wusne}\left(cap^P_{wsne} + \sum_{w' \in W^{\leftarrow}_w} dep^P_{w'wnse} z^P_{w'nse}\right) \end{aligned} \quad [4.6]$$

The problem structure of the three infrastructure service providers presented next is very similar. Each service provider collects fees from renting out the capacity while incurring the operational cost of the infrastructure, emission cost as well as capacity investment expenses. Moreover, each service provider's decision is constrained by the maximum capacity limit and the capacity expansion limit. Due to the price-taking nature assumed for all infrastructure service providers, we can aggregate the capacity and operations for each infrastructure type by geographical location. Hence, there will be (at most) one transmission arc representing electric power transmission between locations A and B, there will be (at most) one transformation unit generating coal-based electricity in location A, etc. As in the supplier's problem above, in each problem the investment cost is weighed by the long-term scenario node probabilities only, whereas the operational and emission cost are additionally weighed by the short-term conditional probabilities. All losses due to transmission, transformation and storage operations are accounted for in the supplier's mass balance (equation [4.4]).

The transmission system operator

Transmission arcs in the model are directional and, naturally, specific to energy carriers. If an oil pipeline and an electricity transmission cable both allow exports from location A to B, they are included in the model as different arcs with their own capacities.

The TSO maximizes the expected net profit from renting out arc capacity f^A while subtracting costs of capacity investment (inv^A_{wa}), arc operation (trf^A_{wa}) and buying emission permits, as formulated in equation [4.7] (see Table 4.3 for relevant notations). Regarding the cost of buying emission permits, it depends on the transmitted quantity

f^A, the emission rate ems^A and the market-clearing price of carbon permits p^G. Moreover, equations [4.8] and [4.9] regulate the transmission quantity limit and the capacity expansion limit, respectively.

$$\max_{f^A, z^A} \sum_{w \in W, u \in U} df_w dur_u pr_w^W pr_{b(u)}^B \Big[(p_{wua}^A - trf_{wa}^A) f_{wua}^A - \sum_{g \in G} p_{wb(u)ng}^G ems_{wag}^A f_{wua}^A - inv_{wa}^A z_{wa}^A \Big] \quad [4.7]$$

$$\text{s.t.} \quad f_{wua}^A \leq cap_{wa}^A + \sum_{w' \in W_w^{\leftarrow}} dep_{w'wa}^A z_{w'a}^A \quad [4.8]$$

$$z_{wa}^A \leq exp_{wa}^A \quad [4.9]$$

Notation	Explanation
Variables:	
f_{wua}^A	Quantity transmitted by the transmission system operator
p_{wua}^A	Market-clearing price of using transmission arc capacity
z_{wa}^A	Transmission arc capacity expansion
Parameters:	
cap_{wa}^A	Existing capacity of arc a
$dep_{ww'a}^A$	Depreciation factor of arc capacity expansion
ems_{wag}^A	Emission rate of type g during transmission process through arc a
exp_{wa}^A	Limit of transmission arc capacity expansion
inv_{wa}^A	Unit cost of arc capacity expansion
$loss_a^A$	Loss rate during transmission process through arc a
trf_{wa}^A	Tariff of using transmission arc a

Table 4.3. *Notations relevant to the transmission system operator*

The transformation technology operator

The transformation function in the model converts one or more fuels (/energy carriers) into one or more other fuels (/energy carriers). For example, a biomass-based power generation plant transforms biomass into electric power. The objective of the TTO is shown in equation [4.10], which is similar to that of TSO. See Table 4.4 for relevant notations.

Moreover, equation [4.11] regulates that the (total) transformed f^C (at a transformation rate $transf^C$) can not surpass the transformation capacity limit (as measured in output fuel). Equation [4.13] states the capacity expansion limit. Moreover, equation [4.12] regulates that at least some minimum share of the aggregate output should be based on specific input fuel(s). This can be used as a technical restriction or policy regulation, for example, a bio-fuel mandate.

$$\max_{f^C, z^C} \sum_{\substack{w \in W \\ u \in U \\ e \in E_c^{C-}}} df_w dur_u pr_w^W pr_{b(u)}^B \Bigg[(p_{wunce}^C - trf_{wnc}^C) f_{wunce}^C$$

$$- \sum_{g \in G} p_{wb(u)ng}^G ems_{wceg}^C f_{wunce}^C - inv_{wnc}^C z_{wnc}^C \Bigg] \quad [4.10]$$

$$\text{s.t.} \quad \sum_{(e,f) \in E_c^C} transf_{wncef}^C f_{wunce}^C \leq cap_{wnc}^C + \sum_{w' \in W_w^{\leftarrow}} dep_{w'wnc}^C z_{w'nc}^C \quad [4.11]$$

$$shr_{wnce}^C \sum_{(e',f) \in E_c^C} transf_{wnce'f}^C f_{wunce'}^C \leq \sum_{f \in E_c^{C+}} transf_{wncef}^C f_{wunce}^C \quad [4.12]$$

$$z_{wnc}^C \leq exp_{wnc}^C \quad [4.13]$$

Notation	Explanation
Variables:	
f_{wunce}^C	Quantity of fuel e put into energy transformation technology c
p_{wunce}^C	Market-clearing price of using transformation technology capacity
z_{wnc}^C	Transformation technology capacity expansion
Parameters:	
cap_{wnc}^C	Existing capacity of transformation technology c (as measured in output fuel)
$dep_{ww'nc}^C$	Depreciation factor of transformation capacity expansion
ems_{wceg}^C	Emission rate of type g during transformation process of (input) fuel e
exp_{wnc}^C	Limit of transformation technology capacity expansion
inv_{wnc}^C	Unit cost of transformation technology expansion
shr_{wnce}^C	Minimum share of fuel e regarding energy transformation technology c
$transf_{wncef}^C$	Transformation rate of technology c from input fuel e to output fuel f
trf_{wnc}^C	Tariff of using energy transformation technology c

Table 4.4. *Notations relevant to the transformation technology operator*

The storage operator

Naturally, storage units are fuel specific. Storage aids suppliers to store an amount of fuel/energy-carrier within the loading/unloading cycle. For instance, commonly, liquefied natural gas is injected into storage in summer and extracted in winter whose cycle is one year. The storage operator maximizes the expected net profit from the revenues of energy injection (f^{O-}) and extraction (f^{O+}) minus the costs for injection operation (trf^{O-}), investment and buying emission permits, as shown in equation [4.14]. Table 4.5 contains the relevant notations. All costs, emissions and losses are accounted for during injection. Limitations for total storage capacity, injection and extraction capacity, respectively, are given by equations [4.15]–[4.17]. In the same order, equations [4.18]–[4.20] regulate the capacity expansion limitations.

Notation	Explanation
Variables:	
f^{O-}_{wuno}	Gross quantity injected into storage o
f^{O+}_{wuno}	Gross quantity extracted from storage o
z^{O}_{wno}	Yearly storage capacity expansion
z^{O-}_{wno}	Injection capacity expansion
z^{O+}_{wno}	Extraction capacity expansion
Parameters:	
cap^{O}_{wno}	Existing capacity for fuel stored in storage technology o over one loading cycle
cap^{O-}_{wno}	Existing capacity for fuel injection into storage
cap^{O+}_{wno}	Existing capacity for fuel extraction from storage
$dep^{O}_{ww'no}$	Depreciation factor of yearly storage capacity expansion
$dep^{O-}_{ww'no}$	Depreciation factor of storage injection capacity expansion
$dep^{O+}_{ww'no}$	Depreciation factor of storage extraction capacity expansion
ems^{O-}_{wog}	Emission rate of type g (accounted at injection) during storage injection/extraction process
exp^{O}_{wno}	Limit of yearly storage capacity expansion
exp^{O-}_{wno}	Limit of storage injection capacity expansion
exp^{O+}_{wno}	Limit of storage extraction capacity expansion
inv^{O}_{wno}	Unit cost of yearly storage capacity expansion
inv^{O-}_{wno}	Unit cost of storage injection capacity expansion
inv^{O+}_{wno}	Unit cost of storage extraction capacity expansion
$loss^{O-}_{o}$	Loss rate (accounted at injection) during storage injection/extraction process
trf^{O-}_{wno}	Tariff for using injection capacity into storage technology o

Table 4.5. *Notations relevant to the storage operator*

$$\max_{\substack{f^{O-},f^{O+}\\ z^{O},z^{O-},z^{O+}}} \sum_{w\in W,u\in U} df_w dur_u pr^W_w pr^B_{b(u)} \Bigg[(p^{O-}_{wuno} - trf^{O-}_{wno}) f^{O-}_{wuno} + p^{O+}_{wuno} f^{O+}_{wuno} - \sum_{g\in G} p^G_{wb(u)ng} ems^{O-}_{wog} f^{O-}_{wuno} - inv^{O}_{wno} z^{O}_{wno} - inv^{O-}_{wno} z^{O-}_{wno} - inv^{O+}_{wno} z^{O+}_{wno} \Bigg] \quad [4.14]$$

$$\text{s.t.} \quad \sum_{u\in U^V_{vo}} dur_u f^{O-}_{wuno} \le cap^{O}_{wno} + \sum_{w'\in W^{\leftarrow}_w} dep^{O}_{w'wno} z^{O}_{w'no} \quad \text{if } v \in V^O_o \quad [4.15]$$

$$f^{O-}_{wuno} \le cap^{O-}_{wno} + \sum_{w'\in W^{\leftarrow}_w} dep^{O-}_{w'wno} z^{O-}_{w'no} \quad [4.16]$$

$$f^{O+}_{wuno} \leq cap^{O+}_{wno} + \sum_{w' \in W^{\leftarrow}_{w}} dep^{O+}_{w'wno} z^{O+}_{w'no} \qquad [4.17]$$

$$z^{O}_{wno} \leq exp^{O}_{wno} \qquad [4.18]$$

$$z^{O-}_{wno} \leq exp^{O-}_{wno} \qquad [4.19]$$

$$z^{O+}_{wno} \leq exp^{O+}_{wno} \qquad [4.20]$$

The emission permit auctioneer

The emission permit auctioneer allocates quotas for environmental emissions (e.g. CO_2) to the other agents. An implicit auction mechanism is adopted in modeling the problem. The model can describe emission ceilings that count at the global, regional and nodal levels, as equations [4.22]–[4.24] regulate (see Table 4.6 for relevant notations). Moreover, emissions price floors at the three levels are also considered, enforcing that emission prices have strictly positive lower bounds even when emission ceilings are not binding. In contrast to the deterministic model formulation (Huppmann and Egging 2014) where the dual variables are with respect to long-term periods, here the dual variables are with respect to short-term scenarios, accounting for emissions price floor values being short-term scenario dependent.

$$\max_{f^G} \sum_{\substack{w \in W, b \in B \\ n \in N, g \in G}} df_w pr^W_w pr^B_b \left(p^G_{wbng} - tax^{glob}_{wbg} - \sum_{r \in R_n} tax^{reg}_{wbrg} - tax^{nod}_{wbng} \right) f^G_{wbng} \qquad [4.21]$$

$$\text{s.t.} \quad \sum_{n \in N} f^G_{wbng} \leq quota^{glob}_{wg} \qquad [4.22]$$

$$\sum_{n \in N_r} f^G_{wbng} \leq quota^{reg}_{wrg} \qquad [4.23]$$

$$f^G_{wbng} \leq quota^{nod}_{wng} \qquad [4.24]$$

Final demand

Each fuel/energy-carrier can be consumed by the final demand sector with some efficiency eff^D to provide services. The optimization problem of the final demand sector is implicitly captured by an inverse demand curve in the following (Huppmann and Egging 2014) (see Table 4.7 for relevant notations).

$$\begin{aligned} p^D_{wunde} = {} & eff^D_{wnde} \left[int^D_{wund} - slp^D_{wund} \left(\sum_{s \in S, f \in E} eff^D_{wndf} q^D_{wusndf} \right) \right] \\ & - eucc^D_{wunde} - eucl^D_{wunde} \left(\sum_{s \in S} q^D_{wusnde} \right) - \sum_{g \in G} p^G_{wb(u)ng} ems^D_{wdeg} \end{aligned} \qquad [4.25]$$

Notation	Explanation
Subsets:	
$n, k \in N_r$	Mapping from region to location
$r \in R_n$	Mapping from location to region
Variables:	
f^G_{wbng}	Quantity of emission type g in location n
p^G_{wbng}	Market-clearing price of environmental emission of type g
Parameters:	
$quota^{glob}_{wg}$	Global emission quota
$quota^{reg}_{wrg}$	Regional emission quota
$quota^{nod}_{wng}$	Nodal emission quota
tax^{glob}_{wbg}	Price floor for global emission of type g
tax^{reg}_{wbrg}	Price floor for regional emission of type g
tax^{nod}_{wbng}	Price floor for nodal emission of type g

Table 4.6. *Notations relevant to the emission auctioneer*

Notation	Explanation
Subsets:	
$c \in C^M_m$	Transformation technology(-ies) satisfying transformation mix constraint m
$d \in D^L_l$	Demand sector(s) where fuel mix constraint l applies
$e \in E^L_l$	Fuel(s) accounting for at least a share of total consumption of involved fuel(s) $e \in \widehat{E}^L_l$ in fuel mix constraint l
$e \in \widehat{E}^L_l$	Fuel(s) involved in fuel mix constraint l
$e \in E^M_m$	Fuel(s) satisfying transformation mix constraint m
Variables:	
p^D_{wunde}	Market-clearing price of fuel e in demand sector d
Parameters:	
eff^D_{wnde}	Efficiency of demand satisfaction in demand sector d at location n by fuel e
ems^D_{wdeg}	Emission rate of type g during consumption process of fuel e in node n
$eucc^D_{wunde}$	Constant end use cost parameter
$eucl^D_{wunde}$	Linear end use cost parameter
int^D_{wund}	Intercept of inverse demand curve of demand sector d in location n
shr^L_{wnl}	Minimum share regarding sector fuel mix constraint l
shr^M_{wnm}	Minimum share regarding generation mix constraint m
slp^D_{wund}	Slope of inverse demand curve of demand sector d in location n
$\Pi^D_{wunde}(\cdot)$	Inverse demand curve of demand sector d regarding fuel e

Table 4.7. *Notations relevant to the demand sector*

Specifically, the first part, that is,

$$eff^D_{wnde}\left[int^D_{wund} - slp^D_{wund}\left(\sum_{s\in S, f\in E} eff^D_{wndf}q^D_{wusndf}\right)\right]$$

on the right hand side of equation [4.25], depicts the composite sector price index (energy service price weighted by the service efficiency). The second part, that is, $-eucc^D_{wunde} - eucl^D_{wunde}\left(\sum_{s\in S} q^D_{wusnde}\right)$, depicts the end use cost of a fuel. The third part, that is, $-\sum_{g \in G} p^G_{wb(u)ng} ems^D_{wdeg}$, represents the emission cost of using a fuel. For more detailed explanations, please refer to Huppmann and Egging (2014).

Moreover, consumption is subject to other constraints of, for example, government regulations and technology restrictions. Equation [4.26] stipulates that at least a share shr^L of total consumption in final demand sector(s) $d \in D^L_l$ of using fuel(s) $e \in \widehat{E}^L_l$ is supplied by the subset of fuel(s) $e \in E^L_l$. For example, in European Commission (2009), Sweden set a target that by 2020, renewable sources ($e \in E^L_l$) should account for 49% (shr^L) of total energy ($e \in \widehat{E}^L_l$) consumption. Moreover, equation [4.27] regulates that at least a share shr^M of total consumption of fuel(s) $e \in E^M_m$ is realized from using transformation technology(s) $c \in C^M_m$. For instance, the EU proposed that by 2020, 10% (shr^M) consumption of the transport fuels ($e \in E^M_m$) come from transformation technologies ($c \in C^M_m$) with renewables as inputs (European Commission 2009), for example, bio-diesel transformed from oil seeds.

$$shr^L_{wnl} \sum_{\substack{s \in S, d \in D^L_l \\ e \in \widehat{E}^L_l}} \mathit{eff}^D_{wnde} q^D_{wusnde} \leq \sum_{\substack{s \in S, d \in D^L_l \\ e \in E^L_l}} \mathit{eff}^D_{wnde} q^D_{wusnde} \quad (\beta^L_{wunl}) \qquad [4.26]$$

$$shr^M_{wnm} \sum_{\substack{s \in S, d \in D \\ f \in E^M_m}} q^D_{wusndf} \leq \sum_{\substack{s \in S, (e,f) \in E^C_c \\ c \in C^M_m}} \mathit{transf}^C_{wncef} q^C_{wusnce} \quad (\beta^M_{wunm}) \qquad [4.27]$$

Since there is no decision variable in the demand sectors, we include the constraints (equations [4.27] and [4.26]) in the suppliers' optimization problems and assume the two constraints to be "shared constraints" among suppliers (Huppmann and Egging 2014).

Market clearing

The optimization problems of all of the agents are linked by the market clearing conditions. Equation [4.28] ensures market balance for transmission capacity between suppliers and the TSO. Equation [4.29] ensures that transformation capacity offered by the TTO equals what is used by the suppliers. Equations [4.30] and [4.31] balance the markets for storage injection and extraction, respectively. Finally, equation [4.32] ensures balance in the emission permit market.

$$\sum_{s \in S} q^A_{wusa} = f^A_{wua} \quad (p^A_{wua}) \qquad [4.28]$$

$$\sum_{s \in S} q^C_{wusnce} = f^C_{wunce} \quad (p^C_{wunce}) \qquad [4.29]$$

$$\sum_{s \in S} q^{O-}_{wusno} = f^{O-}_{wuno} \quad (p^{O-}_{wuno}) \quad [4.30]$$

$$\sum_{s \in S} q^{O+}_{wusno} = f^{O+}_{wuno} \quad (p^{O+}_{wuno}) \quad [4.31]$$

$$\sum_{e \in E, u \in U_b^B} dur_u \Bigg(\sum_{s \in S} ems^P_{wsneg} q^P_{wusne} + \sum_{s \in S, d \in D} ems^D_{wdeg} q^D_{wusnde} + \sum_{a \in A^+_{ne}} ems^A_{wag} f^A_{wua} + \sum_{c \in C} ems^C_{wceg} f^C_{wunce} + \sum_{o \in O} ems^{O-}_{wog} f^{O-}_{wuno} \Bigg) = f^G_{wbng} \quad (p^G_{wbng}) \quad [4.32]$$

4.2.5. *Mixed complementarity problem*

All optimization problems presented above are convex optimization problems with polyhedral feasible regions, therefore the Karush–Kuhn–Tucker (KKT) conditions are necessary and sufficient for optimal solutions (Cottle et al. 1992). By combining the KKT conditions (in section 4.6.4) of all of the agents' optimization problems with the market clearing conditions, we construct an MCP. By solving this MCP, we can find the GNE solution. The existence of the optimal solution has been specified in many literature (Gabriel et al. 2012; Oggioni et al. 2012). However, we cannot guarantee a unique optimal solution due to that not every agent's problem is strictly convex. GAMS software (Brook et al. 1988) is applied to solve the MCP.

Stochastic mixed complementarity programs suffer from scalability problems (Egging 2013). It takes many hours to solve a two-season, five-period, twenty-eight region data set with the deterministic version of the model (Huppmann and Egging 2014). Obviously, incorporating uncertainty increases the model size drastically, and it will take a very long time to solve the model. It is beyond the scope of this chapter to develop a decomposition approach, which may reduce the solution time. Instead, in the following, we introduce synthetic market cases to show and discuss the traits of the model as well as general insights useful for policy development and investment decisions under uncertainty.[3]

3 The multi-horizon stochastic oligopoly data instance presented in the next section contains 41695 variables (and equations) (an MCP is a square system). The model solution time for this data instance is about 10 minutes on a computer with a CPU of 7.88 GB and 3.40 GHz using PATH version 24.2.1 (Ferris and Munson 2000).

4.3. Case study

We introduce a market setup, which reflects characteristics in modern markets. It involves fossil fuel, renewable energy and electricity. The countries rich in fossil fuel resources would export it to countries lacking it. Furthermore, there are energy transformation, transportation and storage. Moreover, the market setup is considered for both a perfectly competitive and a Cournot oligopoly market structure. Generally, we solve three model variants, distinguished by which uncertainty is considered: deterministic (i.e. no uncertainty), long-term uncertainty only, and both long-term and short-term uncertainties. For each stochastic model, we will perform extensive numerical experiments, suggesting how uncertainty variation affects the investments in the markets.

4.3.1. *The market setup*

Element	Comment
Two regions	Northeast, Southwest
Four locations	East, South, West, North
Four suppliers	S^A, S^B, S^C, S^D
Two demand sectors	Industry, commercial
Three types of fuel/energy-carrier	Electricity, natural gas, renewable
Two types of transmission arc	Electricity cable, natural gas pipeline
Two types of storage technology	Natural gas storage, electricity storage
Two types of loading cycle	Yearly for gas, daily for electricity
Two types of transformation technology	Gas-to-power, renewable-to-power
One type of emissions	Carbon dioxide
One type of emissions price floor	Regional emissions price floor

Table 4.8. *General information of the market*

Table 4.8 summarizes the setup of the market. To reflect the real markets, we introduce two distant regions Northeast and Southwest with different local energy sources (each region covers two neighboring geographical locations). In locations North and East (in the region Northeast), there is a production of natural gas as well as renewable (energy) by supplier S^A and S^B, respectively. In locations South and West (in the region Southwest), the two suppliers S^C (in South) and S^D (in West) produce renewable only (renewable could be biomass, geothermal energy, etc.). In each location, there are two demand sectors. Fuel-specific directional transmission arcs (see Figure 4.6) can be used by all suppliers to transmit fuels (or energy carriers) abroad. All locations have a transformation capacity to allow electricity production from natural gas as well as renewable. Gas storage exists in the locations without own production: West and South, whereas electricity storage exists only in North. Within each year, four periods are defined, representing days and nights in summer as well as winter. We have defined a loading/unloading cycle (equation [4.3]) of one day for (pumped) electricity storage: what is injected (extracted) during a summer day must be extracted (injected) during a summer night (the same for winter day and night). For gas storage, the loading cycle covers all periods within a year.

To switch between a perfectly competitive market ("Case-Com") and a Cournot oligopoly ("Case-Oli"), the "Cournot parameter" $cour^S$ in equation [4.1] is used. In Case-Com, $cour^S = 0$ for all suppliers, whereas in Case-Oli, all $cour^S = 1$. In this chapter, the unit of measurement for capacities is GWh/day. The initial transmission capacity is shown in Figure 4.6 (along arcs). The other initial capacities are specified in section 4.6.3.

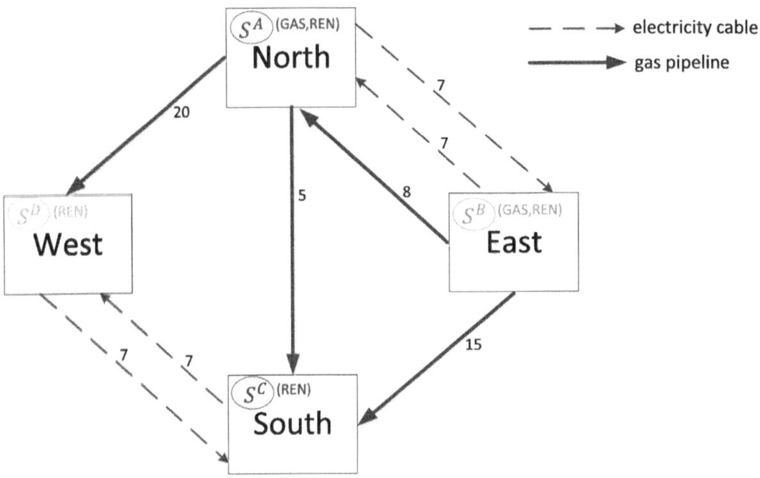

Figure 4.6. *The geographical locations connected*

4.3.2. *The three model variants*

To inspect the traits of our proposed model, we compare it with two other models. One is a deterministic equilibrium model, and the other is a stochastic equilibrium model with only long-term uncertainties. Both these models can be formed by adequately parameterizing the multi-horizon model formulation presented above. In the three models, we assume the discount rate to be 10% per year for investment decisions.

Deterministic model

The first model used for contrasting results is a deterministic parameterization of our model formulation. It is identical to the deterministic formulation in Huppmann and Egging (2014), except that we have omitted the fossil fuel reserves constraints. Figure 4.7 illustrates the deterministic scenario tree represented as a multi-horizon scenario tree with two time resolutions (since there is neither long-term nor short-term uncertainty, this is a degenerated multi-horizon scenario tree). There are four strategic/long-term stages, considered to represent the period from 2010 to 2050 in ten year steps. Figure 4.8 shows how the four representative periods mentioned above (summer day, summer night, winter day and winter night) are connected to each long-term stage.

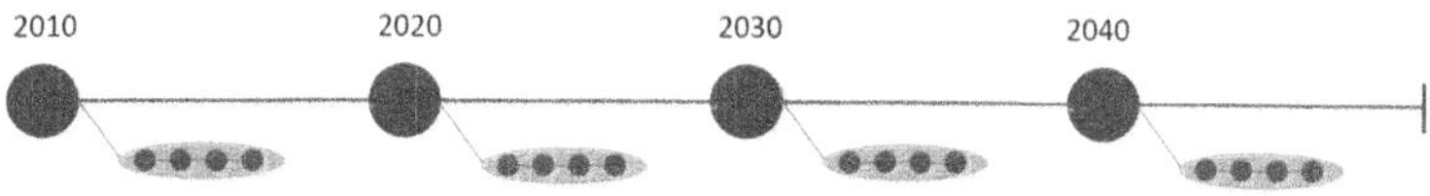

Figure 4.7. *Scenario tree representation of the deterministic equilibrium model. For a color version of this figure, see www.iste.co.uk/gaivoronski/stochastic1.zip*

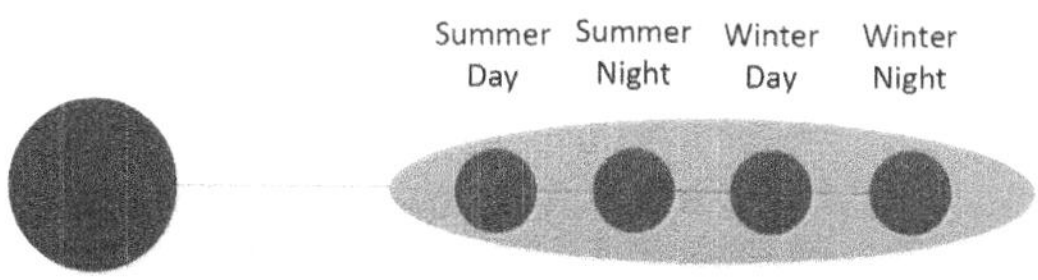

Figure 4.8. *Representative periods. For a color version of this figure, see www.iste.co.uk/gaivoronski/stochastic1.zip*

Stochastic model with only long-term uncertainty

The second model used for comparing results is a four-stage stochastic equilibrium model with long-term uncertainty only. We want to emphasize that this model by itself would have been a significant contribution as there are no publications about stochastic multi-fuel equilibrium models in the current literature. Figure 4.9 shows the scenario tree of the stochastic model with only long-term uncertainty. In each (long-term) investment node, the tree divides into two branches corresponding to different realizations of the uncertain events in the next stage.

Specifically, the considered long-term uncertainty concerns the production cost of natural gas (for all suppliers). In different branches of the tree, the quadratic term in the production cost function (i.e. qud^P_{wsne} in equation [4.6]) is adjusted using parameter $K1$ [4] to depict deviations in parameter values in the stochastic model with

4 In the figure, upward branches face a higher cost adjustment compared to their immediate predecessor and downward branches lower. For example, in investment node w_2 the

only long-term uncertainty relative to the counterpart values used in the deterministic model. The adjustments are assumed symmetrical, as illustrated in Figure 4.9. In the following, we will perform extensive numerical experiments, suggesting how uncertain parameter $K1$ variation affects the investments of all of the agents. To facilitate the experiments, we let $K1 = V_{K1} \times K1_{max}$, and assume $K1_{max} = 0.5$ and V_{K1}, fetching values from the set $\{0, 0.1, 0.2, 0.3, 0.4, 0.5, 0.6, 0.7, 0.8, 0.9, 1.0\}$.

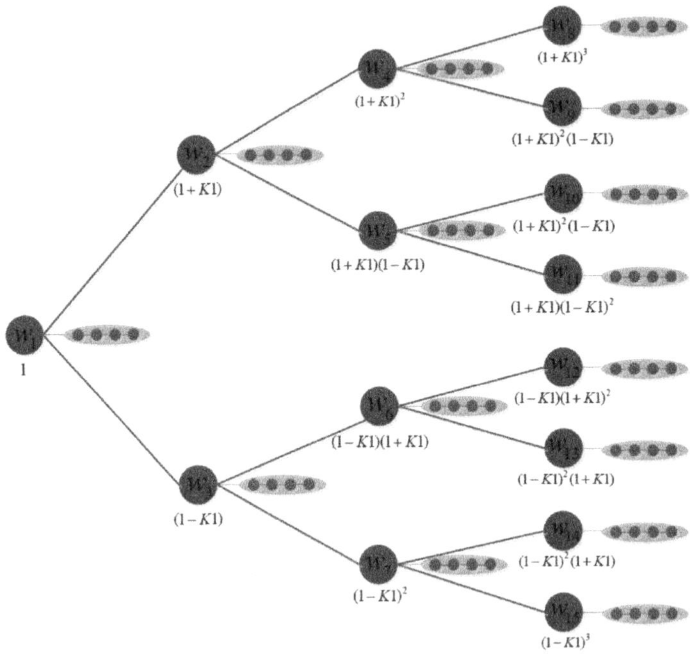

Figure 4.9. *Scenario tree of the stochastic equilibrium model with only long-term uncertainties (note that K1 is the cost parameter adjustment relative to the average value). For a color version of this figure, see www.iste.co.uk/gaivoronski/stochastic1.zip*

Stochastic model with both long-term and short-term uncertainties

The stochastic equilibrium model with both long-term and short-term uncertainties reflects the second contribution of this chapter. To the best of our knowledge, the

---

deterministic quadratic production cost terms used in the deterministic model in 2020 are multiplied by $(1 + K1)$ and in node w_3 multiplied by $(1 - K1)$. In w_2 successor nodes w_4 and w_5, the 2030 values in the deterministic model are multiplied by $(1 + K1)^2$ and $(1 + K1)(1 - K1)$, respectively.

current literature does not present multi-horizon stochastic equilibrium models even for single fuel markets. Figure 4.10 illustrates the four-stage multi-horizon scenario tree, used to reflect uncertainties in long-term production cost of natural gas (as in the stochastic model with only long-term uncertainty), and additionally short-term uncertainties in the availability of renewable production.

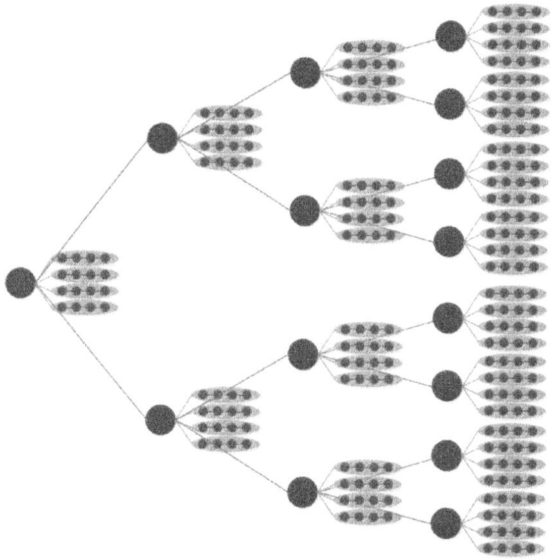

Figure 4.10. *Multi-horizon scenario tree of the stochastic equilibrium model with both long-term and short-term uncertainties. For a color version of this figure, see www.iste.co.uk/gaivoronski/stochastic1.zip*

In the deterministic model and the stochastic model with only long-term uncertainty, the availability of renewable energy production is assumed to be 50%. In the stochastic model with both long-term and short-term uncertainties, we use parameter $K2$ to depict the deviations in availability relative to the counterpart values in the deterministic model. Figure 4.11 displays a sub-tree with four short-term scenarios, that is, b^1, b^2, b^3, b^4, each of which contains four short-term operational nodes (e.g. b^3 containing $u_1^3, u_2^3, u_3^3, u_4^3$). Figure 4.11 shows how, in the stochastic model with both long-term and short-term uncertainties, the values used in the deterministic model are adjusted in each operational node. For instance, in operational node u_1^1 (in short-term scenario b^1), the availability in u_1^1 is the value in the deterministic model multiplied by $(1 + K2)$. Moreover, we will perform extensive numerical experiments, showing how uncertain parameter $K2$ variation affects the investments in the markets. To facilitate the experiments, we let

$K2 = V_{K2} \times K2_{max}$ and assume $K2_{max} = 0.5$ and V_{K2} fetching values from the set $\{0, 0.1, 0.2, 0.3, 0.4, 0.5, 0.6, 0.7, 0.8, 0.9, 1.0\}$. Note that when we vary $K2$, we fix $K1$ to be 0.25.

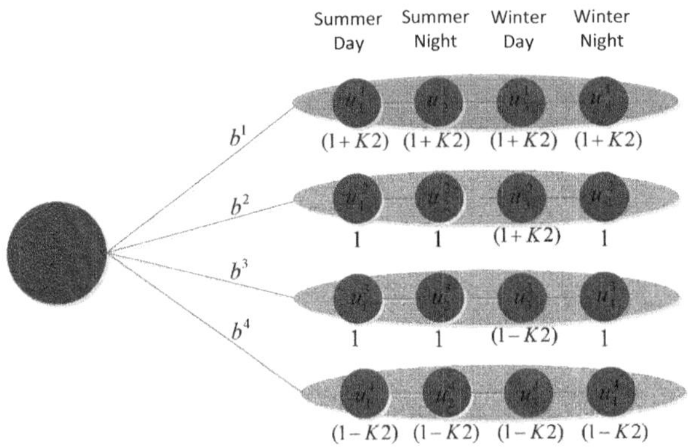

Figure 4.11. *Short-term uncertainty analysis. For a color version of this figure, see www.iste.co.uk/gaivoronski/stochastic1.zip*

The results from these cases allow us to analyze how long-term and short-term uncertainties affect the decisions of market agents and the corresponding profits. The three uncertainty variants, that is, the deterministic model, the stochastic model with only long-term uncertainty and the stochastic model with both long-term and short-term uncertainties, are solved assuming two different market structures. As indicated above, the model is coded in GAMS and we use the PATH solver (Ferris and Munson 2000) to solve all problem instances.

4.4. Results analysis

In the following, we discuss how long-term uncertainty affects investments, before moving to the discussion on the short-term uncertainty. Then, we analyze the VSS.

4.4.1. *How long-term uncertainty affects investments*

To study how long-term uncertainty affects investments in the markets, we compare the results of the deterministic model and the stochastic model with only long-term uncertainty. Specifically, we run the deterministic model once, then we run the stochastic model with only long-term uncertainty 11 times (each time V_{K1} fetches a different value from the set $\{0, 0.1, 0.2, 0.3, 0.4, 0.5, 0.6, 0.7, 0.8, 0.9, 1.0\}$). Note that $V_{K1} = 0$ means no variation. In practice, when $V_{K1} = 0$, the investment solution of the stochastic model with only long-term uncertainty is the same as that of deterministic model.

In the Cournot oligopoly markets

Recall that in the experiments we consider the long-term uncertainty in the natural gas production cost. In this market structure, all suppliers are considered as Cournot oligopoly suppliers. The other agents are price takers. As shown in Figure 4.12(a), the expected total gas production capacity investment in the Cournot oligopoly markets decreases when the long-term uncertainty variation increases. However, the expected total renewable production capacity investment in the Cournot oligopoly markets increases when the long-term uncertainty variation increases (see Figure 4.12(b)). Generally, the results indicate that more uncertainty variation of natural gas production cost favors investment in renewable production over gas production.

As Figure 4.12(c) shows, the expected total investment of gas-power transformation capacity decreases when the long-term uncertainty variation increases. This tendency is similar to the results for gas production capacity. Regarding the expected total investment of renewable-power transformation capacity, Figure 4.12(d) reflects the same increasing tendency as that for renewable production capacity. The midstream energy transformation is closely related to the upstream energy production in the Cournot oligopoly markets.

The transmission expansions present a mixed picture. For the electricity cable, Figure 4.12(e) shows that the expected total investment decreases when the long-term uncertainty variation increases. Regarding the gas pipeline (see Figure 4.12(f)), there is a less explicit relationship between uncertainty and investment.

The expected total gas storage capacity investment, as shown in Figure 4.12(g), has a decreasing tendency as the long-term uncertainty variation increases. This is similar to that of gas production capacity investment. Regarding the electricity storage capacity investment (see Figure 4.12(h)), it does not change as the uncertainty variation increases.

In most of Figures 4.12(a)–(h), there are flat areas when the long-term uncertainty variation is small. However, Figures 4.12(e) and (f) are exceptions, which reflects that the total investment in any type of transmission arc is very sensitive to the long-term uncertainty (in gas production cost) variation. In other words, different agents' investments have different sensitivities to the uncertainty variation. From another perspective, the uncertainty fluctuation range data assigned for the case study can drive the change in energy system investments.

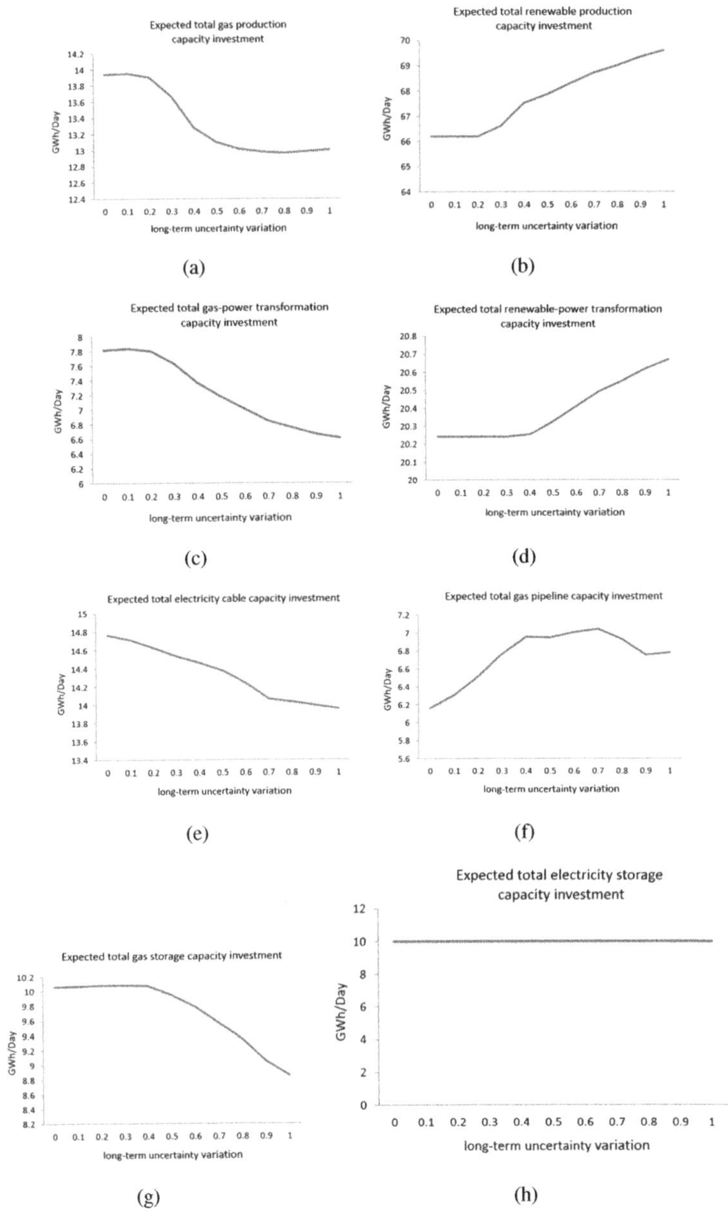

Figure 4.12. *Expected investment as the long-term uncertainty variation changes in the Cournot oligopoly markets*

In the perfectly competitive markets

Generally, the results show that in the perfectly competitive markets there are many more investments in energy production, transformation and storage than those in the Cournot oligopoly markets. As the long-term uncertainty variation increases, there is an increasing tendency of investments in renewable production, renewable-power transformation, electricity cable transmission and electricity storage. There is a decreasing tendency of investments in gas-power transformation, gas pipeline transmission and gas storage. Moreover, the expected total gas production investment generally does not change as the long-term uncertainty increases. This is to say, uncertainty variation of natural gas production cost boosts the investment in renewable production and transformation but reduces the investment in gas transformation and storage, regardless of the market structure.

4.4.2. *How short-term uncertainty affects investments*

To study how short-term uncertainty affects investments in the markets, we compare the results of the stochastic model with only long-term uncertainty and the stochastic model with both long-term and short-term uncertainties. Specifically, we run the stochastic model with only long-term uncertainty one time (with $K1$ fixed to be 0.25) and the stochastic model with both long-term and short-term uncertainties eleven times. Each time we run the stochastic model with both long-term and short-term uncertainties, we fix $K1$ to be 0.25 and let V_{K2} fetch a different value from the set $\{0, 0.1, 0.2, 0.3, 0.4, 0.5, 0.6, 0.7, 0.8, 0.9, 1.0\}$. Note that $V_{K2} = 0$ indicates no variation of short-term uncertainty. In practice, when $V_{K2} = 0$ (and $K1$ fixed to be 0.25), the investment solution of the stochastic model with both long-term and short-term uncertainties is the same as the solution of the stochastic model with only long-term uncertainty (with $K1$ fixed to be 0.25). In other words, we analyze the investment sensitivity to the short-term uncertainty variation while fixing the long-term uncertainty variation to be a certain value.

In the Cournot oligopoly markets

Recall that in the experiments, we consider the short-term uncertainty in the availability of renewable production. As short-term uncertainty variation increases, there is a slowly increasing tendency of the investment in the expected total gas production capacity (see Figure 4.13(a)). However, the investment in the expected total renewable production capacity decreases sharply (from 67.9 to 17.8), as Figure 4.13(b) displays. It reflects the negative impact on the investment of the renewable production due to the short-term uncertainty variation in the renewable production availability.

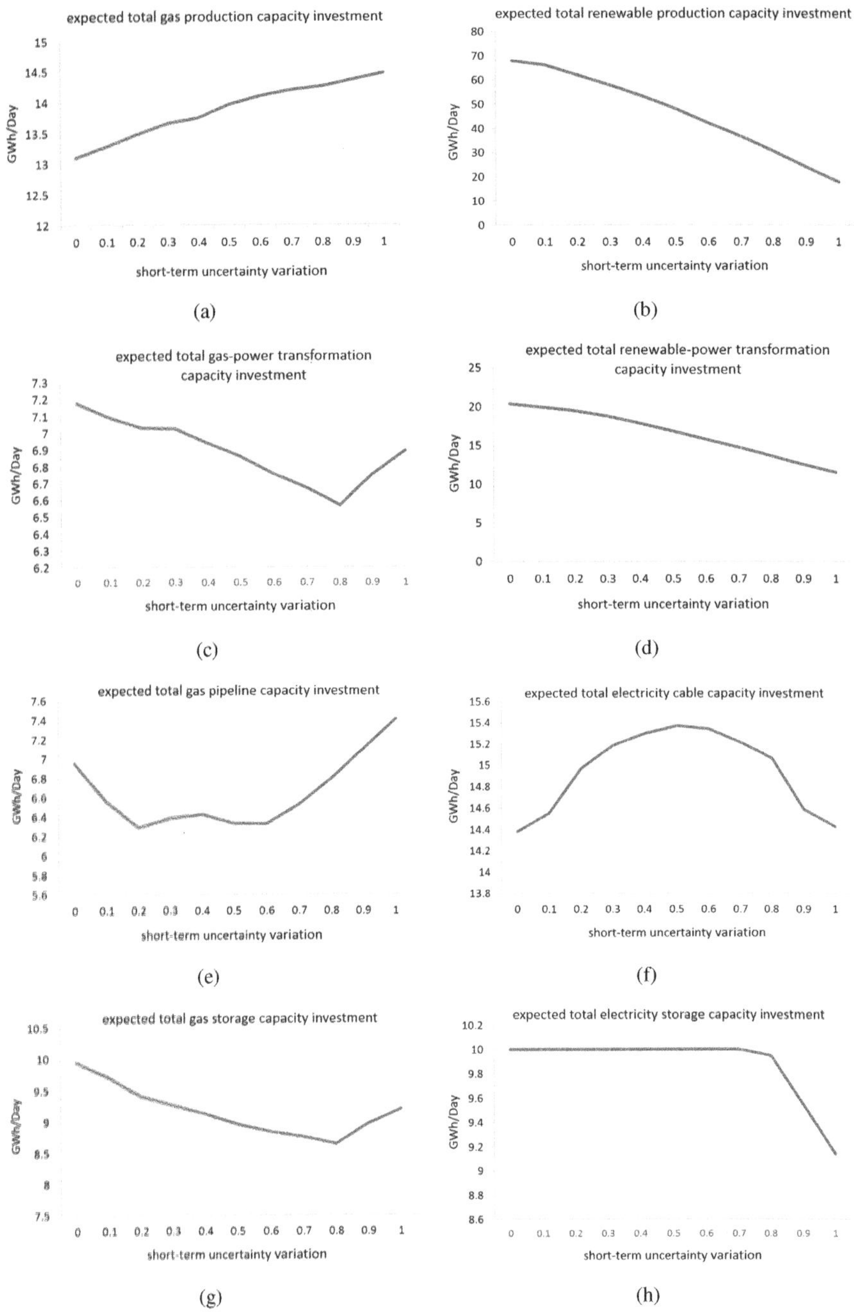

Figure 4.13. *Expected investment as the short-term uncertainty variation changes in the Cournot oligopoly markets*

Moreover, regarding the renewable-power transformation capacity investment, there is a sharp decreasing tendency (from 20.3 to 11.5) as the short-term uncertainty variation increases (see Figure 4.13(d)). However, there is no explicit tendency for the gas-power transformation capacity investment, as Figure 4.13(c) shows. Regarding the transmission, there is no explicit consistent relationship between the short-term uncertainty and the investments, as Figures 4.13(e) and (f) display. The electricity storage capacity investment does not change when the short-term uncertainty variation is moderate (from 0.1 to 0.7) but does decrease when the short-term uncertainty variation becomes bigger (from 0.8), as shown in Figure 4.13(h). Figure 4.13(g) shows no explicit tendency.

In the perfectly competitive markets

Generally, the results show that in the perfectly competitive markets there are many more investments in energy production, transformation and storage than those in the Cournot oligopoly markets. As the short-term uncertainty variation increases, there is a deceasing tendency of investments in renewable production, renewable-power transformation, electricity cable transmission and electricity storage. There is a decreasing tendency of investments in gas-power transformation. Concerning gas production, transmission and storage, there is no explicit tendency. In short, uncertainty variation of renewable production availability reduces the investment in renewable production, transformation and electricity storage, regardless of the market structure.

4.4.3. *The value of the stochastic solution*

In this section, we compare the performance of a multi-horizon stochastic equilibrium solution (from the multi-horizon stochastic equilibrium model with both long-term and short-term uncertainties) with that of the corresponding deterministic equilibrium solution (from the deterministic equilibrium model) in the framework of the multi-horizon stochastic equilibrium model with both long-term and short-term uncertainties. To do so, we refer to the quantification method in the framework of stochastic programming, that is, the VSS, which quantifies how a stochastic solution performs better than the corresponding deterministic solution (Birge and Louveaux 1997). Moreover, the VSS measure for multi-horizon stochastic programs is elaborated on in Maggioni et al. (2020). Furthermore, we elaborate on the VSS measure customized for our multi-horizon stochastic equilibrium model from a mathematical perspective (in section 4.6.5). In the following discussion on the numerical results, we use the notation VSS(DET,STO-LS) instead of VSS to reflect the results in our specific problem. See section 4.6.5 for relevant notations.

For each stochastic equilibrium model with both long-term and short-term uncertainties, we compare the solution's performance with that of the deterministic equilibrium model solution and obtain the VSS(DET,STO-LS). Here, the VSS(DET,STO-LS) for any group J of agents ($i \in J$) is expressed in the form of a percentage of the profit change, that is,

$$\text{VSS(DET,STO-LS)} = \Big(\sum_{i \in J} RP_i - \sum_{i \in J} EEV_i\Big) / \sum_{i \in J} EEV_i. \qquad [4.33]$$

This percentage form can intuitively reflect the profit change percentage from using the deterministic equilibrium model to our multi-horizon stochastic equilibrium model. To calculate the VSS(DET,STO-LS) for any specific group of agents, first, we obtain the profit of the group by using the solution from the stochastic equilibrium model with both long-term and short-term uncertainties. Second, we use the investment solution obtained from the deterministic model in the framework of the stochastic equilibrium model with both long-term and short-term uncertainties to get the profit of the group. Third, we calculate the VSS(DET,STO-LS) according to equation [4.33].

There are, in total, ten stochastic equilibrium models with both long-term and short-term uncertainties, which differentiate in the short-term uncertainty variation level. Note that V_{K2} with a value from the set $\{0.1, 0.2, 0.3, 0.4, 0.5, 0.6, 0.7, 0.8, 0.9, 1.0\}$ reflects the short-term uncertainty variation level of the model and that the long-term uncertainty parameter $K1$ is fixed to be 0.25.

In the perfectly competitive markets

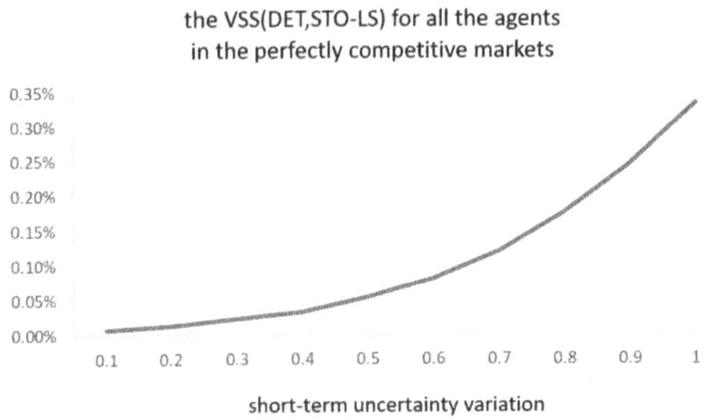

Figure 4.14. *The VSS(DET,STO-LS) for all the agents in the perfectly competitive markets*

Figure 4.14 shows the VSS(DET,STO-LS) for all of the agents in the perfectly competitive markets. As you can see, all values are nonnegative. For an optimization problem this is not a wonder, since in the field of stochastic programming VSS should be nonnegative (Birge and Louveaux 1997). However, our problem is an equilibrium problem. Note that the literature Samuelson (1952) and Barquín et al. (2004) have proven that an equilibrium model in perfectly competitive markets has an equivalent optimization model (solving for maximum total profit). Then, the nonnegative values in Figure 4.14 just coincide with the theory. However, the increasing tendency of the VSS(DET,STO-LS) is a new feature. This suggests that in the perfectly competitive markets, the bigger the short-term uncertainty fluctuation range there is, the bigger the profit change is from using the deterministic model solution to using the multi-horizon stochastic model solution.

Moreover, we notice that the VSS(DET,STO-LS) for all of the agents in the perfectly competitive markets is low, for example, 0.35%. In multi-fuel energy markets, there are a lot of factors together to affect the total profit of all of the agents (i.e. social welfare). Only one or two uncertain factors (fluctuating in a certain range) can not affect the social welfare obviously. However, different agents' VSS(DET,STO-LS) have different sensitivities to uncertainty.

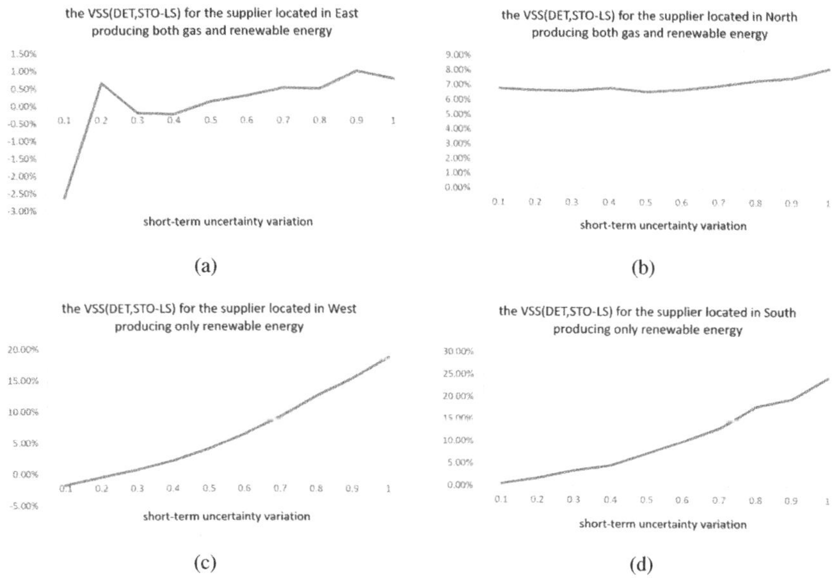

Figure 4.15. *The VSS(DET,STO-LS) for the suppliers in the perfectly competitive markets*

Among the suppliers producing both gas and renewable, the one located in East can have negative VSS(DET,STO-LS) (see Figure 4.15(a)). This means that for the supplier it can be worse off by using the stochastic model considering both uncertainties instead of using the deterministic model. For the suppliers located in South and West producing only renewable, the VSS(DET,STO-LS) has an increasing tendency as the short-term uncertainty variation increases, as shown in Figures 4.15(c) and 4.15(c)(d). Also, negative VSS(DET,STO-LS) occurs (see Figure 4.15(c)).

In the Cournot oligopoly markets

The VSS(DET,STO-LS) for all of the agents in the Cournot oligopoly markets has no consistent tendency as the short-term uncertainty variation increases, as Figure 4.16 displays. Moreover, all of the values are negative, which is different from that in the perfectly competitive markets. To the best of our knowledge, there is no theoretical proof that in imperfect competitive markets the VSS for all of the agents should be nonnegative. Moreover, different agents' VSS(DET,STO-LS) have different sensitivities to uncertainty.

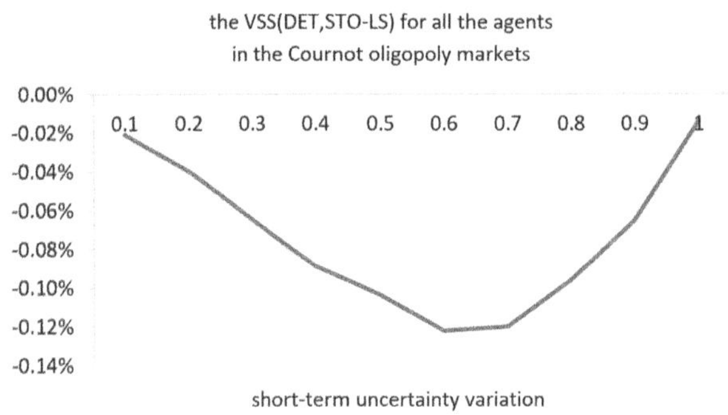

Figure 4.16. *The VSS(DET,STO-LS) for all the agents in the Cournot oligopoly markets*

For the suppliers located in East and North (see Figures 4.17(a) and (b)), the VSS(DET,STO-LS) can be positive or negative as the short-term uncertainty varies. For the suppliers located in West and South producing only renewable, there are increasing tendencies as the short-term uncertainty variation increases (see Figures 4.17(c) and (d)). Also, there are negative VSS(DET,STO-LS) occurring (see Figure 4.17(c)).

In the Cournot oligopoly markets, the negative VSS(DET,STO-LS) for a supplier means that the supplier is worse off by using the stochastic model considering both uncertainties instead of using the deterministic model. Such negative VSS has also been found in Genc et al. (2007), and they hypothesized that a prisoner's dilemma type of effect can be responsible for this in the imperfect market structure. However, in our case study, negative VSS(DET,STO-LS) exists both in the imperfectly competitive markets and perfectly competitive markets (e.g. Figure 4.15(a)). In order to investigate the reason for negative VSS(DET,STO-LS) and the meaning of our multi-horizon stochastic model, in section 4.6.5, we mathematically describe the VSS customized for the multi-horizon stochastic equilibrium model, bring in a hybrid game problem and carry out more experiments to discuss the meaning of our model.

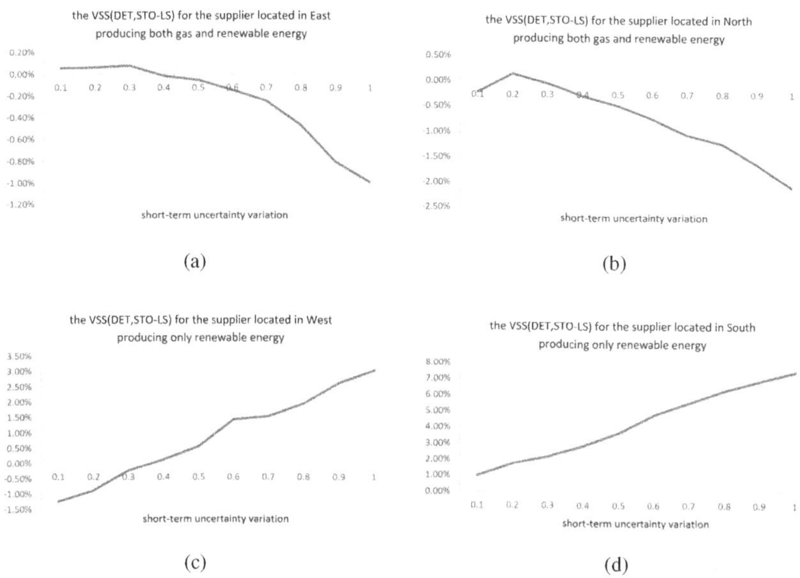

Figure 4.17. *The VSS(DET,STO-LS) for the suppliers in the Cournot oligopoly markets*

When people use the VSS measure for multi-horizon stochastic programming problems (Maggioni et al. 2020), people are able to quantify the performance of an agent's stochastic solution relative to the corresponding deterministic solution, assuming that the other agents' solutions are fixed (in other words, assuming that the market factors/environment possibly affected by the other agents' solutions are fixed). However, the VSS_i measure customized for the multi-horizon stochastic equilibrium model in this chapter has to deal with the case when the other agents' solutions can be changed. We think that strategic behaviors are the key reason for negative VSS_i in our stochastic equilibrium problems. As you can see from equation [4.81], the profit of each agent is affected by the other agents' decisions. When an agent wants to maximize the expected profit by using the stochastic model instead of using the deterministic model, the strategies of the other agents may negatively affect its original intention (in other words, by negatively affecting relevant market prices in the agent's optimization problem), possibly resulting in negative VSS_i. Such negative effects are more serious in a less competitive market structure, due to more serious strategic behaviors. As you can see, the average performance of the VSS_i in the Cournot oligopoly markets (see Figures 4.16 and 4.17) is much worse than that in the perfectly competitive markets (see Figures 4.14 and 4.15).

4.5. Conclusion and outlook for future work

We have presented a multi-stage multi-horizon stochastic equilibrium model for analyzing energy markets. This model provides a twofold contribution to the literature, as it is an equilibrium model considering multiple energy carriers which is (1) *stochastic* and (2) *multi-horizon*. By decoupling short-term operational decisions' feedback from long-term investment decisions, this approach allows consideration of both long-term and short-term uncertainties while maintaining computation tractability. The model can be used for a more comprehensive and robust assessment of potential energy system transformation trajectories as well as the effects of energy and climate policy than permitted by current approaches.

In a four-stage example, considering long-term gas production cost uncertainty and short-term uncertainty in renewable production, we find a significant impact of addressing uncertainties for both the perfectly competitive markets and the Cournot oligopoly markets. When only long-term uncertainty in natural gas production cost is considered, the investment in renewable production and transformation increases, but the investment in gas transformation and storage decreases. However, when the renewable production uncertainty is considered further, it reduces the investment in renewable production, transformation and electricity storage.

Regarding the VSS customized for our multi-horizon stochastic equilibrium model, that is, VSS_i, its mathematical structure is different from the VSS in stochastic programming, which is due to the different nature of stochastic equilibrium problems from that of stochastic optimization problems. VSS_i differs between different market structures.

In the perfectly competitive markets, VSS_i for the aggregate agents is positive and has an increasing tendency as the short-term uncertainty variation increases. This suggests that the bigger the short-term uncertainty fluctuation range there is, the bigger the profit change is from using the deterministic model solution to using the multi-horizon stochastic model solution.

However, in the Cournot oligopoly markets, negative VSS_i appears for the aggregate agents and each separate one. We think that strategic behaviors are the key reason for negative VSS_i. Such negative effects are more serious in a less competitive market structure due to more serious strategic behaviors. Thus, our model can reflect an equilibrium investment strategy portfolio for real markets, wherein negative VSS_i exists as strategic behaviors exist.

Future work may concern efficient ways to incorporate restrictions that naturally couple short-term uncertainty and operational decisions to future (long-term) stages, such as fossil fuel reserves and reservoir levels.

Moreover, we would like to implement our models to real markets. Based on real market data, we would like to comprehensively assess the market performance, for example, prices, emissions and consumer welfare.

Furthermore, we would investigate regional interactions and technological interactions in multi-fuel energy markets. Moreover, we would like to investigate how sensitive markets are to a carbon policy, for example, carbon price floor and emissions quota, so that policymakers can adjust the policy to maximize social welfare.

4.6. Appendix

4.6.1. *Stochastic specification of Golombek production functions*

Equations [4.34]–[4.35] are the probabilistic specification of equations [2b]–[2c] in Huppmann and Egging (2014), which used the specification in Golombek et al. (1995).

$$\frac{\partial\, cost^P_{wusne}(\cdot)}{\partial\, q^P_{wusne}} = lin^P_{wsne} + 2qud^P_{wsne} q^P_{wusne} - gol^P_{wsne} \ln\left(1 - \frac{q^P_{wusne}}{\widehat{cap}^P_{wusne}}\right) \quad [4.34]$$

$$\frac{\partial\, cost^P_{wusne}(\cdot)}{\partial z^P_{w'sne}} = gol^P_{wsne} avl^P_{wusne} dep^P_{w'wnse} \left[\ln\left(1 - \frac{q^P_{wusne}}{\widehat{cap}^P_{wusne}}\right) + \frac{q^P_{wusne}}{\widehat{cap}^P_{wusne}}\right] \text{ if } w' \in W^{\leftarrow}_w \quad [4.35]$$

$$\text{where } \widehat{cap}^P_{wusne} = avl^P_{wusne}\left(cap^P_{wsne} + \sum_{w' \in W^{\leftarrow}_w} dep^P_{w'wnse} z^P_{w'nse}\right)$$

4.6.2. *Dual variable specification*

The following table specifies the dual variables, which show up in the KKTs. Each dual variable is mapped to a constraint.

Notation	Explanation	Mapping
α^P_{wusne}	Dual for available production capacity constraint	Equation [4.2]
α^O_{wvsno}	Dual for injection/extraction balance constraint	Equation [4.3]
ζ^P_{wsne}	Dual for production capacity expansion limit constraint	Equation [4.5]
ϕ_{wusne}	Dual for mass-balance constraint	Equation [4.4]
ζ^A_{wa}	Dual for transmission arc capacity expansion limit	Equation [4.9]
τ^A_{wua}	Dual for transmission arc capacity constraint	Equation [4.8]
β^C_{wunce}	Dual for minimum input share of fuel e regarding transformation technology c	Equation [4.12]
ζ^C_{wnc}	Dual for transformation technology capacity expansion limit constraint	Equation [4.13]
τ^C_{wunc}	Dual for energy transformation technology capacity constraint	Equation [4.11]
ζ^{O-}_{wno}	Dual for injection capacity expansion limitation	Equation [4.19]
ζ^{O+}_{wno}	Dual for extraction capacity expansion limitation	Equation [4.20]
ζ^O_{wno}	Dual for yearly storage capacity expansion limitation	Equation [4.18]
κ^{O-}_{wuno}	Dual for storage injection capacity constraint	Equation [4.16]
κ^{O+}_{wuno}	Dual for storage extraction capacity constraint	Equation [4.17]
τ^O_{wvno}	Dual for storage capacity constraint in loading cycle v	Equation [4.15]
μ^{glob}_{wbg}	Dual for global emission constraint of type g	Equation [4.22]
μ^{reg}_{wbrg}	Dual for regional emission constraint of type g	Equation [4.23]
μ^{nod}_{wbng}	Dual for nodal emission constraint of type g	Equation [4.24]
β^L_{wunl}	Dual of fuel mix constraint l	Equation [4.26]
β^M_{wunm}	Dual of generation mix constraint m	Equation [4.27]
p^A_{wua}	Market-clearing price of using transmission arc capacity	Equation [4.28]
p^C_{wunce}	Market-clearing price of using transformation technology capacity	Equation [4.29]
p^{O-}_{wuno}	Market-clearing price of injection into storage o	Equation [4.30]
p^{O+}_{wuno}	Market-clearing price of extraction from storage o	Equation [4.31]
p^G_{wbng}	Market-clearing price of environmental emission of type g	Equation [4.32]

Table 4.9. *Dual variable specification*

4.6.3. *The initial capacity specification*

The following table specifies most of the initial capacities. Regarding the initial transmission capacity, see Figure 4.6 (along arcs).

Function	Location	Initial capacity
Gas production	North	24
	East	30
Renewable production	North	30
	East	35
	South	60
	West	85
Gas-power transformation	North	10
	East	10
	South	10
	West	10
Renewable-power transformation	North	8
	East	8
	South	10
	West	10
Total gas storage (over one loading cycle)	South	20
	West	20
Injection of gas storage	South	24
	West	24
Extraction of gas storage	South	29
	West	24
Total electricity storage (over one loading cycle)	North	20
Injection of electricity storage	North	20
Extraction of electricity storage	North	24

Table 4.10. *The initial capacities*

4.6.4. *The Karush–Kuhn–Tucker conditions*

$$df_w dur_u pr^W_w \, pr^B_{b(u)} \left[\frac{\partial \, cost^P_{wusne}(\cdot)}{\partial \, q^P_{wusne}} + \sum_{g \in G} p^G_{wb(u)ng} ems^P_{wsneg} \right] + \alpha^P_{wusne} - (1 - loss^P_{sne})\phi_{wusne} \geq 0 \quad \perp \quad q^P_{wusne} \geq 0 \qquad [4.36]$$

$$df_w dur_u pr^W_w \, pr^B_{b(u)} p^A_{wua} + \phi_{wusn^{A-}(a)e} - (1 - loss^A_a)\phi_{wusn^{A+}(a)e} \geq 0 \quad \perp \quad q^A_{wusa} \geq 0 \qquad [4.37]$$

$$df_w dur_u pr^W_w \, pr^B_{b(u)} p^C_{wunce} + \phi_{wusne} - \sum_{f \in E^{C+}_c} transf^C_{wncef} \phi_{wusnf} - \sum_{\substack{m \in M, f \in E^{C+}_c \\ \text{if } c \in C^M_m}} \beta^M_{wunm} transf^C_{wncef} \geq 0 \quad \perp \quad q^C_{wusnce} \geq 0 \qquad [4.38]$$

$$df_w dur_u pr_w^W pr_{b(u)}^B p_{wuno}^{O-} - dur_u(1 - loss_o^{O-})\alpha_{wv^U(uo)sno}^O$$

$$+\phi_{wusne} \geq 0 \ \perp \ q_{wusno}^{O-} \geq 0 \quad [4.39]$$

$$df_w dur_u pr_w^W pr_{b(u)}^B p_{wuno}^{O+} + dur_u \alpha_{wv^U(uo)sno}^O - \phi_{wusne} \geq 0 \ \perp \ q_{wusno}^{O+} \geq 0 \quad [4.40]$$

$$df_w dur_u pr_w^W pr_{b(u)}^B \Bigg\{ \Bigg[-int_{wund}^D$$

$$+slp_{wund}^D \Big(\sum_{s' \in S, f \in E} eff_{wndf}^D q_{wuns'df}^D \Big) \Bigg] eff_{wnde}^D$$

$$+eucc_{wunde}^D + eucl_{wunde}^D \sum_{s' \in S} q_{wus'nde}^D + \sum_{g \in G} p_{wb(u)ng}^G ems_{wdeg}^D$$

$$+cour_{wsnd}^S \Big(eff_{wnde}^D slp_{wund}^D \sum_{f \in E} eff_{wndf}^D q_{wusndf}^D + eucl_{wunde}^D q_{wusnde}^D \Big) \Bigg\}$$

$$+\phi_{wusne} + \sum_{\substack{l \in L \\ \text{if } d \in D_l^L}} \left\{ \begin{array}{ll} (shr_{wnl}^L - 1) eff_{wnde}^D \beta_{wunl}^L & \text{if } e \in E_l^L \\ shr_{wnl}^L eff_{wnde}^D \beta_{wunl}^L & \text{if } e \in \widehat{E}_l^L, e \notin E_l^L \end{array} \right\}$$

$$+ \sum_{\substack{m \in M \\ \text{if } e \in E_m^M}} shr_{wnm}^M \beta_{wunm}^M \geq 0 \ \perp \ q_{wusnde}^D \geq 0 \quad [4.41]$$

$$\sum_{\substack{w' \in W_w^{\rightarrow} \\ u \in U}} \Bigg[df_{w'} dur_u pr_{w'}^W pr_{b(u)}^B \frac{\partial\, cost_{w'usne}^P(\cdot)}{\partial\, z_{wsne}^P}$$

$$-avl_{w'usne}^P dep_{ww'sne}^P \alpha_{w'usne}^P \Bigg] + df_w pr_w^W inv_{wsne}^P$$

$$+\zeta_{wsne}^P \geq 0 \ \perp \ z_{wsne}^P \geq 0 \quad [4.42]$$

$$avl_{wusne}^P \Big(cap_{wsne}^P + \sum_{w' \in W_w^{\leftarrow}} dep_{w'wsne}^P z_{w'sne}^P \Big)$$

$$-q_{wusne}^P \geq 0 \ \perp \ \alpha_{wusne}^P \geq 0 \quad [4.43]$$

$$\sum_{u \in U_{vo}^V} dur_u \Big[(1 - loss_o^{O-}) q_{wusno}^{O-} - q_{wusno}^{O+} \Big] = 0 \ \perp \ \alpha_{wvsno}^O \text{ (free)}$$

$$\text{if } v \in V_o^O \quad [4.44]$$

$$(1 - loss_{sne}^P) q_{wusne}^P - \sum_{d \in D} q_{wusnde}^D + \sum_{c \in C, f \in E_c^{C-}} transf_{wncfe}^C q_{wusncf}^C$$

$$- \sum_{c \in C} q_{wusnce}^C + \sum_{a \in A_{ne}^+} (1 - loss_a^A) q_{wusa}^A - \sum_{a \in A_{ne}^-} q_{wusa}^A$$

$$+\sum_{o\in O_e^E}\left(q_{wusno}^{O+}-q_{wusno}^{O-}\right)=0 \quad \perp \quad \phi_{wusne}\ \text{(free)} \qquad [4.45]$$

$$exp_{wsne}^{P}-z_{wsne}^{P}\geq 0 \quad \perp \quad \zeta_{wsne}^{P}\geq 0 \qquad [4.46]$$

$$-shr_{wnl}^{L}\sum_{\substack{s\in S,d\in D_l^L\\ e\in \widehat{E}_l^L}} e\!f\!f_{wnde}^{D}q_{wusnde}^{D}$$

$$+\sum_{\substack{s\in S,d\in D_l^L\\ e\in E_l^L}} e\!f\!f_{wnde}^{D}q_{wusnde}^{D}\geq 0 \quad \perp \quad \beta_{wunl}^{L}\geq 0 \qquad [4.47]$$

$$-shr_{wnm}^{M}\sum_{\substack{s\in S,d\in D\\ f\in E_m^M}} q_{wusndf}^{D}$$

$$+\sum_{\substack{s\in S,(e,f)\in E_c^C\\ c\in C_m^M}} transf_{wncef}^{C}q_{wusnce}^{C}\geq 0 \quad \perp \quad \beta_{wunm}^{M}\geq 0 \qquad [4.48]$$

$$df_w dur_u pr_w^W pr_{b(u)}^B\Bigg(-p_{wua}^{A}+trf_{wa}^{A}$$

$$+\sum_{g\in G}p_{wb(u)n^{A-}(a)g}^{G}ems_{wag}^{A}\Bigg)+\tau_{wua}^{A}\geq 0 \quad \perp \quad f_{wua}^{A}\geq 0 \qquad [4.49]$$

$$df_w pr_w^W inv_{wa}^{A}-\sum_{w'\in W_w^{\rightarrow},u\in U} dep_{ww'a}^{A}\tau_{w'ua}^{A}+\zeta_{wa}^{A}\geq 0 \quad \perp \quad z_{wa}^{A}\geq 0 \qquad [4.50]$$

$$cap_{wa}^{A}+\sum_{w'\in W_w^{\leftarrow}} dep_{w'wa}^{A}z_{w'a}^{A}-f_{wua}^{A}\geq 0 \quad \perp \quad \tau_{wua}^{A}\geq 0 \qquad [4.51]$$

$$exp_{wa}^{A}-z_{wa}^{A}\geq 0 \quad \perp \quad \zeta_{wa}^{A}\geq 0 \qquad [4.52]$$

$$df_w dur_u pr_w^W pr_{b(u)}^B\Bigg(-p_{wunce}^{C}+trf_{wnc}^{C}+\sum_{g\in G}p_{wb(u)ng}^{G}ems_{wceg}^{C}\Bigg)$$

$$+\sum_{f\in E_c^{C+}} transf_{wncef}^{C}\tau_{wunc}^{C}+\sum_{(e',f)\in E_c^C} shr_{wnce'}^{C}transf_{wncef}^{C}\beta_{wunce'}^{C}$$

$$-\sum_{f\in E_c^{C+}} transf_{wncef}^{C}\beta_{wunce}^{C}\geq 0 \quad \perp \quad f_{wunce}^{C}\geq 0 \qquad [4.53]$$

$$df_w pr_w^W inv_{wnc}^{C}-\sum_{w'\in W_w^{\rightarrow},u\in U} dep_{ww'nc}^{C}\tau_{w'unc}^{C}+\zeta_{wnc}^{C}\geq 0 \quad \perp \quad z_{wnc}^{C}\geq 0 \qquad [4.54]$$

$$cap^{C}_{wnc} + \sum_{w' \in W^{\leftarrow}_{w}} dep^{C}_{w'wnc} z^{C}_{w'nc}$$

$$- \sum_{(e,f) \in E^{C}_{c}} transf^{C}_{wncef} f^{C}_{wunce} \geq 0 \quad \perp \quad \tau^{C}_{wunc} \geq 0 \qquad [4.55]$$

$$-shr^{C}_{wnce} \sum_{(e',f) \in E^{C}_{c}} transf^{C}_{wnce'f} f^{C}_{wunce'}$$

$$+ \sum_{f \in E^{C+}_{c}} transf^{C}_{wncef} f^{C}_{wunce} \geq 0 \quad \perp \quad \beta^{C}_{wunce} \geq 0 \qquad [4.56]$$

$$exp^{C}_{wnc} - z^{C}_{wnc} \geq 0 \quad \perp \quad \zeta^{C}_{wnc} \geq 0 \qquad [4.57]$$

$$df_w dur_u pr^{W}_{w} pr^{B}_{b(u)} \Big(- p^{O-}_{wuno} + trf^{O-}_{wno} + \sum_{g \in G} p^{G}_{wb(u)ng} ems^{O-}_{wog} \Big)$$

$$+ dur_u \tau^{O}_{wv^{U}(uo)no} + \kappa^{O-}_{wuno} \geq 0 \quad \perp \quad f^{O-}_{wuno} \geq 0 \qquad [4.58]$$

$$-df_w dur_u pr^{W}_{w} pr^{B}_{b(u)} p^{O+}_{wuno} + \kappa^{O+}_{wuno} \geq 0 \quad \perp \quad f^{O+}_{wuno} \geq 0 \qquad [4.59]$$

$$df_w pr^{W}_{w} inv^{O}_{wno} - \sum_{\substack{w' \in W^{\rightarrow}_{w} \\ v \in V^{O}_{o}}} dep^{O}_{ww'no} \tau^{O}_{w'vno} + \zeta^{O}_{wno} \geq 0 \quad \perp \quad z^{O}_{wno} \geq 0 \qquad [4.60]$$

$$df_w pr^{W}_{w} inv^{O-}_{wno} - \sum_{\substack{w' \in W^{\rightarrow}_{w} \\ u \in U}} dep^{O-}_{ww'no} \kappa^{O-}_{w'uno} + \zeta^{O-}_{wno} \geq 0 \quad \perp \quad z^{O-}_{wno} \geq 0 \qquad [4.61]$$

$$df_w pr^{W}_{w} inv^{O+}_{wno} - \sum_{\substack{w' \in W^{\rightarrow}_{w} \\ u \in U}} dep^{O+}_{ww'no} \kappa^{O+}_{w'uno} + \zeta^{O+}_{wno} \geq 0 \quad \perp \quad z^{O+}_{wno} \geq 0 \qquad [4.62]$$

$$cap^{O}_{wno} + \sum_{w' \in W^{\leftarrow}_{w}} dep^{O}_{w'wno} z^{O}_{w'no} - \sum_{u \in U^{V}_{vo}} dur_u f^{O-}_{wuno} \geq 0 \quad \perp \quad \tau^{O}_{wvno} \geq 0$$

$$\text{if } v \in V^{O}_{o} \qquad [4.63]$$

$$cap^{O-}_{wno} + \sum_{w' \in W^{\leftarrow}_{w}} dep^{O-}_{w'wno} z^{O-}_{w'no} - f^{O-}_{wuno} \geq 0 \quad \perp \quad \kappa^{O-}_{wuno} \geq 0 \qquad [4.64]$$

$$cap^{O+}_{wno} + \sum_{w' \in W^{\leftarrow}_{w}} dep^{O+}_{w'wno} z^{O+}_{w'no} - \ f^{O+}_{wuno} \geq 0 \quad \perp \quad \kappa^{O+}_{wuno} \geq 0 \qquad [4.65]$$

$$-z^{O}_{wno} + exp^{O}_{wno} \geq 0 \quad \perp \quad \zeta^{O}_{wno} \geq 0 \qquad [4.66]$$

$$-z^{O-}_{wno} + exp^{O-}_{wno} \geq 0 \quad \perp \quad \zeta^{O-}_{wno} \geq 0 \qquad [4.67]$$

$$-z_{wno}^{O+} + exp_{wno}^{O+} \geq 0 \quad \perp \quad \zeta_{wno}^{O+} \geq 0 \qquad [4.68]$$

$$df_w pr_w^W pr_b^B \Big(- p_{wbng}^G + tax_{wbg}^{glob} + \sum_{r \in R_n} tax_{wbrg}^{reg} + tax_{wbng}^{nod} \Big)$$

$$+ \mu_{wbg}^{glob} + \sum_{r \in R_n} \mu_{wbrg}^{reg} + \mu_{wbng}^{nod} \geq 0 \quad \perp \quad f_{wbng}^G \geq 0 \qquad [4.69]$$

$$quota_{wg}^{glob} - \sum_{n \in N} f_{wbng}^G \geq 0 \quad \perp \quad \mu_{wbg}^{glob} \geq 0 \qquad [4.70]$$

$$quota_{wrg}^{reg} - \sum_{n \in N_r} f_{wbng}^G \geq 0 \quad \perp \quad \mu_{wbrg}^{reg} \geq 0 \qquad [4.71]$$

$$quota_{wng}^{nod} - f_{wbng}^G \geq 0 \quad \perp \quad \mu_{wbng}^{nod} \geq 0 \qquad [4.72]$$

4.6.5. *Mathematical descriptions of the VSS customized for the multi-horizon stochastic equilibrium model and further numerical experiments*

The value of the stochastic solution

We first describe a few symbols and notations used in the following discussion. Let $\boldsymbol{\xi}$ ($\boldsymbol{\xi} \in \Xi$) denote a random vector of parameters influenced by the long-term uncertainty process spanning several investment periods. Let also $\boldsymbol{\eta}$ ($\boldsymbol{\eta} \in \mathcal{H}$) denote a random vector of parameters influenced by the short-term uncertainty process spanning every short-term operational period. The realizations of $\boldsymbol{\xi}$ and $\boldsymbol{\eta}$ correspond to the various long-term scenarios and short-term scenarios, respectively. Assume that there are several players in the markets. In the following discussion, we let i ($i \in I$) denote a player and $-i$ the other players. Let $f_i(x_i(\boldsymbol{\xi}, \boldsymbol{\eta}), y_i(\boldsymbol{\xi}, \boldsymbol{\eta}), x_{-i}(\boldsymbol{\xi}, \boldsymbol{\eta}), y_{-i}(\boldsymbol{\xi}, \boldsymbol{\eta}), \boldsymbol{\xi}, \boldsymbol{\eta})$ denote player i's profit function, which is dependent on the realization of ($\boldsymbol{\xi}$,$\boldsymbol{\eta}$), player i's investment solution $x_i(\boldsymbol{\xi}, \boldsymbol{\eta})$, operational solution $y_i(\boldsymbol{\xi}, \boldsymbol{\eta})$, the other players $-i$'s investment solution $x_{-i}(\boldsymbol{\xi}, \boldsymbol{\eta})$ and operational solution $y_{-i}(\boldsymbol{\xi}, \boldsymbol{\eta})$. Moreover, the investment(/operational) solutions are vectors with each component representing the investment(/operational) decision in a stage(/period) under a long-term(/short-term) scenario.

The recourse problem for player i (RP_i) is to find the optimal investment and operational strategies considering uncertainties and the other players' strategies in a market environment, as can be expressed as follows:

$$RP_i := \max_{x_i, y_i} \mathbb{E}_{\boldsymbol{\xi}, \boldsymbol{\eta}} \Big[f_i(x_i(\boldsymbol{\xi}, \boldsymbol{\eta}), y_i(\boldsymbol{\xi}, \boldsymbol{\eta}), x_{-i}^*(\boldsymbol{\xi}, \boldsymbol{\eta}), y_{-i}^*(\boldsymbol{\xi}, \boldsymbol{\eta}), \boldsymbol{\xi}, \boldsymbol{\eta}) \Big] \qquad [4.73]$$

$$\text{s.t. } x_i \in X_i, \qquad [4.74]$$

$$y_i \in Y_i(x_i, y_{-i}^*, \boldsymbol{\xi}, \boldsymbol{\eta}), \qquad [4.75]$$

$$\text{the nonanticipativity constraints.} \qquad [4.76]$$

In equation [4.73], $\mathbb{E}_{\boldsymbol{\xi},\boldsymbol{\eta}}$ denotes mathematical expectation with respect to $\boldsymbol{\xi},\boldsymbol{\eta}$. The feasible set of player i's investment solution is denoted by X_i, as equation [4.74] shows. In equation [4.75], $Y_i(x_i, y^*_{-i}, \boldsymbol{\xi}, \boldsymbol{\eta})$ denotes the feasible set of player i's operational solution, which depends on player i's own investment solution, other players $-i$'s operational solution, and the realizations of the uncertainties. Lastly, the non-anticipativity constraints regulate that each player's scenario-dependent solutions for a stage/period have the same value if only those scenarios pass through the same scenario node (Shapiro et al. 2014). In the recourse problem, player i makes the optimal strategy denoted by $\{(x^*_i(\boldsymbol{\xi},\boldsymbol{\eta}), y^*_i(\boldsymbol{\xi},\boldsymbol{\eta})) \mid \boldsymbol{\xi} \in \Xi, \boldsymbol{\eta} \in \mathcal{H}\}$, while the other players' optimal strategy is $\{(x^*_{-i}(\boldsymbol{\xi},\boldsymbol{\eta}), y^*_{-i}(\boldsymbol{\xi},\boldsymbol{\eta})) \mid \boldsymbol{\xi} \in \Xi, \boldsymbol{\eta} \in \mathcal{H}\}$. The strategy profile $\{(x^*_i(\boldsymbol{\xi},\boldsymbol{\eta}), y^*_i(\boldsymbol{\xi},\boldsymbol{\eta}), x^*_{-i}(\boldsymbol{\xi},\boldsymbol{\eta}), y^*_{-i}(\boldsymbol{\xi},\boldsymbol{\eta})) \mid \boldsymbol{\xi} \in \Xi, \boldsymbol{\eta} \in \mathcal{H}\}$ is obtained by solving the stochastic equilibrium model.

When the players ignore the uncertainties to make decisions, $\boldsymbol{\xi}$ and $\boldsymbol{\eta}$ are replaced by the expectation values $\overline{\xi}$ and $\overline{\eta}$, respectively. Then, the expected value problem for player i (EV_i) is to find the optimal investment and operational solutions considering the other players' solutions in a market environment, as can be expressed as follows:

$$EV_i := \max_{\substack{x_i \in X_i, \\ y_i \in Y_i(x_i, \overline{y}_{-i}, \overline{\xi}, \overline{\eta})}} f_i(x_i, y_i, \overline{x}_{-i}(\overline{\xi},\overline{\eta}), \overline{y}_{-i}(\overline{\xi},\overline{\eta}), \overline{\xi}, \overline{\eta}). \qquad [4.77]$$

In equation [4.77], player i solves for the optimal solution denoted by $(\overline{x}_i(\overline{\xi},\overline{\eta}), \overline{y}_i(\overline{\xi},\overline{\eta}))$. Meanwhile, the other players' solution is denoted by $(\overline{x}_{-i}(\overline{\xi},\overline{\eta}), \overline{y}_{-i}(\overline{\xi},\overline{\eta}))$. The strategy profile $(\overline{x}_i(\overline{\xi},\overline{\eta}), \overline{y}_i(\overline{\xi},\overline{\eta}), \overline{x}_{-i}(\overline{\xi},\overline{\eta}), \overline{y}_{-i}(\overline{\xi},\overline{\eta}))$ is obtained by solving the deterministic equilibrium problem.

To measure how the EV_i investment solution, $\overline{x}_i(\overline{\xi},\overline{\eta})$, performs in the stochastic market environment, allowing the operational solution to be chosen optimally dependent on $\boldsymbol{\xi},\boldsymbol{\eta}$, we define the expected result of using the EV_i investment solution for player i (EEV_i) to be:

$$EEV_i := \max_{y_i} \mathop{\mathbb{E}}_{\boldsymbol{\xi},\boldsymbol{\eta}} \left[f_i(\overline{x}_i(\overline{\xi},\overline{\eta}), y_i(\boldsymbol{\xi},\boldsymbol{\eta}), \overline{x}_{-i}(\overline{\xi},\overline{\eta}), \overline{y}^{\star}_{-i}(\boldsymbol{\xi},\boldsymbol{\eta}), \boldsymbol{\xi}, \boldsymbol{\eta}) \right] \qquad [4.78]$$

$$\text{s.t. } y_i \in Y_i(\overline{x}_i, \overline{y}^{\star}_{-i}, \boldsymbol{\xi}, \boldsymbol{\eta}), \qquad [4.79]$$

$$\text{the nonanticipativity constraints.} \qquad [4.80]$$

In equations [4.78]–[4.80], player i solves for the optimal operational strategy denoted by $\{\overline{y}^{\star}_i(\boldsymbol{\xi},\boldsymbol{\eta}) \mid \boldsymbol{\xi} \in \Xi, \boldsymbol{\eta} \in \mathcal{H}\}$ while the other players' optimal operational strategy is $\{\overline{y}^{\star}_{-i}(\boldsymbol{\xi},\boldsymbol{\eta}) \mid \boldsymbol{\xi} \in \Xi, \boldsymbol{\eta} \in \mathcal{H}\}$. Moreover, all of the players keep using the EV_i investment solutions, for example, $\overline{x}_i(\overline{\xi},\overline{\eta})$, under every scenario. The operational strategy profile $\{(\overline{y}^{\star}_i(\boldsymbol{\xi},\boldsymbol{\eta}), \overline{y}^{\star}_{-i}(\boldsymbol{\xi},\boldsymbol{\eta})) \mid \boldsymbol{\xi} \in \Xi, \boldsymbol{\eta} \in \mathcal{H}\}$ is obtained by solving the stochastic equilibrium model while fixing the investment solutions by the EV_i investment solutions for all of the players.

In stochastic programming, the VSS is

VSS=RP-EEV,

which assesses how better a recourse problem (RP) solution performs, compared to the EV solution. However, in the context of stochastic equilibrium problems, the VSS for player i can be defined as:

$$\begin{aligned} VSS_i =& RP_i - EEV_i \\ =& \mathop{\mathbb{E}}_{\boldsymbol{\xi},\boldsymbol{\eta}} \Big[f_i(x_i^*(\boldsymbol{\xi},\boldsymbol{\eta}), y_i^*(\boldsymbol{\xi},\boldsymbol{\eta}), x_{-i}^*(\boldsymbol{\xi},\boldsymbol{\eta}), y_{-i}^*(\boldsymbol{\xi},\boldsymbol{\eta}), \boldsymbol{\xi},\boldsymbol{\eta}) \\ & - f_i(\overline{x}_i(\overline{\xi},\overline{\eta}), \overline{y}_i^*(\boldsymbol{\xi},\boldsymbol{\eta}), \overline{x}_{-i}(\overline{\xi},\overline{\eta}), \overline{y}_{-i}^*(\boldsymbol{\xi},\boldsymbol{\eta}), \boldsymbol{\xi},\boldsymbol{\eta}) \Big]. \end{aligned} \quad [4.81]$$

As you can see from equation [4.81], player i's profit $f_i(\cdot)$ is affected by the other players $-i$'s solutions, which influence can be treated as the influence of market environment on player i. When player i replaces the EV_i investment solution $\overline{x}_i(\overline{\xi},\overline{\eta})$ with the RP_i investment solution $x_i^*(\boldsymbol{\xi},\boldsymbol{\eta})$, the other players' investment solution changes from the EV_{-i} investment solution $\overline{x}_{-i}(\overline{\xi},\overline{\eta})$ to the RP_{-i} investment solution $x_{-i}^*(\boldsymbol{\xi},\boldsymbol{\eta})$. This is a change in the market environment for player i. Such change does not exist in classical(/multi-horizon) stochastic programming problems.

The hybrid game

In order to reveal the meaning of our multi-horizon stochastic equilibrium model, we bring in a hybrid game problem (HG) (Genc et al. 2007).

In HG, we assume that (1) every player plays EV_i game and makes the investment solution $\overline{x}_i(\overline{\xi},\overline{\eta})$; and (2) an unique player i unilaterally deviates from the EV_i investment solution $\overline{x}_i(\overline{\xi},\overline{\eta})$ and further considers both long- and short-term uncertainties to make the optimal investment and operational strategy denoted by $\{(\widetilde{x}_i^*(\boldsymbol{\xi},\boldsymbol{\eta}), \widetilde{y}_i^*(\boldsymbol{\xi},\boldsymbol{\eta})) \mid \boldsymbol{\xi} \in \Xi, \boldsymbol{\eta} \in \mathcal{H}\}$, while the other players $-i$ keep using the EV_{-i} investment solution $\overline{x}_{-i}(\overline{\xi},\overline{\eta})$ but allow the operational solution $\widetilde{y}_{-i}^*(\boldsymbol{\xi},\boldsymbol{\eta})$ to be chosen optimally dependent on the realization of uncertainties.

The hybrid game problem for the unique player i (HG_i) can be expressed as follows:

$$HG_i := \max_{x_i, y_i} \mathop{\mathbb{E}}_{\boldsymbol{\xi},\boldsymbol{\eta}} \Big[f_i(x_i(\boldsymbol{\xi},\boldsymbol{\eta}), y_i(\boldsymbol{\xi},\boldsymbol{\eta}), \overline{x}_{-i}(\overline{\xi},\overline{\eta}), \widetilde{y}_{-i}^*(\boldsymbol{\xi},\boldsymbol{\eta}), \boldsymbol{\xi},\boldsymbol{\eta}) \Big] \quad [4.82]$$

$$\text{s.t. } x_i \in X_i, \quad [4.83]$$

$$y_i \in Y_i(x_i, \widetilde{y}_{-i}^*, \boldsymbol{\xi}, \boldsymbol{\eta}), \quad [4.84]$$

$$\text{the nonanticipativity constraints.} \quad [4.85]$$

In HG, the other players $-i$'s problem can be expressed as follows:

$$\max_{y_{-i}} \mathbb{E}_{\xi,\eta} \left[f_{-i}(\widetilde{x}_i^*(\xi,\eta), \widetilde{y}_i^*(\xi,\eta), \overline{x}_{-i}(\overline{\xi},\overline{\eta}), y_{-i}(\xi,\eta), \xi, \eta) \right] \quad [4.86]$$

$$\text{s.t. } y_{-i} \in Y_{-i}(\overline{x}_{-i}, \widetilde{y}_i^*, \xi, \eta), \quad [4.87]$$

$$\text{the nonanticipativity constraints.} \quad [4.88]$$

Numerical experiments

We investigate four different hybrid game problems, in each of which we assume that (1) it occurs in the Cournot oligopoly markets; (2) one of the suppliers (i.e. S^A, S^B, S^C, S^D) acts as the unique agent that deviates from the EV_i solution; and (3) each time we run the stochastic model with both long-term and short-term uncertainties, we let $K1 = 0.25$ and $K2 = 0.5$. To obtain the value of HG_i for the unique supplier, we run the stochastic equilibrium model with both long-term and short-term uncertainties after fixing the other agents' solutions by their EV_i investment solutions (obtained by running the deterministic equilibrium model).

	EEV_i	HG_i	$HG_i - EEV_i$
Supplier S^A	10,428	10,233	-195
Supplier S^B	13,149	12,972	-177
Supplier S^C	3,718	3,832	114
Supplier S^D	5,437	5,512	75

Table 4.11. *Contrast of HG_i and EEV_i in the Cournot oligopoly markets*

Table 4.11 compares the value of HG_i with the expected result of using the EV_i solution, EEV_i. Note that each of the four values of HG_i in the third column in Table 4.11 represents the expected profit of the unique agent in each of the four hybrid games. For instance, regarding supplier S^D, $HG_i - EEV_i = 75$ illustrates that to unilaterally deviate from the EV_i solution to the stochastic strategy will win more profit. It is the same with supplier S^C. More profit can be an incentive for an agent to resort to a stochastic model.

However, if S^A or S^B unilaterally deviates from the EV_i solution, it will make less profit (i.e. -195 or -177) in our specified hybrid game. Note that in HG every agent's operational decision $\widetilde{y}_{-i}^*(\xi, \eta)$ interacts with each other, in which interaction affects the market prices (in the whole supply chain) and eventually the profit of every agent. In real energy markets, when a specific agent, for example, a TSO, will use stochastic models, generally it will not consider the price changes in the whole supply chain, for example, gas storage prices. The agent will only consider relevant market factors that can directly affect its profit. There are many examples in

Wallace and Fleten (2003), Gupta and Grossmann (2014) and Lima et al. (2018) which have shown that stochastic models can contribute to higher expected profits compared to the corresponding deterministic models. Thus, though there are negative values of $HG_i - EEV_i$ in our specified hybrid game experiments, in real markets using stochastic models instead of deterministic models for making investment decisions is a trend, especially when renewable energy is playing an increasingly important part in energy systems. For instance, when supplier S^D (with renewable production capacity) is the first to consider uncertainties to make a novel investment strategy instead of using the deterministic investment solution, the good news of increased profit by using a stochastic model will be spread and others will follow, similar to herd behavior. When all of the agents apply stochastic models to make strategies, finally, the markets will reach an equilibrium investment strategy portfolio, which can be obtained by running our stochastic equilibrium model.

Table 4.12 shows the VSS_i (assuming $K1 = 0.25$ and $K2 = 0.5$) for every specific group of agents in the Cournot oligopoly markets. As you can see from the last column, there are positive and negative values of VSS_i for different groups of agents. Some win more profit by using the stochastic equilibrium solutions and some lose. Moreover, the last row shows that the expected profit of all the agents, that is, social welfare, is less (i.e. −9) by using the stochastic equilibrium solutions (i.e. 65,651) than by using the deterministic equilibrium solutions (i.e. 65,660). Such result is also shown in Figure 4.16, where the VSS_i for all of the agents is negative in the Cournot oligopoly markets under the different fluctuation ranges of short-term uncertainty.

	RP_i	EEV_i	VSS_i
Supplier S^A	10,209	10,428	−219
Supplier S^B	13,019	13,149	−130
Supplier S^C	3,995	3,718	277
Supplier S^D	5,603	5,437	166
All of the TSOs	1,244	1,428	−184
All of the TTOs	2,953	3,168	−215
All of the storage operators	502	337	165
All of the consumers	25,826	26,175	−349
The emission permit auctioneer	2,300	1,821	479
All of the agents	65,651	65,660	−9

Table 4.12. *The value of the stochastic solution in the Cournot oligopoly markets*

4.7. References

Abgottspon, H. and Andersson, G. (2016). Multi-horizon modeling in hydro power planning. *Energy Procedia*, 87, 2–10.

Aune, F.R. and Golombek, R. (2021). Are carbon prices redundant in the 2030 EU climate and energy policy package? *The Energy Journal*, 42(3), 233–277.

Aune, F.R., Golombek, R., Moe, A., Rosendahl, K.E., Tissier, H.H.L. (2015). Liberalizing Russian gas markets: An economic analysis. *The Energy Journal*, 36(Adelman Special Issue), 63–97.

Backe, S., Skar, C., del Granado, P.C., Turgut, O., Tomasgard, A. (2022). Empire: An open-source model based on multi-horizon programming for energy transition analyses. *SoftwareX*, 17, 100877.

Baltensperger, T., Füchslin, R.M., Krütli, P., Lygeros, J. (2016). Multiplicity of equilibria in conjectural variations models of natural gas markets. *European Journal of Operational Research*, 252(2), 646–656.

Barquín, J., Centeno, E., Reneses, J. (2004). Medium-term generation programming in competitive environments: A new optimisation approach for market equilibrium computing. *IEE Proceedings-Generation, Transmission and Distribution*, 151(1), 119–126.

Berk, I. and Çam, E. (2020). The shift in global crude oil market structure: A model-based analysis of the period 2013–2017. *Energy Policy*, 142, 111497.

Birge, J. and Louveaux, F. (1997). *Introduction to Stochastic Programming*. Springer, New York.

Boots, M.G., Rijkers, F.A., Hobbs, B.F. (2004). Trading in the downstream European gas market: A successive oligopoly approach. *The Energy Journal*, 25(3), 73–102.

Brook, A., Kendrick, D., Meeraus, A. (1988). GAMS: A user's guide. *ACM Signum Newsletter*, 23(3–4), 10–11.

Cottle, R.W., Pang, J.S., Stone, R.E. (1992). *The Linear Complementarity Problem*. Academic Press, Boston.

Devine, M.T. and Bertsch, V. (2018). Examining the benefits of load shedding strategies using a rolling-horizon stochastic mixed complementarity equilibrium model. *European Journal of Operational Research*, 267(2), 643–658.

Devine, M.T. and Russo, M. (2019). Liquefied natural gas and gas storage valuation: Lessons from the integrated Irish and UK markets. *Applied Energy*, 238, 1389–1406.

E3MLab (2016). PRIMES Model 2016–2017 Detailed Model Description. National Technical University of Athens, Athens.

Egging, R. (2010). Multi-period natural gas market modeling applications, stochastic extensions and solution approaches. PhD Thesis, University of Maryland, College Park.

Egging, R. (2013). Benders decomposition for multi-stage stochastic mixed complementarity problems – Applied to a global natural gas market model. *European Journal of Operational Research*, 226(2), 341–353.

EC (2009). Directive 2009/28/EC of the European Parliament and of the Council of 23 April 2009 on the promotion of the use of energy from renewable sources and amending and subsequently repealing Directives 2001/77/EC and 2003/30/EC. *Official Journal of the European Union*, 140, 47.

Facchinei, F. and Kanzow, C. (2007). Generalized Nash equilibrium problems. *4OR*, 5(3), 173–210.

Ferris, M.C. and Munson, T.S. (2000). Complementarity problems in GAMS and the PATH solver. *Journal of Economic Dynamics and Control*, 24(2), 165–188.

Fodstad, M., Crespo del Granado, P., Hellemo, L., Knudsen, B.R., Pisciella, P., Silvast, A., Bordin, C., Schmidt, S., Straus, J. (2022). Next frontiers in energy system modelling: A review on challenges and the state of the art. *Renewable and Sustainable Energy Reviews*, 160, 112246.

Gabriel, S.A., Conejo, A.J., Fuller, J.D., Hobbs, B.F., Ruiz, C. (2012). *Complementarity Modeling in Energy Markets*. Springer, New York.

Genc, T.S., Reynolds, S.S., Sen, S. (2007). Dynamic oligopolistic games under uncertainty: A stochastic programming approach. *Journal of Economic Dynamics and Control*, 31(1), 55–80.

Giocoli, N. (2005). The escape from conjectural variations: The consistency condition in duopoly theory from Bowley to Fellner. *Cambridge Journal of Economics*, 29(4), 601–618.

Golombek, R., Gjelsvik, E., Rosendahl, K.E. (1995). Effects of liberalizing the natural gas markets in western Europe. *The Energy Journal*, 16(1), 85–111.

Golombek, R., Lind, A., Ringkjøb, H.-K., Seljom, P. (2022). The role of transmission and energy storage in European decarbonization towards 2050. *Energy*, 239(Part C), 122159.

Gupta, V. and Grossmann, I.E. (2014). Multistage stochastic programming approach for offshore oilfield infrastructure planning under production sharing agreements and endogenous uncertainties. *Journal of Petroleum Science and Engineering*, 124, 180–197.

Haftendorn, C. and Holz, F. (2010). Modeling and analysis of the international steam coal trade. *The Energy Journal*, 31(4), 201–225.

Hellemo, L., Midthun, K., Tomasgard, A., Werner, A.T. (2013). Multi-stage stochastic programming for natural gas infrastructure design with a production perspective. In *Stochastic Programming: Applications in Finance, Energy, Planning and Logistics*, Gassmann, H.I. and Ziemba, W.T. (eds). World Scientific, Singapore, 259–288.

Huppmann, D. and Egging, R. (2014). Market power, fuel substitution and infrastructure – A large-scale equilibrium model of global energy markets. *Energy*, 75, 483–500.

Jacoby, H.D., O'Sullivan, F.M., Paltsev, S. (2011). The influence of shale gas on US energy and environmental policy. Technical Report, MIT Joint Program on the Science and Policy of Global Change, Cambridge, MA.

Kasina, S. and Hobbs, B.F. (2020). The value of cooperation in interregional transmission planning: A noncooperative equilibrium model approach. *European Journal of Operational Research*, 285(2), 740–752.

Kaut, M., Midthun, K.T., Werner, A.S., Tomasgard, A., Hellemo, L., Fodstad, M. (2014). Multi-horizon stochastic programming. *Computational Management Science*, 11(1–2), 179–193.

Li, R., Wei, W., Mei, S., Hu, Q., Wu, Q. (2019). Participation of an energy hub in electricity and heat distribution markets: An MPEC approach. *IEEE Transactions on Smart Grid*, 10(4), 3641–3653.

Lima, C., Relvas, S., Barbosa-Póvoa, A. (2018). Stochastic programming approach for the optimal tactical planning of the downstream oil supply chain. *Computers & Chemical Engineering*, 108, 314–336.

Loulou, R., Remme, U., Kanudia, A., Lehtila, A., Goldstein, G. (2005). Documentation for the TIMES model, part II. Energy technology systems analysis programme.

Lynch, M.Á., Nolan, S., Devine, M.T., O'Malley, M. (2019). The impacts of demand response participation in capacity markets. *Applied Energy*, 250, 444–451.

Maggioni, F., Allevi, E., Tomasgard, A. (2020). Bounds in multi-horizon stochastic programs. *Annals of Operations Research*, 292, 605–625.

Oggioni, G., Smeers, Y., Allevi, E., Schaible, S. (2012). A generalized Nash equilibrium model of market coupling in the European power system. *Networks and Spatial Economics*, 12(4), 503–560.

Oliveira, F.S. and Ruiz, C. (2021). Analysis of futures and spot electricity markets under risk aversion. *European Journal of Operational Research*, 291(3), 1132–1148.

Rad, V.Z., Torabi, S.A., Shakouri G.H. (2019). Joint electricity generation and transmission expansion planning under integrated gas and power system. *Energy*, 167, 523–537.

Rhodes, R. (2007). Energy transitions: A curious history. Working Paper, Center for International Security and Cooperation, Stanford University, Stanford.

Riepin, I., Möbius, T., Müsgens, F. (2021). Modelling uncertainty in coupled electricity and gas systems – Is it worth the effort? *Applied Energy*, 285, 116363.

Ringkjøb, H.-K., Haugan, P.M., Solbrekke, I.M. (2018). A review of modelling tools for energy and electricity systems with large shares of variable renewables. *Renewable and Sustainable Energy Reviews*, 96, 440–459.

Samuelson, P.A. (1952). Spatial price equilibrium and linear programming. *American Economic Association*, 42(3), 283–303.

Shafiekhani, M., Badri, A., Shafie-khah, M., Catalão, J.P. (2019). Strategic bidding of virtual power plant in energy markets: A bi-level multi-objective approach. *International Journal of Electrical Power & Energy Systems*, 113, 208–219.

Shapiro, A., Dentcheva, D., Ruszczyński, A. (2014). *Lectures on Stochastic Programming: Modeling and Theory*. SIAM, Philadelphia.

Wallace, S.W. and Fleten, S.E. (2003). Stochastic programming models in energy. *Handbooks in Operations Research and Management Science*, 10, 637–677.

Yu, J., Ryu, J.-H., Lee, I.-b. (2019). A stochastic optimization approach to the design and operation planning of a hybrid renewable energy system. *Applied Energy*, 247, 212–220.

5

Modeling for Diversification and Optimization of the Electricity Generation Capacities in the Energy Sector

The power generation industry is a critical infrastructure (CI) that significantly affects the functioning of all sectors of the economy, social sphere and security, and its failure leads to significant negative consequences. To ensure the effective management of processes in the energy sector, it is necessary to collect, process and analyze information from various sources, as well as take into account various scenarios for the occurrence of adverse incidents. The objective of the current study is to model the structure of electricity generation in order to create an information technology (IT) for diversification and optimization of the energy portfolio. The concept of the approach is to manage and optimize the structure of the electricity generation portfolio in order to mix various electricity generation technologies to maximize the value of the portfolio, ensure its safety, minimize risks and comply with the strategic direction. The developed approach is based on the type-variety principle, the analytic hierarchy process (AHP) method developed by Thomas Saaty as a tool for multi-factor decision-making processes that helps to solve such problems. The AHP method and the Markowitz modern portfolio theory (MPT) method are used for balancing the structure of electricity generation. The calculation results are illustrated in graphs.

5.1. Introduction

Problem statement. The power industry is a complex, cybernetic-type system with the features of non-static components and uncertainty in their parameters. The deployment of innovative energy generating technologies results in change management and requires decision making within multiple tasks, structuring of

---

Chapter written by Volodymyr A. ZASLAVSKYI and Maya PASICHNA.

input data, etc. (Stetsyuk 2012). Moreover, it requires revision of the whole enterprise architecture of the company, accounting for its business, data, technology and infrastructure levels.

It is forecasted that in 2035, the global electricity demand is expected to increase 70% to 34 TWh, as compared to the 2010 consumption, and the world's total water withdrawals are expected to climb to 790 bcm, which is 35% higher than in 2010. Desalination processes as a result of the operation of fossil fuel power plants are among the major sources of CO_2 emissions. These days, desalination capacities throughout the globe contribute 76 million tons of CO_2 per year, and this is expected to increase to 218 million tons of CO_2 per year by 2040 (Shahzad et al. 2017, pp. 52–64).

Given that energy objects belong to CI (Zaslavskyi et al. 2010, pp. 161–173), innovative IT to manage, support and monitor their operations is key to the economic stability and national security of the country. To ensure the functioning of such systems, the type-variety principle (TVP) is applied. TVP is an application of different components, for example, systems, technologies, models, methods and software. These components act in a similar way, but have different principles of operation and each of them can solve the task separately. As a joint effort, they could improve the resilience of a system, exclude the possibility of its failure and result in its reliable and long-term performance (Zaslavskyi 2006, pp. 136–147).

The TVP ideology was a basis for the development of a mathematical model and a two-level discrete optimization algorithm for solving the problem of optimal redundancy of complex critical systems in the space industry (Volkovich et al. 1986, pp. 54–61, 81; Volkovich et al. 1993). To achieve high reliability and long-term performance in space technology, it is necessary to take measures to ensure them at all stages of the lifecycle – design, production, testing and operation – although their importance is not equivalent. At the stages of operation, the possibilities for improving the reliability of spacecraft are limited, since it is difficult to achieve the desired results without changing the structure, design solutions, replacing unreliable elements, operating time of component equipment and elements. Therefore, at the design stage, it was proposed to use different types of redundant units, elements in subsystems and assemblies of complex systems as backup elements, which made it possible to eliminate a common cause failure and to increase the reliability of the systems being created (Volkovich et al. 1993).

Ukraine's economic development and reconstruction requires the active involvement of the enterprises from the critical infrastructure sector. At the same time, conflicts arise around limited resources, the inability for enterprises to carry out timely renewal and the technical re-equipment of existing complex systems and their components due to a difficult financial condition and political situation. Many complex critical systems such as nuclear power plants (NPPs) were designed and built decades ago, so their technical resource is exhausted.

In the current challenging economic and political conditions, the organizations that are developing systems cannot generally take responsibility for security guarantees when extending the life of systems and their high-quality operation, since some enterprises have legally ceased to exist. Therefore, ensuring the safety of the functioning of such systems and extending the terms of their functioning is an important problem.

To identify many defects in critical systems, based on the developed mathematical mechanisms for the formation of diverse options, an approach was developed to form a diverse set of non-destructive testing methods. The use of these methods made it possible to increase the probability of detecting defects, significantly reduce the time to detect these defects and take into account economic indicators when replacing equipment (Zaslavskyi et al. 1999, pp. 5–22). The quality of the natural environment directly depends on the quality of water resources of territories in various countries and continents. The problem of planning the construction of the structure of the system of treatment facilities and monitoring the quality of water in river basins is of high importance. The idea of constructing different types of solutions for a territorially distributed water purification system, the formation of which takes into account various economic conditions and territorial features, was implemented in the formation of a system of treatment facilities in a river clearing (Zaslavskyi 2011, pp. 18–22).

The development of international (VISA and MasterCard) and national payment systems puts forward ever-growing requirements for security, technical and software improvement of systems, methods to ensure information security on an international scale. The classification of the risk sources and methods for their evaluation, as well as the analysis of methods to identify fraudulent activities, were proposed in Zaslavskyi (2011, pp. 18–22) from a system point of view.

The idea of the TVP was used for the analysis of regional management and identification of depressive territories (Zaslavskyi et al. 2006, pp. 48–63; Zaslavskyi 2011, pp. 93–105), as well as for the protection of critical systems (Norkin et al. 2018).

In this regard, the factor of creating an effective energy mix – the structure of electricity generation capacity (GC) for power plants (i.e. distribution [diversification] of GCs by types of technologies for producing electricity) – is a central issue for countries and their energy companies. As such, a task to provide the automation of the intellectual decision-making process for the generation of electricity is currently a priority on the agenda.

The purpose of this chapter is to study the peculiarities of the creation of IT to support decision making in the strategic planning of the structure of all installed electricity GCs of energy companies. The IT is intended to facilitate the assessment of the electricity GCs of power stations through systematization, formalization and consistent aggregation of information about their operation.

Previous research. IT for the optimization of tasks in the energy industry started to develop in the late 1960s, when a number of high-level modeling systems (MPL, LINGO), model generators (MARKAL, TIMES), and optimization and simulation software tools (POLES, ENPEP-BALANCE) were created. Modern versions of these pieces of software have a predominantly macroeconomic approach, the representation of the energy sector is simplified and data input is not flexible (Dyachuk 2013, pp. 98–103).

Novelty. With the advent of the concept of "Smart Grid" technology at the end of the first decade of the 21st century, there was a need to develop new approaches to the management of diverse fuel and energy resources that allows them to be used safely and in an efficient manner in existing and future energy systems. The current research aims to contribute to solving non-formalized weakly structured problems in the energy sector. It combines approaches for the optimization of electricity generation structure such as multi-criteria decision-making (MCDM) techniques (Lehtveer et al. 2015, pp. 45–55; Celikbilek et al. 2016, pp. 1246–1258), Markowitz mean-variance portfolio (MVP) analysis (Awerbuch et al. 2007, pp. 45–55; Lang et al. 2010) and risk level evaluation into one IT. This has not been widely applied in the previous research. Furthermore, the current study focuses on different countries and companies (Madlener et al. 2009, pp. 45–55; Cucciella 2012, pp. 673–692). As such, the current research is a continuation of the previous works (Zaslavskyi et al. 2018, pp. 545–555).

5.1.1. *Methods of the research: description of the model of the research*

Given the complexity of the energy industry, its study should be carried out meticulously, correctly identifying the importance of the criteria and the reliability of critical components that ensure its functioning. To assess risks and maintain the security of CI, it is necessary to apply the principles of systems analysis, mathematical models and algorithms for qualitative and quantitative assessment of systems efficiency.

First, given the importance of choosing (giving priority to) the most appropriate energy technology, which is determined by a set of certain factors and conditions, the approach of multi-criteria decision making should be applied. The AHP method developed by Thomas Saaty as a tool for multi-factor decision-making process helps to solve such problems. In the energy sector, AHP has been used within the context of rational evaluation and as a basis for the fixation of alternatives in meeting energy demand, taking into account the limited supply. In recent years, approaches with the application of AHP to the energy sector have been considered by a number of researchers. In 2011, much attention was paid to reliability theory and risk analysis, conducting reliability analyses and assessments of risks of energy systems and their components, such as thermal power plants or NPPs. In 2015, the attention was focused on the issue of rational placement of CI objects within the task of coherent location of the power stations (Zaslavskyi et al. 2016, pp. 3–20).

Second, given the need to balance the advantages and disadvantages of using a particular set/configuration of energy technologies, the MPT has to be considered. The second step provides an analysis of the balancing of the composition of generation assets (capacities) by the types of technologies for electricity generation. It is to be carried out through the evaluation of the following three components: (1) competitiveness on the basis of construction of an effective frontier (EF) of the electricity generation portfolio to visualize the ratio of physical returns and standard deviations (risk), (2) energy security as a distinction of possible risks directly related to the reliability of energy supply, and (3) impact on the environment as an analysis of electricity generation sources through inherent greenhouse gas emissions and efficiency of electricity generation. Construction of an EF was performed using Solver software based on MVP theory. Weighted LCOE (levelized cost of generation electricity) values for existing energy technologies in different countries for the period 2009–2014 were calculated for this purpose (Zaslavskyi et al. 2018, pp. 555–560).

Third, the introduction of the new technologies has to be taken step by step, so there is a suggestion on taking this into account.

In the fourth step, since there is a need to re-assess the constellation of the energy portfolio in terms of other possible dangers, an assessment of the strategic alignment of the energy mix is performed. Additionally, the analysis of the risks of different electricity sources and their possible impact is studied.

The architecture that describes various types of input data, mechanisms for their collection, storage, processing and management is presented.

The concept of the main objects and their interconnections within the diversification and optimization of the structure of GCs can be represented through the following diagrams (Figures 5.1 and 5.2).

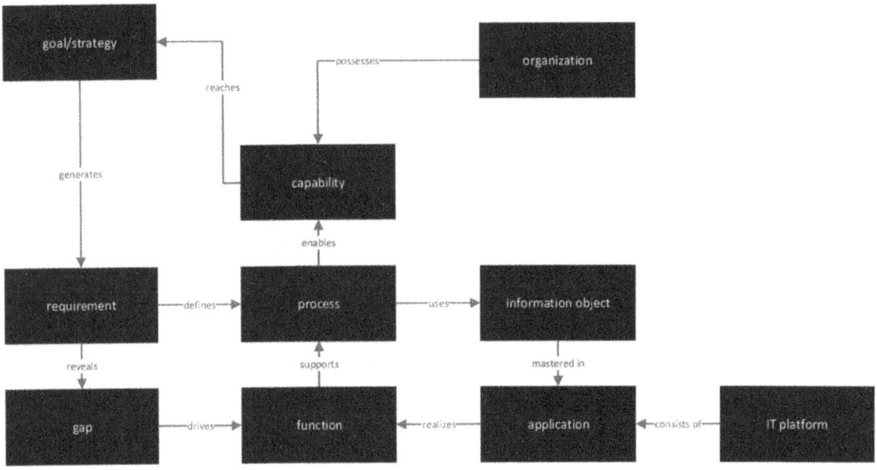

Figure 5.1. *Concept modeling – basis*

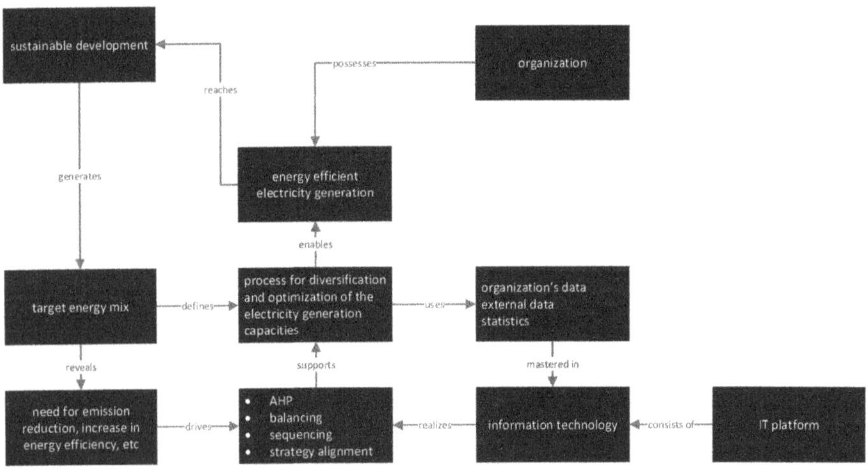

Figure 5.2. *Concept modeling – example*

Electricity generation should be considered within the framework of the modeling of complex systems of CI using the TVP (Zaslavskyi et al. 2018, pp. 555–560). In this context, the use of the TVP is to combine bottom-up and top-down approaches, a multi-criteria approach to decision making, concepts of optimization and qualitative decision analysis.

5.1.2. *First part of the IT*

In the first stage, according to the AHP (analytical hierarchy process) (Celikbilek et al. 2016, pp. 1246–1258) and based on subjective expert assessments, criteria and factors that are crucial for energy companies in choosing the technologies (alternatives) for generation electricity are determined. Based on the existing set of alternatives, criteria and factors, a hierarchy is constructed and appropriate calculations are carried out to evaluate elements of the hierarchy.

The purpose of the AHP hierarchy is the ranking of sources of electricity generation (the first level of the hierarchy), influenced by a number of criteria F_1–F_8 and their corresponding groups of factors F_{11}–F_{82} (second and third level of the hierarchy, respectively). The number of sources of electricity generation Z_1–Z_7 (alternatives to the hierarchy) is the fourth level of the hierarchy.

Let Z_1–Z_m be the set of alternative variants of power generation sources (m = 7), which consists of elements: coal (Z_1), natural gas (Z_2), hydropower (Z_3), wind energy (Z_4), solar energy (Z_5), biomass use (Z_6) and nuclear energy (Z_7). Let F_1–F_8 be eight complex multi-type criteria and F_{11}–F_{13}, F_{21}–F_{22}, F_{31}–F_{32}, F_{41}–F_{43}, F_{51}–F_{52}, F_{61}–F_{62}, F_{71}–F_{73}, F_{81}–F_{82} are 19 relevant factors influencing decision making in companies regarding the set of alternatives. Thus, the task of AHP is described by the system of the following equations – a matrix of pair-wise comparisons of general form:

$$A^k = \begin{pmatrix} a^k{}_{11} & \dots & a^k{}_{1n} \\ \dots & \dots & \dots \\ a^k{}_{n1} & \dots & a^k{}_{nn} \end{pmatrix}, \quad [5.1]$$

in which the elements of the matrix A^k must satisfy the properties of the inverse symmetry $a_{ij} = \frac{1}{a_{ji}}$, and on the diagonal of the matrix there are 1.

For each matrix of judgments, the normalized vector of local priorities $a^k_{norm} = (a^k_1, a^k_2 \dots a^k_n), k = \overline{1,28}$ is determined, which is calculated by three known methods:

a) the method of the priority vector:

$$A^k a^k_{norm} = \lambda^k_{max} a^k_{norm}, \qquad [5.2]$$

where λ^k_{max} is the maximal eigen value of the matrix A^k;

b) the method of the average geometric element of each of the rows of the matrix A^k:

$$a^k_{norm\_i} = \frac{\sqrt[n]{\prod_{j=1}^{n} a^k_{ij}}}{\sum_i^n \left(\sqrt[n]{\prod_{j=1}^{n} a^k_{ij}}\right)}, i = \overline{1,n}; \qquad [5.3]$$

c) the method of averaging over normalized columns of the matrix A^k:

$$a^k_{norm\_ij} = \frac{a^k_{ij}}{\sum_{i=1}^{n} a^k_{ij}}, a^k_{norm\_i} = \frac{\sum_{j=1}^{n} a^k_{norm\_ij}}{n}. \qquad [5.4]$$

Normalized vectors of judgment matrix were calculated for obtaining global alternatives priorities:

$$b^{Z_m} = \sum_{i=1}^{8} \sum_{j=1}^{19} b^{N_O} \cdot b^{N_{F_i}} \cdot b^{N_{F_{ij}}}, \mathrm{m} = \overline{1,7}, \qquad [5.5]$$

where n is the dimension of the matrix; a^k_{ij} is the element of i raw of the matrix (each of the matrices of pair-wise comparisons corresponds to the vector a^k, $k = \overline{1.28}$); b^{Z_m} is the vector of alternative priorities; b^{N_O} is a normalized vector of priorities of pair-wise comparisons matrix relative to the main goal; $b^{N_{F_i}}$ is the normalized vector of priorities of pair-wise comparisons matrix of factors with respect to complex criteria; $b^{N_{F_{ij}}}$ is the normalized vector of the priorities of matrix of pair-wise comparisons of alternatives with respect to the factors.

The matrix consistency estimation was calculated as:

$$CR = \frac{CI}{RI}, \qquad [5.6]$$

where CI is the index of matrix coherence, which is determined as:

$$CI = \frac{\lambda^k_{max} - n}{n-1}, k = \overline{1.28}, \qquad [5.7]$$

Here, RI is the estimate of random coincidence for a random matrix of dimension n × n. The calculations were carried out using matrix algebra and software developed in the MATLAB environment.

5.1.3. *Second part of the IT*

The second part of the proposed IT aims to balance the structure of electricity generation. Taking into account Markowitz MPT, an assessment of the structure of GCs is being studied. It searches for such a set of electricity generation structure that is able to provide the lowest level of risk (or fluctuation of generation costs) for the specified return level (or electricity output per unit of cost) or maximize the expected return at an acceptable level of risk.

Thus, an analysis of the structure of electricity GCs performed within the quadratic optimization problem under linear constraints and an efficiency frontier (EF), indicating the Sharpe ration, was constructed.

This modeling is defined by the following main variables:

a) expected electricity generation portfolio return:

$$E_{R_p} = \sum_{i=1}^{m} w_i E_{R_i}, \qquad [5.8]$$

where m is the set of alternative variants of power generation sources ($m = 7$);

b) standard deviation (σ_p), or aggregate risk of the electricity generation portfolio:

$$E_{\sigma_p} = \sqrt{\sum_{i=1}^{m} w_i^2 \sigma_i^2 + 2\sum_{i=1}^{m-1} \sum_{j=i+1}^{m} w_i w_j \sigma_i \sigma_j \rho_{ij}}, \qquad [5.9]$$

where w_i is the share of ith sources of electricity generation in the structure of generating capacity i; E_{R_i} is the expected returns of the ith source of electricity generation (the physical output of the electricity per unit of value); σ_i and σ_j are the standard deviations in the costs of electricity generation by ith and jth sources of electricity generation, respectively; ρ_{ij} is the correlation coefficient (takes values from −1 to +1).

The Sharpe ratio is calculated as:

$$\frac{E_{R_p} - r_0}{E_{\sigma_p}}, \qquad [5.10]$$

where r_0 is the no risk factor. At the same time, the optimization problem is as follows:

$$\min E_{\sigma_p} = \sqrt{\sum_{i=1}^{m} w_i^2 \sigma_i^2 + 2\sum_{i=1}^{m-1} \sum_{j=i+1}^{m} w_i w_j \sigma_i \sigma_j \rho_{ij}}, \qquad [5.11]$$

$$\sum_{i=1}^{n} w_i = 1, \qquad [5.12]$$

$$w_i \geq 0, i = 1, \dots, n, \qquad [5.13]$$

and

$$\max E_{R_p} = \sum_{i=1}^{m} w_i E_{R_i}, \qquad [5.14]$$

$$\sigma_p^2 = \sum_{i=1}^{n} \sum_{j=1}^{n} w_i w_j \sigma_{ij} \leq \sigma^2, \qquad [5.15]$$

$$\sum_{i=1}^{n} w_i = 1, \qquad [5.16]$$

$$w_i \geq 0, i = 1, \dots, n. \qquad [5.17]$$

The calculations were carried out using matrix algebra and software developed in the MATLAB environment.

5.1.4. *Third part of the IT*

Given the different capacities at the power plants, it is necessary to estimate the sequence of the introduction of the new technologies, so that there is a step-by-step introduction of the new facilities and smooth phase out of the old ones.

5.1.5. *Fourth part of the IT*

To get an insight into the strategic alignment of the energy companies, the analysis was performed on how changes in electricity GC reflect the goals stated in the strategies of the companies. Considering a variety of different types of risks for different sources of electricity, their classification is constructed and the absolute magnitude of the risk (absolute loss level) for each source of electricity generation Z_m $(m = 7)$ is calculated:

$$W_m = p_m x_m, \qquad [5.18]$$

where p_m and x_m are the probability of occurrence of the event of losses and the size of possible damage from it, respectively.

5.2. Data collection

The study reviews academic literature and companies' reports (that cover the period 2007–2016). Additionally (for AHP purposes), a survey from the company experts within different European companies (and different countries) was carried out – semi-restrictive, open-ended interviews were conducted and closed, and fixed-response questionnaires were filled in. These experts were senior level managers with an engineering degree and 15–30 years of experience in the energy field.

5.3. Conclusion

A. Ranking of electricity generation sources

The calculation of the ranking of elements of the AHP hierarchy according to three methods of calculating the priority vector was delivered. According to the most closely approximated result, the ranking of sources of electricity generation is presented. A significant difference between the regions can be seen, which can be explained by the difference in the ranking of the criteria that are influencing the final ranking of the alternatives.

B. Balancing electricity generation sources

The construction of an EF of the structure of electricity GCs with regards to a balance between energy portfolio risk and return defines that the most efficient energy portfolio is the one which is more diversified and where the predominant electricity source has a lower level of fluctuation in LCOE[1]. So, in its predominance in the EU, hydropower, solar, wind energy, biomass energy and sometimes nuclear energy (in particular, in France) show the greatest dynamics of fluctuations in LCOE. In Ukraine, a portfolio with a predominance of nuclear energy is the least risky because of the relatively low dynamics of LCOE for nuclear energy.

C. Strategic alignment of the structure of electricity generation sources

A qualitative analysis of the dynamics of the companies' energy mixes indicates that the activities in traditional and nuclear energy sectors remain high despite statements of the companies about the transition to renewable energy (Figure 5.3). This can be justified by a large production capacity, related infrastructure, current resources (constraints) and dependent customers.

The analysis of the risks indicates that sources of electricity generation with a lower level of LCOE are characterized by lower levels of other risks.

$$S_{b=}B_r - B_{capacity}, \qquad [5.19]$$

1 LCOE: levelized cost of generating (producing) electricity.

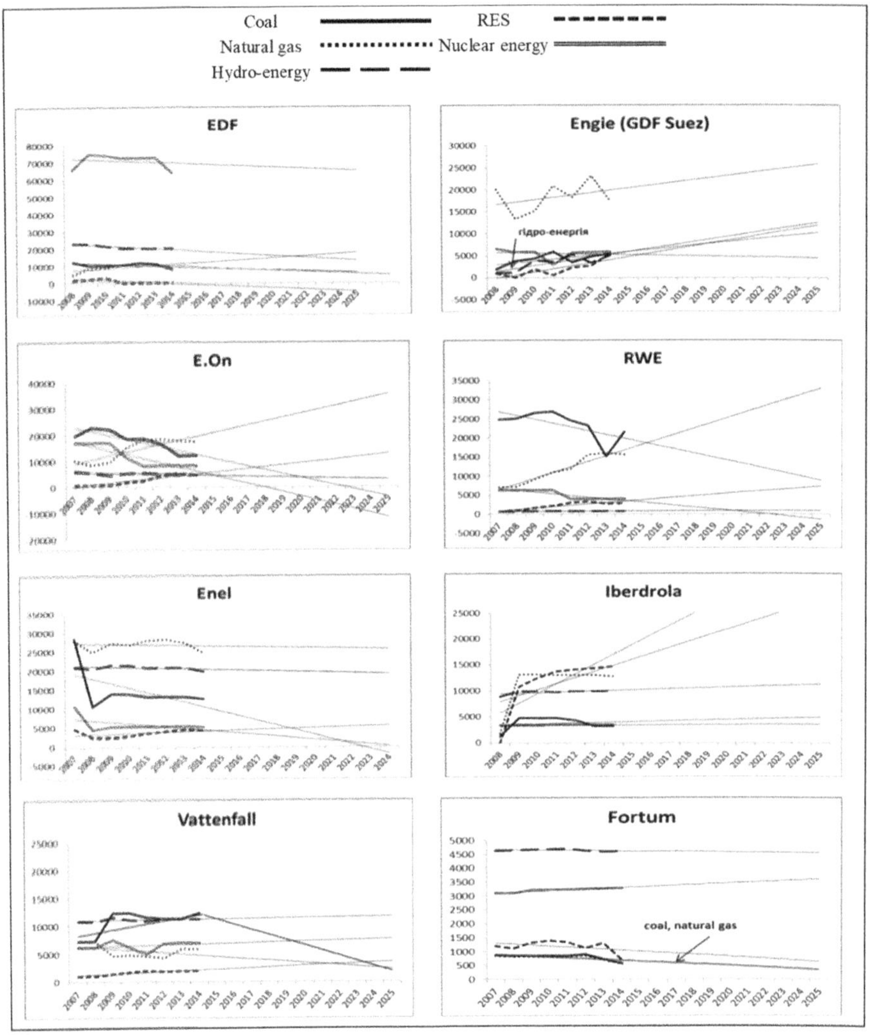

Figure 5.3. *Past, present and projected composition of electricity generation portfolio (%)*

where S_b is the distance between the balancing indicator according to the AHP rating B_r and the balancing indicator of the current structure of the GCs $B_{capacity}$:

$$B_{capacity} = \frac{\sum_{Z=1}^{m} c_Z r_{F_4}}{\sum_{Z=1}^{m} c_Z r_{F_8}}, \qquad [5.20]$$

where c_Z is the normalized weight of the source of electricity generation Z in the current structure of generating electricity, and r_{F_4} and r_{F_8} are weights of criteria F_4 and F_8 for each source of electricity generation.

Let $\Delta d_y = d_y/d_{y-1} - 1$ and $\Delta g_y = g_y/g_{y-1} - 1$, where Δd_y and Δg_y are the change in the volume of consumption and generation of electricity, respectively, over the years y and $y-1$, $S_{str\_y} = \Delta d_y$-Δg_y, then

$$S_{str} = \sum_{y=1}^{u} S_{str\_y}, \qquad [5.21]$$

where u is the number of years. Thus, the total distance is

$$S = \sqrt{S_r^{\,2} + S_b^{\,2} + S_{str}^{\,2}}, \qquad [5.22]$$

Let $P = \sum_{y=1}^{u} p_y$, where P is the company's profit for the period, p_y is the company's profit in year y and u is the number of years. When comparing D and P, the following experimental rule is obtained.

Experimental rule 1: Minimization of the coherence coefficient S between the results of the research model and the indicators of real practice leads to an increase in the profitability of companies P.

It can be summarized that according to the company's goals, and also taking into account the trends of the power market, the optimal structure of electricity GC would depend on the economic and political availability of fuels for the next decade (decades), electricity price predictability and state support.

The presented algorithm delivers an assessment of how to construct a structure of electricity generation, which is an important element of strategic energy planning. Decision-making techniques in the field of energy generation, economic effectiveness and risk adherence to the electricity generation portfolio, the level of strategic alignment – all this has to account for the specifics of different countries. The specifics which might have influence include the costs of the energy technologies, governmental regulation in energy policy, final energy demand and the level of available capacity in the country.

5.4. References

Awerbuch, S. and Spencer, Y. (2007). Efficient electricity generating portfolios for Europe: Maximising energy security and climate change mitigation. *EIB Papers*, 12(2), 8–37.

Celikbilek, Y. and Tuysuzb, F. (2016). An integrated grey based multi-criteria decision making approach for the evaluation of renewable energy sources. *Energy*, 115(1), 1246–1258.

Cucciella, F. (2012). Modeling optimal investments with portfolio analysis in electricity markets. *Energy Education Science and Technology Part A: Energy Science and Research*, 30(1), 673–692.

Dyachuk, O. (2013). Practical use of MARKAL/TIMES models for modeling, forecasting and analysis of energy systems development. *Economic Analysis*, 12(1), 98–103.

Lehtveer, M., Makowski, M., Hedenus, F. (2015). Multi-criteria analysis of nuclear power in the global energy system: Assessing trade-offs between simultaneously attainable economic, environmental and social goals. *Energy Strategy Reviews*, 8, 45–55.

Madlener, R., Glensk, B., Westner, G. (2009). Applying mean-variance portfolio analysis to E.ON's power generation portfolio in the UK and Sweden. E.ON Energy Research Center, RWTH Aachen University.

Norkin, V., Gaivoronski, A., Zaslavskyi, V.A., Knopov, P. (2018). Models of the optimal resources allocation for the critical infrastructure protection. *Cybernetics and Systems Analysis*, 5, 13–26.

Shahzad, M., Burhan, M., Ang, L., Choon, K. (2017). Energy-water-environment nexus underpinning future desalination sustainability. *Desalination*, 413, 52–64.

Stetsyuk, P. (2012). Mathematical models and software in energy tasks. National Academy of Sciences of Ukraine, Kyiv.

Volkovich, V.L. and Zaslavskyi, V.A. (1986). Algorithm to solve reliability optimization problem for complex systems using type-variety redundant elements in subsystems. *Kibernetika*, 5, 54–61, 81.

Volkovich, V.L., Voloshin, A.F., Zaslavskyi, V.A., Ushakov, I.A. (1993). *Models and Algorithms for Reliability Optimization of Complex Systems*. Naukova Dumka, Kyiv.

Zaslavskyi, V.A. (2005). Multi-stage optimization model of the problem of water management in the river basin. *Scientific and Practical Journal World of Information Technologies*, 2, 18–22.

Zaslavskyi, V.A. (2006). Type variety principle and peculiarities of study of complex systems with a high cost of failure. *Bulletin of Kyiv National Taras Shevchenko University,* 1, 136–147.

Zaslavskyi, V.A. (2011). Systems approach for risk management in regional systems. In *Proceedings of the International Conference "Research & Development as the Basis for Innovation in Creating the Competitive Region"*, 12–13 November, Podgorica.

Zaslavskyi, V.A. and Ievgiienko, Y. (2010). Risk analyses and redundancy for protection of critical infrastructure. In *Monographs of System Dependability*. Oficyna Widawnicza Politechniki Wroclawskiej, Wrocław.

Zaslavskyi, V.A. and Kadenko, I. (1999). The role and place of non-destructive testing methods to ensure the reliability and durability of complex systems with a high price of failure. *Non-Destructive Testing*, 1, 5–22.

Zaslavskyi, V.A. and Pasichna, M. (2018a). Optimization techniques for modelling energy generation portfolios in Ukraine and the EU: Comparative analysis. *Advances in Intelligent Systems and Computing*, 761, 545–555.

Zaslavskyi, V.A. and Pasichna, M. (2018b). Strategic evaluation of electricity generation structure in the European Union and Ukraine: Geographical focus. In *Proceeding of Dependable Systems, Services and Technologies*. Banking University, Kyiv.

Zaslavskyi, V.A. and Strizak, A. (2006). Credit card fraud detection using self-organizing maps. *Information & Security*, 18, 48–63.

Zaslavskyi, V.A., Kadenko, I., Sakhno, N. (1999). Application of the complex NDT approach for inspection of NPP power system. In *Proceedings of International Symposium on Nondestructive Testing Contribution to the Infrastructure Safety Systems in the 21st Century*, 22–26 November, Torres, RS.

Zaslavskyi, V.A., Krasovska, K., Pasichna, M. (2016). Towards the creation of a competitive, diversified energy portfolio for electricity generating companies in EU energy market conditions. *European Data Q*, 1(1), 3–20. doi: 10.11610/edq.01101.

PART 2

Reliability Theory for Ensuring Safety of Critical Infrastructure Facilities

Introduction to Part 2

In the methods of risk assessment that arise when solving many of the problems of identification and control theory, the functioning of ecologically hazardous objects are considered. This part of the book will mainly focus on the assessment of unknown reliability parameters in the presence of small samples. Models for searching for robust Bayesian estimates are proposed in the presence of insufficient a priori information. Particular attention is paid to the case when the class of functions of a priori distributions is specified using linear constraints. It is shown that the developed models are reduced to optimization problems in the space of distribution functions. Quantile regression models and cases of linear constraints on a priori distributions that have fixed first moments are considered in detail. These results are of significant importance in the analysis of critical situations in the functioning of high-tech industries.

Applications of the type-variety principle for developing non-destructive testing technologies of critical infrastructure facilities and for optimization of the reliability of parallel-sequential critical infrastructure systems are discussed.

Introduction written by Pavel S. KNOPOV and Volodymyr A. ZASLAVSKYI.

6

Methods of Risk Assessment in Environmentally Hazardous Industries

In the methods of risk assessment that arise when solving many of the problems of identification and control theory, the functioning of ecologically hazardous objects are considered. This chapter will mainly focus on the assessment of unknown reliability parameters in the presence of small samples. Models for searching for robust Bayesian estimates in the presence of insufficient a priori information are proposed.

6.1. Introduction

The past decade has been accompanied by numerous accidents that have resulted in technological and financial catastrophes. The Chernobyl disaster demonstrated that neglecting the need to assess the risk of accidents can lead to consequences on a planetary scale.

Typically, individuals making decisions under conditions of risk and uncertainty are unable to make informed decisions, even in the simplest and frequently recurring situations. In the operation of high-tech industries, the probability of failure of each individual system is very low, and therefore decision-makers often disregard it. However, such a low-probability system failure can lead to catastrophic consequences. After the Chernobyl accident, the attitude to risk assessment problems dramatically changed, which prompted numerous studies in different countries.

Chapter written by Pavel S. KNOPOV, Aleksandr N. GOLODNIKOV, Volodumir A. PEPELYAEV and Liliia B. VOVK.

Analysis of critical technogenic situations has shown that the main factors influencing the occurrence of accidents are the imperfection of production technologies, design miscalculations in technological equipment and insufficiently substantiated strategies for technical maintenance of objects with a high level of environmental hazard. Factors such as the location of environmentally hazardous objects, the availability of pre-developed protective measures and their implementation on time in emergency situations under conditions of acute time shortage have a significant impact on the scale of accident consequences.

To scientifically substantiate the possibility of locating environmentally hazardous production, the following tasks need to be solved:

1) Conduct a safety examination of the proposed location of environmentally hazardous production to identify the occurrence of accidents and critical points that most affect the system's safety. Since absolute safety does not exist in nature, an acceptable option may be a process or production with a safety level not lower than a certain threshold.

2) Develop an optimal strategy for the technological maintenance of production equipment with the aim of increasing the safety level.

Solving this task is necessary because any system safety decreases over time due to wear and tear of its components. In order to prevent system failures, technical maintenance is performed, which involves monitoring subsystems and elements that make up the system, as well as troubleshooting. The quality of technical maintenance is influenced by both the frequency and the extent of inspections.

Therefore, the task of optimal planning for technical system maintenance lies in determining the periodicity and volume of inspections at which the level of safety for the environmentally hazardous production under consideration is maximized.

3) Make a forecast of possible accident consequences at a given production facility and plan protective actions that will protect the population and environment from the effects of harmful emissions that may occur as a result of an accident. In solving this task, it is necessary to model the entire chain of dispersion of pollutants from a source to a human, taking into account various meteorological, physicochemical, radiological aspects, among others. Individual and collective, or population, doses are used as indicators of the impact of harmful emissions on the population.

All three tasks are interconnected and can be formulated as a two-stage stochastic programming problem. Two-stage stochastic programming problems model a two-stage decision-making process under conditions of risk and uncertainty. In the first stage, before the random realization of the state of nature ϖ becomes known (in our case, the occurrence of an accident, emission and dispersion of pollutants in the environment, harmful impact of pollutants on the population, etc.), a strategic decision x is made, which involves choosing a specific project for environmentally hazardous production, its location, as well as a strategy for equipment maintenance.

After the realization of one of the possible states of nature ϖ, when the degree and extent of environmental pollution become known, the second stage of decision-making is implemented – the selection of a set of protective actions $y(\varpi)$, which depend on the realization of the state of nature ϖ and are aimed at mitigating damages. Such a choice is made by taking into account the criteria developed in advance before the accident. Protective actions are characterized by effectiveness (the degree of reduction of the expected individual dose and the level of material costs $z_1(y(\varpi))$). Material costs include expenses for organizing dosimetric control, population evacuation, decontamination work, etc.

In addition to the material costs of implementing protective actions, direct losses $z_2(\varpi)$ need to be taken into account. These losses consist of expenses for reconstruction, the value of remaining fixed assets in the contaminated area. The total losses after the realization of the state of nature ϖ are represented as $z(\varpi) \rightleftarrows= z_1(\varpi) + z_2(\varpi)$.

To calculate radiation risk in the case of radiation contamination risk, it is necessary to estimate the expected collective dose, determined by the following formula:

$$s(\varpi) = \sum_i N_i(\varpi) H_i(\varpi),$$

where $N_i(\varpi)$ is the number of individuals for whom the expected equivalent dose is $H_i(\varpi)$.

The radiation risk R and expected losses Z are determined by the following formulas:

$$R = \sum_i s\,(\varpi_i) P_i$$

$$Z = \sum_i z\,(\varpi_i) P_i$$

where ϖ_i is the expected realization of the state of nature and P_i is the probability of realization of ϖ_i.

The set of nature states is defined by possible values of parameters ϖ representing emissions at the environmentally hazardous production facility and parameters describing weather conditions. Additionally, the probabilities P_i may depend on various unknown parameters.

The aim of the two-stage problem of stochastic programming is to determine, for an admissible set of solutions X, such a solution $x \in X$, which consists of choosing an environmentally hazardous production project, a place for its location, as well as maintenance parameters, in which the radiation risk would be lower than some predetermined value ρ_0 $(R(\mathrm{x}) \leq \rho_0)$ and the sum of costs and expected material losses is minimized:

$$Z^1(x) + \rightleftarrows Z^{11}(x) \rightarrow \min,$$

where $Z^1(x)$ denotes costs of technical maintenance and $Z^{11}(x)$ denotes the expected losses, corresponding to the solution x.

Thus, the solution to the overall two-stage stochastic programming problem is reduced to solving several subproblems. Let us focus on some of them in more detail. As an example, consider the estimation of the probability of accidents at nuclear power plants (NPPs).

There are two possible approaches to this problem. The first one involves collecting and processing statistical data on failures at NPPs. By analyzing the statistical data, the probabilities of accidents can be estimated. However, in practice, this method cannot be applied effectively because NPPs are complex high-tech systems and accidents are relatively rare events. Therefore, most potential accidents have not yet occurred in practice.

The other approach involves modeling NPPs as complex systems composed of interconnected elements, where each element failure affects the occurrence of accidents to some degree. In this approach, the probabilities of the individual system elements failures are used to calculate the probabilities of accidents to some degree. The algorithm for calculating the probabilities of accidents is determined by the logical structure of the system. Thus, when using the second approach, the reliability of estimating accident probabilities depends on the completeness and adequacy of modeling a NPP safety system as a complex system of interconnected elements, as well as the reliability of estimating the probabilities of failures of its components.

Calculating the probabilities of failures of individual NPP elements is much simpler than statistically estimating accidents at NPPs as a whole. This approach is based on the well-known fault tree method (e.g. Fussel 1988; Idaho National Engineering Laboratory 1989; Konda 1989). A fault tree is a graphical model representing various combinations of parallel and sequential processes and the logical relationships between events that can lead to accidents.

We will not touch on the algorithmic description of the fault trees method. There are numerous publications on this subject, and a significant contribution to the development of this method is made in the proceedings (e.g. Kuznetsov 1985; Kovalenko and Kuznetsov 1988; Kuznetsov 1994; Kovalenko and Kuznetsov 1997). These results were used to solve a number of applied problems.

Let us dwell on some problems related to the solution of the above-mentioned tasks. One of the important stages of the existing risk assessment methodology at environmentally hazardous facilities is the determination of parameters characterizing equipment reliability. Such parameters include, for example, the intensity of failures and the probability of failures that occur at the moment of receiving a request for the activation of the equipment. The accuracy of the parameter estimates obtained at this stage significantly affects the final result – the risk assessment of the entire environmentally hazardous object.

Statistical methods that are widely used to estimate reliability parameters are based on two main approaches: classical sampling theory methods and Bayesian estimation procedures.

The classical approach provides a satisfactory estimate in those cases where there is sufficient primary information on technological equipment failures. However, sampling methods are not suitable for processing small samples, which often have to be dealt with when evaluating the parameters of high-reliability equipment. In the practice of evaluating NPP equipment reliability parameters, there were instances where no failure was registered for some types of equipment for many reactor-years. The use of classical sampling methods in such cases leads to inaccurate assessments and a decrease in the degree of confidence in the results obtained.

One way to overcome the problem of small samples is to use not only the information obtained in the current equipment reliability study, but also additional analysis information from various sources. Such sources include the results of previous studies of similar equipment, the results of bench tests, engineering calculations, etc. This circumstance is significant and allows us to obtain samples of large volumes, which makes it possible to use a sufficiently well-developed apparatus of asymptotic statistical analysis. Unfortunately, classical methods cannot simultaneously use current and additional information when making statistical conclusions. In contrast to sampling theory methods, the Bayesian approach allows the natural combination of data from different sources to obtain estimates of reliability parameters. At the same time, each source is perceived as a sample from one population. The a priori distribution density accumulates everything known about the reliability parameter before obtaining empirical data. A priori information is transformed into an a priori distribution function and can be either objective or subjective in nature. Operative information about the equipment functioning at previous time moments, as well as information obtained from similar experiments with the same equipment can be included in objective a priori information. Subjective information can be supplemented by expert estimates based on specialists' own experience, their opinions and project decisions.

In fact, as a rule, the available a priori information is not sufficient to accurately determine an a priori distribution function. Under such conditions, the problem of choosing an a priori distribution function and calculating Bayesian estimates becomes non-trivial.

Empirical Bayesian decision-making procedures are an effective means of combining data that have been collected from different sources. Attractive properties of these methods include their asymptotic optimality. However, the rate of convergence of the empirical Bayesian risk to the minimum of the true Bayesian risk can be very slow. Therefore, in the case of small samples, the accuracy of approximation of Bayesian estimates by empirical Bayesian estimates is not always known in practice.

In such cases, it is desirable to assess how far the estimate obtained by applying the empirical Bayesian approach is from the true Bayesian estimate.

A similar problem arises when calculating a two-sided probability interval, which is used in uncertainty analysis. Since this requires knowledge of the true posterior distribution, there may be situations where the probability interval differs significantly from the interval corresponding to the true prior distribution.

Given the fact that in practice the true a priori distribution is not always known, it is natural to assume that any distribution function that does not contradict the available a priori information can be used as an a priori distribution on the same grounds.

The use of the beta distribution as an a priori one in the binomial model and the gamma distribution in the Poisson model in Bayesian evaluation procedures is often justified by the fact that it is convenient to perform analytical transformations with them. However, this evidence is not conclusive now that most researchers have access to high-speed computers. Therefore, in cases of lack of a priori information, the most attractive Bayesian estimator is the robust Bayesian estimator, which was obtained under the assumption that the true a priori distribution corresponds to the available a priori information.

In this context, there is a need to develop new methods for solving these problems. Mathematical methods that can be used to solve these problems are given in Mikhalevich et al. (1994), Golodnikov et al. (2004, 2009, 2010, 2019) and Pepelyaev et al. (2022a, 2022b).

The obtained results confirm the assumption that Bayesian estimates are sufficiently sensitive to the choice of a priori distribution function that corresponds to the available a priori information. The examples with analysis of data on rejections given in these proceedings demonstrate that the use in Bayesian estimation procedures as a prior distribution of the beta distribution leads to an estimate that may differ from other estimates that can be obtained from another distribution with the same priors average and variance by more than an order of magnitude.

Since there is no reason to prefer the beta distribution, using this distribution as a prior leads to an underestimation of the failure probability of a component by more than one order of magnitude. At the same time, the degree of underestimation of the entire system increases with the increase in the level of duplication of this component in this system. The results of the study showed that such a situation is not uncommon.

An approach based on the approximation of the unknown distribution function with limited moments and the corresponding criterion function is proposed in Martz and Waller (1991). At the same time, it becomes necessary to solve the problem of stochastic programming, and the unknown parameters of the distribution are estimated using an empirical Bayesian approach.

For this problem, on the one hand, the convergence of the proposed methods is proven and, on the other hand, numerical experiments confirm its effectiveness.

At the same time, there are still many unsolved problems related to the solution of specific problems, both in risk assessment, and in the assessment of the parameters of the distribution of random variables characterizing the elements or blocks of elements of the functional system under consideration.

6.2. Analysis of publications

The following structure of safety indicators is based on the results of the works by Barlow and Lambert (1975), IEEE (1983) and Department of Nuclear Energy Brookhaven National Laboratory (1984).

6.2.1. *Quantitative safety indicators*

Quantitative indicators of safety are radiation and probabilistic indicators. Radiation indicators characterize the extent of damage or the extent of consequences associated with radiation exposure to an individual, a part of the population and/or the environment. In practice, the following radiation indicators are used:

– values of radionuclide emissions C;

– equivalent effective radiation doses D.

Radiation indicators can take different values depending on the state of the NPP, ranging from values corresponding to normal operating conditions to post-design accidents, in which most of the radioactive substances contained in it may be released from the reactor. Individual states may arise as a result of the realization of a certain set of events, each of which represents operational or non-operational states of systems and components of a nuclear plant. The full set of possible states is determined when performing a probabilistic safety analysis. At the same time, for each individual state, the values of radiation indicators and the probabilities of their implementation at a certain time interval of the operation of the NPP under consideration are determined.

6.2.2. *Probable safety indicators*

The probabilities of realization of individual states $P_i(T)$ in the time interval $[0, T]$ are probabilistic safety indicators. The set of probability indicators determined for the entire set of possible states of the nuclear plant can be represented as a probability distribution of a discrete random variable – the size of the radiation consequences of the operation of the nuclear plant. This distribution is a sufficiently complete quantitative characteristic of the level of safety of NPPs. It can be used to determine indicators characterizing off-station risk.

Off-station risk indicators are as follows:

1) Individual risk of fatality $R(T)$: this is defined as the probability of death of an individual person located in the territory close to the NPP as a result of its operation during a period of time T^*. This indicator is the average value or mathematical expectation of a discrete random variable – the conditional probability of a person's death, when irradiated by dose D_i, and is determined by the following formula:

$$R(T) = \sum_{i=1}^{n} P_i(T, D_i) r_i(D_i),$$

where $P_i(T, D_i)$ is the probability of a person receiving a dose D_i at a time interval $[0, T]$, $r_i(D_i)$ is a person's death probability when exposed to its dose D_i and N is the number of possible states of the NPP differing from each other in the value of the dose.

2) The average expected dose (or the average expected emission), $\bar{D}(T)$: this is defined as the mathematical expectation of the dose according to the following formula:

$$\bar{D}(T) = \sum_{i=1}^{N} P_i(T, D_i) D_i,$$

where $P_i(T, D_i)$ is the probability of occurrence in the time interval $p_i' = \bar{p}_i, i = m + 2, \dots, k + r$, of the ith state of the NPP, in which the dose value is D_i.

Probability indicators of the station safety level include the probability of damage to the active zone. Damage means partial or complete destruction or melting of the active zone. This indicator is the main indicator in the case where the probabilistic safety analysis is limited to the statistical evaluation of damage to the core. The assessment of the probability of damage to the core is also a convenient tool in determining the importance for the safety of systems and equipment of the normal operation of the reactor plant and protective safety systems.

The quantitative safety indicators discussed above refer to the indicators characterizing the level of safety of the NPP as a whole. In addition, we can use functional and system level indicators. They are indicators of the reliability of the performance of certain security functions and indicators of the reliability of individual security systems. Such indicators are the probability of non-fulfillment of the specified safety functions or the probability of failure of safety systems in the event of requirements for operation.

As mentioned above, quantitative safety indicators are determined as a result of performing probabilistic analyses. A list of quantitative indicators can be found in the following.

6.2.3. *Reliability of safety-critical systems*

Safety indicators are listed as follows:

– the probability of failure to perform a given function, that is, the probability that a given function will not be performed within a certain period, starting from an arbitrary moment in time;

– the probability of system failure on demand, that is, the probability that this system will be in an inoperable state at any moment of NPP operation if there is a demand for its operation at that moment;

– intensity, frequency of initial events, that is, conditional probability density of the occurrence of an initial event at the current time (intensity), mathematical expectation of the number of initial events per unit of time (frequency).

6.2.4. *Safety indicators and probability of active zone damage*

Safety indicators are listed as follows:

– degree of damage (destruction or melting of the active zone);

– the probability of damage of the active zone in the considered range;

– probability distribution of active zone damage.

6.2.5. *Values and probabilities of radioactive emissions into the environment*

Safety indicators are listed as follows:

– value of emissions of a separate group of radionuclides into the environment;

– probability distribution of emissions of individual groups of radionuclides.

6.2.6. *Risk to the population*

Safety indicators are listed as follows:

– magnitude of equivalent effective dose $D(S)$ at a distance S from the NPP;

– probability of dose D_i, $P(T, D_i)$, that is, the probability that, in the interval $p_i' = \bar{p}_i$, $i = m + 2, \dots, k + r$, at least one state of the NPP will occur, in which the dose value will be in the range $[D_j, D_j + \Delta D_j]$;

– probability distribution of dose $P\{T, D_i\}$ on the interval $p_i' = \bar{p}_i$, $i = m + 2$, $\dots, k + r$, of each of the considered ranges;

– average expected dose $\bar{D}(T)$ on the interval $p_i' = \bar{p}_i$, $i = m + 2, \dots, k + r$, which is the mathematical expectation of the dose on the interval $p_i' = \bar{p}_i$, $i = m + 2$, $\dots, k + r$,: $\bar{D}(T) = \sum_D D_i P(T, D_i)$, where the sum is taken over the entire set of states with different values D_i;

– individual lethal risk $R(T)$:

$$R(T) = \sum P(T, D_i) r_i(D_i),$$

where $r_i(D_i)$ is the conditional probability of death for a person exposed to a dose D_i. The sum is taken over the entire set of states of the NPP.

It follows from the above that the definition of probable safety indicators is based on the calculations of the probabilities of realization of various emergency sequences or the corresponding final states of the NPP. Therefore, these probabilities are the main indicators for the calculation of which it is necessary to use appropriate models.

6.2.7. *Reliability indicators of security systems*

Some reliability indicators of security systems in standby mode are:

– unreadiness of the security system $Q_s(t)$, which is equal to the probability that the system is faulty at a moment in time $t \in [0, T]$ and will not be able to start performing the given security function when the initial event occurs at this moment in time;

– the average unreadiness of the security system $\bar{Q}_s(T)$ over the entire interval of the standby mode $(0, T)$:

$$\bar{Q}_s(T) = \int_0^T Q_s(t)dt;$$

– the component of the average unreadiness of the security system $\bar{Q}_{test}$, which is caused by the control of its components:

$$\bar{Q}_{test} = \frac{1}{T}\sum_{i=1}^{n} \int_{t_i}^{t_i+\tau_i} Q_s(t)dt,$$

where$(t_i, t_i + \tau_i)$ is the ith interval on which at least one component is monitored;

– the component of the average unreadiness of the security system $\bar{Q}_{rep}$, which is caused by the repair of components that have failed:

$$\bar{Q}_{rep} = \frac{1}{T}\sum_{i=1}^{n} \int_{t_i+\tau_i}^{t_i+\tau_i+T_{r_i}} Q_s(t)dt,$$

where $(t_i + \tau_i, t_i + \tau_i + T_{R_i})$ is the ith interval at which at least one failed component is repaired;

– the component of the average unreadiness of the security system $\bar{Q}_h$, which is caused by failures occurring between two consecutive checks:

$$\bar{Q}_h = \bar{Q}_s - \bar{Q}_{test} - \bar{Q}_{rep}.$$

The point unreadiness of the safety system $Q_s(t)$ is calculated using the values $q(t)$ of the point unreadiness of the components included in it using the apparatus of minimum intersections, that is, sets of minimum sets of failures of system components that lead to the failure of the entire system. Let $A_1, A_2, \dots, A_N$ be the set of minimum intersections that were constructed based on the analysis of the fault tree. If it is assumed that the failures of the components that make up any minimum intersection are independent of each other, then the unreadiness of the jth minimum intersection is calculated by the following formula:

$$Q_j(t) = q_1(t)q_2(t) \cdots q_{n_j}(t),$$

where n_j is the number of components that make up the minimum cross-section A_j, and $q_1(t), q_2(t), \dots q_{n_j}(t)$ are their point failures. If we ignore the probability of simultaneous implementation of more than one minimum intersection, then the unreadiness of the system is expressed by the unreadiness of the minimum intersections according to the following formula:

$$Q_s(t) = \sum_{j=1}^{N} Q_j(t) = \sum_{j=1}^{N} \prod_{k=1}^{n_j} q_k(t).$$

Further, we will assume that minimal intersections are known. Thus, to determine the point unreadiness of the security system $Q_s(t)$, it is necessary to identify expressions for the point unavailability of individual components $q(t)$. The type $q(t)$ is based on the type of model and type of component. As a rule, three types of models are considered: (1) the component uncontrolled in standby mode, (2) the component continuously controlled in standby mode and (3) the component periodically controlled in standby mode. In general, any minimal intersection may contain components that are described by three different types of model.

It is assumed that the time of the component's failure-free operation is described by the exponential law with a constant intensity of failures λ. We will also assume that for each repairable component, the duration of its failure elimination T_r is known.

The state of non-readiness of a component is the state in which it is unable to perform its function.

The unreadiness of an uncontrolled component is calculated by the following formula:

$$q(t) = 1 - e^{-\lambda t}$$

for any $t,\ 0 \leq t \leq T$.

The unreadiness of a continuously controlled component in standby mode is calculated by the following formula:

$$q(t) = \begin{cases} 1 - e^{-\lambda t}, & 0 \leq t \leq T_r, \\ \dfrac{\lambda T_r}{1 + \lambda T_r}, & t > T_r. \end{cases}$$

We introduce the following notations to calculate the unreadiness of a periodically controlled component:

– ϕ is the time interval until the first control of the component. The duration of this interval for the first channel elements is equal to t_0. For other channels elements, $\phi_m = \frac{(m-1)t_0}{M}$, where M is the number of security system channels.

– t_0 is the interval between subsequent scheduled maintenance of the component (periodicity of control).

– τ is the duration of component verification.

– p is the probability of failure to start at the time of the request for activation receipt.

– q_0 is the probability of the inoperable condition of the component caused by its disconnection during scheduled maintenance.

Then

$$q(t) = \begin{cases} p + (1-p)(1 - e^{-\lambda t}), & t \leq \phi, \\ q_0 + (1 - q_0)P_n^n, & \phi + (n-1)t_0 < t \leq \phi + (n-1)t_0 + \tau, \\ P_n^n + (1 - P_n^n)\left[p + (1-p)\left(1 - e^{-\frac{\lambda T_r}{2}}\right)\right], & \phi + (n-1)t_0 + \tau < t \leq \phi + (n-1)t_0 + \tau + T_r, \\ P_n^n\left[p + (1-p)\left(1 - e^{-\lambda(t - \phi - (n-1)t_0 - \tau - T_r)}\right)\right] & \\ +(1 - P_n^n)\left[p + (1-p)\left(1 - e^{-\lambda(t - \phi - (n-1)t_0 - \tau)}\right)\right], & \phi + (n-1)t_0 + \tau + T_r < t \leq \phi + nt_0, \end{cases}$$

where

$$P_n^n = p + (1-p)Q_n,$$

$$Q_n = P_{n-1}^{n-1}\left(1-e^{-\lambda(t_0-\tau-T_r)}\right) + \left(1-P_{n-1}^{n-1}\right)\left(1-e^{-\lambda(t_0-\tau)}\right), \quad Q_1 = 1-e^{-\lambda\phi}.$$

To implement these models, it is necessary to estimate the main parameters:

– intensity of failures λ;

– the probability p of failure to start at the time when f request for activation is received.

Later, we will consider the methods of estimating these parameters.

6.3. Evaluation methods with a limited amount of statistical information

This section discusses methods based on a non-asymptotic formulation of the problem when it is necessary to construct the best estimates with a limited amount of statistical information.

6.3.1. *Methods of estimating parameters of risk models based on classical sampling theory*

One of the important stages of the existing risk assessment methodology is the assessment of the parameters characterizing the equipment reliability (the intensity of failures and the probability of failures that occur when a request for activation is received). The accuracy of the parameter estimates obtained at this stage significantly affects the accuracy of the final result – the risk assessment of the entire object.

Statistical methods that are widely used to estimate reliability parameters are based on two main approaches: methods of classical sampling theory and the Bayesian approach.

6.3.1.1. *Sample methods of point estimation of reliability parameters*

Let $f(x;\theta)$ be the distribution of the random variable X, where θ is the unknown parameter to be estimated. Consider the method of calculating a point estimate of an unknown parameter. Let $X_1, X_2, \dots, X_n$ be a random sample according to $f(x;\theta)$. The likelihood function for this random sample is the joint probability density

$$L(\theta; x_1, x_2, \dots, x_n) = \prod_{i=1}^{n} f(x_i; \theta),$$

which is considered as a function of θ.

The maximum likelihood estimation of the parameter θ is the value $\hat{\theta}$ such that $L(\hat{\theta}; x_1, x_2, \dots, x_n) \geq L(\theta; x_1, x_2, \dots, x_n)$ for all values of the parameter θ. The maximum likelihood estimate is a function of the random sample $x_1, x_2, \dots, x_n$, that is, it is a random variable.

Let $T_1, T_2, \dots, T_n$ be a set of n random variables that indicate the duration of equipment operation until the first failure. Let them be modeled using an exponential distribution function that depends on the failure intensity parameter λ. With the help of the exponential distribution law, the failures of the equipment that is in working condition (after a successful start) are modeled. According to this model, the probability that the equipment will not fail during the time interval $(1, t)$ is calculated by the following formula:

$$P\{X(t) = 0\} = e^{-\lambda t}.$$

Then the maximum likelihood estimation of the parameter λ is

$$\hat{\lambda} = \frac{n}{\sum_{i=1}^{n} t_i},$$

where t_i is the implementation of a random variable T_i (e.g. Martz and Waller 1991).

The method of moments uses sample moments m_j' as estimates of the moments of the distribution function $\mu_j' = E(X^j)$

$$m_j' = \frac{\sum_{i=1}^{n} X_i^j}{n}$$

for $j = 1,2, \dots, k$.

Using this method, it is easy to obtain an estimate of the parameter p for the binomial distribution law, which simulates the failures of the transition of the equipment from the standby state to the operating state at the moment of the request for activation. According to this model, the probability P that a failure is observed upon receipt of activation requirements is calculated by the following formula:

$$P(x) = \frac{n!}{(n-x)!\,x!} p^x (1-p)^{n-x}.$$

The estimation of this probability is calculated according to the following formula (e.g. Martz and Waller 1991):

$$R_S^i = \left(x_{1,i}^S, x_{2,i}^S, \dots, x_{i_S,i}^S\right)$$

6.3.1.2. *Sample methods of interval estimating of reliability parameters*

The practice of using sample estimations of reliability parameters shows that in many cases it is not possible to limit yourself to point estimates only. For example, in the case of highly reliable systems, the number of failures observed during testing is very small. In such cases, the value of the estimates varies dramatically from trial to trial and cannot be used as a stable characteristic of reliability. That is why the point estimate of the reliability parameter should be supplemented with an estimate of the degree of uncertainty, that is, confidence intervals. A two-sided confidence interval for estimating the reliability parameter ε with a confidence coefficient not less than γ is called a random interval $(\varepsilon_1(x), \varepsilon_2(x))$ depending only on the test result x such that

$$P\{\varepsilon_1(x) < \varepsilon < \varepsilon_2(x)\} \geq \gamma.$$

Consider two-sided confidence intervals for binomial and exponential failure models, which are the most common in the methodology of probabilistic safety analysis.

The lower and upper limits, $\varepsilon_1(x), \varepsilon_2(x)$, of the two-sided confidence interval for parameter p estimation in the binomial model are calculated according to the following formulas:

$$\varepsilon_1(x) = \frac{x}{x + (n-x+1)F_{1-\frac{\gamma}{2}}(2n-2x+2,2x)},$$

$$\varepsilon_2(x) = \frac{(x+1)F_{1-\frac{\gamma}{2}}(2x+2,2n-2x)}{(n-x) + (x+1)F_{1-\frac{\gamma}{2}}(2x+2,2n-2x)},$$

where $F_{1-\gamma/2}(n_1, n_2)$ is $(1-\gamma/2)$ – quantile of the F distribution with (n_1, n_2) degrees of freedom (e.g. Jeffreys 1961; Barlow and Lambert 1975; IEEE 1983; Department of Nuclear Energy Brookhaven National Laboratory 1984).

The lower and upper bounds $\varepsilon_1(x), \varepsilon_2(x)$ of the two-sided confidence interval for parameter λ estimation in the exponential model are calculated by the following formulas:

$$\varepsilon_1(x) = \frac{\chi^2_{\gamma/2}(2x)}{2t},$$

$$\varepsilon_2(x) = \frac{\chi^2_{1-\gamma/2}(2x+2)}{2t},$$

where $\chi^2_\gamma(n)$ is γ – quantile of the distribution with n degrees of freedom.

6.3.2. *Bayesian methods of estimating reliability parameters*

The classical approach allows satisfactory estimates to be obtained in cases when there is sufficient information on failures of technological equipment. As noted above, in contrast to the methods of sampling theory, the Bayesian approach allows for the natural combination of data from different sources of obtaining estimates of reliability parameters, and at the same time, each source is treated as a sample from the same population. If in the classical approach the parameters of the distribution function are considered constants to be estimated, then in the Bayesian approach the parameters are considered as random variables described by some a priori distribution function. In practice, as a rule, the available a priori information is not enough to accurately determine the a priori distribution function. Under these conditions, the problem of choosing an a priori distribution function and calculating Bayesian estimates becomes non-trivial (e.g. Bennet and Martz 1972; Carota and Ruggeri 1994; Bernardo 1998; Ruggeri and Sivaganesan 2000).

To avoid arbitrariness when choosing an a priori distribution function, based on the available partial a priori information, it is advisable to use the minimax approach (e.g. Vidakovic 2000). This approach takes into account the fact that when using Bayesian procedures in practice, we have to deal not with one a priori distribution function, but with a whole class Γ of such functions. At the same time, each distribution function from this class has the same reasons for being chosen a priori.

If for each distribution function from the class Γ we calculate the value of some posterior function (e.g. posterior risk and mathematical expectation), we will get a whole range of such values. This range is used as a measure of robustness. A narrow range means that the value of the posterior function does not change significantly for any choice of the prior distribution function from the specified class, that is, it is robust to the choice of the prior distribution function. Conversely, when this range is wide, the values of the posterior function are sensitive to the choice of the a priori distribution function, that is, it is not robust. In the latter case, it is necessary to pay special attention to the least favorable a priori distribution function in the class Γ and use the minimax approach to find a robust estimate.

As part of the Γ-minimax approach, an estimate is chosen that minimizes the supremum of the objective functional by the distribution functions belonging to the class Γ. If there is a small amount of a priori information, then the class Γ of a priori distribution functions is very large, and the results obtained using this method are close to the results obtained with the minimax approach. In another limiting case, when there is sufficient a priori information, the class Γ can consist of only one a priori distribution function and the Γ-minimax approach coincides with the traditional Bayesian approach.

To investigate the sensitivity of Bayesian estimates to the choice of an a priori distribution function from the class Γ, it is necessary to learn to find the lower and upper bounds of the range of possible values of the objective functional. A natural choice of the objective functional can be the mathematical expectation of the parameter θ at fixed sample data x

$$E\{\theta|x\} = \frac{\int_{\Theta} \theta\, f(x|\theta)dH(\theta)}{\int_{\Theta} f(x|\theta)dH(\theta)}.$$

When a quadratic loss function is used, this objective function coincides with the Bayesian estimate $\hat{\theta}_H$ of the parameter θ being estimated. If we calculate the value of the Bayesian estimate $\hat{\theta}_H$ for any prior distribution function $H \in \Gamma$, we get a range of possible values (θ_*, θ^*). The width of this range is a measure of the sensitivity of the Bayesian estimator to the choice of the prior distribution.

The main elements of the Bayesian approach are the sample model $f(x_i|\theta)$: the conditional density of the distribution of a random variable X_i, which depends on the parameter θ; the a priori model $g(\theta)$: the a priori density of the parameter θ distribution, and the a posteriori model $g(\theta|x)$: the posterior density of the parameter θ distribution, if x is fixed. According to the Bayesian approach, the posterior model is related to the sample and a priori models by the following relation:

$$g(\theta|x) = \frac{[\prod_{i=1}^{n} f(x_i|\theta)]g(\theta)}{f(x)} = \frac{f(x|\theta)g(\theta)}{f(x)},$$

where the marginal distribution $f(x)$ is defined as

$$f(x) = \int f(x|\theta)g(\theta)d\theta.$$

The a priori distribution density $g(\theta)$ accumulates all known information about the parameter θ until the moment of obtaining empirical data. A priori information, which is transformed into an a priori distribution function, can have an objective or subjective nature, or be both objective and subjective at the same time.

Objective a priori information can include operational information about the functioning of the equipment in previous periods of time, as well as information obtained during the conduct of relevant experiments with this equipment.

Subjective information can include expert assessments based on the specialists' own experience, their reasoning and project decisions.

When there is no a priori information about the parameter θ, or such information is too little, a non-informative a priori distribution function is used. Such a choice is based on the "principle of insufficient reason" according to which the distribution over a finite set of possible values of parameter θ should be uniform if there is no reason to believe that one parameter value is more likely than another. This principle was first formulated by Jeffreys (1961).

If the parametric space is a bounded interval, or an infinite interval $(-\infty, \infty)$, Jeffries suggested taking the a priori density of the distribution as a constant over the entire interval. In the case of an infinite parametric interval, such a choice led to a non-proprietary distribution, the integral of which over the entire parametric space is infinite. Jeffries did not believe that such a complication is fundamental, because often a statistician, based on such a choice of a priori distribution, can obtain a posterior distribution that no longer has such a disadvantage.

In the case where the parameter space is the interval $(0, \infty)$, which is associated with the variance σ^2, he used the a priori density distribution $g(\sigma) = 1/\sigma$. In Jeffreys (1961), a "general rule" for choosing a non-informative a priori distribution function was proposed, which is based on the use of Fisher's information matrix, which is defined as follows. Let $\theta = (\theta_1, \ldots, \theta_k)$ be a vector parameter with values in the parameter space Ω and $L(\theta|\tilde{x}) = \ln\prod_{j=1}^{n} f(x_i|\theta)$ denote the logarithmic probability of the sample. Then the element of Fisher's information matrix is determined by the following formula:

$$I_{ij}(\theta) = E_{\tilde{x}|\theta}\left(-\frac{\partial^2 L}{\partial\theta_i \partial\theta_j}\right),$$

and the uninformative a priori distribution density is chosen proportional to the square root of the determinant of the Fisher information matrix:

$$g(\theta) \sim \det(I(\theta))^{\frac{1}{2}}.$$

In the case when a random variable X is observed, which is described by a normal distribution law $N(\mu, \sigma^2)$ with unknown parameters of mathematical expectation μ and variance σ, the logarithmic probability has the following form:

$$L(\theta|x) = -\frac{n}{2}\ln(2\pi) - n\ln\sigma - \frac{1}{2\sigma^2}\sum(x_i - \mu)^2,$$

where $\theta = (\mu, \sigma)$, i $x = (x_1, x_2, \dots, x_n)$.

Then the elements of Fisher's information matrix are determined by the following formulas:

$$I_{11}(\theta) = \frac{\partial^2 L}{\partial \mu^2} = -\frac{n}{\sigma^2},$$

$$I_{12}(\theta) = I_{21}(\theta) = \frac{\partial^2 L}{\partial \mu \partial \sigma} = -\frac{2}{\sigma^3}\sum(x_i - \mu),$$

$$I_{22}(\theta) = \frac{\partial^2 L}{\partial \sigma^2} = \frac{n}{\sigma^2} - \frac{3}{\sigma^4}\sum(x_i - \mu)^2,$$

from which it follows that the uninformative a priori density of the distribution, which is chosen according to the "general rule" is $g(\mu, \sigma) \sim det(I(\theta))^{1/2} \sim 1/\sigma^2$, which does not coincide with the previously proposed choice $g(\sigma) = 1/\sigma$. To resolve this contradiction, Jeffries proposed that the mathematical expectation μ and variance σ should be considered independent a priori and thus treated independently of each other. When the general rule is used at a fixed value of σ, we get a uniform prior distribution with respect to μ as a result, and when it is used at a fixed value of μ, we get $g(\sigma) \sim 1/\sigma$.

More common is the situation when there is some information about the unknown parameter θ, but it is not enough to accurately determine the a priori distribution function. In such situations, in the process of transforming this incomplete a priori information into an a priori distribution function, there is always a danger of introducing additional subjective information that does not belong to the available a priori information.

A priori information is mostly used to determine a specific distribution function from some selected class of distribution functions. According to this method, a class of distribution functions is first selected, and then a specific distribution function is selected from it by selecting the values of its parameters so that they correspond to a priori values of the moments or quantiles. For example, when studying the safety level of a reactor, the upper and lower limits of component failure intensities are first evaluated, and then the parameters of the lognormal distribution function are selected so that these limits correspond to the 95% and 5% percentiles of this distribution function. This example shows that the choice of a class of distribution functions is a clear introduction of additional subjective information that does not belong to the available a priori information.

To prevent the introduction of additional subjectivism when choosing an a priori distribution function, it was suggested in Jeffreys (1961), Bennet and Martz (1972), and Bernardo (1998) to use the principle of maximum entropy. According to this principle, the a priori density $g(\theta)$ of the parameter θ distribution is chosen to provide the maximum Shannon–Jaynes entropy value

$$H(g) = -\int^{\int} g(\theta)\, ln(g(\theta))d\theta \rightarrow \max$$

among all distribution functions that satisfy the available a priori information:

$$S(g(\theta)) = 0,$$

where $S(g(\theta))$ is a functional restriction on $g(\theta)$, resulting from the available a priori information. The maximum entropy principle ensures the selection of an a priori distribution function that would be as uninformative as possible given partial a priori information.

The above results were obtained for the case of the absence of any a priori information about the unknown parameter θ. Bernardo (1998) extends these results to the case when some a priori information is available, for example, it is known that the a priori density of the distribution belongs to some class Q.

The following concept is used below.

DEFINITION 6.1.– Any positive function $g(\theta)$ such that for some $c(x) > 0$, all $\theta \in \Theta$ and the distribution of the random variable $p(x, \theta)$, the identity holds

$$g(\theta|x) = c(x)p(x|\theta)g(\theta),$$

which is called the reference a priori density for the parameter θ.

In Jeffreys (1961), it was shown that when the class Q of a priori distribution densities can be represented in the form of constraints

$$\int h_i(\theta)\, g(\theta)d\theta = \beta_i, \quad i = 1, \dots, m,$$

then reference a priori density of the parameter θ distribution Q has the form

$$g^Q(\theta) \sim g(\theta) \exp\left\{\sum_{i=1}^{m} \lambda_i h_i(\theta)\right\},$$

where $g(\theta)$ is the reference a priori density of the distribution of the parameter θ, which is obtained in the absence of any a priori information, and the constants λ_i are determined from the constraints that describe the class Q.

The experience of using Bayesian procedures shows that it is almost impossible to accurately determine the a priori distribution function based on the available a priori information. In practice, a priori information is obtained from both objective and subjective sources. The objective sources are the results of previous experiments, which were conducted with the same or similar equipment, historical data related to previous operation, reference data, etc. Subjective data are generated by polling experts for the values of various numerical characteristics of the prior distribution function, such as moments and/or quantiles.

Unfortunately, the volume of such data, as a rule, is not enough to accurately determine the a priori distribution function. Therefore, when implementing Bayesian methods, we do not have to deal with one a priori distribution function, but with a whole class Γ of such functions. Each distribution function from this class has the same reason to be chosen as a priori. If for each distribution function from the class Γ we calculate the value of a certain posterior function (e.g. posterior risk, mathematical expectation, etc.), we will get a whole range of such values.

This range of values is used as a measure of robustness (e.g. Vidakovic 2000). A narrow range means that the value of the posterior function does not change significantly with any choice of the prior distribution function from the specified class, that is, it is robust to the choice of the prior distribution function. And vice versa, when this range is wide, the value of the posterior function is sensitive to the choice of the a priori distribution function, that is, it is not robust. The methods of solving these optimization problems depend on the type of classes Γ of distribution functions.

Further, we consider a class of distribution functions that can be represented by the following linear constraints:

$$\int_{\Theta} dH(\theta) = 1,$$

$$\int_{\Theta} f_i(\theta) dH(\theta) \leq d_i, i = 1,2, \ldots, m_1,$$

$$\int_{\Theta} g_j(\theta)dH(\theta) = \mu_j,\ j = 1, \dots, m_2,$$

where functions $f_i(\theta),\ i = 1,2, \dots, m_1,\ g_j(\theta),\ j = 1,2, \dots, m_2,$ may be discontinuous.

If the parametric space is one dimensional, $\Theta = [a, b]$, and the functions $g_j(\theta) = \theta^j,\ j = 1,2, \dots, m_2$, then this class consists of all distribution functions that have given moment restrictions. If $f_i(\theta),\ i = 1,2, \dots, m_1$, are indicative functions for some intervals of the parametric space $\Theta = [a, b]$, then this class consists of all distribution functions that have given restrictions on quantiles.

Below, we focus on two cases of optimization of linear functionals in the class of distribution functions that have fixed moments or given quantile restrictions.

6.3.2.1. *Algorithms for the optimization of linear functionals in the class of distribution functions with fixed m moments*

Consider the problem of minimization of the functional

$$\phi(H) = \int_a^b f_0(x)dH(x) \qquad [6.1]$$

with restrictions

$$\int_a^b dH(x) = 1, \int_a^b x^i dH(x) = \mu_i, i = 1, \dots, m, \quad -\infty < a < b < \infty. \qquad [6.2]$$

We denote by $K_m(a, b)$ the set of distribution functions that satisfy [6.1]. Let us consider only the case when $f_0(x)$ is semicontinuous from below. The solution of problem [6.1]–[6.2] is achieved on the step distribution function, in which the number of jumps does not exceed $m + 1$. The following algorithm is proposed to solve our problem.

At the sth iteration, we construct a division $R_s = (x_1, x_2, \dots, x_{n_s})$ of the segment $[a, b]$ so that intervals of length r_s centered at points $x_i \in [a, b],\ i = 1, \dots, n_s$ cover the segment $[a, b]$; $a = x_1 \le x_2 \le \dots \le x_{n_s} = b$; $R_s \subset R_{s+1}$ and $r_s \to 0$ at $s \to \infty$.

Then, we solve the problem of linear programming:

$$\sum_{j=1}^{n_s} f_0(x_j)p_j \to \min \qquad [6.3]$$

with restrictions

$$\sum_{j=1}^{n_s} p_j = 1, \sum_{j=1}^{n_s} x_j^i p_j = \mu_i, i = 1,2, \ldots, m,\ p_j \geq 0, x_j \in R_s, j = 1,2, \ldots, n_s. \qquad [6.4]$$

Let $p^s = (p_1^s, p_2^s, \ldots, p_{n_s}^s)$ be the solution of problem [6.3]–[6.4]. Since the number of basic variables in problem [6.3]–[6.4] is $m + 1$, no more than $m + 1$ components of the vector p^s can be non-zero. Without loss of generality, we can assume that the first $m + 1$ components $p_1^s, p_2^s, \ldots, p_{m+1}^s$ are non-zero.

Therefore, it is possible to present the solution of problem [6.3]–[6.4] in the following form:

$$H_s(x) = (x_1^s, \ldots, x_{m+1}^s, p_1^s, \ldots, p_{m+1}^s), \qquad [6.5]$$

where the base variable p_i^s corresponds to a point x_i^s and the corresponding base column $(1, x_i^s, (x_i^s)^2, \ldots, (x_i^s)^m)'$.

On the other hand, [6.5] can be considered as the representation of the distribution function $H_s(x)$, which has a jump p_i^s at a point x_i^s, $i = 1,2, \ldots, m$.

We will use the solution $H_s(x)$ that was found on the sth iteration as the initial basic variables when solving problems [6.3]–[6.4] on the $(s + 1)$-th iteration. The convergence of the described procedure is based on the following statement (e.g. Golodnikov et al. 2009).

THEOREM 6.1.– Suppose that

1) The function $f_0(x)$ in [6.1] is semicontinuous from below, is bounded on the segment $[a, b]$ and has a finite number of discontinuity points.

2) The point $(\mu_1, \ldots, \mu_m)$ in [6.2] is an interior point of the moment space.

Then

$$\lim_{s \to \infty} \phi(H_s) = \phi(H^*)$$

and the limit of any convergent subsequence $\{H_{s_k}\}$ of the sequence $\{H_s\}$ belongs to the set X^*, where

$$X^* = \left\{H^*(x) : \phi(H^*) = \min_{H(x) \in K_m(a,b)} \phi(H)\right\}.$$

6.3.2.2. *Optimization of linear functionals under quantile constraints*

When solving many applied estimation and optimization problems, the constraints on the distribution function have a quite simple structure. Very often, a class of distribution functions with fixed quantiles is considered, for example, with two fixed quantiles: γ_1-quantile x_{γ_1} and γ_2-quantile x_{γ_2}. If the distribution function $H(x)$ is continuous, then its γ -quantile $(0 < \gamma < 1)$ coincides with the root of the equation

$$H(x_\gamma) = \gamma.$$

If the function $H(x)$ is discontinuous, then γ-quantile does not exist for every γ, that is, as a rule, given γ will be found only such x_γ, that

$$H(x_\gamma - 0) \le \gamma < H(x_\gamma + 0).$$

To investigate the sensitivity of Bayesian estimates to the choice of an a priori distribution function belonging to some class of functions Γ, it is necessary to learn to find the lower and upper bounds of the range of possible values of the target functional. A natural choice of the target functional can be the mathematical expectation of the parameter θ at fixed sample values x

$$\int_\Theta \theta \, dG(\theta|x) = \frac{\int_\Theta \theta \, f(x|\theta) dH(\theta)}{\int_\Theta f(x|\theta) dH(\theta)}.$$

In the case where a quadratic loss function is used, this target functional coincides with the Bayesian estimate of the parameter being estimated. If we calculate the value of the Bayesian estimate for any prior distribution function, we get a range of possible values. The width of this range is a measure of the sensitivity of the Bayesian estimator to the choice of the prior distribution.

Let us consider the problem of estimation on the example of the exponential distribution of equipment failures. Thus, the following problem of minimization of the fractional-linear functional is considered:

$$\phi(H) = \frac{\psi_1(H)}{\psi_2(H)} = \frac{\int_0^\infty \lambda^{s+1} e^{-\lambda t} dH(\lambda)}{\int_0^\infty \lambda^s e^{-\lambda t} dH(\lambda)} \to \inf_{H \in \Gamma}, \qquad [6.6]$$

where λ is the parameter of the exponential distribution with which equipment failure is modeled, and t is the duration of the time interval during which failures are observed; $H(\lambda)$ is a priori distribution function of the parameter λ, about which it is known only that it belongs to the class Γ.

In a non-degenerate case, the denominator of the functional [6.6] is strictly positive, so it exists

$$u^* = \inf_{H\in\Gamma} \frac{\int_0^\infty x^{s+1} e^{-xt} dH(x)}{\int_0^\infty x^s e^{-xt} dH(x)}, \qquad [6.7]$$

If there is a smallest value (exact lower bound) of the fractional-linear functional [6.7] equal to u^*, then problem [6.6] is equivalent to the following problem:

$$\inf_{H\in\Gamma} \psi(H) = \inf_{H\in\Gamma} [\psi_1(H) - u^*\psi_2(H)] = 0. \qquad [6.8]$$

Since the functional $\phi(H)$ is positive and bounded from above, there will be a number $b > 0$ such that any value $H \in \Gamma$ of the functional $\phi(H)$ belongs to the segment $[0, b]$. Considering these remarks, the algorithm for solving problem [6.8] is given as follows:

Step 1. Let $s = 1$; $a_1^0 = 0$; $a_2^0 = b$.

Step 2. Calculate the value

$$u_s = \frac{a_1^{s-1} + a_2^{s-1}}{2}.$$

Step 3. Solve the problem

$$w_s = \inf_{H\in\Gamma} [\psi_1(H) - u_s\psi_2(H)].$$

Step 4. If $w_s = 0$, then a solution to problem [6.8] has been found. Otherwise:

– If $w_s > 0$, then we assume that $a_1^s = u_s$, $a_2^s = a_2^{s-1}$.

– If $w_s < 0$, then we assume that $a_1^s = a_1^{s-1}$, $a_2^s = u_s$.

Put $s = s + 1$ and proceed to step 2.

It follows from the results of Vidakovic (2000), that in the case when the class consists of all distribution functions with two given quantiles, the solution to problem [6.6] is achieved (or as close as you like) on step distribution functions with no more than three growth points. Therefore, when solving problem [6.6], we will further consider only the class Γ_3 of all three-stage distribution functions $H(x) = (x_1, x_2, x_3, p_1, p_2, p_3)$ in which the γ_1-quantile is equal to x_{γ_1} and the γ_2-quantile is equal to x_{γ_2}. Here, x_i is the growth point, the jump which is equal to p_i.

Thus, when solving problem [6.6] using the modified algorithm, it is enough at step 3 to solve the following problem:

$$w_s = \inf_{H \in \Gamma_3} [\psi_1(H) - u_s \psi_2(H)].$$

Below we will focus on one more approach related to solving quantile regression problems. In general, quantile regression is a generalization of classical regression. It (unlike classical regression) can be used even in cases where the type of data distribution differs from normal. In this sense, quantile regression is a non-parametric method. At the same time, for the use of this method, it is assumed that the variance can be a variable value, while classical regression requires a constant value of this statistical indicator.

Let Y be a random variable, $F_Y(y) = P(Y \leq y)$ is its distribution function and γ is a fixed number, $0 \leq \gamma \leq 1$.

Let us define the quantile function

$$Q_Y(\gamma) = F_Y^{-1}(\gamma) = \inf\{y | F_Y(y) \geq \gamma\}.$$

Consider a random sample $Y_1, \dots, Y_n$ from the empirical distribution function $\hat{F}_Y(y)$ and the empirical γ-quantile function

$$\hat{Q}_Y(\gamma) = \hat{F}_Y^{-1}(\gamma) = \inf\{y | \hat{F}_Y(y) \geq \gamma\}.$$

This function can be constructed by solving the following optimization problem:

$$\hat{Q}_Y(\gamma) = \arg\min_y \left\{ \sum_{i|Y_i \geq y} \gamma |Y_i - y| + \sum_{i|Y_i < y} (1-\gamma) |Y_i - y| \right\}$$

at different values of γ from the interval $0 \leq \gamma \leq 1$.

If the number of observations is large enough, then using this formula for different values from the interval $0 \leq \gamma \leq 1$, we can construct an empirical distribution function and determine all its parameters. However, with small samples, this approach cannot be used.

In Koenker and Bassett (1978), the γ-quantile regression function is considered, which generalizes the empirical γ-quantile function to the case when Y is a linear function of $K+1$ independent variables $\vec{x}' = [1, x_1, \dots, x_K]$

$$Y = \vec{x}'\vec{\beta} + \varepsilon, \qquad [6.9]$$

where $\vec{\beta}' = [\beta_0, \beta_1, ..., \beta_K]$ is the vector of linear function coefficients, and ε is a random error, whose mathematical expectation is zero. A random error is introduced into a regression to model excess variability or scatter in the dependent variable Y that cannot be explained by the independent variables $x_1, ..., x_K$. This error models the cumulative effect of variables that cannot be measured or predicted. Thus, γ is the quantile regression function and can be written as

$$Q_Y(\gamma|\vec{x}) = \inf\{y|F_Y(y|\vec{x}) \geq \gamma\} \equiv \vec{x}'\vec{\beta}_\gamma,$$

where $\vec{x}' = (1, x_1, ..., x_{1K})$ is a vector of independent variables, and $\vec{\beta}_\gamma = (\beta_0^\gamma, \beta_1^\gamma, ..., \beta_K^\gamma)'$ is a vector of coefficients of function [6.9], which can be found by minimizing the normalized Koenker–Basset error (e.g. Koenker and Bassett 1978):

$$\frac{1}{n}\left\{\sum_{i:Y_i \geq \vec{x}_i'\vec{\beta}_\gamma} \frac{\gamma}{(1-\gamma)}\left|Y_i - \vec{x}_i'\vec{\beta}_\gamma\right| + \sum_{i:Y_i \leq \vec{x}_i'\vec{\beta}_\gamma} \left|Y_i - \vec{x}_i'\vec{\beta}_\gamma\right|\right\}.$$

6.4. Conclusion

The probability of failure is the main indicator of the reliability of complex systems and their components. In the conditions of operation of high-tech industries, the probability of failure of each individual system is very small. However, such an unlikely failure can lead to catastrophic consequences. The analysis of critical man-made situations showed that the main factors affecting the occurrence of accidents are the imperfection of production technologies, structural miscalculations in technological equipment and an insufficiently substantiated maintenance strategy for objects with a high level of environmental danger.

One of the important stages of the methodology of probabilistic analysis of the security level is the evaluation of the parameters characterizing the reliability of the equipment. The accuracy of the estimates of reliability indicators obtained at this stage greatly affects the level of validity of criteria, requirements and conditions regarding safety.

Bayesian evaluation procedures require an accurate definition of the a priori distribution function, which accumulates all available a priori information about the equipment reliability parameters. But when analyzing high-reliability equipment, researchers are usually faced with limited information that is not sufficient to accurately determine the a priori distribution function. Therefore, under conditions of limited information, the use of the traditional Bayesian approach to estimate equipment reliability parameters is the weakest point in the existing methodology of probabilistic safety analysis. This work considers approaches that will allow us to overcome the mentioned difficulties. Other approaches to assessing the risk of unwanted situations are given, for example, in works by Butenko et al. (2005), Atoyev et al. (2017), Norkin et al. (2018), Ermoliev et al. (2022a, 2022b) and Zagorodny et al. (2024).

6.5. Acknowledgments

The development of the methodologies and models is supported by a joint project between the International Institute for Applied Systems Analysis (IIASA) and the National Academy of Sciences of Ukraine (NASU) on "Integrated robust modeling and management of food–energy–water–land use nexus for sustainable development (22-501). Moreover, this work was supported by the projects 0122U000552 and 2.3/25-P of the National Academy of Sciences of Ukraine.

6.6. References

Atoyev, A., Knopov, P., Pepeliaev, V., Kisala, P., Romaniuk, R., Kalimoldayev, M. (2017). The mathematical problems of complex systems investigation under uncertainties. In *Recent Advances in Information Technology*, Wojcik, W. and Sikora, J. (eds). CRC Press/Balkema, Taylor & Francis Group, London.

Barlow, R.E. and Lambert, H.E. (1975). Introduction to fault tree analysis. In *Reliability and Fault Tree Analysis*, Barlow, R.E., Fussel, I.B., Singpurwalla, N.D. (eds). SIAM, Philadelphia.

Bennet, G.K. and Martz, H.F. (1972). A continuous empirical bayes smoothing technique. *Biometrika*, 59, 361–368.

Bernardo, J.M. (1998). Bayesian reference analysis. A postgraduate tutorial course [Online]. Available at: https://www.uv.es/~bernardo/Monograph.pdf [Accessed 4 November 2024].

Butenko, S., Golodnikov, A., Uryasev, S. (2005). Optimal security liquidation algorithms. *Comput Optim Applic*, 32, 9–27.

Carota, C. and Ruggeri, F. (1994). Robust Bayesian analysis given priors on partition sets. *Test*, 3, 73–86.

Department of Nuclear Energy Brookhaven National Laboratory (1984). Probabilistic safety analysis procedures guide (NUREG/CR-2815) [Online]. Available at: https://www.nrc.gov/reading-rm/doc-collections/nuregs/contract/cr2815/index.html [Accessed 9 November 2024].

Ermoliev, Y., Zagorodny, A., Bogdanov, V., Ermolieva, T., Havlik, P., Rovenskaya, E., Komendantova, N., Obersteiner, M. (2022a). Linking distributed optimization models for food, water, and energy security nexus management. *Sustainability*, 14(3), 1255.

Ermoliev, Y., Zagorodny, A.G., Bogdanov, V.L., Ermolieva, T., Havlik, P., Rovenskaya, E., Komendantova, N., Obersteiner, M. (2022b). Robust food-energy-water-environmental security management: Stochastic quasigradient procedure for linkage of distributed optimization models under asymmetric information and uncertainty. *Cybern Syst Anal*, 58(1), 45–57.

Fussel, I.B. (1988). Computer aided fault tree construction for electrical systems. *IEEE Trans. Reliability*, R-37, 37–56.

Golodnikov, A.N., Knopov, P.S., Pepelyaev, V.A. (2004). Estimation of reliability parameters under incomplete primary information. *Theor Decis*, 57, 331–344.

Golodnikov, A.N., Knopov, P.S., Pepelyaev, V.A. (2009). *Robust Risk Assessment*. V.M. Gluskov Institute of Cybernetics, Kyiv.

Golodnikov, A.N., Ermoliev, Y.M., Knopov, P.S. (2010). Estimating reliability parameters under insufficient information. *Cybern Syst Anal*, 46, 443–459.

Golodnikov, A., Kuzmenko, V., Uryasev, S. (2019). CVaR regression based on the relation between CVaR and mixed-quantile quadrangles. *J. Risk Financial Manag.*, 12, 107.

Idaho National Engineering Laboratory (1989). A review of the three mile Island-1 Probabilistic Risk Assessment (NUREG/CR-5457) [Online]. Available at: https://www.nrc.gov/reading-rm/doc-collections/nuregs/contract/cr5457/index.html [Accessed 9 November 2024].

IEEE (1983). *A Guide to the Performance of Probabilistic Risk Assessments for Nuclear Power Plants*. The Institute of Electrical and Electronics Engineers, New York.

Jeffreys, H. (1961). *Theory of Probability*, 3rd edition. Clarendon Press, Oxford.

Koenker, R. and Bassett, G. Jr. (1978). Regression quantiles. *Econometrica*, 46, 33–50.

Konda, T. (1989). Tinding modules in fault trees. *IEEE Trans. Reliability*, R-38, 165–176.

Kovalenko, I.N. and Kuznetsov, N.Y. (1988). *Methods for Calculating Highly Reliable Systems*. Radio i Sviaz, Moscow.

Kovalenko, I.N. and Kuznetsov, N.Y. (1997). *Mathematical Theory of Reliability of Time-Dependent Systems with Practical Applications*. Wiley, Chichester.

Kuznetsov, N.Y. (1985). General approach to determine the probability of failfree operation of compound systems by an analytical-statistical method. *Cybern Syst Anal*, 21, 380–391.

Kuznetsov, N.Y. (1994). Fault trees – Problems and the modern state of investigations. *Cybern Syst Anal*, 30, 419–439.

Martz, H.F. and Waller, R.A. (1991). *Bayesian Reliability Analysis*. Krieger Publishing Company, Malabar, FL.

Mikhalevich, V.S., Knopov, P.S., Golodnikov, A.N. (1994). Mathematical models and methods of risk assessment in ecologically hazardous industries. *Cybern Syst Anal*, 30, 259–273.

Norkin, V.I., Gaivoronski, A.A., Zaslavsky, V.A., Knopov, P.S. (2018). Models of the optimal resource allocation for the critical infrastructure protection. *Cybern Syst Anal*, 54, 696–706.

Pepelyaev, V.A., Golodnikov, A.N., Golodnikova, N.A. (2022a). Reliability optimization method alternative to bPOE. *Cybern Syst Anal*, 58, 593–597.

Pepelyaev, V.A., Golodnikov, A.N., Golodnikova, N.A. (2022b). A new method of reliability optimization in the classical problem statement. *Cybern Syst Anal*, 58, 917–922.

Ruggeri, F. and Sivaganesan, S. (2000). On a global sensitivity measure for Bayesian inference. *Sankhya: The Indian Journal of Statistics*, 62A(1), 110–127.

Vidakovic, B. (2000). Γ-Minimax: A paradigm for conservative robust Bayesians. In *Robust Bayesian Analysis*, Insua, D.R. and Ruggeri, F. (eds). Springer, New York.

Zagorodny, A., Bogdanov, V., Ermolieva, T., Komendantova, N. (2024). Modeling for managing food-energy-water-social-environmental – NEXUS security: Novel systems' analysis approaches. In *Nexus of Sustainability. Studies in Systems, Decision and Control*, Zagorodny, A., Bogdanov, V., Zaporozhets, A. (eds). Springer, Cham.

7

Application of the Type-Variety Principle in the Formation of a Complex of Non-Destructive Testing Technologies for Critical Infrastructure

In scientific and technical support of complex systems, critical facilities and critical infrastructures (CIs), the problem of defect detection is an important task. In order to effectively solve the problems of detecting various types of defects, increasing the probability of their detection in conditions of limited resources, this chapter proposes to purposefully use and combine various types of devices (according to the type-variety principle) that implement various non-destructive testing (NDT) methods, which determines the quality and cost of "diagnostic" solutions. The mechanism of the type-variety principle is the basis for the mathematical models presented in the work, computational procedures and an optimization algorithm for forming a set of NDT methods built on various physical bases. The developed approach to constructing type-variety sets of NDT methods, the formulated optimization problems and the algorithm for their optimization, emphasizing maximum reliability in defect detection alongside technical and economic parameters, such as sensitivity, suitability for different control facilities, time limitations and considerations of adverse diagnostic conditions, are used in forming sets of NDT devices to detect defects in units and systems of aircraft, NPPs, spacecraft and other CI objects. This can be used for various types of OC, as well as in training NDT specialists.

7.1. Introduction

In the scientific and technical support of complex systems, critical facilities and CIs, the task of defect detection presents specific challenges, as outlined by some

---

Chapter written by Volodymyr A. ZASLAVSKYI.

previous studies (Klyuev 1995; Hetman and Kozin 1997; Zaslavsky and Kadenko 1999, pp. 5–22; Zaslavsky et al. 2000, pp. 33–41):

– High stakes of defect detection: detecting defects is crucial, as even a small number of defects or their combinations can result in large-scale catastrophic consequences.

– Challenges in accessibility: certain control objects (COs) may be inaccessible to humans due to aggressive or harmful environments, necessitating the development of specialized methods and technologies for defect detection.

– Leveraging experience: effective NDT requires incorporating accumulated experience, which involves selecting appropriate sets of devices, technologies, rules and sequencing various NDT methods.

– NDT computerization: the computerization of NDT enhances control quality and facilitates the accumulation and transfer of data throughout the CO lifecycle stages.

This necessitates the systematic application of a specially designed suite of NDT methods, considered as tools for systemic research. These methods enable the execution of specific control tasks under varying modes and external conditions to detect a range of potential defects with corresponding result reliability. To address the diverse challenges of defect detection effectively, different types of devices and NDT methods are purposefully utilized, implementing the principle of heterotype. This approach directly influences the quality and cost of diagnostic solutions.

The complexity of systems throughout their lifecycle results in the emergence and accumulation of engineering and design errors, technological deviations and physical defects in structural elements. These issues diminish reliability and reduce the planned operational lifespan of such systems. Consequently, system risk management becomes critically important in lifecycle support. Addressing this requires a scientifically grounded program to ensure safety, eliminate errors and mitigate the aging processes of high-cost systems.

Such a program demands a thorough analysis and revision of existing approaches, alongside the development of new principles, models and decision-making procedures. These innovations are essential for effective defect detection, strategic maintenance planning and timely equipment replacement to sustain the system's operational integrity.

The following subsection applies the type-variety principle (Zaslavsky 2006, pp. 136–147) to develop optimization models for a suite of NDT methods, each with distinct physical principles. These models consider efficiency criteria alongside technical and economic constraints (Kadenko et al. 1999). The significance of integrating diverse NDT methods to enhance defect detection has been highlighted in previous studies (Hetman and Kozin 1997; Troitsky and Zagrebelny 1999, pp. 117–118).

7.2. Optimization algorithm for a heterogeneous set of non-destructive testing methods for defect detection in complex systems

Problem statement: let there be a known finite set of possible types of defects $D = \{d_l, l \in L = \{1, 2, ..., l^*\}\}$ that may be present in the OC (the complex system under investigation, such as a nuclear power plant (NPP) or spacecraft subsystems) or in individual elements. Let L be the set of indices of these defect types. Different defect types $d_l \in D$ are characterized by indicators such as potential hazard and geometric features (e.g. defect length, such as crack length, surface opening width, penetration depth, etc.).

Let us denote $f(d_l, w_l)$ as the distribution of the number of defects d_l in OC, where $w_l \in \left\{0, 1, ..., w_l^*\right\}$, $l \in L$, represents the possible number of defects, and w_l^* – denotes the maximum number (where $w_l = 0$ indicates the absence of defects in d_l in OC) (Klyuev 1995).

Let us denote $h(d_l)$ as an indicator of the potential probability of a defect $d_l \in D$ in OC (potential risk). Defects $d_l \in D$ can then be categorized into acceptable defects, for which $h(d_l) = 0$, and unacceptable defects $h(d_l) = 1$.

Various NDT methods and their types are used for diagnosing $d_l \in D$ defects, each with different probabilities of defect detection and resource expenditures during testing. Let $M_{jl} = \{m_{jk}, k \in K_{jl}\}$ denote the set of j-type NDT methods that can be used to detect defect d_l, where $j \in J_l \subseteq J$ is the set of NDT type indices and m_{jk} represents the kth modification of the j-type NDT, with $K_{jl} \subseteq K_j = \{1, 2, ..., k_j^*\}$ being the set of modification indices for the j-type NDT (see Figure 7.1).

Let $p_j(m_{jk}, d_l)$ denote the a priori probability of detecting defect $d_l \in D$ by method m_{jk}, and let $g_{il}(m_{jk}, d_l)$, $i \in I$ represent the corresponding resource costs. The values $p_j(m_{jk}, d_l)$, which indicate the probabilities of detecting different defect types, are specified in the technical documentation of the equipment, known from studies on similar OCs, or determined based on experimental research.

The construction of heterogeneous sets of NDT methods is carried out, taking into account a certain set of technologies, which are determined and developed based on the practice and specifics of the OC, as well as the strategies for their combination and integrated application. These technologies are selected for their appropriateness in defect detection D.

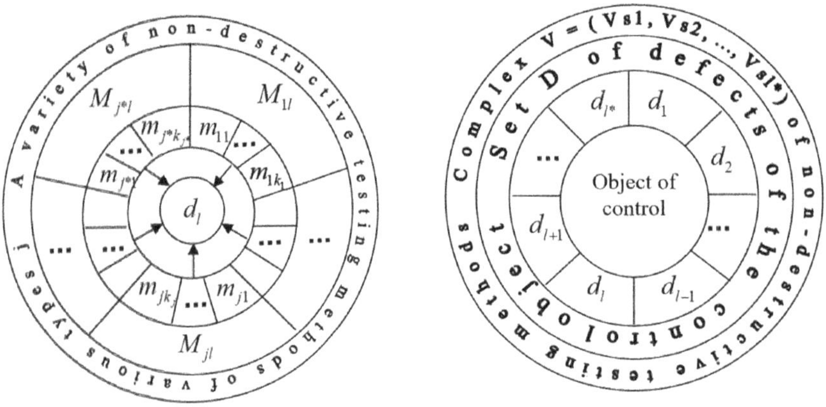

Figure 7.1. *Method for constructing the optimal composition of an NDT method complex for assessing the technical condition of CI aggregates and systems*

The set of alternative defect $d_l \in D$, $l \in L$ detection technologies for the NDT method complex is defined as follows:

$$S_l = \{\{j_1^1,...,j_{r_1}^1\},\{j_1^2,...,j_{r_2}^2\},...,\{j_1^{\tau_l},...,j_{r_{\tau_l}}^{\tau_l}\}, j_1^1,...,j_{r_1}^1, j_1^2,...,j_{r_2}^2,...,j_1^{\tau_l},...,j_{r_{\tau_l}}^{\tau_l} \in J_l\}$$

The elements of S_l are combinations of indices $j_1,...,j_r \in J_l \subseteq J$ of various types of NDT methods $M_{j_1 l},...,M_{j_r l}$, which define a fixed inspection technology. Thus, each combination $s_l = \{j_1,...,j_r\} \in S_l$ represents a specific technology for detecting defect $d_l \in D$, involving certain types of NDT methods. This approach accounts for the specifics of both OC (system components) and the equipment used to ensure effective testing.

Each technology $s_l \in S_l$ can be implemented with various modifications of methods $m_{jk} \in M_{jl}, j \in s_l$ and is represented by a possible option (NDT complex)

$v_{s_l} = (m_{j_1k_1},...,m_{j_rk_r}) \equiv (m_{jk})_{j \in s_l, k \in K_{jl}}$, used in detecting defect $d_l \in D$. Thus, $V_{s_l} = \prod_{j \in s_l} M_{jl}$ is the set of possible options for implementing technology $s_l \in S_l$, and $V_l = \bigcup_{s_l \in S_l} V_{s_l}$ represents the set of all alternative NDT complexes for detecting defect $d_l \in D$. Consequently, $V = \prod_{l \in L} V_l$ is the set of alternative NDT complexes $v = (v_{s_1},...,v_{s_l},...,v_{s_{l^*}}) \equiv (v_{s_l})_{l \in L}$, $v_{s_l} \in V_l, l \in L$, $v \in V = \prod_{l \in L} V_l$, which are used for detecting all defects $d_l \in D$.

An objective assessment of the technical condition of CI is significantly complicated by the interdependence of elements, which intensifies with prolonged operation. Under these conditions, to increase the reliability of technical condition monitoring of OC, the principle of "redundancy" (multi-type) control is employed.

This principle involves using various NDT methods of differing physical nature to evaluate the same parameter or defect, thereby implementing the principle of diversity in testing.

The probability of avoiding an emergency situation in OC after the detection and elimination of defect $d_l \in D$ is defined as follows (Davis et al. 1982):

$$P_l(p(v_{s_l}), h(d_l), f(d_l, w_l)) = \sum_{w_l=1}^{w_l^*} \left[(1 - h(d_l) \cdot (1 - p(v_{s_l}))\right]^{w_l} \cdot f(d_l, w_l), \quad [7.1]$$

where $p(v_{s_l})$ is the probability of detecting defect d_l, when using the set v_{s_l}, for technology s_l (considering that the sequential independent application of various methods and technologies increases the probability of defect detection), and is determined as follows:

$$p(v_{s_l}) = 1 - \prod_{j \in J_l} (1 - p_j(m_{jk}, d_l)). \quad [7.2]$$

If there is a possibility of a single unacceptable defect $d_l \in D$, occurring in OK, that is, $f(d_l, w_l) = 1$, $w_l = 1$, $h(d_l) = 1$, then expression [3.1] can be rewritten as follows (assuming that $f(d_l, 0) = 0$):

$$P_l(p(v_{s_l}), 1, f(d_l, 1)) = p(v_{s_l}) \quad [7.3]$$

Given that the control systems (CS) are nearing the end of their designated technical service life, the issue of defect detection and monitoring is especially critical for them. The time available for organizing and conducting NDT on CS is limited due to the requirements for preparation and execution of launches, and other resources are also constrained.

With prolonged operation of the CS, defects that arise may either worsen or remain minor. Therefore, within the set *D*, defects are distinguished by importance into critical and insignificant, allowing for consideration of the acceptability or unacceptability of their undetection. In this regard, the following formal formulations of optimization problems are considered in the analysis of this applied issue.

It is necessary to determine, for the set of possible defects *D*, an optimal complex of NDT methods (a set of instruments and their order of use) that will be most effective for detecting $d_l \in D$ defects.

– *Task 1*: in performing NDT, the failure to detect any defect is not permissible.

If we consider the task of detecting all defects from the set *D* simultaneously and assume that the values $h(d_l)$, $f(d_l, w_l)$, $w_l \in \{0,1,...,w_l^*\}$, $d_l \in D$ are known, and different $v_{s_l} \in V_l$ sets are used for their detection, then expression [3.1] can be rewritten as follows:

$$P_D(v, h_D, f_D) = \prod_{l \in L} P_l(p(v_{s_l}), h(d_l), f(d_l, w_l)), \tag{7.4}$$

where $v = (v_{s_1}, v_{s_2}, ..., v_{s_{l^*}}) \in V$, and $h_D = (h(d_1),...,h(d_l),...,h(d_{l^*}))$, $f_D = (f(d_1, w_1),..., f(d_l, w_l),..., f(d_{l^*}, w_{l^*}))$.

If in the CS the existence of one defect of each type is allowed, then [7.4], taking into account expression [7.3], can be rewritten as follows:

$$P_D(v, h_D, f_D) = \prod_{l \in L} p(v_{s_l}) \tag{7.5}$$

In terms of complex system design, the task of selecting an NDT complex has the following interpretation. The set of defects *D* is viewed as a set of subsystems (the l^* subsystems), which, in this case, form a "series system". The probability of reliable operation of this system is represented by equation [7.5], and the

$v = (v_{S_1}, v_{S_2}, ..., v_{S_{l}^{*}}) \in V$ complex represents a variant of the series system structure. The value of $P_D(v, h_D, f_D)$ serves as a lower bound for the probability of detecting the set of defects D.

Since the potential risk $h(d_l)$ in expression [3.2] is considered as the probability of defect $d_l \in D$ independently of the potential risks $h(d_k)$, $k \neq l$ of other defects $d_k \in D$, the simultaneous occurrence of certain combinations of two, three, etc., defects can differently impact the state of the CS. Therefore, for systems with a high cost of failure, accounting for these possible combinations is essential when assessing system operability, scheduling maintenance, determining required resources and evaluating economic impact.

This creates the need to gather data and solve the problem of detecting "critical" defects in the CS, which, in terms of determining potential risk $h(d_l)$, means that for critical elements $h(d_l)=1$ (i.e. those whose undetection is unacceptable). In this case, the set D is divided into two subsets: $D = D_k \cup D_d$, where D_k is the set of critical defects $h(d_l)$, and D_k is the set of acceptable defects.

Then, for the set of critical defects D_k, $h(d_l)=1$, $d_l \in D_k$, and for the set of acceptable defects $h(d_l)=0$, $d_l \in D_d$, expression [3.4] can be rewritten as follows:

$$P_{D_k \cup D_d}(v, (h_{D_k}, f_{D_k}), (h_{D_d}, f_{D_d})) = \prod_{l \in L_k} \left\{ \sum_{w_l=0}^{w_l^*} \left[(1-(1-p(v_{S_l})) \right]^{w_l} \cdot f(d_l, w_l) \right\} \cdot$$

$$\cdot \prod_{l \in L_d} \left\{ \sum_{w_l=0}^{w_l^*} f(d_l, w_l) \right\},$$

where L_k is the set of indices of critical defects $d_l \in D_k$, and L_d is the set of permissible/possible defects.

For $w_l = 1$ in the case of $d_l \in D_k$

$$P_{D_k \cup D_d}(v, (h_{D_k}, f_{D_k}), (h_{D_d}, f_{D_d})) = \prod_{l \in L_k} \left(p(v_{S_l}) \cdot f(d_l, 1) \right) \cdot \prod_{l \in L_d} f(d_l, 1) =$$

$$= A_{D_k} \cdot A_{D_d} \cdot \prod_{l \in L_k} p(v_{S_l}), \qquad [7.6]$$

where $A_{D_k} = \prod_{l \in L_k} f(d_l, 1)$, $A_{D_d} = \prod_{l \in L_d} f(d_l, 1)$.

Thus, equation [7.6] can be used as a criterion when forming an NDT complex for the simultaneous detection of all critical defects $d_l \in D_k$. Possible combinations of acceptable and unacceptable situations when detecting defects are not considered in this case, but in practice, this is important, as the occurrence of defect combinations is possible and may lead to negative, and sometimes catastrophic, consequences.

Thus, Task 1 involves forming an NDT complex in the case where it is necessary to detect simultaneously the entire set of unacceptable defects D, and the quality of defect detection is evaluated by the indicator $P_D(v, h_D, f_D)$.

At the same time, the CS may be a complex, geographically distributed system, with its elements potentially having large sizes, and its subsystems may be located at remote distances, etc. Therefore, it is necessary to prevent combinations of dangerous defects, which could be much fewer in number, from occurring.

For systems with a high cost of failure, the occurrence of combinations of 2, 3, or more defects, which, for example, are part of the set of critical elements D_k, may be unacceptable. Therefore, it is necessary to consider combinations of defects of different types. However, taking these factors into account requires refining the indicator [7.4] for the quality of defect detection.

– *Task 2*: when performing NDT, it is necessary to consider the possible combinations of different types of defects in the CS.

This task can be interpreted in terms of the reliability optimization problem of complex structured systems (monotonic and non-sequential systems) (Volkovich et al. 1992). For such systems, in general, the failure of individual subsystems does not always lead to an emergency situation or a system-wide failure. This means that the non-detection of some (insignificant) defects from the set D in the CS may be acceptable and not lead to dangerous consequences. In other words, the failure of an individual unit may be a minor event for the overall system's operability.

Let x_l, $l \in L$ be a Boolean variable such that:

$$x_l = \begin{cases} 0, & \textit{if it is permissible for a defect not to be detected } d_l \\ 1, & \textit{if it is not permissible for a defect not to be detected } d_l \end{cases}$$

Then $x = (x_1, \ldots, x_l, \ldots, x_{l^*}) \in X$ is a vector with l^* components that defines the possible combinations (states) of defect detection, where X is the set of all such combinations.

Let us define a Boolean indicator function $x \in X$ on the set of combinations $W(x)$ such that:

$$W(x) = \begin{cases} 0, \textit{if the combination } x \textit{ is not allowed for } OC, \\ 1, \textit{if the combination } x \textit{ is allowed for } OC. \end{cases}$$

For example, the state $x = (1,1,\ldots,1)$ means that no undetected defects are allowed in the CS. In this case, $W(x) = 1$ for $x = (0,0,\ldots,0)$ is true when no defects are present, and $W(x) = 0$ when $x = (1,\ldots,1,0_l,1,\ldots,1)$ – $W(x) = 1$ means that the defect d_l is insignificant.

In the general case, the values of $W(x)$ can be defined within the interval $0 \leq W(x) \leq 1$ and represent the indicator of the conditional probability of state x or the "weight" of the x combination.

It is necessary to form a version of the NDT complex $v = (v_{s_l})_{l \in L} \in \prod_{l \in L} V_l$ that has the maximum probability of detecting the set of defects ("covers the entire set D") while considering the specified resource constraints b_i, $i \in I = \{1,\ldots,i^*\}$ allocated for forming the complex.

The mathematical model for the problem of selecting the NDT complex for the set of defects D in the general case is formulated as follows:

$$\begin{gathered} P_D(v) = P_D(P_1(p(v_{s_1}), h(d_1), f(d_1, w_1)), \ldots, \\ P_l(p(v_{s_l}), h(d_l), f(d_l, w_l)), \ldots, P_{l^*}(p(v_{s_{l^*}}), h(d_{l^*}), f(d_{l^*}, w_{l^*}))) \to \max, \end{gathered} \quad [7.7]$$

under restrictions

$$G_i(v) = G_i(g_{i1}(v_{s_1}), \ldots, g_{il}(v_{s_l}), \ldots, g_{il^*}(v_{s_{l^*}})) \leq b_i, \; i \in I, \quad [7.8]$$

$$v = (v_{s_1}, v_{s_2}, \ldots, v_{s_{l^*}}) \in V = \prod_{l \in L} V_l. \quad [7.9]$$

From now on, the vector $v = (v_{s_l})_{l \in L} \in V$ will be called a possible least squares complex for the set of defects *D*, and v_{s_l} will be referred to as a set for defect detection d_l when using the $s_l \in S_l$ technology.

A possible complex $v \in V$, that satisfies the constraints [7.8] is called acceptable, and an acceptable complex v^*, that maximizes the criterion [7.7] is called the optimal complex or the optimal solution to the problem [7.7]–[7.9].

The criterion [7.7], considering the notation for states x and $W(x)$, is represented as follows:

$$P_D(v) = \sum_{x \in X} W(x) \prod_{l \in L} \left[P_l(p(v_{s_l}), h(d_l), f(d_l, w_l)) \right]^{x_l} \times \\ \times \left[1 - P_l(p(v_{s_l}), h(d_l), f(d_l, w_l)) \right]^{1-x_l} \rightarrow \max . \quad [7.10]$$

In the case where $d_l \in D$ and $h(d_l) = 0,\ w_l^* = 1$ the criterion for the problem of selecting the optimal multi-type NDT complex takes the following form:

$$P_D(v) = \max_{v \in V} \left\{ \sum_{x \in X} W(x) \prod_{l \in L} p(v_{s_l})^{x_l} (1 - p(v_{s_l}))^{1-x_l} \right\} \quad [7.11]$$

For defects of increased hazard, requirements $p_l^*,\ l \in L$ can be set for their detection probability in CS systems. In this case, the following constraint is added to the model [7.7]–[7.9]:

$$p(v_{s_l}) \geq p_l^*, l \in L, \quad [7.12]$$

which sets additional requirements for forming the $v_{s_l} \in V_l$ complex.

In the constraints [7.8], the values of $b_i,\ i \in I$ are determined based on available resources but must be sufficient to carry out NDT operations, as cost savings may lead to emergency situations and be accompanied by losses that could be incomparably greater than the costs of performing the NDT.

When considering and taking into account the technical and economic indicators of the NDT complex, issues arise related to the formulation of constraints in optimization problems.

1) The resource indicators $G_i(v),\ i \in I$ for the $v \in V$ complex are determined, for example, by the total cost of the instruments that make up the V complex, the cost of control using the methods included in the NDT complex; they depend on the $s_l \in S_l$ technology, auxiliary operations that accompany the inspection, energy and facility usage costs, the cost of spare parts, potential losses due to over-inspection, etc.

2) In the case where different methods and technologies $d_l \in D$ can be used to detect a single defect $s_l \in S_l$, the following optimization problem is considered:

$$p(v_{s_l}) \to \max,$$

$$g_{il}(v_{s_l}) \le b_{il}, \quad i \in I,$$

$$v_{s_l} \in V_l.$$

In this case, a separate complex is formed for $d_l \in D$.

3) If a separate group of methods and technologies $d_l \in D$ is used for detecting each type of defect $s_l \in S_l$, in this case, the total resource $b_i,\ i \in I$ is allocated to create individual complexes (subsystems) used for detecting specific types of defects. The complexes formed in this way have independent compositions and are applied separately, for example, by different teams or individual specialists. This management approach in forming the complex may be beneficial when performing NDT for geographically distributed systems.

In practice, the indicators $G_i(v),\ i \subset I$ are often considered as additive functions of the form (Volkovich et al. 1992):

$$G_i(v) = \sum_{l \in L} g_{il}(v_{s_l}), \quad i \in I,$$

where $g_{il}(v_{s_l})$ are the resource indicators of the $v_{s_l} = (m_{jk})_{j \in s_l}$ complex, which are determined as follows:

$$g_{il}(v_{s_l}) = \sum_{j \in s_l} g_{il}(m_{jk}, d_l), \quad i \in I,\ l \in L.$$

4) If there is a frequent need to simultaneously inspect multiple identical OKs in practice, the question arises of creating "backup NDT complexes", and their construction involves its own optimization problems.

5) To detect different types of defects $d_l \in D$, NDT methods can be used together, meaning that the same m_{jk} method can be applied to detect various types of $d_{l_1}, d_{l_2}, \ldots, d_{l_s} \in D$ defects. Therefore, this must be taken into account when formulating the constraints of the optimization problems [7.7]–[7.9].

To detect different defects from a certain set of defects $D' \subseteq D$, a group of NDT methods may be used, which also needs to be considered when constructing the overall NDT complex variant for the entire OC.

The consideration of the aforementioned methods for constructing and using NDT complexes for defect detection and their optimization requires conducting research and adapting exclusion procedures (for unpromising solutions) to the specific constraints of such problems.

The formulated problem ([7.7]–[7.9]) is a special two-level problem of discrete monotonic programming with large dimensionality (Volkovich et al. 1992) and is considered in this formulation for the first time. The relevance of such a problem was highlighted in Hetman and Kozin (1997). This problem ([7.7]–[7.9]) can be viewed in a multi-criteria formulation.

The application of standard discrete optimization methods is limited for solving it, because first, the objective function [7.2] is a non-separable function of the discrete argument, and second, the problem has many constraints and variables (complexes), which are formed according to a specific mechanism (defined by the technologies $s_l \in S_l$, $l \in L$ and the use of NDT methods).

The explicit construction of the V_l, $l \in L$ set of possible solutions is not feasible due to their large number, and therefore, the application of known "single-level" discrete programming methods (such as dynamic programming; Bellman and Dreyfus 1965) and other methods (Volkovich et al. 1984; Alekseev 1987; Zaslavsky 1988, pp. 72–77) is complicated.

To solve the problems [7.8], [7.9] and [7.11], a two-level algorithmic scheme is used, which is based on the method of sequential analysis and elimination of variants (based on rules and procedures for excluding unpromising and suboptimal solutions (Volkovich et al. 1992). This method was developed for solving the problem of multi-type redundancy (Volkovich and Zaslavsky 1986, pp. 54–61) and generalized in the study of maintenance planning tasks and optimization of multi-level complex systems (Zaslavsky 1988, pp. 72–77; Volkovich et al. 1992). The use of the specified method requires the specification of mechanisms for forming sets of possible solutions at each level and taking into account the type and properties of the criterion and constraint functions. According to the general scheme of the sequential analysis method of variants (Volkovich et al. 1992), we consider the adaptation of procedures for analyzing and eliminating variants of complexes, as well as the rules for calculating tolerances at the first and second levels to narrow down the sets of possible solutions and form an aggregated problem.

When solving the problems [7.8], [7.9] and [7.11] at the first level, tolerances at the first level are computed for the sets V_l based on resources (using the E_1 procedure), and tolerances at the second level are determined for the elements of the sets M_{jk} based on resources (using the E_2 procedure). Using the computed tolerances, exclusion is carried out by the following:

– Types of $m_{jl} \in M_{jk}$ that form different complexes $v_{s_l} \in V_{s_l}$ for detecting the defect d_l, which leads to narrowing down the sets V_{s_l}, and therefore V_l, $l \in L$.

– Possible technologies $s_l \in S_l$, which leads to narrowing down the sets V_{s_l} and V_l, $l \in L$.

The first-level tolerances for the set V_l based on the i-resource are calculated as follows (Volkovich et al. 1992):

$$g_i^l = b_i - \min_{g_{il}^{s_l} \in H_{g_{il}}(V_{s_l})} G_i \ (g_{i1}(v_{s_1}^*), \ldots, g_{il-1}(v_{s_{l-1}}^*), g_{il}^{s_l}, g_{il+1}(v_{s_{l+1}}^*), \ldots, g_i(v_{s_{l^*}}^*)), \ i \in I, \qquad [7.13]$$

where $v^* = \arg\min_{v \in V} G_i(v)$, $i \in I$ and $H_{g_{il}}(V_{s_l}) = \{g_{il}^{s_l} \,|\, g_{il}^{s_l} \equiv g_{il}(v_{s_l}),\ v_{s_l} \in V_{s_l}\}$, $i \in I$ is the set of values of the function $g_{il}(v_{s_l})$ on the variants $v_{s_l} \in V_{s_l}$.

The calculated tolerances g_i^l, $i \in I$, $l \in L$ are used in the following subsystems of constraints, through which the analysis of the sets V_l based on the tolerances g_i^l is carried out (Volkovich et al. 1992):

$$g_{il}(v_{s_l}) \le g_i^l, \ i \in I, \qquad [7.14]$$

$$v_{s_l} \in V_l. \qquad [7.15]$$

Let $Q_l = \{g_i^l, i \in I\}$, $l \in L$ be the set of tolerances for the constraint subsystems [7.14] and [7.15] and $Q = \bigcup_{l \in L} Q_l$ be the tolerance system. A preference relation $Q_l = \{g_i^l, i \in I\}$ is defined on the sets of tolerances "$\succ$". The set of tolerances $Q_l^1 = \{g_i^{1l}, i \in I\}$ is preferred over $Q_l^2 = \{g_i^{2l}, i \in I\}$, denoted as $Q_l^1 \succ Q_l^2$, if $g_i^{1l} \le g_i^{2l}$ and for at least one $i \in I$, the inequality is strict. The preference relation is similarly extended to the tolerance system Q.

The calculation and refinement of the tolerance system Q is carried out using the E_1 procedure through the refinement of the tolerance values as the sets V_l are narrowed.

Based on the constraint subsystems [7.14] and [7.15], when analyzing the sets M_{jl} based on the second-level tolerances, the E_2 procedure performs the exclusion of m_{jk} types of NDT methods from the M_{jl} set and technologies s_l that are unpromising in the construction of complexes.

The second-level tolerances for the set M_{jl} based on the constraint for the resource [7.15] are calculated as follows:

$$g_{ij}^l = g_i^l - \sum_{r \in s_l \setminus \{j\}} g_{il}(m_{rk}^*, d_l),\ j \in J_l, \qquad [7.16]$$

where $v_{s_l}^* = (m_{jk}^*)_{j \in s_l} = \arg\min_{v_{s_l} \in V_l} g_{il}(v_{s_l}),\ i \in I.$

– *Statement 1*: let g_{ij}^l be the tolerance [7.16]. If for at least one $i \in I$, the condition is satisfied

$$g_{ij}(m_{jk}, d_l) > g_{ij}^l,\ k \in K_{jl}, \qquad [7.17]$$

then the k th modification m_{jk} of the j type method cannot be used to construct the v_{s_l} complex, which implements the s_l technology.

If, according to condition [7.17], all M_{jl} methods are excluded from the set m_{jk}, then the technologies $s_l \in S_l$ that use this method are excluded from the sets S_l and $J_l' = J_l \setminus \{j\}$. If all s_l technologies are excluded from the set S_l, then the defect d_l cannot be detected by the existing set of NDT methods with the given resources.

Let $M'_{jl} \subseteq M_{jl}$, $j \in J_l'$ be the set of modifications of the NDT methods that remain in the set M_{jl}, and $S_l' \subseteq S_l$ be the set of technologies that remain in the set S_l after checking the conditions [7.17]. Then, the number of possible variants of constructing complexes that implement the S_l technology for detecting the $d_l \in D$ defect is determined by $\left|V'_{s_l}\right| = \prod_{j \in J_l} \left|M'_{jl}\right|$, and $\left|V_l'\right| = \sum_{s_l \in S_l'} \left|V'_{s_l}\right|$ is the number of possible complexes for the d_l defect, where $|\bullet|$ is the number of elements in the corresponding set.

Clearly, if there exists $l \in L$ such that $V_l' = \varnothing$, then the problems [7.8], [7.9] and [7.11] have no solution. If the number of variants $|V_l'|$ in the sets V_l', $l \in L$ does not exceed a predefined number N_0 ($|V_l'| \le N_0$), then the following aggregated problem $A^{(0)}$ is formulated and solved.

According to the general scheme of the sequential analysis method for two-level discrete optimization problems, the construction of the aggregated problem is the implementation of the construction operator, which consists of the following steps:

– the following sets of complexes are formed, in which the methods m_{jk} and technologies $s_l \in S_l$ are fixed.

$$Z_l^Q = \left\{ z_{lr_l} = v_{s_l} \,\middle|\, g_{il}(v_{s_l}) \le g_i^l,\ i \in I,\ v_{s_l} \in V_l^{(0)} = \bigcup_{s_l \in S_l^{(0)}} V_{s_l}^{(0)} \right\},\quad l \in L,$$

$$Z_l^* = \left\{ z_{lr_l} \equiv v_{s_l} \,\middle|\, p(v_{s_l}) \ge p_l^*,\ i \in I,\ v_{s_l} \in V_l^{(0)} = \bigcup_{s_l \in S_l^{(0)}} V_{s_l}^{(0)} \right\},\quad l \in L.$$

On the sets $Z_l = Z_l^Q \cap Z_l^*$, $l \in L$, the explicit values of the functions $g_{il}(v_{s_l})$ and $p(v_{s_l})$ are calculated, and the following sets are formed:

$$H_{g_{il}}(Z_l) = \{g_{il}(z_{lr_l}) \big| z_{lr_l} \equiv v_{s_l}, v_{s_l} \in V_l^{(0)}\}, \ l \in L,$$

$$H_p(Z_l) = \{p(z_{lr_l}) \big| z_{lr_l} \equiv v_{s_l}, v_{s_l} \in V_l^{(0)}\}, \ l \in L.$$

Based on these data, the following *aggregated* discrete monotonic programming *problem* $A^{(0)}$ is formed:

$$P_D(z) = P_D(p(z_{1r_1}),..., p(z_{lr_l}),..., p(z_{l^*r_{l^*}})) =$$

$$= \sum_{x \in X} W(x) \prod_{l \in L} p(z_{lr_l})^{x_l} (1 - p(z_{lr_l}))^{1-x_l} \to \max,$$

under resource constraints

$$g_i(z) = \sum_{l \in L} g_{il}(z_{lr_l}) \le b_i, \ i \in I,$$

$$z = (z_{1r_1},..., z_{lr_l},.., z_{l^*r_{l^*}}) \in Z = \prod_{l \in L} Z_l.$$

According to the general scheme of the sequential analysis method, the optimal solution to the problem $A^{(0)}$ is the optimal solution to the problem [7.8], [7.9] and [7.11] (Volkovich et al. 1992).

If $\left|V_l'\right| > N_0$, then to continue the search for the optimal solution, the following additional constraint on the criterion (effectiveness indicator of the complex) is considered (Volkovich et al. 1992):

$$P_D(v) \ge P^*, \qquad [7.18]$$

where the magnitude $P^* \in \left[P_{\min}, P_{\max}\right]$, $P_{\min} = \min_{v \in V} P_D(v)$, $P_{\max} = \max_{v \in V} P_D(v)$.

Considering that the probability of detecting defects $P_D(v)$ is a monotonically increasing function of the values $p(v_{s_l})$, the general solution scheme for two-level monotonic discrete programming problems is used, where the tolerances according to criterion [7.18] are calculated as follows.

Let the indicator $P_D(v)$ be represented in the form $P_D(v) = P_D(p^1,..., p^l,..., p^{l^*})$, which is defined on the set $H_{P_D}(V) = \prod_{l \in L} H_{p_l}(V_l)$. Here, the ordered set of values $p(v_{s_l})$ is determined by $H_{p_l}(V_l) = \{p^l_{v_{s_l}} \mid p^l_{v_{s_l}} \equiv p(v_{s_l}),\ v_{s_l} \in V_{s_l},\ s_l \in S_l\}$, $l \in L$.

The tolerances of the first and second levels according to the constraint [3.18] are determined as follows.

The magnitude

$$p_l^* = \min_{p_l \in H_{p_l}(V_l)} P_D(\tilde{p}_1,..., \tilde{p}_{l-1}, p_l, \tilde{p}_{l+1},..., \tilde{p}_{l^*}) \geq P^*, \qquad [7.19]$$

is the tolerance of the first level for the set V_l according to the constraint [3.18], where $\tilde{p}_l = \max_{v_{s_l} \in V_l} p(v_{s_l})$, $l \in L$.

To the subsystem of constraints [7.14] and [7.15] with the set of tolerances Q_l, we add the following constraint on the probability of defect detection:

$$p(v_{s_l}) \geq p_l^*, \qquad [7.20]$$

Then, $\bar{Q} = \bigcup_{l \in L} \bar{Q}_l$ - is a complete system of tolerances for the subsystem of constraints [3.14], [3.15] and [3.20] with the set of tolerances $\bar{Q}_l = Q_l \cup \{p_l^*\}$, $l \in L$.

Using the tolerances $\bar{Q}$ of the subsystem of constraints [7.14], [7.15] and [7.20], further analysis of the sets M_{jl} and the exclusion of elements from them can be performed using the procedure E_2.

– *Statement 2*: let p_l^* be the tolerance [7.20]. The value

$$p_{jl}^* = \lg(1 - p_l^*) - \sum_{r \in s_l \setminus \{j\}} \lg(1 - p(m_{rk}, d_l)) \qquad [7.21]$$

is the tolerance of the second level for the elements of the set M_{jl}.

– *Statement 3*: let p^*_{jl} be the tolerance [7.21]. If

$$\lg(1 - p(m_{jk}, d_l)) > p^*_{jl}, \qquad [7.22]$$

then an element m_{jk} of the *k*th type is not used when constructing sets v_{s_l} that implement the d_l defect detection technology s_l.

If, as a result of checking condition [7.22] for the elements of m_{jk}, we obtain for some $j \in J_l$ that $M_{jl} = \varnothing$, then the s_l technologies that use methods from the set M_{jl} are excluded from S_l and from further consideration.

Thus, as a result of applying the procedures E_1 and E_2 to exclude unpromising variants according to criterion [7.18], we obtain the set V'' such that $V'' \subseteq V$, which is further analyzed for the presence of optimal complexes. The procedure E_2 for analyzing the variants of $v_{s_l} \in V_l$ consists of the following steps.

– *Procedure* E_2

Step 0: let us assume $M_{jl}^{(0)} = M_{jl}, S_l^{(0)} = S_l,\ J_l^{(0)} = J_l,\ l \in L,\ r = 1$.

Step 1: using formula [3.16], we calculate the tolerances $g_{ij}^{l(r-1)}$, $i \in I$, $j \in J_l$, $s_l \in S_l^{(v-1)}$. As a result of checking conditions [7.17], we obtain the sets

$$M'^{(r-1)}_{jl},\ S'^{(r-1)}_l,\ j \in J_l^{(r-1)},\ l \in L.$$

Step 2: if the set $S'^{(r-1)}_l = \varnothing$, then we stop the calculation.

Step 3: we calculate the tolerances $p_l^{*(r-1)}$, $l \in L$ using formula [7.19]. As a result of checking condition [7.22], we obtain the sets $M_{jl}^{(r)}$, $S_l^{(r)}$, $j \in J_l^{(r)}$, $l \in L$.

Step 4: if $S_l^{(r)} = \varnothing$, then we stop the calculation.

Step 5: if $M_{jl}^{(r)} = M_{jl}^{(r-1)}$, $S_l^{(r)} = S_l^{(r-1)}$, $J_l^{(r)} = J_l^{(r-1)}$, then we stop the calculation. Otherwise, we proceed to step 1, setting $r = r+1$.

In step 5 of the E_2 procedure, the conditions $M_{jl}^{(r)} = M_{jl}^{(r-1)}$, $S_l^{(r)} = S_l^{(r-1)}$, $J_l^{(r)} = J_l^{(r-1)}$, $l \in L$ are equivalent to $V_l^{(r)} = V_l^{(r-1)}$, where $V_l^{(r)}$ is the set of options obtained after r iterations. It is obvious that $V_l^{(r)} \subseteq V_l$ $(V_l^{(0)} = V_l)$, $l \in L$.

Narrowing the sets V_l, $l \in L$ may lead to an improvement in the complete system of tolerances $\bar{Q}$. The recalculation of the tolerance system $\bar{Q}$ is carried out by the E_1 procedure.

– *Procedure* E_1

Step 0: let $V_l^{(0)} \subseteq V_l$, $l \in L$, $V^{(0)} = \prod_{l \in L} V_l^{(0)}$ and determine the tolerance system on the set $V^{(0)}$

$$\bar{Q}^{(0)} = \bigcup_{l \in L} \bar{Q}_l^{(0)},\ \bar{Q}_l^{(0)} = Q_l^{(0)} \cup \{p_l^{*(0)}\},\ Q^{(0)} = \{g_i^{l(0)}\},\ l \in L,$$

where the tolerances $g_i^{l(0)}$ and $p_l^{*(0)}$ are calculated using formulas [7.13] and [7.19], respectively.

Step 1: to the subsystems of constraints of the forms [7.14], [7.15] and [7.20] with tolerances $\bar{Q}_l^{(r-1)}$, $l \in L$, we apply the E_2 procedure and determine the new tolerance system $\bar{Q}^{(r)} = \bigcup_{l \in L} \bar{Q}_l^{(r)}$, where the tolerances $g_i^{l(r)}$ and $p_l^{(r)}$ are calculated using formulas [7.16] and [7.21], respectively. We proceed to step 2.

Step 2: if $\bar{Q}^{(r)} = \bar{Q}^{(r-1)}$, then we stop the calculation. If $\bar{Q}^{(r)} \succ \bar{Q}^{(r-1)}$, then we set $r = r+1$ and proceed to step 1.

The *algorithm* for solving problems [7.8], [7.9] and [7.11] is based on the E_1 and E_2 procedures and consists of the following steps:

Step 0: we apply the E_1 procedure to the set V and obtain the set $V^{(0)} = \prod_{l \in L} V_l^{(0)}$ and the tolerance system $\bar{Q}^{(0)} = \bigcup_{l \in L} \bar{Q}_l^{(0)}$.

If $\left|V^{(0)}\right| < N_{(0)}$, then problems [7.8], [7.9] and [7.11] are solved by directly enumerating the options of the set $V^{(0)}$. Otherwise, proceed to step 1.

Step 1: if $\sum_{l \in L} \left|V^{(0)}\right| > N_1$, then we set $\gamma = 1$, $P^{*(\gamma)} = (P_{\min} + P_{\max})/2$, where $P_{\min} = \min_{v \in V^{(0)}} P(v)$, $P_{\max} = \max_{v \in V^{(0)}} P(v)$, and proceed to step 2 (the value of N_1 is determined considering the resources of the computer system).

If $\sum_{l \in L} \left|V^{(0)}\right| \leq N_1$, then an aggregated problem $A^{(0)}$ is formed. If, in the problem, for at least one $l \in L$, the set $Z_l^{(0)} = \varnothing$ is empty, or the problem $A^{(0)}$ has no solution, then problems [7.8], [7.9] and [7.11] have no solution.

If $\left|Z^{(0)}\right| < N_0$, we solve the problem $A^{(0)}$ by directly enumerating the options, which may be the most computationally efficient approach.

If $\left|Z^{(0)}\right| > N_0$, we use established methods of discrete optimization (Volkovich et al. 1992) to solve the problem $A^{(0)}$.

If $z^{*(0)} = (z_{1r_1}^{*(0)}, \ldots, z_{lr_l}^{*(0)}, \ldots, z_{l^* r_{l^*}}^{*(0)})$, $z_{lr_l}^{*(0)} \in Z_l^{(0)}$, $l \in L$ – is the optimal solution to the problem $A^{(0)}$, then we set $v_{s_l}^{*} = z_{lr_l}^{*(0)}$, which is the optimal solution to problems [7.8], [7.9] and [7.11].

If solving the problem $A^{(0)}$ is complicated, we set $\gamma = 1$, $P^{*(\gamma)} = (P_{\min} + P_{\max})/2$, and proceed to step 2.

Step 2: we apply the E_1 procedure, taking into account the value of $P^{*(\gamma)}$ in constraint [3.18], and obtain a new tolerance system $\bar{Q}^{(\gamma)}$ and the set $V^{(\gamma)} = \prod_{l \in L} V_l^{(\gamma)}$. The following cases are possible:

1) The set $V^{(\gamma)} = \varnothing$, then proceed to step 3.

2) $\sum_{l \in L} \left| V_l^{(\gamma)} \right| \leq N_1$. With the obtained tolerances $\bar{Q}^{(\gamma)}$ on the set $V^{(\gamma)}$, we form the aggregated problem $A^{(\gamma)}$ (similar to the $A^{(0)}$ problem). As a result of solving the $A^{(\gamma)}$ problem, the following cases are possible.

2.1) An $z^{*(\gamma)}$, an optimal solution of the $A^{(\gamma)}$ problem, has been obtained. Option $z^{*(\gamma)}$ is checked for optimality using optimality criteria (Volkovich et al. 1992). If the optimality criteria are not met, then $z^{*(\gamma)}$ is an approximate solution to the $A^{(\gamma)}$ problem.

If $z^{*(\gamma)}$ is the optimal or accepted approximate solution of problems [7.8], [7.9] and [7.11], then we stop the calculation. Otherwise, set $P_{\min} = P_D(z^{*(\gamma)})$, $P^{*(\gamma+1)} = P_{\min}$, $\gamma = \gamma + 1$ and proceed to step 2.

2.2) The $A^{(\gamma)}$ problem has no feasible solutions. Proceed to step 3.

(If the $A^{(\gamma)}$ problem has no feasible solutions, or $Z^{(\gamma)} = \varnothing$, then the feasible solution of problems [7.8], [7.9] and [7.11] satisfies the condition $P(v) \leq P^{*(\gamma)}$).

2.3) Solving the $A^{(\gamma)}$ problem is complicated. Proceed to step 4 (in this case, it is advisable to tighten constraint [3.18] without solving the $A^{(\gamma)}$ problem).

3) $\sum_{l \in L} \left| V_l^{(\gamma)} \right| > N_1$. Option $\bar{v} = \arg\max_{v \in V^{(\gamma)}} P_D(v)$ is checked for optimality according to optimality criterion 1 (Volkovich et al. 1992); if it does not meet this criterion, proceed to step 4.

Step 3: decrease the value of $P^{*(\gamma)}$, set $P^{*(\gamma+1)} = (P_{\min} + P^{*(\gamma)}) / 2$, $P_{\max}^{(\gamma)} = P^{*(\gamma)}$, and proceed to step 2 if $\gamma = \gamma + 1$. Here, $P_{\max}^{(\gamma)}$ is the upper bound of the criterion value at step γ.

Step 4: increase the value of $P^{*(\gamma)}$, setting $P^{*(\gamma+1)} = (P_{\min} + P^{*(\gamma)}) / 2$, $\gamma = \gamma + 1$. If $P_*^{(\gamma+1)} - P_*^{(\gamma)} > \varepsilon_1$ (where $\varepsilon_1 \geq \varepsilon_0$, ε_0 - is a certain positive value defined taking into account rounding error, calculation accuracy, etc.), then proceed to step 2. If $\left|P_*^{(\gamma+1)} - P_*^{(\gamma)}\right| \leq \varepsilon_1$, but if $\left|V^{(\gamma)}\right| > N_0$, and $\sum_{l \in L} \left|V_l^{(\gamma)}\right| > N_1$, and then either increase the parameters N_0, N_1, or limit the search to finding approximate options for the complexes.

7.3. Conclusion

The methodology for constructing type-variety NDT complexes, alongside the optimization problems outlined in this section and the corresponding optimization algorithms, has been applied in designing NDT systems for detecting defects in CI. These include aircraft, NPPs, spacecraft and other high-stakes systems. Furthermore, this approach is adaptable for diverse operational contexts OCs and is integral in training specialists in NDT methods.

Given the significant effort required to ensure reliability and perform NDT, as well as the potential catastrophic consequences of undetected defects, the emphasis on automation and advanced NDT methodologies is paramount. This includes leveraging mathematical models, decision-making techniques and modern information technologies (Gosselin and Gore 1999; Ostap et al. 1999, pp. 3–8; Zaslavsky et al. 2003, pp. 19–25). Although the cost of an NDT system can be substantial – driven by the complexity of methods and devices employed – the benefits far outweigh the expenses. Effective NDT systems mitigate risks associated with critical defects, significantly reducing the likelihood of hazardous events (Afanasiev et al. 1993; Zaslavsky et al. 2000, pp. 33–41).

7.4. References

Afanasiev, V.G., Verkhoturov, V.I., Zaslavsky, V.A., Zelentsov, V.A., Mironov, A.N., Franchuk, O.V. (1993). *Design of Reliable Communication Satellites*. MGP 'RASKO', Tomsk.

Alekseev, O.G. (1987). *Complex Application of Discrete Optimization Methods*. Nauka, Moscow.

Bellman, R. and Dreyfus, S. (1965). *Applied Problems of Dynamic Programming*. Nauka, Moscow.

Davis, D., Barber, D., Price, C., Solomodines, S. (1982). *Computer Networks and Network Protocols*. Mir, Moscow.

Gosselin, S. and Gor, B. (eds) (1999). *Optimization of the Procedure for Conducting Inspection of Pipelines and Equipment Based on the Concept of Risk. Transfer of the Inspection Methodology to the Ukrainian NPPs*. Kyiv.

Hetman, A. and Kozin, Y. (1997). *Non-Destructive Control and Safety of Operation of Pressure Vessels and Pipelines*. Energoatomizdat, Moscow.

Kadenko, I., Zaslavsky, V.A., Sakhno, N. (1999). Application of the complex NDT approach for inspection of NPP power system. In *Proceedings of the International Symposium on Nondestructive Testing Contribution to the Infrastructure Safety Systems in the 21st Century*, 22–26 November, Torres, RS.

Klyuev, V.V. (ed.) (1995). *Non-Destructive Testing and Diagnostics. Directory*. Mashinostroenie, Moscow.

Ostap, O.P., Uchanin, V.M., Andreyko, I.M., Makoviychuk, I.R. (1999). Technical diagnostics and service life of structures after long-term operation. In *Physical Methods and Means of Control of Environments, Materials and Products*. Leotest – Medium Center, Kyiv-Lviv, 3–8.

Troitsky, V. and Zagrebelny, V. (1999). Application of visual and eddy current methods of non-destructive testing for defectoscopy assessment of welded structural elements operated in space. In *Physical Methods and Means of Monitoring Environments, Materials and Products*, Leotest – Medium Center, Kyiv-Lviv, 117–118.

Volkovich, V.L. and Zaslavsky, V.A. (1986). Algorithm to solve reliability optimization problem for complex systems using type-variety redundant elements in subsystems. *Kibernetika*, 5(81), 54–61.

Volkovich, V.L., Voloshin, A.F., Gorlova, T.M. (1984). *Methods and Algorithms for Automated Design of Complex Control Systems*. Naukova Dumka, Kyiv.

Volkovich, V.L., Voloshin, A.F., Zaslavsky, V.A., Ushakov, I.A. (1992). *Models and Algorithms for Reliability Optimization of Complex Systems*. Naukova Dumka, Kyiv.

Zaslavsky, V.A. (1988). Sequential analysis of variants in multi-level problems of optimization of reliability of complex systems. *Bulletin of Kyiv University, Modeling and Optimization of Complex Systems*, 7, 72–77.

Zaslavsky, V.A. (2006). Type variety principle and peculiarities of study of complex systems with a high cost of failure. *Bulletin of Taras Shevchenko National University of Kyiv*, 1, 136–147.

Zaslavsky, V.A. and Kadenko, I. (1999). The role and place of non-destructive testing methods to ensure the reliability and durability of complex systems with a high price of failure. *Non-Destructive Testing*, 1, 5–22.

Zaslavsky, V.A., Kadenko, I., Sakhno, N. (2000). Methodological aspects of ensuring the safety of complex technical facilities in conditions of limited resources (Message 2). *Nuclear and Radiation Safety*, 4, 33–41.

Zaslavsky, V.A., Kadenko, I.M., Sakhno, N.V. (2003). Problems of planning and organizing work during restoration and extension of the resource of elements of complex systems using non-destructive testing methods. *Bulletin of Kyiv University, Ser. Cybernetics*, 4, 19–25.

8

The Type-Variety Principle, Mathematical Models and Algorithms for the Optimization of the Reliability of Series–Parallel and Parallel–Series Systems, the Elements of Which Allow Two Types of Failures

This chapter considers two problems of optimal redundancy of complex systems (CS) in which elements (subsystems) admit two types of inoperability states – "open circuit" and "short circuit" – as well as algorithms for their solution. The probability of failure due to an "open circuit" is reduced by connecting elements in parallel, while connecting elements in series increases the system's reliability with respect to failures such as "short circuits". The first optimization problem explores the design of a system using identical (single-type) reserved elements for redundancy, while the second problem considers a more complex formulation involving optimal redundancy with type-variety elements.

The problems under consideration arose from the practical needs to ensure longer periods of active existence of spacecraft and other CS. The developed models and algorithms are based on the type-variety principle, as a method used in system studies to eliminate the possibility of failures caused by common factors. The practical implementation of these algorithms enables the generation of qualitatively new, innovative project solutions for ensuring the reliability of CS, taking into account various constraints related to technical and economic parameters. The formulations of mathematical models and algorithms for solving problems are considered.

Chapter written by Volodymyr A. ZASLAVSKYI and Oleg FRANCHUK.

8.1. Introduction

In the design of complex electronic systems used in spacecraft, communication systems, and similar applications, challenges of optimal redundancy arise when subsystems (components) can experience two types of failure states: "open circuit" and "short circuit" (Barlow and Proschan 1965; Epifanov 1976; Nakagava and Hattory 1981; Druzhynin 1986; Jenney and Sherwin 1986; Page and Perry 1988). The probability of failure due to an "open circuit" is reduced by connecting components in parallel, while connecting components in series enhances the system's reliability with respect to "short circuit" failures.

The reliability analysis of structurally complex systems, where the components can fail in two types – "open circuit" and "short circuit" (relay-contact circuits) – and the study of probabilistic performance indicators for such systems, were addressed in the foundational work of Moore and Shannon (1960). Their research focused on developing exact calculation formulas for the probability of failure-free operation (reliability) of parallel-series systems and computing the upper and lower bounds for the system reliability indicator.

The study of the reliability indicator properties of parallel-series systems consisting of m parallel chains, each containing n serially connected identical elements, and the task of maximizing the reliability of such structural schemes, were analyzed in the works of Barlow and Proschan (1965), Jenny and Sherwin (1986), Nakagawa and Hattori (1981), and Paige and Perry (1988). However, due to the complex combinatorial nature of the problem, where it is necessary to form a parallel-series structure and the parameters m and n are variables, finding the optimal structure presents computational challenges.

8.2. Models and algorithms for optimizing the reliability of series–parallel systems the elements of which allow two types of failures

Considering the problem of synthesis of the structure of the system, and when given a fixed number of identical items, we must select the parallel–serial (Figure 8.1) or series–parallel (Figure 8.1(b)) block diagram, providing maximum system reliability. It is assumed that the probability of failures is statistically independent. Let each element of the system under consideration be in one of three states: working with probability p, in a state of failure of "open-circuit" with the probability $q_O = 1 - p_O$ or in a state of failure or condition such as "short-circuiting" of probability $q_{K3} = 1 - p_{K3}$. Because of the incompatibility of pair of states there is equality, from where:

$$p = p_0 + p_{K3} - 1 = p_0 - q_{K3} = p_{K3} - q_0 \qquad [8.1]$$

Formula [8.1] shows that, in spite of addiction p_0 and p_{K3}, because of the incompatibility of the two types of failures, failure operation element is determined by unconditional p_0 and p_{K3}. Then the obvious restrictions on p_0 and p_{K3}:

$$p_0 + p_{K3} > 1, p_0 > q_{K3}, p_{K3} > q_0 .$$

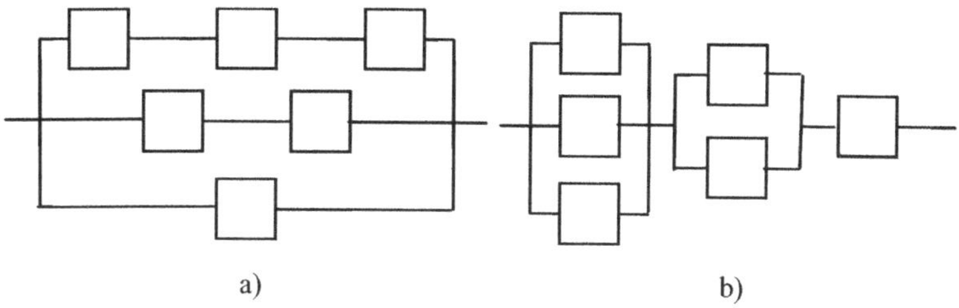

Figure 8.1. *Parallel–series (a) and series–parallel (b) block diagram*

Consider a parallel–serial and serial–parallel flow diagrams that pair r parallel chains (width scheme) and l identical elements (Figure 8.2).

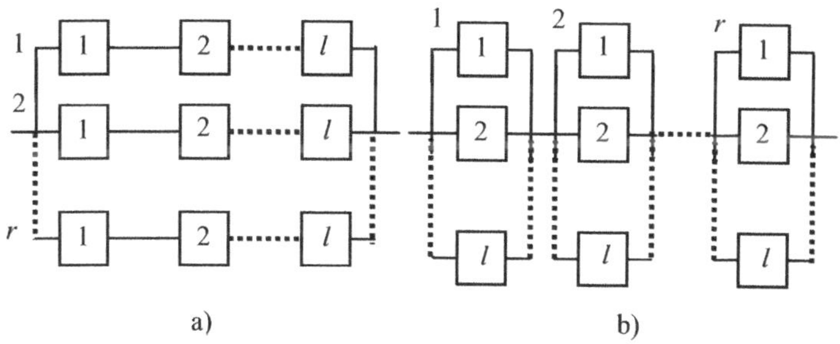

Figure 8.2. *Parallel sequential circuit with r parallel chains and l identical elements in them (a); series–parallel circuit with r sequential circuits on the l same type of parallel elements (b)*

Reliability P_{ps} of parallel–serial and P_{sp} serial–parallel systems, as shown in Figure 8.2, are calculated in accordance with (Barlow and Proschan 1965):

$$P_{ps} = \left(1 - q_{K3}^{l}\right)^{r} - \left(1 - \left(1 - q_{o}\right)^{l}\right)^{r} \quad [8.2]$$

$$P_{sp} = \left(1 - q_o^l\right)^r - \left(1 - \left(1 - q_{K3}\right)^l\right)^r \qquad [8.3]$$

Since the reliability functions P_{ps} and P_{sp} in [8.1] and [8.2] are symmetrical with respect to the indicators q_0 and q_{K3}, we will focus on parallel-series structures in the studies, as everything that holds true for them also applies to series-parallel systems. Vtorova-Karyevskaya and Litvak (1979) proposed upper and lower bounds for systems with complex structure, whose elements are two types of failures, and lead an example to assess the reliability bridged circuit under certain conditions on q_0 and q_{K3}. If the problem of maximizing reliability P_{ps} viewed without restrictions on the technical and economic parameters (number of reserve elements), it is known from Barlow and Proschan (1965) that there is a limit to the number of elements in the block diagram, which maximizes reliability. With a fixed number of elements l in successive chains and fixed values q_0 and q_{K3} there exists a number r^* of parallel chains in the scheme that maximizes P_{ps}, presented in (Barlow and Proschan 1965):

$$r^* = [r] + 1,$$

$$r = l\frac{\lg(1 - q_o) - \lg(q_{K3})}{\lg(1 - q_{K3}{}^l) - \lg\left(1 - (1 - q_O)^l\right)}$$

If r is an integer, then function of reliability P_{ps} maximizes r as well as $r + 1$.

Using different types and methods of redundancy is necessary in designing spacecrafts, and therefore a need for a practical implementation problem of optimal redundancy with two types of failures – which will be considered below – was found.

In the study of optimal redundancy with two types of failures in Voloshin (1977b, 1977a), the total number of variants of the structure of such systems is estimated by the number of partitions of whole into parts. In Zaslavsky and Franchuk (1989), task of reliability optimization of structure of series–parallel systems with elements that have two types of failures has been formalized and examined on a set of solutions that are lexicographically ordered partition of an integer into parts (Andrews 1982) (see options block diagrams in Figures 8.1 and 8.2). Formalizing the problem of optimal redundancy proposed in Zaslavsky and Franchuk (1989) is also used in Franchuk (1994).

Partition of integer n is called arbitrary nonincreasing sequence of numbers $x_1, x_2, ..., x_r \in N$ for which $\sum_{i=1}^{r} x_i = n$. Suppose x_i is number of elements in a consistent configuration (length of the ist string) and r is number of all of the parallel chains (the width of the block diagram) (for the circuit in Figure 8.1, we have r=3, $x_1 = 3$, $x_2 = 1$, $x_3 = 1 =$ 3). Let $x = (x_1, ..., x_i, ..., x_r)$ is vector that corresponds to block diagram in Figure 8.3.

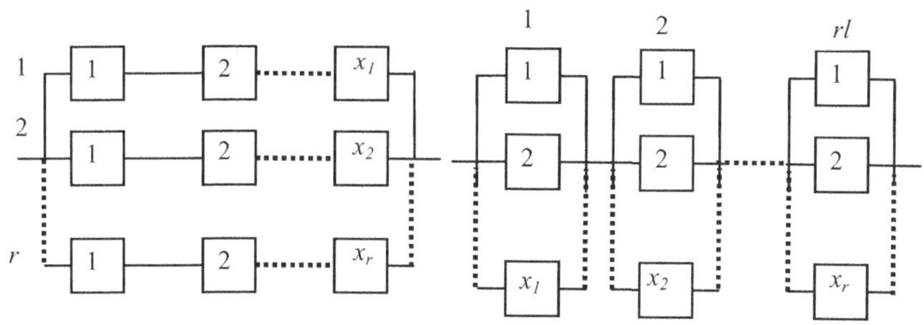

Figure 8.3. *Parallel sequential circuit with r-parallel chains and x_i identical elements in them (a); series–parallel circuit with sequential circuits r on the x_i same type of parallel elements (b)*

Reliability of parallel–serial block diagram (see Figure 8.3(a)) is defined as:

$$P_{ps}(r, x) = \prod_{i=1}^{r}(1 - q_{K3}^{x_i}) - \prod_{i=1}^{r}(1 - (1 - q_o)^{x_i})$$

Problem that optimizes the structure of the system is formulated for a fixed number of elements n, and fixed values q_0 and q_{K3} and $r > 0$. It is necessary to find a vector $x = (x_1, ..., x_i, ..., x_r)$ such that:

$$P_{ps}(r, x) = \prod_{i=1}^{r}(1 - q_{K3}^{x_i}) - \prod_{i=1}^{r}(1 - (1 - q_o)^{x_i}) \to \max, \quad [8.4]$$

$$\sum_{i=1}^{r} x_i = n, \quad [8.5]$$

$$x = (x_1, ..., x_i, ..., x_r), \; x_i \in N. \quad [8.6]$$

As the nonlinear function [8.4] is symmetric in x (Kovalev 1997), lexicographically ordered partition that determines the set of possible solutions of the problems [8.4]–[8.6] are considered, and their number represents dimension of the problem. For example, for $n = 5$, we have seven partitions of 5, 4 + 1, 3 + 2, 3 + 1 + 1, 2 + 2 + 1, 2 + 1 + 1 + 1 and 1 + 1 + 1 + 1 + 1. Generation of lexicographically ordered partitions uses an algorithm (Andrews 1982). For smaller n, generation algorithm partitions allows us to find quickly the optimal solution of problems [8.4]–[8.6] by brute force. The rise of n search requires generating a large number of partitions, whose number is estimated at (Andrews 1982):

$$p(n) \approx \frac{\exp(\pi\sqrt{2n/3})}{4n\sqrt{3}}. \qquad [8.7]$$

So $p(10) = 42, p(20) = 627, p(50) = 204{,}266, p(100) = 190{,}569{,}292$.

This approach to finding solutions of problems posed the question of the reliability analysis values $P_{ps}(r,x)$ for partitioning with different number of terms r (the width of the circuit). We conducted analytical studies and a large amount of computational experiments to determine:

– properties of reliability functions for different values r;

– the values of system reliability depending on the number of elements n;

– the values of system reliability depending on the values of q_0 and q_{k3}.

As a result, it was found for the problems that were considered in the experiments: optimal reliability block diagrams were those in which the length of the chains differ from each other not more than one unit or the same.

For the first time, for problems [8.4]–[8.6], *Rule of Thumb 1* was formulated (Zaslavsky and Franchuk 1989; Volkovich et al. 1992; Afanasiev et al. 1993):

$$\left|x_i - x_j\right| \le 1, \quad 1 \le i,\ j \le r,\ r = 1,\ldots,n, \qquad [8.8]$$

which means that for set of solutions of the problem, it is necessary to search among partitions, which satisfy the condition [8.8].

Satisfying the conditions in [8.8] for the partition components that form the solution variants of the problem leads to a sharp reduction in the number of possible solutions. To find the solution with maximum reliability P_{ps}, it is necessary to evaluate $n - 1$ possible variants. Using this rule and taking into account the properties of the function [8.4], an effective algorithm for solution of problems [8.4]–[8.6] has been developed, which is discussed below.

The following properties are important in function $P_{ps}(q_0, q_{k3}, r, n)$, depending on the parameters q_0, q_{k3}, r, n:

1) During conducting experiments, the local maximum of the function P_{ps} coincided with the global maximum. In Figure 8.4, given the graph $P_{ps}(q_0, q_{k3}, r, n)$ of the elements $n = 50$ and three different values of the failure probability of "break" and "short circuit" ($q_o^1 = 0.05$, $q_{k3}^1 = 0.1$, $q_o^2 = 0.1$, $q_{k3}^2 = 0.05$, $q_o^3 = 0.075$, $q_{k3}^3 = 0.075$), the r-width of the scheme (the number of parallel chains) is plotted on the x-axis, while the maximum values of the reliability indicators for a fixed r-width of the scheme are plotted on the y-axis.

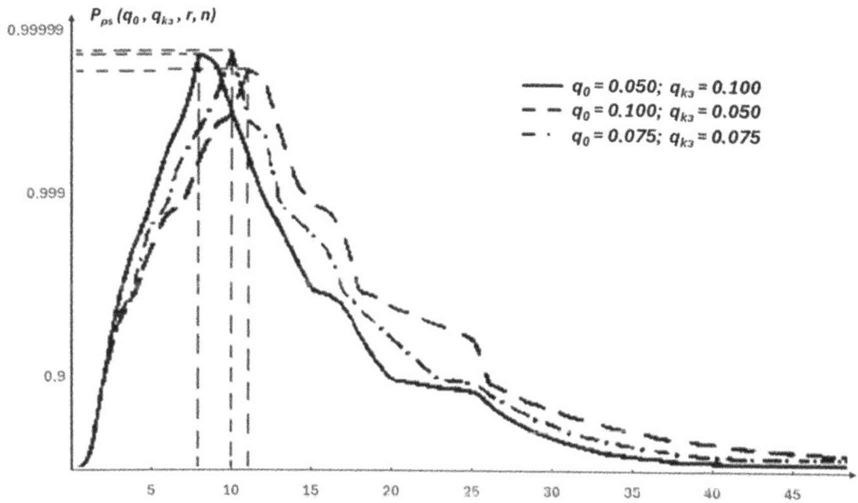

Figure 8.4. *Graph of the function* $P_{ps}(q_0, q_{k3}, r, n)$

It should be noted that for fixed values q_0 and q_{K3}, maximum reliability is at optimum width r^*. Localization of the optimal width is a separate task. Considering the kind of graphics functions, we can have argued that if the reliability value comes after the passage of the optimal width of the circuit, then search solutions of the problem can be stopped.

2) Reliability of parallel-sequential system depends on the number of items n and not necessarily increases with increasing number of reserve elements (Figure 8.5 illustrates this fact). In the graph (Figure 8.5), the number of elements in the structural scheme is shown on the horizontal (x) axis, while the maximum reliability of the structural scheme for the optimal configuration is shown on the vertical (y) axis, with fixed values, $q_o = 0.030$, $q_{k3} = 0.070$, and a maximum number of elements $n = 50$. Since increasing the number of reserve elements in problems [2.4]–[2.6], as demonstrated by computer experiments, does not always lead to an increase in the system reliability indicator (Figure 8.5), this fact is special and, unlike the standard understanding, increasing the reserve leads only to an increase in technical and economic indicators, and not to the reliability of the system as a whole (Volkovich et al. 1992).

3) The graph in Figure 8.6 show the values of the reliability indicator, which are illustrated for three fixed values of the r-width of the structural schemes.

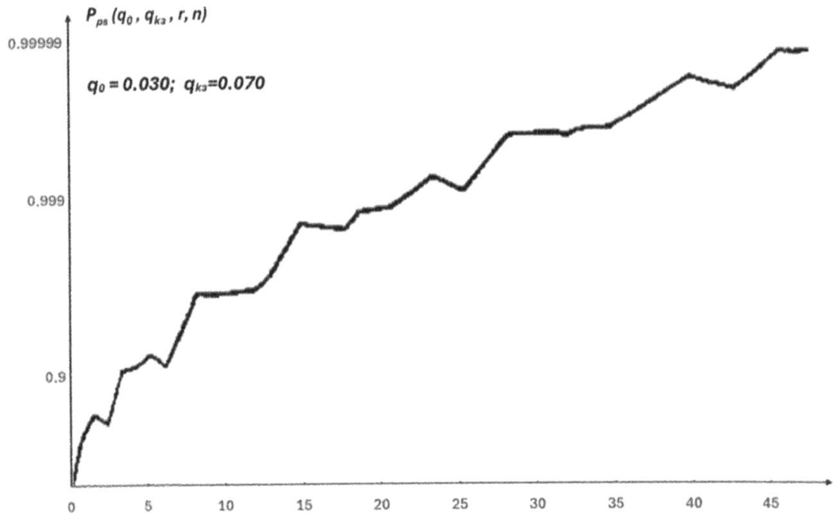

Figure 8.5. *Graph of function* $P_{ps}(q_0, q_{k3}, r, n)$ *for* $q_0 = 0.03$, $q_{k3} = 0.07$

For $r = 3$, the maximum of the reliability function is achieved at $n = 9$, P_{ps} $(q_0, q_{k3}, r, n) = 0.9839$ and the optimal structure is determined by the partition 3 + 3 + 3. For $r = 4$, the maximum value is P_{ps} $(q_0, q_{k3}, r, n) = 0.9927$ and is achieved at $n = 16$ (4 + 4 + 4 + 4). Thus, after reaching the maximum for a fixed width, an increase n in the number of elements in the structure leads to a decrease in the reliability indicator of the structures, which is shown in the graphs for $r = 3$ and $r = 4$. For $r = 5$, the maximum of the reliability function in this case ($n = 20$) is not yet achieved.

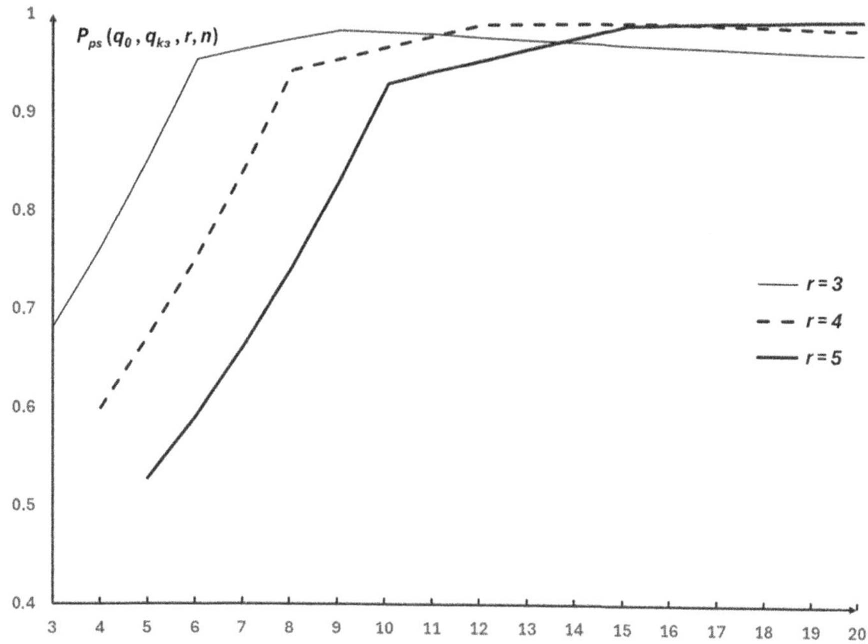

Figure 8.6. *Graphs of the function* $P_{ps}(q_0, q_{k3}, r, n)$ *with* $q_0 = 0.08$, $q_{k3} = 0.12$, *and parallel circuits of fixed width* $r = 3,4,5$

Denote $a \operatorname{div} b$ as a function whose value is the integer part from a / b. The algorithm of the solution of problems [8.4]–[8.6] consists of the following steps:

– **Step 0**: for a fixed n, we pin $r = 2$ and $P_{ps}^{\max} = 0$.

– **Step 1**: for fixed r, we find $m = n \operatorname{div} r$, the length of the smallest circuit. Using [8.8], we have chain lengths m and $m+1$. Calculate $l_1 = n - m \cdot r$ – number of chain length $m+1$ – and $l_0 = r - l_1$ – the number of chain lengths m. In $x = (x_1, ..., x_i, ..., x_r)$, we lay components $x_i = m+1$ for $i = 1, 2, ..., l_1$ and $x_i = m$ for $i = l_1 + 1, ..., r$ and go to step 2.

– **Step 2**: unless $P_{ps}(r, x) > P_{ps}^{\max}$, we lay $P_{ps}^{\max} = P_{ps}(r, x)$, $r = r + 1$ and go to step 1, otherwise we go to step 3.

– **Step 3**: then, we lay $x^* = x$, $r^* = r$ and finish the algorithm.

The complexity of this algorithm linearly depends on n, which allows us to find the solution to problems [8.4]–[8.6].

These results of Zaslavsky and Franchuk (1989) and Volkovich et al. (1992) were reported at the International Institute for Applied Systems Analysis seminars (IIASA, Laxenburg, Austria) and aroused interest because of the unusual specificity of combinatorial problems and the properties of solutions, which made it the basis for further discussion and research. Hypothesis [8.8] was carried out in Gutjahr et al. (1996, 1993), where it was proposed to consider the continuous analogue of the problem in order to find the length and width of the block diagram. This is the starting point in the algorithm, which was proposed in these works, chosen by hypothesis [8.8]. Research results were also reported at the seminar at the V.M. Glushkov Institute of Cybernetics of NASU. Discussion of the problem and the properties of its solutions initiated the appearance of Kirilyuk (1995, 1997, 2000). The proposed algorithms in these papers are based on empirical rule 1. Kirilyuk (1997) provided an example where hypothesis [8.8] does not provide the optimal solution, and the value of reliability marginally deviates from the optimum where $n = 26$, $q_0 = 0.1$, $q_{K3} = 0.1$.

A numerical experiment was carried out to investigate research exemptions from Rule of Thumb 1 when finding optimal solutions of problems [8.4]–[8.6]. In the experiment, all possible block diagrams were generated for a given number of items that were changed from 14 to 27. The unreliable indicator value q_0, q_{K3} of 0.002 increments changed at specified intervals.

Each problem was solved by the proposed algorithm and brute force. For example, in Table 8.1, for $n = 14$ and the values q_0, q_{K3} that were selected in steps of 0.002 in the interval (0.001, 0.2), the optimal structure does not meet the criteria of Rule of Thumb 1. In every row of Table 8.1, the following information is provided: your current problem (which is the exception), values q_{K3} and q_0, $P_{ps}^{\max}$ are reliability optimal structure $x^* = (x_1,...,x_i,...,x_r)$, r^* is the optimum width, P_{ps}^1 is the reliability of structures as per Rule of Thumb 1 and r^1 is the width. Table 8.2 summarizes the results of the experiments.

In Table 8.2, we can generalize experimental results. For $n = 14$ by indicated conditions of formation of tasks of the number of exceptions Rule of Thumb 1 is 42 tasks from 9801. It should be noted that the solutions within the bounds of Rule of Thumb 1 are, in most cases, optimal (for $n = 14$, this is 99.6%, as confirmed by experiments) or are approximate solutions, are close to optimal.

Number of tasks	q_{K3}	q_0	P_{ps}^{max}	r^*	x^*	P_{ps}^1	r^1
4,452	0.08900	0.10300	0.9888468128	4	5,3,3,3	0.9888382	4
4,453	0.08900	0.10500	0.9882232786	4	5,3,3,3	0.9881741	4
4,501	0.09100	0.00100	0.9999517145	2	8,6	0.9999512	2
4,553	0.09100	0.10500	0.9880770312	4	5,3,3,3	0.9880654	4
4,554	0.09100	0.10700	0.9874254671	4	5,3,3,3	0.9873715	4
4,601	0.09300	0.00100	0.9999516345	2	8,6	0.9999512	2
4,614	0.09300	0.02700	0.9982209617	3	6,4,4	0.9982147	3
4,654	0.09300	0.10700	0.9872726325	4	5,3,3,3	0.9872576	4
4,701	0.09500	0.00100	0.9999515454	2	8,6	0.9999512	2
4,714	0.09500	0.02700	0.9982075838	3	6,4,4	0.9982065	3
4,755	0.09500	0.10900	0.9864329466	4	5,3,3,3	0.9864142	4
4,801	0.09700	0.00100	0.9999514463	2	8,6	0.9999511	2
4,856	0.09700	0.11100	0.9855573159	4	5,3,3,3	0.9855345	4
4,901	0.09900	0.00100	0.9999513364	2	8,6	0.9999511	2
4,915	0.09900	0.02900	0.9978108158	3	6,4,4	0.9978058	3
4,957	0.09900	0.11300	0.9846450953	4	5,3,3,3	0.9846178	4
5,001	0.10100	0.00100	0.9999512147	2	8,6	0.9999511	2

Table 8.1. *Result of experiments for calculation of maximum reliability of systems*

n	Problems count	Number of exclusions	Percentage of the total number of exemptions	P(n)	Total solutions, X	Best percentage among the total number	Number of different chain widths	The mean difference of reliability	The average deviation from the optimum percentage
14	9,801	42	0.4285	135	1,323,135	0.003174279	0	0.0000175997	0.0017775979
15	9,801	16	0.1632	176	1,724,976	0.000927549	2	0.0000008955	0.0000895622
...									
17	4,356	42	0.9641	297	1,293,732	0.003246422	6	0.0000372997	0.0037439330
18	4,096	34	0.8300	385	1,576,960	0.002156047	2	0.0000009712	0.0000971387
...									
22	1,444	42	2.9085	1,002	1,446,888	0.002902782	3	0.0000022964	0.0002297581
23	1,444	42	2.9085	1,255	1,812,220	0.002317599	1	0.0000053464	0.0005348367
27	1,444	42	2.9085	3,010	4,346,440	0.000966308	3	0.0000009102	0.0000910331

Table 8.2. *Examples excluded from Rule of Thumb 1*

Experimental research and analysis of the structure of optimal solutions are allowed to formulate the following Rule of Thumb 2.

Rule of Thumb 2: the optimal solution of problems [8.4]–[8.6] (for system elements n) consists only of two types of chains of components x', x'' such as

$$x' + kx'' = n\ ,\ x' - x'' > 1, \qquad [8.9]$$

where x', x'', k are integers, x' and x'' are length of the chain and k is factor of multiplicity chain length x''. That is, the optimal value $x^* = (x_1,...,x_i,...,x_r)$ seems so $x^* = (x', x''^1,..., x''^k)$. For example, at n=14, x'=5, x''=3 and k=3, $x^* = (5,3,3,3)$. So according to Rule of Thumb 1, the proposed algorithm allows us to quickly find a close to optimal solution to the problems [8.4]–[8.6] that, according to the computational experiments, is optimal in most tasks, but Rule of Thumb 2 (equation [8.9]) specifies the structure of the optimal solution.

8.3. Optimal type-variety redundancy of parallel–serial systems, the element of which allows two types of failures

In this section, the type-variety principle applies (a mechanism that eliminates failures of due to common causes) in constructing new mathematical model of the problem of optimal redundancy systems with different types of redundant elements that allow for two types of failures "break" and "short circuit". The need for research of such models was related to their practical importance in optimizing the structure and reliability of spacecraft components. Experience with models of different types of redundancy (loaded reservation (Volkovich and Zaslavsky 1986; Volkovich et al. 1992)) and laid them opportunities possible to find new and better quality for the technical and economic performance design solutions, which also confirms the relevance of the problem. Revyakov (1988) considered the problem of constructing optimal parallel-sequential system of n groups for m elements (loaded backup) that are reliable p_{ij}, $i = \overline{1,m}$, $j = \overline{1,n}$, and each string must be one element from each group.

In developing mathematical models for complex combinatorial problems of optimal heterogeneous redundancy in parallel-series systems, where the components allow for two types of failures, the results from section 8.1, the properties of the reliability function [8.4], and the solution algorithm from problems [8.4]–[8.6] are used. Suppose when creating the block diagram of different type of redundant elements used k item types that have different technical and economic parameters and the same functionality and are consistent with structural implementation. Suppose we are given n_j^* elements of j type, $j \in J = \{1, 2, ..., k\}$, which have probabilities of failures like $q_{0,j}$ "break" and $q_{k3,j}$ type "short-circuit", $n^* = \sum_{j \in J} n_j^*$ is the total number of different types of items. For values n^* and n_j^*, $j \in J$ are determined by constraints on resources for optimal redundancy problem (Volkovich and Zaslavsky 1986).

The problem of optimal type-variety redundancy for parallel-series (or series-parallel) systems, where the components allow for two types of failures, involves forming configurations of structural schemes, selecting the number of type-variety elements, and determining their arrangement in the structural schemes. The goal is to optimize the structural schemes in order to find the one with the maximum reliability.

This problem can be considered as a sub-problem of the general problem of optimal redundancy, which is necessary to determine both the number of different types of elements in the sub-systems and their location in the structural diagram.

The problem of optimal type-variety redundancy for parallel-series systems, where the components allow for two types of failures, is a complex combinatorial problem of large dimensionality. It was first discussed and formally formulated in the works of Afanasiev et al. (1993) and in Franchuk (1994).

The solution scheme of this formulated problem is based on the ideas of decomposition and construction of a hierarchy of simpler optimization problems and rules for excluding unpromising solutions. Thus, the problem is divided into three interrelated subproblems, which form the basis of the computational scheme considered as follows:

1) *Subproblem 1*: this includes the formation set of possible configurations, block diagrams of different sizes based on the conditions and rules that define the structure of heterogeneous elements, perspective on the subject of optimality.

2) *Subproblem 2*: this includes choosing a multiplicity of diverse redundancy elements.

3) *Subproblem 3*: this includes generation of fixed block diagram of accommodation options diverse elements in a chain considering equivalence of block diagrams options.

The combinatorial complexity of the problem and its specific nature lead to the need for a multi-level (three-level) approach, where at each level, the corresponding subproblem is considered and solved. For each structural scheme obtained from solving subproblem 1, sets of heterogeneous backup elements and their redundancy multiples (subproblem 2) are formed. Then, at each level, subproblem 3 is addressed, forming the arrangement of a fixed number of heterogeneous elements in the selected structural scheme to ensure maximum reliability. Heuristic evaluation rules are applied at each level to assess alternatives and eliminate unpromising ones. Let us consider these subproblems separately.

Subproblem 1: suppose n (integer) is represented as $l^n = (l_1^n,...,l_i^n,...,l_r^n)$ – lexicographically ordered partition $n = l_1^n + l_2^n + ... + l_r^n$ $(n = 1,...,n^*)$ on r components, $l_1^n \geq l_2^n \geq ... \geq l_i^n \geq ... \geq l_r^n$, $l_i^n > 0$, l_i^n – integers, $i = \overline{1,r}$.

Every partition l^n corresponds to the parallel-sequential block diagram $s(l^n,r)$ of components l_i^n (length of the i_rst string) and r (wide scheme) (Figure 8.7), which then filled with elements of fixed type.

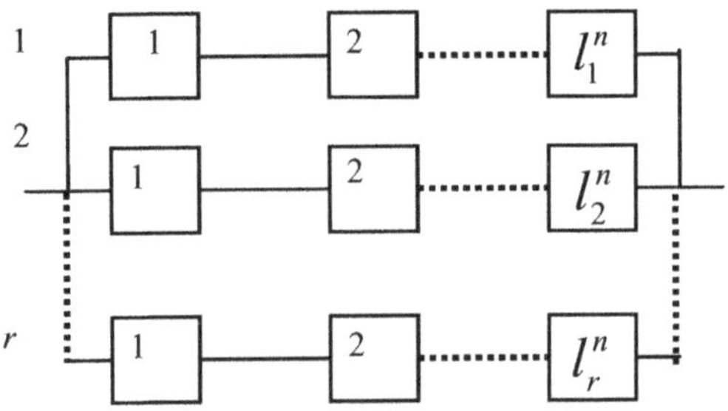

Figure 8.7. *Parallel–serial block diagram $s(l^n,r)$ with n elements and r chains $l_1^n,...,l_i^n,...,l_r^n$ of elements in each*

For each n considered $S_n = \{s(l^n,r)\}$, the set of all block diagrams corresponds to breakdown l^n of the different number of chains r. The number of such schemes is estimated at $p(n)$ (equation [8.7]). If the total number of elements $n = 6$, then $p(n) = 11$, thus there are 11 variants of parallel-serial structures (Figure 8.8).

The number of elements n of structural schemes varies between 1 and n^*. For each $n \in [1, n^*]$, relevant S_n (set of block diagrams) are formed and their total number is $\sum_{n=1}^{n} p(n)$ (coinciding with the number of variants of parallel-serial systems with identical elements). The identical elements circuit $s(l^n,r)$ is represented by graphical objects □, and, in the case of different types of items, they may be a different color. Reliability block diagram depends on the location of diverse elements in the chain.

In constructing block diagrams of heterogeneous elements (e.g. $n = 6$, see Figure 8.8), taking into account the results of section 8.1, not all flow diagrams should be considered in terms of maximizing the reliability of their structure. For example, structures 1 and 5 in Figure 8.8 are last resorts and thus hopeless, whereas structures 6–10 are possible candidates for constructing optimal configuration of heterogeneous elements.

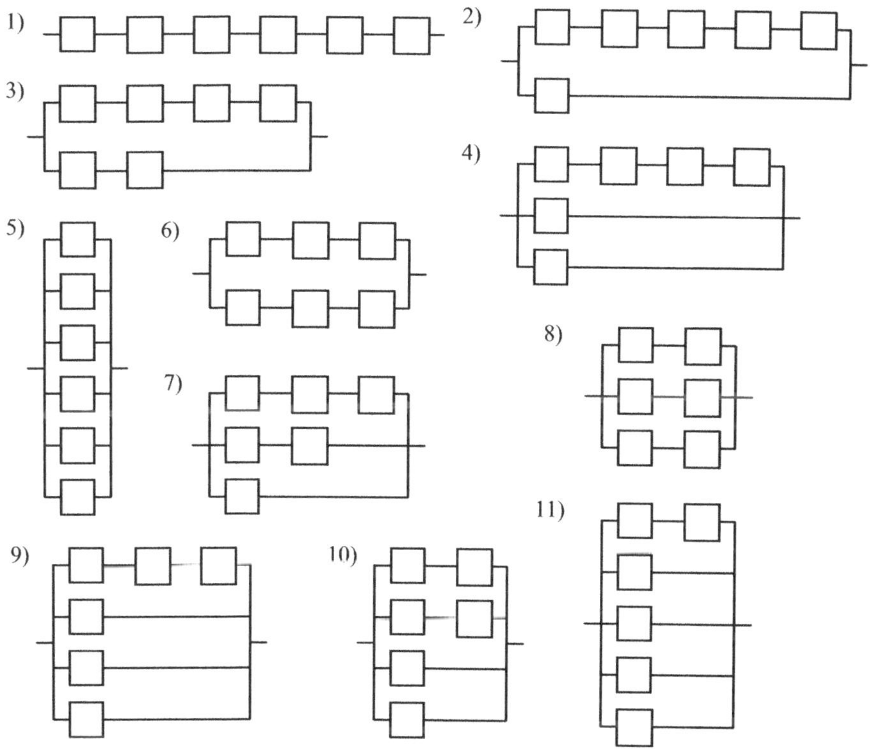

Figure 8.8. *Variants of parallel structure consistent with* $n = 6,\ S_6 = \{s(l^6, r)\}$

The idea of exclusion from further consideration of unpromising structural schemes is based on the use of an empirical approach and results which are discussed in section 8.1 through discussing the research of systems with identical elements. This idea sees us using block diagrams $s(l^n, r)$ with identical items as "approximations" options block diagrams of the heterogeneous elements of perspective for consideration.

As discussed in section 2.1, flow diagrams with identical elements with fixed values q_0 and q_{K3} that have optimal "width" of the block diagram r^* (number of parallel strings). Restrictions for $\overset{=}{r}$ - the maximum width $s(l^n, r)$ that is built from diverse elements, are given inequality $r^{\min} \le \overset{=}{r} \le r^{\max}$. Value $r^{\min}$ - minimum and $r^{\max}$ - maximum width $s(l^n, r)$ that "approximate" the desired scheme with heterogeneous elements are found as a result of solving problems [8.4]–[8.6] with failure probability $(q_0^{\max}, q_{K3}^{\max})$ and $(q_0^{\min}, q_{K3}^{\min})$ respectively, where $q_0^{\max} = \max\{q_{0,j}, j = \overline{1,k}\}$, $q_{K3}^{\max} = \max\{q_{K3,j}, j = \overline{1,k}\}$, $q_0^{\min} = \min\{q_{0,j}, j = \overline{1,k}\}$, $q_{K3}^{\min} = \min\{q_{K3,j}, j = \overline{1,k}\}$.

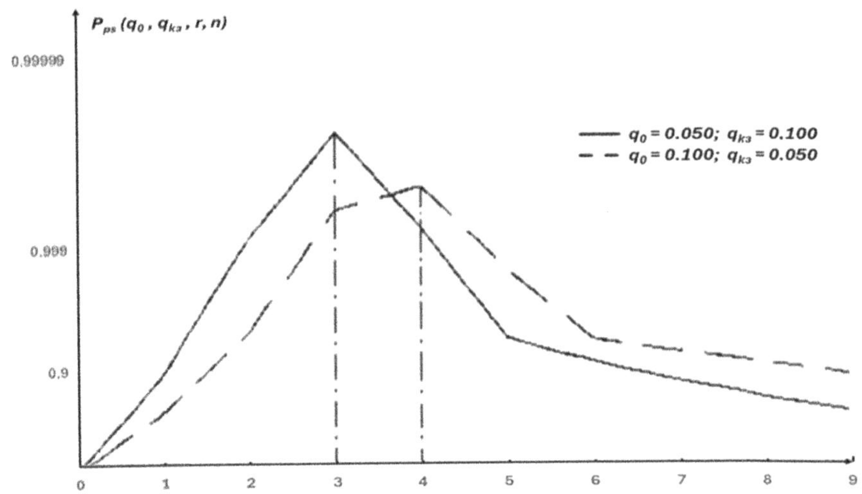

Figure 8.9. *The dependence of the reliability from the width of the circuit*

In Figure 8.9, graphs of the system of reliability of the width (number of parallel strings) when $q_0^{\min} = q_{K3}^{\min} = 0.050$, $q_0^{\max} = q_{K3}^{\max} = 0.100$, for the elements of the failure probability $q_{o,1} = 0.050$, $q_{K3,1} = 0.100$ and $q_{o,2} = 0.100$, $q_{K3,2} = 0.050$ $(n = 9)$ are presented.

For this example, the width of perspective of different types of schemes $s(l^9, r)$ can be 3 or 4. When we find $P_{ps}(q_0^{\min}, q_{K3}^{\min})$ and $P_{ps}(q_0^{\max}, q_{k3}^{\max})$, we get the upper and lower level of reliability scheme (Figure 8.10). Thus, for parameter of reliability block diagram of the heterogeneous elements, an inequality is performed:

$$\overline{P}_{ps}(q_0^{\max}, q_{k3}^{\max}) \le P_{sp}^{R}(\bullet) \le \overline{P}_{ps}(q_0^{\min}, q_{K3}^{\min}),$$

where $\overline{P}_{ps}(q_0^{\max}, q_{k3}^{\max})$ and $\overline{P}_{ps}(q_0^{\min}, q_{K3}^{\min})$ are optimal values of criterion [8.4] for problems [8.4]–[8.6] (see section 8.1).

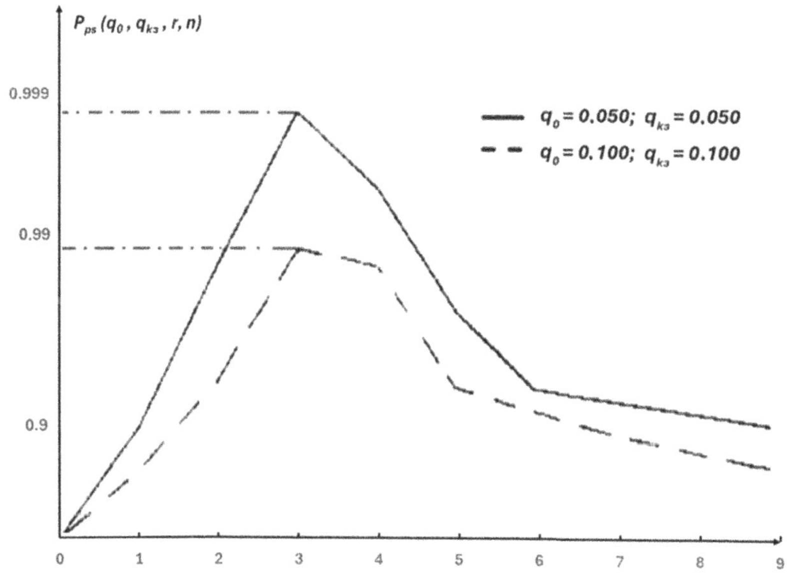

Figure 8.10. *The top and bottom borders of the reliability of the circuit*

From the set of all possible configurations of structural patterns of homogeneous elements, it is necessary to choose scheme $s(l^n, \overline{\overline{r}})$, the width of which $\overline{\overline{r}}$ satisfies inequality $r^{\min} \le \overline{\overline{r}} \le r^{\max}$. This inequality is an "approximation" of width r of block diagrams $s(l^n, r)$ and a rule of exclusion of possible solutions that can significantly reduce the total number of possible variants of block diagrams, among which seek the best of heterogeneous elements.

Thus, as a result of solving subproblem 1, subsets of sets $S_n = \left\{s(l^n, r)\right\}$, $n \in [1, n^*]$ of block diagrams are formed, which are promising for further consideration.

Consider following subproblem 2: although n is the number of elements in the circuit, then in the case of the use of diverse elements it consists of elements of k types, $n = n_1 + ... + n_j + ... + n_k$, where n_j is a number of elements of j type, $n_j \in [0, n_j^*]$, $j \in J$. Formation of value $n = \sum_{j \in J} n_j$ is a generating of sets $(n_1, n_2, ..., n_k)$, where $n_j \in [0, n_j^*]$, $j \in J$. The upper estimate of the number of such sets is variable C_{n+k-1}^{k-1}. Since the reliability of homogeneous elements are multi-extremal function, it must be considered in the formation of structures and sets. Thus, the total number of possible subproblem 3 is estimated, which is defined in equation [8.7].

Because the system reliability with identical elements is a many-extreme function, it must be considered in the formation of structures $s(l^n, r)$ and sets $(n_1, n_2, ..., n_k)$. Thus, the total number of possible subproblem 3 is estimated as $\sum_{n=1}^{n^*} p(n) \cdot C_{n+k-1}^{k-1}$, where $p(n)$ is defined in equation [8.7].

Consider a subproblem 3, whose essence is to determine the optimum layout different types elements in a fixed block diagram $s(l^n, r)$. Let x_{ij} be number of elements of j type in i chain of scheme $s(l^n, r)$, $0 \le x_{ij} \le n_j$, $j = \overline{1,k}$; $X = \left\| x_{ij} \right\|_{i=\overline{1,r}, j=\overline{1,k}}$ are matrix of layout options. Reliability of scheme $s(l^n, r)$ with heterogeneous elements is defined by:

$$P_{ps}^{R}(X, s(l^n, r), q_0, q_{k3}) = \prod_{i=1}^{r}\left(1 - \prod_{j=1}^{k}(q_{k3,j})^{x_{ij}}\right) - \prod_{i=1}^{r}\left(1 - \prod_{j=1}^{k}(1 - q_{0,j})^{x_{ij}}\right)$$

where $q_0 = (q_{0,1}, q_{0,2}, ..., q_{0,k})$ and $q_{k3} = (q_{k3,1}, q_{k3,2}, ..., q_{k3,k})$. These are vectors of probabilities of failures.

Then, the mathematical model of 3 subproblems has the form:

$$P_{ps}^{R}(X,s(l^{n},r),q_0,q_{k3})=\prod_{i=1}^{r}\left(1-\prod_{j=1}^{k}(q_{k3,j})^{x_{ij}}\right)$$
$$-\prod_{i=1}^{r}\left(1-\prod_{j=1}^{k}(1-q_{0,j})^{x_{ij}}\right)\rightarrow \max \qquad [8.10]$$

$$\sum_{i=1}^{r} xij = n_j,\ j=\overline{1,k}. \qquad [8.11]$$

$$\sum_{j=1}^{k} xij = l_i^n,\ i=\overline{1,r}. \qquad [8.12]$$

Condition [8.11] means that all n_j elements of j type should be used in the circuit $s(l^n,r)$, and condition [8.12] means that each chain ought to be equal of l_i^n elements, including elements x_{i1} of type 1, items x_{i2} of type 2, etc. If $x_{ij}=0$, then j-type of elements does not uses i chain. For the construction scheme $s(l^n,r)$, executed ratio $\sum_{i=1}^{r}\sum_{j=1}^{k} xij = n$.

Thus, the value parameter of reliability [8.10] depends on the structure $s(l^n,r)$, recruitment $(n_1,n_2,...,n_k)$ and placement of different types of elements in chains.

Let us consider the question of equivalence of different types of structural patterns considering reliability. Block diagrams of heterogeneous elements are equivalent if they are:

– formed by rearrangement of chains in $s(l^n,r)$ without changing the number and composition of different types elements in the chain (Figure 8.11(a));

– constructed by permutations of elements of different types of chain of structure $s(l^n,r)$ without changing their number and composition (Figure 8.11(b));

– formed by permutation in $s(l^n,r)$ by the same number of identical elements (Figure 8.11(c)).

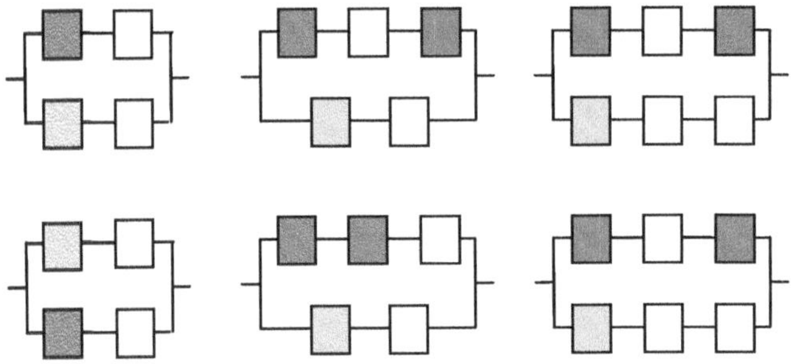

Figure 8.11. *Pairs of equivalent block diagrams*

Equivalence of schemes (solutions) should be considered in generating possible variants of structure with diverse elements by permutations of elements.

In the case where the construction $s(l^k, r)$ used one item of each type $n_1 = ... = n_k = 1$, in the optimization problems [8.10]–[8.12], constraint [8.11] takes the next form:

$$\sum_{i=1}^{r} xij = 1\,,\ j = \overline{1,k}, \qquad [8.13]$$

and the matrix elements are defined as Boule variables:

$$x_{ij} = \begin{Bmatrix} 1, \textit{if element } j \textit{ of type } i \textit{ in chain,} \\ 0, \textit{else.} \end{Bmatrix} \qquad [8.14]$$

In problems [8.10] and [8.12]–[8.14], finding the best options for the location of different types of elements is much easier as compared to problems [8.10]–[8.12]. The number of possible variations of the elements in the structure $s(l^k, r)$, that is, the number of solutions of [8.10] and [8.12]–[8.14], is $\dfrac{k!}{r! \cdot \prod_{i=1}^{r} l_i^k !}$. In this case, the condition of equivalence of solutions is defined as the following: solutions X_1 and X_2 are equivalent in case of equivalent circuits of heterogeneous elements (X_2 can be obtained from X_1 by permutation of rows).

Possible variants of placement of identical elements can lead to equivalent circuits, for example, the rearrangement of such elements within one chain. For the structure $l_9 = (3,3,3)$, consisting of nine elements of three types, with three elements of each type, there are 280 different ways to form structural schemes. But for the structure $l_9 = (2,2,5)$ with two elements of type 1, two elements of type 2, and five elements of type 3, the number of nonequivalent placement variants within a fixed structural scheme is seven (see Figure 8.12).

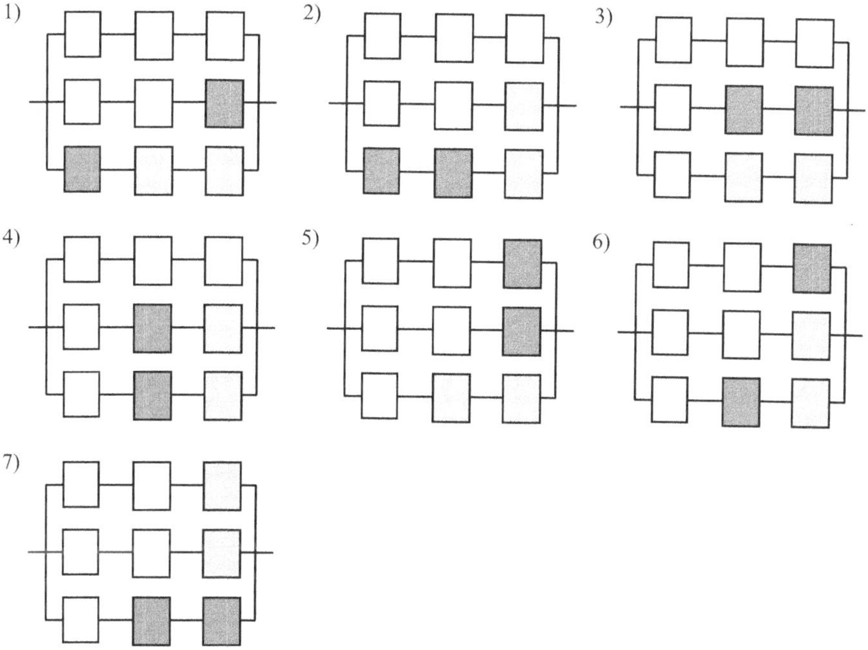

Figure 8.12. *The structure* $s(l^9,3)$, $l^9 = (3,3,3)$ *of the three types of elements*

The solution of problems [8.10]–[8.12] is carried out in the course of an iterative process with a step-by-step improvement of the reliability indicator. In this case, for a fixed structural diagram $s(l^n,r)$, such a rearrangement of elements is carried out that leads to an increase in the reliability indicator of the structure.

The function of reliability $P_{ps}^R(X, q_0, q_{k3}, r)$ is written as

$$P_{ps}^{R}(X,s(l^n,r),q_0,q_{k3}) = A\left(1-\prod_{j\in J}(q_{k3,j})^{x_{i_1 j}}\right)\left(1-\prod_{j\in J}(q_{k3,j})^{x_{i_2 j}}\right)-$$

$$-B\left(1-\prod_{j\in J}(p_{o,j})^{x_{i_1 j}}\right)\left(1-\prod_{j\in J}(p_{o,j})^{x_{i_2 j}}\right), \qquad [8.15]$$

therefore $p_{o,j} = 1-q_{o,j}$, $A = \prod_{i\in I/\{i_1,i_2\}}\left(1-\prod_{j\in J}(q_{k3,j})^{x_{ij}}\right)$,

$$B = \prod_{i\in I/\{i_1,i_2\}}\left(1-\prod_{j\in J}(p_{o,j})^{x_{ij}}\right)$$

After permutation of element of j_1 type from i_1 -string with j_2 -type from i_2 of chain, function [8.10] will be written as

$$P_{ps}^{R}(X',s(l^n,r),q_0,q_{k3}) = A\left(1-(q_{k3,j_1})^{x_{i_1 j_1}-1}(q_{k3,j_2})^{x_{i_1 j_2}+1}\prod_{j\in J/\{j_1,j_2\}}(q_{k3,j})^{x_{i_1 j}}\right)\times$$

$$\times\left(1-(q_{k3,j_1})^{x_{i_1 j_1}+1}(q_{k3,j_2})^{x_{i_1 j_2}-1}\prod_{j\in J/\{j_1,j_2\}}(q_{k3,j})^{x_{i_2 j}}\right)$$

$$-B\left(1-(p_{o,j_1})^{x_{i_1 j_1}-1}(p_{o,j_2})^{x_{i_1 j_2}+1}\prod_{j\in J}(p_{o,j})^{x_{i_1 j}}\right)$$

$$\times\left(1-(p_{o,j_1})^{x_{i_1 j_1}+1}(p_{o,j_2})^{x_{i_1 j_2}-1}\prod_{j\in J}(p_{o,j})^{x_{i_2 j}}\right). \qquad [8.16]$$

Considering the difference between [8.16] and [8.15], we find Δ_{ps}^{R} growth of function [8.10] after the permutation

$$\Delta_{ps}^{R}(X,s(l^n,r),q_0,q_{k3},r,i_1,i_2,j_1,j_2) = P_{ps}^{R}(X',s(l^n,r),q_0,q_{k3})$$
$$-P_{ps}^{R}(X,s(l^n,r),q_0,q_{k3}) =$$

$$= A\left[\left(1-\frac{q_{k3,j_2}}{q_{k3,j_1}}\prod_{j\in J}(q_{k3,j})^{x_{i_1j}}\right)\times\left(1-\frac{q_{k3,j_1}}{q_{k3,j_2}}\prod_{j\in J}(q_{k3,j})^{x_{i_2j}}\right)-\left(1-\prod_{j\in J}(q_{k3,j})^{x_{i_1j}}\right)\times\right.$$

$$\left.\times\left(1-\prod_{j\in J}(q_{k3,j})^{x_{i_2j}}\right)\right]-B\left[\left(1-\frac{p_{o,j_2}}{p_{o,j_1}}\prod_{j\in J}(p_{o,j})^{x_{i_1j}}\right)\times\left(1-\frac{p_{o,j_1}}{p_{o,j_2}}\prod_{j\in J}(p_{o,j})^{x_{i_2j}}\right)-\right.$$

$$\left.-\left(1-\prod_{j\in J}(p_{o,j})^{x_{i_1j}}\right)\times\left(1-\prod_{j\in J}(p_{o,j})^{x_{i_2j}}\right)\right]$$

Having opened the brackets and lifted the same elements, we have

$$\Delta_{ps}^{R}(X,s(l^n,r),q_0,q_{k3},r,i_1,i_2,j_1,j_2)=$$

$$= A\left[\left(1-\frac{q_{k3,j_2}}{q_{k3,j_1}}\right)\prod_{j\in J}(q_{k3,j})^{x_{i_1j}}+\left(1-\frac{q_{k3,j_1}}{q_{k3,j_2}}\right)\prod_{j\in J}(q_{k3,j})^{x_{i_2j}}\right]-$$

$$-B\left[\left(1-\frac{p_{o,j_2}}{p_{o,j_1}}\right)\prod_{j\in J}(p_{o,j})^{x_{i_1j}}+\left(1-\frac{p_{o,j_1}}{p_{o,j_2}}\right)\prod_{j\in J}(p_{o,j})^{x_{i_2j}}\right]. \qquad [8.17]$$

Expression [8.17] makes it possible to identify such elements, in which permutation achieves maximum increase reliability. This is why we apply the permutation of two elements, where the values of i_1, i_2, j_1, j_2 are the solution of the optimization problem

$$\max_{i_1,i_2,j_1,j_2}\ \Delta_{ps}^{R}(X,s(l^n,r),q_0,q_{k3},r,i_1,i_2,j_1,j_2),$$

in terms of:

$$\Delta_{ps}^{R}(X,s(l^n,r),q_0,q_{k3},r,i_1,i_2,j_1,j_2)>0,$$

$$x_{i_1j_1}>0,\ x_{i_2j_2}>0,$$

$$i_1\neq i_2,\ i_1,\ i_2\in I\ ,\ j_1\neq j_2, j_1,\ j_2\in J.$$

Tha algorithm solving the problem of optimal redundancy systems with different types of redundancy elements consists of the following steps:

– **Step 1**: solve a *subproblem* 1 (forming a plurality of configuration of block diagrams $S_n = \left\{ s(l^n, r) \right\}$ of various sizes $n \in [1, n^*]$ and promising in terms of optimality).

Perform step 2 for each structural scheme $s(l^n, r) \in S_n$.

– **Step 2**: solve a *subproblem* 2 for fixed n (forming sets $(n_1, n_2, ..., n_k)$, of $n = \sum_{j \in J} n_j$ values of multiplicities of booking heterogeneous elements). For each set $(n_1, n_2, ..., n_k)$, perform step 3.

– **Step 3**: for fixed structural scheme $s(l^n, r)$ and set $(n_1, n_2, ..., n_k)$, solve a subproblem 3 of the third form [8.10]–[8.12]. Obtained solution is compared with the best solution obtained in a previous iteration.

8.4. Conclusion

In this section, the conducted research allowed us to develop constructive models and algorithms for solving the problem of optimal redundancy of series–parallel and parallel–series systems with both the same type and different types of elements that have two types of failure: open-circuit failure and short-circuit failure. The optimization algorithms are based on the identified properties of the reliability indicator of parallel–series systems with the same type of redundancy elements, identified as a result of numerous computational experiments. The models and algorithms for optimizing the reliability of parallel–series and series–parallel systems presented in this section are included in the DSS and are used to solve real problems of designing complex systems.

8.5. References

Afanasiev, V.G., Verhoturov, V.I., Zaslavsky, V.A. (1993). *Designing Reliable Communication Satellites*. MGP 'RASKO', Tomsk.

Andrews, G. (1982). *Partition Theory*. Nauka, Moscow.

Barlow, R. and Proschan, F. (1965). *Mathematical Theory of Reliability*. John Wiley & Sons, New York.

Druzhynin, G.V. (1986). *Reliability of Automated Production Systems*. Energoatomizdat, Moscow.

Epifanov, A.D. (1976). *Reliability of Control Systems*. Mashynostroenie, Moscow.

Franchuk, O.V. (1994). Development of optimal algorithms and software complexes backup and maintenance of complex systems. PhD Thesis, Taras Shevchenko National University of Kyiv, Kyiv.

Gutjahr, W., Pflug, G.C., Ruszscinsky, A. (1993). Configuration of series-parallel networks with maximum reliability. Report WP-93-60, IIASA, Laxenburg.

Gutjahr, W., Pflug, G.C., Ruszscinsky, A. (1996). Configuration of series-parallel networks with maximum reliability. *Microelectron. Reliab.*, 36(2), 247–253.

Jenney, B.W. and Sherwin, D.J. (1986). Open and short circuits reliability of systems of identical items. *IEEE Trans. Reliab.*, 35(5), 388–394.

Kirilyuk, V.S. (1995). On the most reliable structure of a parallel-sequential circuit of elements with two types of failures. *Cybernetics and Systems Analysis*, 1, 34–46.

Kirilyuk, V.S. (1997). On optimal structures of parallel-sequential systems with two types of failures. *Dop. NASU. Ser. A*, 109–114.

Kirilyuk, V.S. (2000). On maximum reliability problem in parallel-series systems with two failure modes. In *Probabilistic Constrained Optimization. Methodology and Applications*, Uryasev, S.P. (ed.). Kluwer Academic Publisher, Dordrecht.

Kovalev, M.M. (1997). *Matroids in Discrete Optimization*. Izd-vo 'Universitetskoe', Minsk.

Moore, E. and Shannon, K. (1960). *Reliable Systems from Unreliable Relays*. Foreign Languages Publishing House, Moscow.

Nakagava, N. and Hattory, Y. (1981). Discussion of constrained reliability problems with several models of failure. *IEEE Trans. Reliab.*, 30(5), 424–428.

Page, L.B. and Perry, J.E. (1988). Optimal series-parallel networks of 3-state devices. *IEEE Trans. Reliab.*, 37(4), 388–394.

Revyakov, M.I. (1988). Optimal reliability arrangement of redundant systems from elements of different reliability. *Technical Cybernetics*, 1988, 72–76.

Volkovich, V.L. and Zaslavsky, V.A. (1986). Algorithm for solving reliability optimization of complex systems using different types of redundant elements subsystems. *Kibernetika*, 5(81), 54–61.

Volkovich, V.L., Voloshin, A.F., Zaslavsky, V.A., Ushakov, I.A. (1992). *Models and Algorithms for Optimizing the Reliability of Complex Systems*. Naukova Dumka, Kyiv.

Voloshin, A.F. (1977a). On one algorithm for optimizing the structure of the designed system according to the reliability criterion. In *First International Conference of Young Scientists 'Problems of Design and Application of Discrete Control Systems*. BSU, Minsk.

Voloshin, A.F. (1977b). Sequential variants analysis in discrete optimization problems and its application. PhD Thesis, Taras Shevchenko National University of Kyiv, Kyiv.

Vtorova-Karyevskaya, E.I. and Litvak, E.I. (1979). On the reliability of systems that allow two types of failures. *Izvestiya AN SSSR, Tekhn. Cybernet.*, 4, 150–152.

Zaslavsky, V.A. and Franchuk, O.V. (1989). Optimal redundancy of a complex system with two types of inoperative states of elements. *Bulletin of Taras Shevchenko National University of Kyiv*, 64–68.

List of Authors

Iuliana ARMAS
Department of Geomorphology, Pedology and Geomatics
University of Bucharest
Romania

Konstantin ATOYEV
Department of Mathematical Methods of Operations Research
V.M. Glushkov Institute of Cybernetics of the NAS of Ukraine
Kyiv
Ukraine

Juraj BALKOVIČ
Agriculture, Forestry and Ecosystem Services Research Group
International Institute for Applied Systems Analysis (IIASA)
Laxenburg
Austria

Viacheslav L. BOGDANOV
National Academy of Sciences of Ukraine (NASU)
S.P. Timoshenko Institute of Mechanics of NASU
Center for evaluation of activity of research institutions and scientific support of regional development of Ukraine NASU
Kyiv
Ukraine

Andre DEPPERMANN
International Institute for Applied Systems Analysis (IIASA)
Laxenburg
Austria

Tatiana Y. ERMOLIEVA
IIASA Integrated Biosphere Futures Research Group (IBF)
International Institute for Applied Systems Analysis (IIASA)
Laxenburg
Austria

Oleg FRANCHUK
Department of Network Technologies
Faculty of Informatics
National University of
"Kyiv-Mohyla Academy"
Kyiv
Ukraine

Stefan FRANK
International Institute for Applied
Systems Analysis (IIASA)
Laxenburg
Austria

Alexei A. GAIVORONSKI
Department of Industrial Economy
and Technology Management
Norwegian University of
Science and Technology
Trondheim
Norway

Aleksandr N. GOLODNIKOV
Department of Mathematical
Methods of Operations Research
V.M. Glushkov Institute of
Cybernetics of the NAS of Ukraine
Kyiv
Ukraine

Petr HAVLIK
Biodiversity and Natural Resources
Program (BNR)
International Institute for Applied
Systems Analysis (IIASA)
Laxenburg
Austria

Marcel HÜRLIMANN
Department of Civil and
Environmental Engineering,
UPC-BarcelonaTECH
Spain

Pavel S. KNOPOV
National Academy of Sciences
of Ukraine (NASU)
Department of Mathematical
Methods of Operations Research
V.M. Glushkov Institute of
Cybernetics of the NAS of Ukraine
Kyiv
Ukraine

Nadejda KOMENDANTOVA
Cooperation and Transformative
Governance Research Group
International Institute for Applied
Systems Analysis (IIASA)
Laxenburg
Austria

Andrey LESSA-DERCI-
AUGUSTYNCZIK
IIASA Integrated Biosphere Futures
Research Group (IBF)
International Institute for Applied
Systems Analysis (IIASA)
Laxenburg
Austria

Andrè (Mahdi) NAKHAVALI
IIASA Integrated Biosphere Futures
Research Group (IBF)
Research Group International
Institute for Applied Systems
Analysis (IIASA)
Laxenburg
Austria

Vladimir I. NORKIN
Department of Mathematical Methods of Operations Research
V.M. Glushkov Institute of Cybernetics of the NAS of Ukraine
Kyiv
Ukraine

Maya PASICHNA
SCANIA
Stockholm
Sweden

Volodumir A. PEPELYAEV
Department of System Modeling Methods
V.M. Glushkov Institute of Cybernetics of the NAS of Ukraine
Kyiv
Ukraine

Elena ROVENSKAJA
Advancing Systems Analysis (ASA)
International Institute for Applied Systems Analysis (IIASA)
Laxenburg
Austria

Rastislav SKALSKY
National Agricultural and Food Centre
Soil Science and Conservation Research Institute (NPPC-VUPOP)
Bratislava
Slovakia

Zhonghua SU
Norwegian University of Science and Technology
Trondheim
Norway

Dragos TOMA-DANILA
National Institute for Earth Physics
Măgurele
Ilfov
Romania

Asgeir TOMASGARD
Department of Industrial Economics and Technology Management
Norwegian University of Science and Technology
Trondheim
Norway

Liliia B. VOVK
Department of Applied Mathematics
Igor Sikorsky Kyiv Polytechnic Institute
National Technical University of Ukraine
Ukraine

Anatoly G. ZAGORODNY
National Academy of Sciences of Ukraine (NASU)
Bogolyubov Institute for Theoretical Physics of NASU
Center for evaluation of activity of research institutions and scientific support of regional development of Ukraine NASU
Kyiv
Ukraine

Volodymyr A. ZASLAVSKYI
Department of Computer Science and Cybernetics
Taras Shevchenko National University of Kyiv
Ukraine

Taher ZOBEIDI
International Institute for Applied Systems Analysis (IIASA)
Laxenburg
Austria

9

Mathematical Models for the Study of Critical Infrastructure Vulnerability

This chapter presents a mathematical approach developed to assess the critical infrastructure (CI) vulnerability and the consequences of disruptions in CI objects for interconnected economic sectors. A risk assessment is conducted using smooth function theory methods and a six-sector Lorenz model with variable coefficients. The study explores the economic consequences of CI disruptions, sensitivity to small changes and the dependency of CI vulnerability in various economic sectors on control parameters.

9.1. Introduction

Global changes in recent decades have significantly deformed the global security landscape across various dimensions – technological, economic, environmental and social. As a result, the vulnerability of CI has increased substantially. CI includes facilities, systems, networks or parts thereof, whose malfunction or destruction leads to serious consequences for a country's economic development and significantly impacts national security. CI objects include (1) energy facilities and networks; (2) communication and information technology; (3) finance (banking, securities and investment); (4) healthcare; (5) food security; (6) hydraulic structures (dams, levees and canals); (7) storage, processing and distribution networks; (8) transport (airports, ports, intermodal facilities, rail and transit networks, and traffic management systems); (9) production, storage and transportation of hazardous materials (chemical, biological, radiological and nuclear materials); and (10) government administration (information networks, assets and national landmarks and monuments).

Chapter written by Konstantin ATOYEV.

The increase in the number of technogenic disasters, along with the scale of the damage they cause, has focused attention on the problem of a crisis in management systems. This crisis is associated with a narrowing of the forecasting horizon, manifesting in the fact that low-probability events occur much more frequently than predicted by traditional safety assessment methods. Due to globalization, the technosphere has transformed into a system characterized by the following features: (1) the presence of multiple development trajectories and "windows of vulnerability"; (2) a limited timeframe for decision making; (3) the rapid pace of changes in order parameters that define human safety; and (4) a strong dependence on initial conditions, making it so that small influences can lead to significant divergences in development trajectories (Wilkinson et al. 2002).

The increasing role of minor impacts expands the scope of traditional risks and gives rise to fundamentally new ones. These are associated with events of enormous destructive power, prolonged in time, unfolding on a transnational scale, where their effects are felt in geographical zones far from the incident site (Renn 2003). This has led to a sharp increase in the vulnerability of CI. Until recently, security policy in the field of CI protection was based on addressing issues related only to the crisis in management systems (Ermoliev and von Vinterfeldt 2012; Golodnikov et al. 2013a, 2013b; Norkin et al. 2018; Zgurovsky 2024). However, in the context of military conflicts, it is necessary to approach the problem of CI protection from a new perspective. There is a need to significantly revise the old security paradigms, considering the role that CI has come to play in modern warfare as a target for attacks. It is essential to consider the likelihood of deliberate destruction of energy facilities, hydraulic structures and hazardous enterprises in the nuclear and chemical industries. Therefore, the task of developing and implementing automated systems that enable forecasting and prevention of crisis phenomena, ranking threat levels and identifying weak points that significantly influence the deformation of the security space, has become highly relevant. The development of mathematical models and methods to address these tasks is the goal of this work.

9.2. The general approach to CI risk assessment

Since the issue of sustainable functioning of CI involves a complex set of technological, environmental, economic and social factors, its solution requires an integrated approach that considers the development trajectory of a complex system in the space of the aforementioned factors. The effectiveness of CI management can be seen as a complex set of interactions within the "security square" (Atoyev 2005), defined by technological, environmental, economic and social impacts, which are assessed by the corresponding indices W_T, W_{EN}, W_{EC} and W_S, respectively. Thus, risk represents a vector in the four-dimensional space of these factors.

In recent years, the issue of improving the effectiveness of the CI vulnerability assessment has come to the forefront, mainly due to the global rise in terrorist threats. According to the approach proposed by RAND Corporation (Willis et al. 2005, p. 10), the risk of a terrorist act on a CI object R_{CI} consists of three components: the probability of choosing a particular target P_T, the probability that the attack will be successful P_V and the extent of human and material losses from a terrorist attack E.

$$R_{CI} = P_T P_V E. \qquad [9.1]$$

Each component contributes to the overall uncertainty in risk assessment. The greatest uncertainty is associated with the terrorists' choice of targets P_T, while the least uncertainty is related to estimating the damage from the attack, which depends on the material or physical factors characterizing the target at the time of the attack (Willis et al. 2005, p. 13).

Let us consider that the choice of a target for an attack largely depends on the ability to cause maximum destruction with minimal resource expenditure, as well as inflicting maximum economic damage from the attack. Therefore, we will assume that the choice of a target for an attack on CI is made by assessing the overall vulnerability of the object, which depends on its technological, environmental, economic and social characteristics. The probability that the attack will be successful also largely depends on the level of vulnerability. Therefore, we will combine these two probabilities and use the probability of the destruction of a CI object as a result of an adversary's attack as a function $P_{CI}(W_T, W_{EN}, W_{EC}, W_S)$.

In Atoyev et al. (2017) and Atoyev and Knopov (2022), mathematical models for analyzing the vulnerability of CI have been developed based on the theory of smooth mappings using examples from housing and communal services, potentially hazardous facilities and environmentally polluting enterprises. The main advantages of the proposed approach include the ability to (1) forecast and manage complex risks; (2) rank different types of threats, identify weak links in CI and quantitatively assess the proximity to critical parameter values indicating increase in risk; (3) calculate, using optimal control theory, the trajectories of changes in CI parameters to reduce the risks of man-made disasters and minimize the costs of their elimination.

In Atoyev (2005) and Atoyev and Knopov (2023), multi-sector Lorenz models were developed to study the interconnections between different sectors of the economy and determine the conditions for instability in such complex systems. These models are integrated in a holistic structure from various economic sectors, described in the same way. Each sector is considered in terms of productivity levels, the number of jobs and structural disruptions. They allow for the calculation of the losses from instability in the functioning of such complex systems as CI. The measure of these losses is the level of structural disruptions.

To assess risks for CI, we will combine these two approaches. The model should include (1) a block for evaluating the proximity of parameters characterizing CI to their bifurcation values, the attainment of which sharply increases the probability of its destruction; (2) an economic block for assessing the impact of CI destruction on the economy. Furthermore, the system of interconnections between these blocks should be considered.

9.3. The model for assessment of CI vulnerability

The analysis of rare events shows that they are typically associated with sudden, discontinuous changes that result from small continuous impacts on the system. Traditional forecasting methods are not sufficiently effective for events of this kind. The emergence of new forms of global problems related to a wide range of asymmetric threats, high sensitivity to initial conditions and the increasing likelihood that a small disturbance can lead to unpredictable consequences necessitates the development of new mathematical approaches for studying systems with these properties.

To study the processes of instability emergence in complex systems, whose behaviour exhibits discontinuous changes or phase transitions due to small continuous changes in the variables characterizing the system, the mathematical formalism of catastrophe theory was employed in Sergienko et al. (1997) and Atoyev et al. (2017). This approach allows for the calculation of bifurcation values, curves and surfaces of control parameters. The risk of transitioning the system from one steady state (normal) to another (catastrophe) is assessed by the proximity of the values of control parameters to their bifurcation values.

Let us consider a bistable oscillatory system that describes the motion of a material point of mass m in a potential field $U(x)$ with friction γ, represented as follows:

$$m\frac{d^2x}{dt^2} + \gamma\frac{dx}{dt} = F(x) = k(x - x^3) \qquad [9.2]$$

The first term on the left side of [9.2] represents the inertial force, while the second term represents the frictional force, which is proportional to the velocity. In the absence of friction ($\gamma = 0$), equation [9.2] describes undamped oscillations (the Lyapunov numbers in this case are purely imaginary). In this situation, we have a conservative or Hamiltonian system in which the law of conservation of energy applies. In the case with the presence of friction ($\gamma > 0$), there is partial dissipation of energy. When the dissipation is very strong, we can neglect the inertial force in [9.2].

Thus, we have

$$\frac{dx}{dt_1} = F(x) = k(x - x^3)\text{, where } \gamma = 0,\ t_1 = t / \gamma.$$

The function $U(x)$, called the potential, will be introduced as follows:

$$U(x) = -\int F(x)dx,$$

where $F(x)$ is function describing the motion in potential field $U(x)$.

In mechanics, quantum mechanics and field theory, Hamiltonian systems are primarily considered. However, in "real life", we often deal with dissipative systems. To study the system behavior near local extrema function $U(x)$, the function $F(x)$ is expanded into a series in the neighborhood of stationary states, and the expansion is limited to a few small terms.

The minimum number of dimensions n and parameters k that need to be considered is determined by the degree of degeneracy of the stationary state. They are connected by the usual relationship: $k = n-1$. In catastrophe theory, this number is referred to as the co-dimension of the catastrophe. For the investigation of a wide range of phenomena, the "cusp" catastrophe is most commonly used, which involves the merging of three special points (Poston and Stewart 1978), for which $n = 3,\ k = 2$.

To assess risk, we will use the "cusp" catastrophe, whose potential has the following form:

$$U(x) = -x^4 / 4 - Ax^2 / 2 - Bx$$

The manifold of the catastrophe is defined by the following equation:

$$-\frac{\partial U(x)}{\partial x} = x^3 + Ax - B. \qquad [9.3]$$

The polynomial [9.3], according to Sturm's theorem regarding the number of real roots of a polynomial (Andronov et al. 1959), has at most three and at least one real root. The number of roots depends on the discriminant $\Delta = 4A^3 + 27B^2$. If the condition $\Delta < 0$ is satisfied, there are three real roots. The system has three steady states, two of which are stable. The first stable steady state represents the norm (an acceptable level of vulnerability of the system), while the second represents a crisis (a dangerous level of vulnerability). When $\Delta > 0$, there is one real root and two imaginary ones. The bifurcation curve has the following form:

$$\Delta(A, B) = 0. \quad [9.4]$$

The measure of the risk for the transition of the system from one steady state, corresponding to the norm, to another, corresponding to a crisis, is the degree of proximity of parameters A and B to their bifurcation values A^* and B^*, whose achievement leads to a sharp change in the trajectory of development. Since the parameter characterizes rapid impacts on the system, it was used to assess the risk in Atoyev et al. (2007). The bifurcation value of this parameter is determined from equation [9.4]

$$B^* = \pm 2A\sqrt{A / 27}$$

The risk value R can be assessed as follows:

$$R = 1 - (B^* - B) / B^* \quad [9.5]$$

If $B = 0$, then $R = 0$, and if $B = B^*$, then $R = 1$. If $B > B^*$, we will also consider $R = 1$. For the chosen acceptable level of risk R_{AC}, the corresponding value B_{AC} is determined from [9.5], which will be used in further research to determine the strategy for ensuring the specified level of CI security.

Risk assessment for CI requires reliable information about the objects being studied. The absence of such information, due to incomplete sampling or the stochastic nature of the research object, leads to uncertainty (Pepelyaev et al. 2024). In this situation, the effectiveness of deterministic models decreases, making the issue of accounting for stochasticity particularly relevant (Wagenmakers et al 2005). There are several approaches to addressing this issue. In Ebeling and Engel-Herbert (1982), the case of non-equilibrium stochastic systems approaching a stationary state was examined. It was shown that for gradient systems, the set of transitions (catastrophes) coincides under both deterministic and stochastic descriptions and consists of all points in the control space where the number and type of extremal points change. When the modeled process is stochastic and governed by the Langevin equation, equation [9.3] transforms into the following form:

$$-\partial U(x) / \partial x = dx / dt = x^3 + Ax + B + D^{(1/2)}\xi(t),$$

where D is a constant and $\xi(t)$ is an independent Gaussian δ-correlated fluctuating quantity. According to Ebeling and Engel-Herbert (1982), the system is described using a single, globally stable stationary probability distribution $P^0(x, A, B)$, which is related to $U(x, A, B)$, as follows:

$$P^0(x, A, B) = (1 / n)[2U(x, A, B) / D]$$

9.4. Assessing the consequences of CI disruptions

For the economic block of the model, we will use a multi-sector Lorenz model. In this context, as in Atoyev and Knopov (2023) and Atoyev et al. (2024), we will consider the following assumptions: (1) there is competition for labor among different sectors of the economy, so the growth of the production function in one sector hinders job creation in others; (2) fluctuations in energy prices, changes in the balance of natural and material resources, changes due to the disruption of CI and the introduction of new technologies that significantly alter productivity – all of these provoke random disturbances that become additional factors for increasing the level of structural disruptions; (3) processes in different sectors of the economy may proceed at different rates; (4) an increase in the vulnerability level of CI x leads to a decrease in the system's capacity to recover from structural disruptions; (5) parameters A and B from [9.3] change with an increase in structural disruptions.

The mathematical model that integrates the economic and security blocks has the following form:

$$\varepsilon_{Xi} \frac{dX_i}{dt} = \sigma_i (Y_i - X_i) + \delta_i \dot{w}_{ij}$$

$$\varepsilon_{Yi} \frac{dY_i}{dt} = [r_i (1 - \sum a_{ij} X_i) - Z_i] X_i - Y_i + \delta_i \dot{w}_{ij} \qquad [9.6]$$

$$\varepsilon_{Zi} \frac{dZ_i}{dt} = X_i Y_i - b_i (1 - k_i x) Z_i + \delta_i \dot{w}_{ij}$$

$$\varepsilon_x \frac{dx}{dt} = x^3 + (A + \sum_{i-1}^{6} l_i Z_i)x + B + \sum_{i-1}^{6} m_i Z_i + \delta_i \dot{w}_{ij},$$

where X_i are normalized levels of productivity, Y_i are normalized jobs and Z_i are normalized level of structural disturbances in the following sectors: energy facilities and networks (i = *E*); transport service (i = *T*); hydraulic structures, water supply networks (i = *H*); chemical industry, production, transportation and storage of hazardous materials (i = *C*); food and medical supply facilities (i = *FM*); communication and information technology (i = *I*); x is normalized levels of vulnerability of CI; $\sigma_i, r_i, b_i (i = \overline{1,6})$ are parameters of the Lorenz model, which are functions of specific demands and supplies for the products of the respective production systems and the number of jobs occupied in them; a_{ij} are parameters characterizing competition between different sectors of the economy in labor markets $i \neq j$); k_i, l_i and m_i are parameters characterizing the impact of CI vulnerability on economic sectors, and the impact of structural disruptions on the dynamics of CI vulnerability, respectively; $\varepsilon_{Xi}, \varepsilon_{Yi}, \varepsilon_{Zi}, \varepsilon_x$ are parameters that allow for considering the time hierarchy; $w_{ij}(t)$ are independent standard Wiener processes with parameters $E(w_{ij}(t) - w_{ij}(s)) = 0$, $E(w_{ij}(t) - w_{ij}(s))^2 = |t-s|$; δ_i are intensities of disturbance.

According to the results obtained in Atoyev (2005), the parameters σ_i, r_i, b_i are related to the characteristics that determine the functioning of economic sectors as follows:

$$\sigma_i = (\alpha_{1i}\beta_{2i}) / (\alpha_{2i}\gamma_{2i}), \; r_i = (\beta_{1i}\gamma_{1i}) / (\beta_{2i}\gamma_{2i})), \; b_i = \zeta_i / (\alpha_{2i}\gamma_{2i}), \quad [9.7]$$

where α_{1i} and α_{2i} are parameters that characterize adaptive capabilities; β_{1i} is the demand for activity of the *i*th manufacturing system normalized to the unit of material production system, that is, to a job in the corresponding branch of manufacturing Y_i; β_{2i} is the level of supply, normalized to the unit of function of the *i*th manufacturing system X_i; γ_{1i} is the demand for increasing the number of jobs, normalized to the unit of X_i; γ_{2i} is the level of supply for increasing the number of jobs, normalized to the unit of Y_i; and ζ_i is the specific rate of disruption elimination.

The investigation of the Lorenz model (Lorenz 1963) shows that increasing the parameter r is crucial for the onset of turbulence. The operating modes change at the following bifurcation values of parameter r: $r = 13.926$, $r = 24.06$, $r = 24.74$. When $r > 24.74$, the system transitions to a regime of metastable chaos – a strange attractor emerges (Kaplan and Yorke 1979). As follows from [9.7], the transition of parameters r_i to the range of values corresponding to the regime of metastable chaos is achieved by increasing the specific demand for the products of the manufacturing system and the number of jobs employed (parameters β_{1i} and γ_{1i}) or by reducing their specific supply (parameters β_{2i} and γ_{2i}).

Let us consider how the rate of disruption elimination affects the level of security of CI. As follows from [9.7], a decrease in the rates of disruption elimination ζ_i leads to decline in parameters b_i. Rates ζ_i change significantly faster than the adaptive capabilities α_{2i} and the supply of increasing the number of jobs γ_{2i}. Within short time intervals, α_{2i} and γ_{2i} can be consider constants. In these conditions, we will associate the decrease in b_i only with the reduction in ζ_i.

Figures 9.1 and 9.2 show how the dynamics of vulnerability x, the proximity of the current values of the parameter B to bifurcation value B^* and the discriminant Δ change with the decrease in the parameters b_i of model [9.6].

The study presented in these figures was conducted with the following values for parameter b_i: $b_i = 16/3$ (a); $b_i = 12/3$ (b); $b_i = 8/3$ (c); $b_i = 5/3$ (d).

As follows from Figure 9.1, the decrease in b_i leads to transformation of dynamics for variables of model [9.6]. The operating modes transit to chaotic regime. The modeling results also indicate changing in the sign of the discriminant, meaning the number of steady states of the system changes. The sign of the function $B^* - B$ also changes, causing the system to abruptly shift to a new steady state. Thus, the modeling results indicate that reduction in b_i leads to a disruption in system synchronization and the gradual onset of chaotic modes.

The simulation results indicate that reducing the rate of eliminating structural disruptions leads to changes in the sign of the discriminant Δ, meaning the number of stationary states of the system changes.

For simplicity in modeling, it was assumed that the coefficients for all sectors are the same: $A = 2$, $B = 1$, $r_i = 24$, $k_i = 0.5$, $\varepsilon_{Xi} = \varepsilon_{Yi} = \varepsilon_{Zi} = \varepsilon_x = 0.2$, $l_i = m_i = 0.015$.

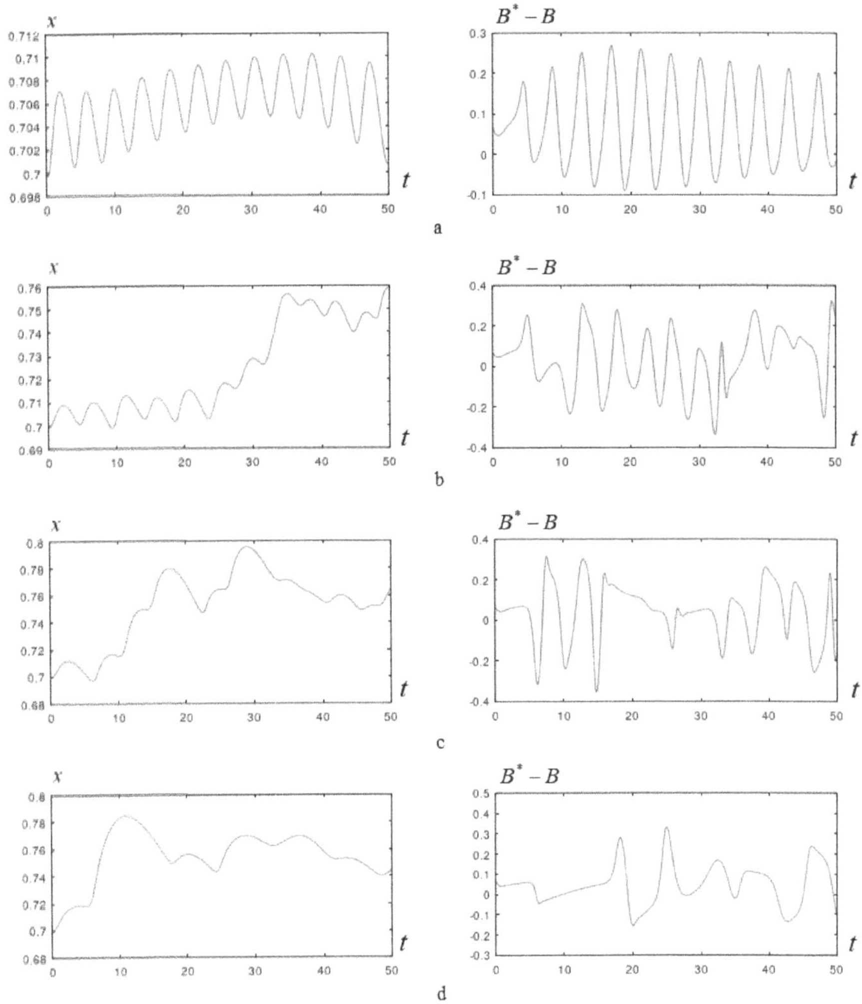

Figure 9.1. *The impact of changes in b on changes in the CI vulnerability*

Figure 9.3 shows how the level of the total structural disruption of the CI $\sum\int Z_i dt$ changes with the variation of the parameters r_i. The results of the research show that there are regions of parameters r_i, in which the level of structured disruption increases sharply. For the energy sector (i = E), when the demand-to-supply ratio reaches a level corresponding to the values of parameters r_i in the range from $r_i = 22$ to $r_i = 24$, the level of total disruption increases from

3,856.4 to 8,077.6. A further increase in r_i initially reduces this level to 3,925.9 at $r_i = 26$, but then the level of structural disturbances begins to rise again.

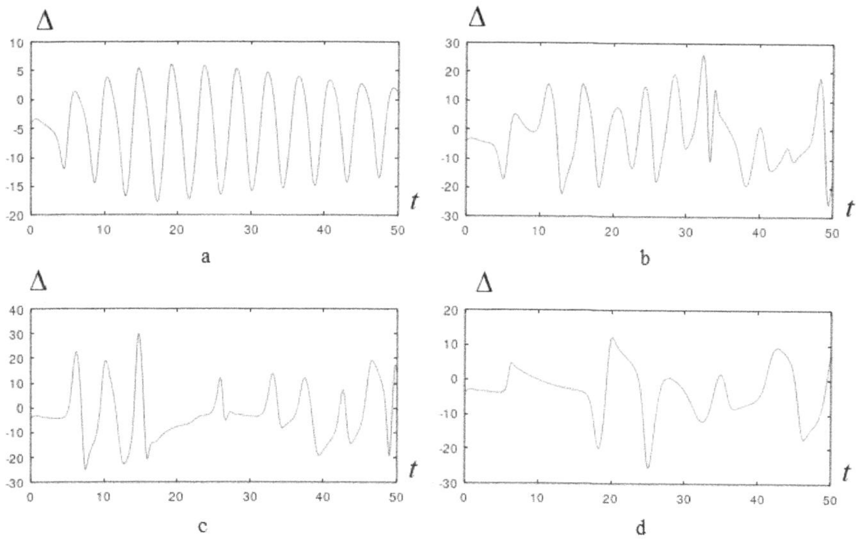

Figure 9.2. *The impact of changes in b on changes in discriminant of [9.3]*

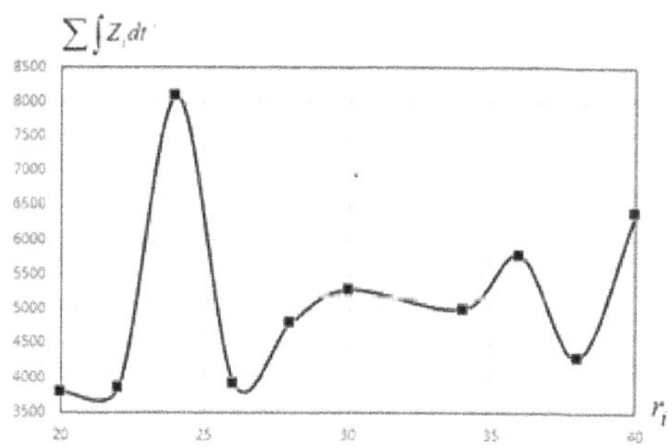

Figure 9.3. *Dependence of total structural disturbances of CI on parameter r*

In Figure 9.4, it is shown how the dynamics of disturbances Z_E change with a decrease in parameters b_i: $b_i = 16/3$ (a); $b_i = 8/3$ (b)), as well as the projections of the phase space of system [9.6] onto the planes $Z_E - X_E$, using one of the sectors of the economy related to the energy system as an example $i = E$.

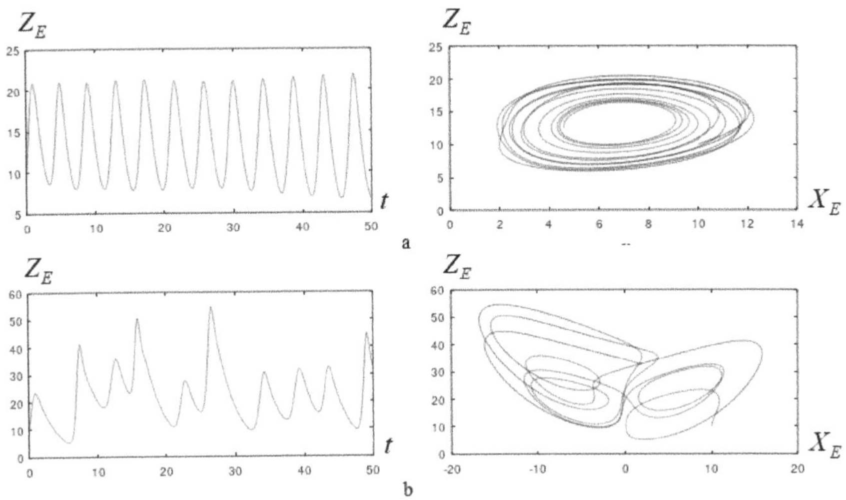

Figure 9.4. *Dependence of disturbances in energy system on parameter b*

9.5. Dependence on small changes in model parameters

The formation of a complex and interconnected network of modern society significantly deforms the fields of natural, technological and economic risks. The nodes of this network serve as unique acupuncture points of vulnerability for CI, where small influences can lead to unforeseen consequences on a large scale with irreversible damage (a kind of domino effect). This occurs due to the density of connections between nodes, unprecedented lengthening of causal relationships and the speed at which material values and information circulate through the links of this network. The behavior of such systems often becomes unstable (Laszlo 1993; Kröger and Zio 2011).

Therefore, the network society can be seen as a system near an unstable stationary state within a bifurcation zone, where the likelihood of sudden and unforeseen events increases.

Very small fluctuations can lead to abrupt changes in the socioeconomic and natural-technological characteristics of society, with the amplitude of these jumps potentially being quite significant (Zgurovsky and Pankratova 2007; Ermoliev and von Vinterfeldt 2012).

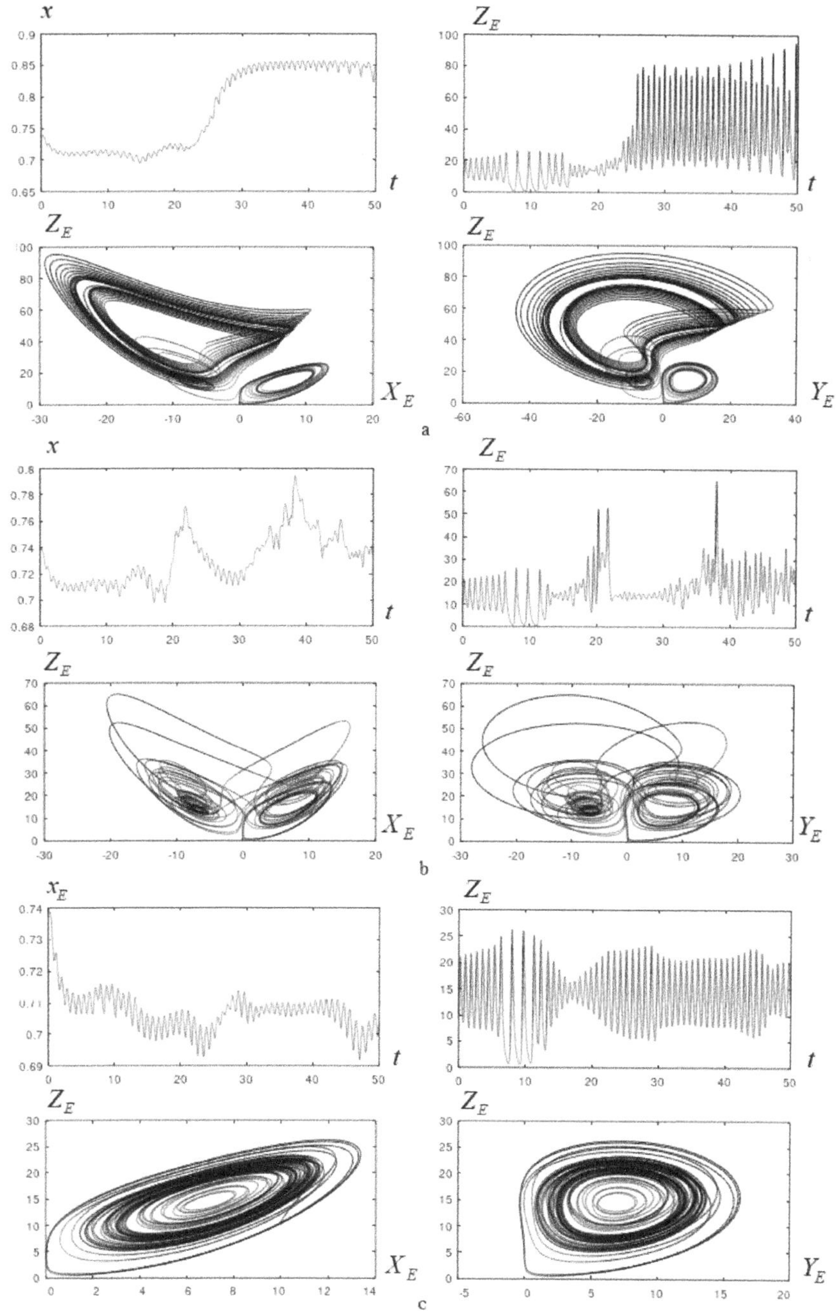

Figure 9.5. *Dependence of disturbances in energy system on parameter B*

Figure 9.5 illustrates the results of modeling, where a very slight change in the parameter B leads to a significant shift in the operating mode of system [9.6]. When $B = 1$, the level of structural disruptions reaches maximum (Figure 9.5(a)).

With a small increase or decrease in B by a value of 10^{-9} (as shown in Figures 9.5(b) and (c)), the total structural disruptions significantly decrease to levels $\sum \int Z_i dt = 5192.8$ and $\sum \int Z_i dt = 3870.9$, respectively.

Moreover, the phase portraits of the system differ significantly. These results were obtained at $\varepsilon_{Xi} = \varepsilon_{Yi} = \varepsilon_{Zi} = \varepsilon_x = 1.0$.

Thus, a slight change in the balance of supply and demand can significantly alter the development trajectory of the system, change the vulnerability of CI and affect the scale of negative consequences in case of its disruption. At the same time, due to this high sensitivity to small parameter changes under chaotic conditions, it is possible to shift the system from one unstable limit cycle to another, thereby qualitatively altering the system's behavior with minimal costs for changes in the interconnected sectors of the economy.

Thus, a transformation of the chaos management process from actions aimed at stopping it to the choice of controls stabilizing some unstable periodic trajectories (Magnitskii and Sidorov 2006) has occurred.

The further development of this work will be aimed at determining the dependence of the control parameters A and B of model [9.3] on the technological, economic, environmental and social factors that characterize the functioning of CI. These parameters may be determined using approaches elaborated in Atoyev et al. (2017), Ermoliev et al. (2020), Pepelyaev et al. (2023) and Shulzhenko et al. (2024).

Thus, using the proposed model [9.6], the risk assessment function [9.1] is transformed as follows:

$$R_{CI} = P_T P_V E \rightarrow P_{CI}(W_T, W_{EN}, W_{EC}, W_S)E = R \sum_{i=1}^{6} \int Z_t dt \,.$$

Using model [9.5], R is determined, and with model [9.6], $\sum_{i=1}^{6} \int Z_t dt$ is determined.

9.6. Assessment of CI risks for separate economic sectors

In constructing model [9.6], we started from the assumption that the level of structural disruptions to CI in each economic sector is influenced by the overall vulnerability of CI. We will modify model [9.6] to enable an assessment of the vulnerability of CI in each specific economic sector.

To achieve this, the equations for Z_t and x in [9.6], will be transformed as follows:

$$\varepsilon_{Zi}\frac{dZ_i}{dt} = X_i Y_i - b_i(1-k_i x_i)Z_i + \delta_i \dot{w}_{ij}$$

$$\varepsilon_{ix}\frac{dx_i}{dt} = x_i^3 + (A + l_i Z_i)x_i + B + m_i Z_i + \delta_i \dot{w}_{ij},$$

where x_i represents the normalized levels of CI vulnerability in each of the economic sectors under consideration; ε_{ix} denotes parameters that account for the varying rates of change in CI vulnerability across individual economic sectors.

Figure 9.6 shows the dynamics of changes in the functions x_i and Z_i for six economic sectors, obtained using the modified model with the following parameter values: $A_E = 1.96$, $A_i = 2.0$ ($i \neq E$), $B_i = 1$, $r_i = 28$, $b_i = 15.45064047/3$, $k_i = 0.5$, $l_i = m_i$ $m_i = 0.015$ $\varepsilon_{Xi} = \varepsilon_{Yi} = \varepsilon_{Zi} = \varepsilon_x = 0.2$.

Let us assume that the vulnerability of the ith economic sector V_i is defined as $V_t = \int x_t dt$.

Figure 9.7 present the modeling results obtained for various values of parameters A_E. For $i = T$, $i = C$, $i = I$, $i = H$ and $i = PM$, the vulnerability functions exhibit uniform behavior. They have two local minima over the selected range of variation and a local maximum at 1.965, except for $i = PM$, where the maximum occurs at 1.96 and is less pronounced (Figures 9.7(a) and (b)). For $i = E$, the function has only one local minimum, after reaching which, it begins to increase very slightly compared to other sectors. Figure 9.7(c) shows the dependence of the total structural disruption on parameter A_E.

The simulation results indicate that the modified model is also sensitive to small changes in parameters. As shown in Figure 9.7, a slight change in A_E leads to significant transformations in the vulnerability of CI, not only within the energy sector but across the entire system as a whole.

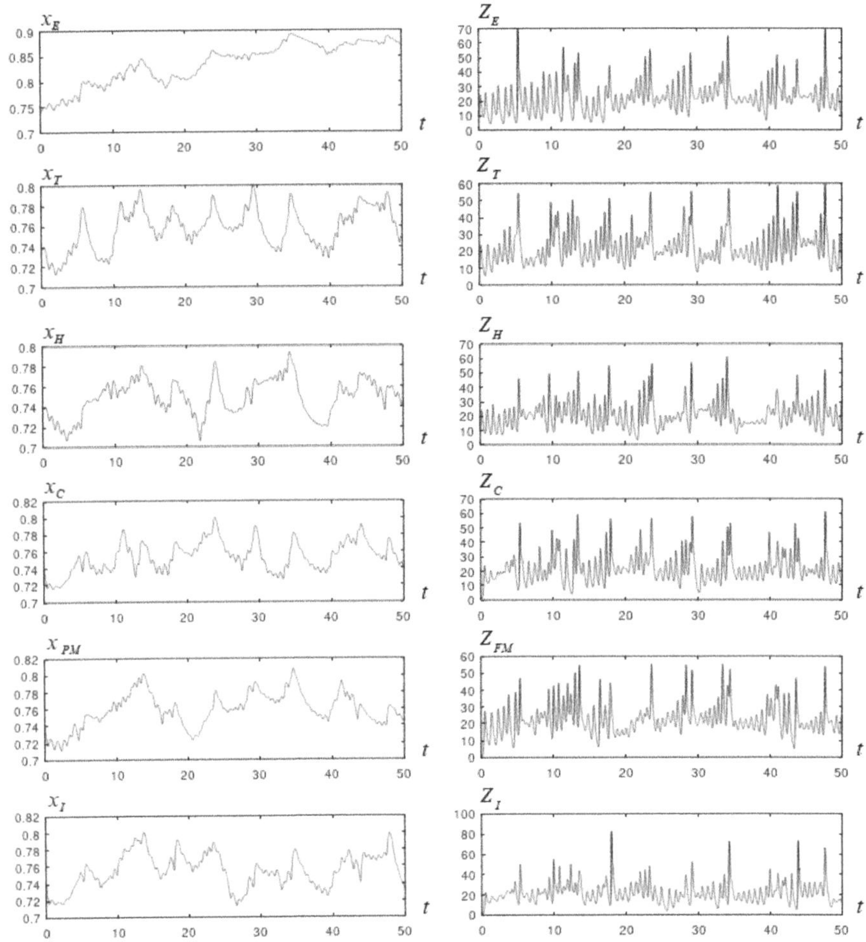

Figure 9.6. *Dynamics of vulnerability and structural disturbances in various sectors*

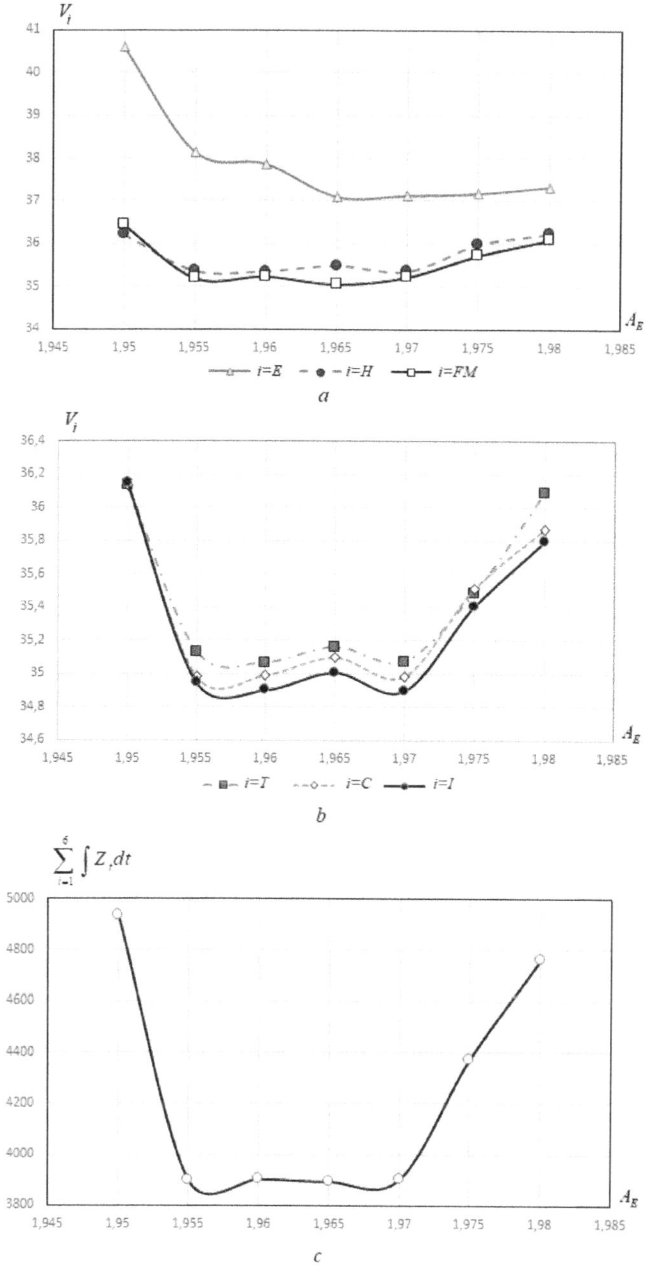

Figure 9.7. *Vulnerability for separate sectors of CI. For a color version of this figure, see www.iste.co.uk/gaivoronski/stochastic1.zip*

9.7. Conclusion

This chapter presented a mathematical approach that has been elaborated to assess the security level of CI objects and the consequences of their destruction for interrelated sectors of the economy.

This approach allows for the evaluation of threat levels, defined using the formalism of smooth function theory, based on the proximity of CI parameters to their bifurcation values, the achievement of which sharply increases the likelihood of their destruction. This way, the "safety margin" of objects is calculated. It is assumed that the probability of an attack on a CI object is higher, the greater its vulnerability level.

The assessment of the impact of CI destruction consequences on the economy is carried out using a multi-sectoral Lorenz model, which determines the dynamics of productivity levels, employment and structural disruptions in sectors directly related to CI activities: energy, transportation, hydraulic structures and water supply networks, chemical industry, production, storage and transportation of hazardous materials, food and medical supply facilities, and information technology.

The study investigated the impact of changes in the speed of eliminating structural disruptions on the dynamics of vulnerability levels in CI. Conditions for the transition of interrelated sectors of the economy into a state of deterministic chaos were identified as a result of changes in the specific demands and supplies of products in production systems and the number of occupied jobs, as well as changes in the speed of eliminating structural disruptions. It was demonstrated that there are regions of parameter values in the model where minor changes can lead to significant transformations in the CI system and its security space.

9.8. Acknowledgments

The development of the methodologies and models is supported by a joint project between the International Institute for Applied Systems Analysis (IIASA) and the National Academy of Sciences of Ukraine (NASU) on "Integrated robust modeling and management of food-energy-water-land use nexus for sustainable development" (22-501). Moreover, this work was supported by the projects 0122U00052 and 2.3/25-P of the National Academy of Sciences of Ukraine.

9.9. References

Andronov, A., Witt, A., Khaikin, S. (1959). *Theory of Oscillations*. Fizmatgiz, Moscow.

Atoyev, K. (2005). The challenges to safety in the East Mediterranean: Mathematical modeling and risk management of marine ecosystems. In *Strategic Management of Marine Ecosystems*, Levner, E., Linkov, I., Proth, J.-M. (eds). Springer, Dordrecht.

Atoyev, K. and Knopov P.S. (2022). Application of robust methods for estimation of distribution parameters with a prioriary constraints on parameters in economics and engineering. *Cybern. Syst. Anal.*, 58(5), 713–720.

Atoyev, K. and Knopov, P.S. (2023). Mathematical modeling of climate change impact on relationships of economic sectors. *Cybern. Syst. Anal.*, 59(4), 535–545.

Atoyev, K., Tomin, A., Aksionova, T. (2007). Global changes, new risks, and novel methods and tools of their assessment. Modeling and management of environmental security in Ukraine. In *Managing Critical Infrastructure Risks*, Linkov I., Wenning R.J., Kiker G.A. (eds). Springer, Netherlands.

Atoyev, K., Knopov, P., Pepeliaev, V., Kisała, P., Romaniuk, R., Kalimoldayev, M. (2017). The mathematical problems of complex systems investigation under uncertainties. In *Recent Advanced in Information Technology*, Wojcik, W. and Sikora, J. (eds). CRC Press, Boca Raton.

Atoyev, K., Ermolieva, T., Knopov, P. (2024). Mathematical modelling of interconnections between ecological, food, and economic dimensions of security. In *Nexus of Sustainability, Studies in Systems, Decision and Control*, Zagorodny, A. Bogdanov, V., Zaporozhets, A. (eds). Springer, Cham.

Ebeling, W. and Engel-Herbert, H. (1982). Extremal principles and catastrophe theory for stochastic models of nonlinear irreversible processes. In *Thermodynamics and Kinetics of Biological Processes*, Lamprect, I. and Zotin, A.I. (eds). Walter de Gruyter, Berlin/ New York.

Ermoliev, Y.M. and von Vinterfeldt, D. (2012). Systemic risk and security management. In *Managing Safety of Heterogeneous Systems*, Ermoliev, Y.M, Makowski, M., Marti, K. (eds). Springer-Verlag, Berlin.

Ermoliev, Y.M., Zagorodny, A.G., Bogdanov, V.I., Ermolieva, T.Y., Havlik, P., Obersteiner, M., Rovenskaya, E. (2020). Linking distributed sectorial optimization models under asymmetric information: Towards robust food-water-environmental nexus. In *FEW Nexux for Sustainable Development: Integrated Modeling & Robust Management*, Ermoliev, Y.M., Zagorodny, A.G., Bogdanov, V.I., Ermolieva, T.Y., Kostyuchenko, Y.V. (eds). Akademperiodika, Kyiv.

Golodnikov, A.N., Ermoliev, Y.M., Ermolieva, T.Y., Knopov, P.S., Pepelyaev, V.A. (2013a). Integrated modeling of food security management in Ukraine. I. Model for management of the economic availability of food. *Cybern. Syst. Anal.*, 49, 26–35.

Golodnikov, A.N., Ermoliev, Y.M., Ermolieva, T.Y., Knopov, P.S., Pepelyaev, V.A. (2013b). Integrated modeling of food security management in Ukraine. II. Model for structural optimization of agricultural production under risk. *Cybern. Syst. Anal.*, 49, 217–228.

Kaplan, J. and Yorke, J. (1979). Preturbulence: A regime observed in a fluid flow model of Lorenz. *Comm. Math. Phys.*, 67(2), 93–108.

Kröger, W. and Zio, E. (2011). *Vulnerable Systems*. Springer, London.

Laszlo, E. (1993). *Age of Bifurcation: Understanding the Changing World*. Gordon and Breach, London.

Lorenz, E. (1963). Deterministic nonperiodic flow. *Journal of Atoms. Sci.*, 20, 130–141.

Magnitskii, N.A. and Sidorov, S.V. (2006). *New Methods for Chaotic Dynamics*. World Scientific, Singapore.

Norkin, V.I., Gaivoronski, A.A., Zaslavsky, V.A., Knopov, P.S. (2018). Models of the optimal resource allocation for the critical infrastructure protection. *Cybern. Syst. Anal.*, 54(5), 696–706.

Pepelyaev, V.A., Golodnikov, A.N., Golodnikova, N.A. (2023). Reliability optimization method alternative to bPOE. *Cybern. Syst. Anal.*, 58, 593–597.

Pepelyaev, V.A., Golodnikov, A.N., Golodnikova. N.A. (2024). Method of optimizing the structure of sowing areas for the adaptation of crop production to climate changes. *Cybern. Syst. Anal.*, 60, 415–421.

Poston, T. and Stewart, J. (1978). *Catastrophe Theory and Its Application*. Pitman Publishing Ltd., London.

Renn, O. (2003). Typology of risks. *Journal of Risk Research*, 6 (4–6), 519–524.

Sergienko, I.V, Yanenko, V.M., Atoev, K.L. (1997). A conceptual framework for managing the risk of ecological, technogenic, and sociogenic disasters. *Cybern. Syst. Anal.*, 33(2), 203–219.

Shulzhenko, S., Nechaieva, T., Leshchenko, I. (2024). The application of the optimal unit commitment problem for the studies of the national power sector development under system risks. In *Nexus of Sustainability, Studies in Systems, Decision and Control*, Zagorodny, A. Bogdanov, V., Zaporozhets, A. (eds). Springer, Cham.

Wagenmakers, E., Molenaar, P., Grasman, R., Hartelman, P., van der Maas, H. (2005). Transformation invariant stochastic catastrophe theory. *Physica D*, 211, 263–276.

Wilkinson, A., Elani, S., Eidinow, E. (2002). Risk world scenarios. *Journal of Risk Research*, 6(4–6), 297–334.

Willis, H.H., Morral, A.R., Kelly, T.K., Medby, J.J. (2005). Estimating terrorism risk. *Rand Corporation*, 94 [Online]. Available at: https://www.rand.org/content/dam/rand/pubs/monographs/2005/RAND_MG388.pdf.

Zgurovsky, M.Z. (2024). World transformation after the COVID-19 pandemic: The European context. In *Nexus of Sustainability, Studies in Systems, Decision and Control*, Zagorodny, A., Bogdanov, V., Zaporozhets, A. (eds). Springer, Cham.

Zgurovsky, M.Z. and Pankratova, N.D. (2007). System control of complex objects. In *System Analysis: Theory and Applications. Data and Knowledge in a Changing World*. Springer, Berlin.

Index

I, K

L, M

N, O

P, Q

R, S

T, U, V

Summary of Volume 2

Preface
Alexei A. GAIVORONSKI, Pavel S. KNOPOV,
Vladimir I. NORKIN and Volodymyr A. ZASLAVSKYI

Part 1. Mathematical Models and Methods for Risk Mitigation and Defending Critical Infrastructure

Introduction to Part 1
Pavel S. KNOPOV and Vladimir I. NORKIN

Chapter 1. Three Approaches to Decision-making Under Risk and Uncertainty for the Critical Infrastructure Protection
Vladimir S. KIRILYUK

Chapter 5. Making Decisions and Motion Control in Conditions of Conflict

Arkadii CHIKRII

Chapter 6. Contemporary Stochastic Quasi-gradient Algorithms

Vladimir I. NORKIN, Alexei A. GAIVORONSKI, Pavel S. KNOPOV and Anton KOZYRIEV

Chapter 7. Two Classes of Optimization Problems for Arcs Capacities Modernization for Fault-tolerant Networks

Petro STETSYUK, Viktor STOVBA and Volodymyr ZHYDKOV

Chapter 10. Cybersecurity Investments in Networks
Vasyl GORBACHUK, Maksym DUNAIEVSKYI and Seit-Bekir SULEIMANOV

Other titles from

iSTE

in

Mathematics and Statistics

2024

BOURLÈS Henri
System Theory – A Modern Approach 1: Linear Ordinary and Functional Differential Equations

MAKAROV Volodymyr, MAYKO Nataliya
Traditional Functional-Discrete Methods for the Problems of Mathematical Physics: New Aspects

2023

AIT BEN HASSI El Mustapha
The Theory of Distributions: Introduction

KOROLIOUK Dmitri, SAMOILENKO Igor
Asymptotic and Analytic Methods in Stochastic Evolutionary Systems

PARROCHIA Daniel
Graphs, Orders, Infinites and Philosophy

2022

CHAKRAVARTHY Srinivas R.
Introduction to Matrix-Analytic Methods in Queues 1: Analytical and Simulation Approach – Basics
Introduction to Matrix-Analytic Methods in Queues 2: Analytical and Simulation Approach – Queues and Simulation

LESFARI Ahmed
Integrable Systems

RADCHENKI Vadym M.
General Stochastic Measures: Integration, Path Properties and Equations

DE SAPORTA Benoîte, ZILI Mounir
Martingales and Financial Mathematics in Discrete Time

SIMON Jacques
Distributions
(Analysis for PDEs Set – Volume 3)

2021

KOROLIOUK Dmitri, SAMOILENKO Igor
Random Evolutionary Systems: Asymptotic Properties and Large Deviations

MOKLYACHUK Mikhail
Convex Optimization: Introductory Course

POGORUI Anatoliy, SWISHCHUK Anatoliy, RODRÍGUEZ-DAGNINO Ramón M.
Random Motions in Markov and Semi-Markov Random Environments 1: Homogeneous Random Motions and their Applications
Random Motions in Markov and Semi-Markov Random Environments 2: High-dimensional Random Motions and Financial Applications

PROVENZI Edoardo
From Euclidean to Hilbert Spaces: Introduction to Functional Analysis and its Applications

2020

BARBU Vlad Stefan, VERGNE Nicolas
Statistical Topics and Stochastic Models for Dependent Data with Applications

CHABANYUK Yaroslav, NIKITIN Anatolii, KHIMKA Uliana
Asymptotic Analyses for Complex Evolutionary Systems with Markov and Semi-Markov Switching Using Approximation Schemes

KOROLIOUK Dmitri
Dynamics of Statistical Experiments

MANOU-ABI Solym Mawaki, DABO-NIANG Sophie, SALONE Jean-Jacques
Mathematical Modeling of Random and Deterministic Phenomena

SIMON Jacques
Continuous Functions
(Analysis for PDEs Set – Volume23)

2019

BANNA Oksana, MISHURA Yuliya, RALCHENKO Kostiantyn, SHKLYAR Sergiy
Fractional Brownian Motion: Approximations and Projections

GANA Kamel, BROC Guillaume
Structural Equation Modeling with lavaan

KUKUSH Alexander
Gaussian Measures in Hilbert Space: Construction and Properties

LUZ Maksym, MOKLYACHUK Mikhail
Estimation of Stochastic Processes with Stationary Increments and Cointegrated Sequences

MICHELITSCH Thomas, PÉREZ RIASCOS Alejandro, COLLET Bernard, NOWAKOWSKI Andrzej, NICOLLEAU Franck
Fractional Dynamics on Networks and Lattices

VOTSI Irene, LIMNIOS Nikolaos, PAPADIMITRIOU Eleftheria, TSAKLIDIS George
Earthquake Statistical Analysis through Multi-state Modeling
(Statistical Methods for Earthquakes Set – Volume 2)

2018

AZAÏS Romain, BOUGUET Florian
Statistical Inference for Piecewise-deterministic Markov Processes

IBRAHIMI Mohammed
Mergers & Acquisitions: Theory, Strategy, Finance

PARROCHIA Daniel
Mathematics and Philosophy

2017

CARONI Chysseis
First Hitting Time Regression Models: Lifetime Data Analysis Based on Underlying Stochastic Processes
(Mathematical Models and Methods in Reliability Set – Volume 4)

CELANT Giorgio, BRONIATOWSKI Michel
Interpolation and Extrapolation Optimal Designs 2: Finite Dimensional General Models

CONSOLE Rodolfo, MURRU Maura, FALCONE Giuseppe
Earthquake Occurrence: Short- and Long-term Models and their Validation
(Statistical Methods for Earthquakes Set – Volume 1)

D'AMICO Guglielmo, DI BIASE Giuseppe, JANSSEN Jacques, MANCA Raimondo
Semi-Markov Migration Models for Credit Risk
(Stochastic Models for Insurance Set – Volume 1)

GONZÁLEZ VELASCO Miguel, del PUERTO GARCÍA Inés, YANEV George P.
Controlled Branching Processes
(Branching Processes, Branching Random Walks and Branching Particle Fields Set – Volume 2)

HARLAMOV Boris
Stochastic Analysis of Risk and Management
(Stochastic Models in Survival Analysis and Reliability Set – Volume 2)

KERSTING Götz, VATUTIN Vladimir
Discrete Time Branching Processes in Random Environment
(Branching Processes, Branching Random Walks and Branching Particle Fields Set – Volume 1)

MISHURA Yuliya, SHEVCHENKO Georgiy
Theory and Statistical Applications of Stochastic Processes

NIKULIN Mikhail, CHIMITOVA Ekaterina
Chi-squared Goodness-of-fit Tests for Censored Data
(Stochastic Models in Survival Analysis and Reliability Set – Volume 3)

SIMON Jacques
Banach, Fréchet, Hilbert and Neumann Spaces
(Analysis for PDEs Set – Volume 1)

2016

CELANT Giorgio, BRONIATOWSKI Michel
Interpolation and Extrapolation Optimal Designs 1: Polynomial Regression and Approximation Theory

CHIASSERINI Carla Fabiana, GRIBAUDO Marco, MANINI Daniele
Analytical Modeling of Wireless Communication Systems
(Stochastic Models in Computer Science and Telecommunication Networks Set – Volume 1)

GOUDON Thierry
Mathematics for Modeling and Scientific Computing

KAHLE Waltraud, MERCIER Sophie, PAROISSIN Christian
Degradation Processes in Reliability
(Mathematial Models and Methods in Reliability Set – Volume 3)

KERN Michel
Numerical Methods for Inverse Problems

RYKOV Vladimir
Reliability of Engineering Systems and Technological Risks (Stochastic Models in Survival Analysis and Reliability Set – Volume 1)

2015

DEVOLDER Pierre, JANSSEN Jacques, MANCA Raimondo
Basic Stochastic Processes

LE GAT Yves
Recurrent Event Modeling Based on the Yule Process (Mathematical Models and Methods in Reliability Set – Volume 2)

DE SAPORTA Benoîte, DUFOUR François, ZHANG Huilong
Numerical Methods for Simulation and Optimization of Piecewise Deterministic Markov Processes

2014

COOKE Roger M., NIEBOER Daan, MISIEWICZ Jolanta
Fat-tailed Distributions: Data, Diagnostics and Dependence (Mathematical Models and Methods in Reliability Set – Volume 1)

MACKEVIČIUS Vigirdas
Integral and Measure: From Rather Simple to Rather Complex

PASCHOS Vangelis Th
Combinatorial Optimization – 3-volume series – 2nd edition
Concepts of Combinatorial Optimization / Concepts and Fundamentals – volume 1
Paradigms of Combinatorial Optimization – volume 2
Applications of Combinatorial Optimization – volume 3

2013

COUALLIER Vincent, GERVILLE-RÉACHE Léo, HUBER Catherine, LIMNIOS Nikolaos, MESBAH Mounir
Statistical Models and Methods for Reliability and Survival Analysis

JANSSEN Jacques, MANCA Oronzio, MANCA Raimondo
Applied Diffusion Processes from Engineering to Finance

SERICOLA Bruno
Markov Chains: Theory, Algorithms and Applications

2012

BOSQ Denis
Mathematical Statistics and Stochastic Processes

CHRISTENSEN Karl Bang, KREINER Svend, MESBAH Mounir
Rasch Models in Health

DECREUSEFOND Laurent, MOYAL Pascal
Stochastic Modeling and Analysis of Telecom Networks

DEVOLDER Pierre, JANSSEN Jacques, MANCA Raimondo
Stochastic Methods for Pension Funds

2011

MACKEVIČIUS Vigirdas
Introduction to Stochastic Analysis: Integrals and Differential Equations

MAHJOUB Ridha
Recent Progress in Combinatorial Optimization – ISCO2010

RAYNAUD Hervé, ARROW Kenneth
Managerial Logic

2010

BAGDONAVIČIUS Vilijandas, KRUOPIS Julius, NIKULIN Mikhail
Nonparametric Tests for Censored Data

IOSIFESCU Marius, LIMNIOS Nikoloas, OPRISAN Gheorghe
Introduction to Stochastic Models

VASSILIOU P.C.G.
Discrete-time Asset Pricing Models in Applied Stochastic Finance

2008

ANISIMOV Vladimir
Switching Processes in Queuing Models

FICHE Georges, HÉBUTERNE Gérard
Mathematics for Engineers

HUBER Catherine, LIMNIOS Nikolaos, MESBAH Mounir, NIKULIN Mikhail
Mathematical Methods in Survival Analysis, Reliability and Quality of Life

JANSSEN Jacques, MANCA Raimondo, VOLPE Ernesto
Mathematical Finance

2007

HARLAMOV Boris
Continuous Semi-Markov Processes

2006

CLERC Maurice
Particle Swarm Optimization

Printed and bound by CPI Group (UK) Ltd, Croydon, CR0 4YY
13/09/2026
14961012-0005